Costume Craftwork

on a Budget

Costume Craftwork

on a *Budget*

Clothing, 3-D Makeup, Wigs, Millinery & Accessories

Tan Huaixiang

Focal Press
Taylor & Francis Group

NEW YORK AND LONDON

First published 2007
This edition published 2013 by Focal Press
70 Blanchard Road, Suite 402, Burlington, MA 01803

Simultaneously published in the UK
By Focal Press
2 Park Square, Milton Park, Abingdon, Oxon OX14 4RN

Focal Press is an imprint of the Taylor & Francis Group, an informa business

Notices

Practitioners and researchers must always rely on their own experience and knowledge
in evaluating and using any information, methods, compounds, or experiments
described herein. In using such information or methods they should be mindful of their
own safety and the safety of others, including parties for whom they have a professional
responsibility.

To the fullest extent of the law, neither the Publisher nor the authors, contributors, or
editors, assume any liability for any injury and/or damage to persons or property as a
matter of products liability, negligence or otherwise, or from any use or operation of
any methods, products, instructions, or ideas contained in the material herein.

Library of Congress Cataloging-in-Publication Data
Tan, Huaixiang.
   Costume craftwork on a budget: clothing, 3-D makeup, wigs, millinery & accessories/Tan Huaixiang.
      p.   cm.
   ISBN-13: 978-0-240-80853-6 (pbk.: alk. paper)
   ISBN-10: 0-240-80853-3 (pbk.: alk. paper) 1. Costume. 2. Costume design. I. Title.
   PN2067.T37 2007
   792.02′6 — dc22   2006100482

British Library Cataloguing-in-Publication Data
A catalogue record for this book is available from the British Library.

ISBN 13: 978-0-240-80853-6 (pbk)

Table of Contents

Preface

This book is based on my years of experimental executions of costume and makeup designs in theatrical productions. I consider this book to be a companion book to my *Character Figure Drawing* book, published two years ago by Focal Press. The drawing book emphasized drawing and rendering techniques; this craftwork book focuses on the execution process and on techniques for creating craftwork for costume designs.

My purpose in writing this book is to stress the importance of the steps that turn 2-D costume designs into 3-D physical objects. In my opinion, experience creating craftwork from designs is essential for anybody who wants to be a better costume and makeup designer. The creation of the actual crafts may be delegated to others, but the costume designer should understand the craft-production process.

I consider myself to be a hands-on person. (I believe my crafting skills are much better than my writing skills.) This book is a summary of the executions of my designs that worked effectively on stage. It covers broad-based craft subjects, useful information, instructions, and ideas.

Unfortunately, I don't possess all the process photos showing every step for each creation in the book. To make up for this, I have included many drawings illustrating the most important processes; I hope the sketches make sense to you. The lesson here is: DO NOT FORGET TO TAKE PROCESS PICTURES OF YOUR WORK! You never know when you may need them later.

In addition, some of the photos that appear in this book are of poor quality, and I apologize for this; I was not able to replace them. I am also unfortunately unable to list all the names of the people related to every photo.

The methods and techniques presented in this book are rather primitive and simple, and can be done using basic equipment. Creating craftwork involves problem solving, exploring media, and cost control.

My book on character figure drawing has been well received by the readers, and I hope readers who are interested in creating craftwork will find this craftwork book even more useful.

Acknowledgments

I thank Focal Press for giving me this opportunity to write and publish my costume craftwork book and for their unending support and encouragement along the way.

I extend a special thanks to Bonnie J. Kruger, who introduced me to Focal Press for my first book; without her, I wouldn't have had the opportunity to write this second book.

I thank all my professors at the Central Academy of Drama in Beijing, China, including Hou Qidi, Ma Chi, Xing Dalun, Wang Ren, Li Chang, Zhang Bingyao, Qi Mudong, Zhang Chongqing, He Yunlan, Yie Ming, An Lin, Wang Xiping, Sun Mu, and Li Dequan. They are the ones who laid the foundation for me to pursue and achieve what I have today. They nurtured and motivated me to start my costume and makeup design career, and their influence has changed my life.

I thank the professors in the Department of Theatre Arts at Utah State University — Colin B. Johnson, Sid Perks, Voce Call, and Bruce E. McInroy — for their kindness, advice, patience, and support. They helped me endure and overcome graduate school, a difficult period in my life. They provided opportunities for me to work on many productions and created many learning experiences for me. Their guidance has led me to accomplish what I have today.

I thank all my former chairmen in the United States with whom I've worked for encouraging and guiding me: Sid Perks, Utah State University; Bruce A. Levitt, Cornell University; Buck Favorony, University of Pittsburgh; Wesley Van Tassel, Central Washington University; and Donald Seay, Joseph Rusnock, and Roberta Salon, University of Central Florida.

I thank Ryan Retherford, Dr. Ruth Marshall, Meg Shell, and Margie Garland-Aguilar at the Faculty Multimedia Center at University of Central Florida for all your help and availability whenever I needed them.

I thank Arlene Flores, Georgia Culp, Etelka Palmer, and Samuel Waters at the University of Central Florida for helping me when I needed it most.

I thank the entire faculty and staff at the University of Central Florida Conservatory Theatre Department for your support.

I thank my dear friends Xiangyun Jie, Julia Zheng, Helen Huang, Peiran Teng, Dunsi Dai, Liming Tang, Haibou Yu, Lu Yi, and Rujun Wang for their unconditional support and wise advice. You all put a smile on my face when I needed it most.

I thank my parents for teaching and disciplining me to become the strong person I am today. I owe a big thanks to my daughter, Yingtao Zhang, for proofreading my manuscript. Her inspiration and creativity continually sparked ideas for the book. I owe additional thanks to my husband, Juli Zhang, for helping me succeed in my professional career.

I thank Mark Brotherton, Michaeleen Melida, Nina Blankenship, Yingtao Zhang, and all students mentioned in the text for all your help making this book happen.

Finally, I thank all my students for their tolerance in allowing me to be their instructor and allowing me to continue to learn and grow in my career.

Introduction

I received positive feedback from readers after Focal Press published my book *Character Costume Figure Drawing*. This interest from my readers encouraged me to write a second book. *Character Costume Figure Drawing* demonstrated drawing techniques for portraying characters with lifelike body language and facial expression; *Costume Craftwork on a Budget* is a continuation, focusing on the development and execution of craftwork. It shows the techniques for moving from 2-D designs to 3-D pieces of theater craftwork that I have designed, built, and used effectively on stage. My goal is to make this an instructional and technical book that is easy to follow and fun to read.

This book covers broad topics, including 3-D makeup, false teeth, beards and wigs, masks, millinery, armor, soft leather shoes, nonhuman costumes, aging and altering garments, and Halloween costumes. There is no other book available that comprehensively covers everything I cover here. Some of the methods I developed had never been used before. Many other techniques I improved and enhanced to make my project work in a particular situation, producing end results that were beautiful, economical, and quick and easy to make. I have made many crafts throughout my career, and for this book I

have chosen examples that use a diverse array of techniques.

This book demonstrates straightforward step-by-step procedures with many illustrations. It also includes my designs, construction photos and illustrations, materials and tools, production photos, and some of my students' creative work for productions I designed. I am very proud of my students' work, and I am delighted to be able to share our experiences with other theater craft creators.

Although you may not make the same crafts I show in this book, I hope you pick up some useful techniques that will help you along your creative pathway. I hope this book will inspire new ideas in your craft-creating adventures. Although certain details covered here may seem elementary, I include them in order to thoroughly display the creation of the craft. Unfortunately, I don't have photos of all the steps. The book covers productions from throughout my career, and many of them took place many years ago; I illustrated these older productions with line drawings.

The techniques for creating the craftwork in this book are only one way to execute the projects, and of course they are not the only

way. Craftwork should not all be done the same way; otherwise, it won't be unique. We must always keep trying and learning nonstop, continually experimenting and developing, and imaginatively inventing new techniques and technologies.

This book is for anyone who is interested in craftwork, such as theater costume professionals, students, craft specialists, or people interested in Halloween costumes; it can be used in the classroom as an instructional tool or in a theater company's craft department. It is for anyone who needs specific craft techniques for theater productions or for anyone whose goal is to create fast, easy, and practical crafts that are durable. If you don't have a big budget for a production but still want beautiful products, this book imparts some inspiration, methods, and ideas to get you started and help you create dramatic and unique pieces of affordable artwork.

I hope this book is enjoyable to read and brings out the readers' creativity, imagination, ideas, and inspiration as it tells a story of how to cleverly make durable products in a short amount of time in simple, easy-to-follow steps using a wide array of illustrations and photographs.

Chapter 1   3-D Makeup — Prosthetic Pieces

I have experimented with different materials such as: liquid latex, cold foam latex, hot foam latex, and gel-foam. And I have made various prosthetic pieces for numerous productions such as full and half masks, individual facial features, and animal faces. Liquid latex is used for creating scars or fine wrinkles on the face. Liquid latex prosthetic pieces are the simplest of all to make since no mold release is required and no heating is needed to cure it; the product is quite strong and stiffer than other materials. Using gel-foam is the second easiest and fastest way to produce prosthetic pieces. Gel-foam possesses an excellent natural skin texture; however, it is heavier in weight and therefore is suitable for small prosthetic pieces.

Cold foam latex does not need to be baked and prosthetic pieces are easy to make, but cold foam lacks flexibility compared to hot foam latex. Hot foam latex must be baked to cure the prosthetic piece. Both cold and hot foam prosthetic pieces are lightweight; however, hot foam prosthetic pieces are softer, more durable and flexible, and excellent in conforming to the actor's facial movements. All the material kits include instructions. A precise working operation is the key to creating good usable prosthetic pieces.

FULL-HEAD LIFE CASTING AND HOT FOAM MASK

Here I use the hot foam mask I made for *Dracula* to demonstrate the process of full-head life casting and making a hot foam mask.

The production *Dracula* was staged at the Theatre Arts Department at Central Washington University, Ellensburg, WA. It was one of the productions for which I designed the costumes and 3-D makeup. The director of *Dracula* requested that I create two distinct characters, old and young Dracula, both played by a 20-year-old theatre performance student. Old Dracula had to transform into young Dracula within a few minutes. A prosthetic mask (3-D makeup) was required for the character to achieve the special look and to solve the quick makeup-change problem. Dracula's mask provides an example of using life casting, positive and negative molds, and sculpture to make a 3-D prosthetic piece.

Summary of Procedures for Creating 3-D Makeup or Prosthetic Mask

- Make actor's full-head life casting.
- Make a positive mold from the life casting mold.
- Sculpture the old Dracula face with modeling clay.
- Make a negative mold from the clay sculpture mold.
- Make a hot foam prosthetic mask.
- Add hair to the mask.
- Paint the mask.
- Apply the mask to the actor's face.

MAKING A FULL-HEAD LIFE CASTING

Life casting is the first step in making prosthetic products. It can be done on just the face or on the full head and is the foundation for 3-D makeup. It duplicates the actor's face with detailed impressions and provides an accurate fit for the actor. Life casting is a long two-part process that involves making positive and negative molds. A casting mold is a mold made from any object or human. In this case, it is made from a human head. To create different characters and to change the physical appearance of an actor using 3-D makeup, life casting is a necessary step.

In my experience, the best life casting material is Alginate. I've also worked with plaster of paris and plaster bandages for life casting many years ago but this has its limitations and dangers because when the plaster hardens it is difficult to remove from the face, especially from a face with big jaws. Alginate is flexible, captures impressions from any subject amazingly well, and is safely removed.

PROCEDURE FOR LIFE CASTING

Materials Required:

- Alginate, 5- or 8-minute setting (2.5 lb)
- Plaster bandage (2 or 3 rolls, 4″ × 6 yd rolls)
- Water
- Vaseline or petroleum jelly
- Bald cap
- Hair gel
- Comb
- Hair pins
- Spirit gum
- Dental chair (optional)
- Cotton balls
- Large drinking straw (for breathing through the nose)
- Nose putty
- Haircut mockup
- Scissors
- Terry cloth (about eight pieces, precut 1″ × 2″ or 2″ × 2″)
- Container for measuring alginate and water
- Container for water
- Container for mixing plaster or alginate
- Rubber spatula
- Butter knife or screwdriver
- Eyeliner pencil
- Brush to apply Vaseline
- Knife for cutting and trimming

Alginate. Dental alginate is used by dentists to cast teeth. Prosthetic alginate is used to cast the face, limbs, and body parts. Dental alginate usually comes in flavors that set in 50–60 seconds. Prosthetic alginates, with tinted color and no flavor, set in 2–10 minutes. I used 5-minute setting alginate so I would have enough time to manage the life casting.

Plaster bandage. This is a gauze material sized with plaster used to cast broken arms and legs. It comes in 4″ × 6 yd rolls. It can be applied on the skin to make a life casting mold, but sometimes it's hard to remove from the face because of its rigidness. Its other purpose is to provide a rigid shell over the alginate for support — alginate is in a soft form by itself and will not maintain its shape when it is removed from face.

Step One: Flattening the Hair

A bald cap is applied to the actor's head for protection and to get an accurate shape and size of the actor's head for making the prosthetic appliances. If the actor has short hair, it will be easy to cover. But if the actor has long hair, you first need to flatten the hair to the skull in order to make it fit underneath the bald cap.

The method of flattening hair is demonstrated next; it can be also used for applying a regular bald cap (without making a mask). When I teach the advanced makeup class, I purposely schedule applying a bald cap and life casting on the same day to kill two birds with one stone. However, these two processes combined can take from 6 to 8 hours and can be exhausting. You may want to bring your favorite music, food, and drinks to the working room in preparation for the long day or practice this on a weekend.

- Start from the top crown or center of the skull and work your way down. Apply hair gel to the hair and spread it down to the roots. First create the flattened center spiral, and then continue making spirals on alternating sides of the first spiral, wrapping them toward the center spiral (Figures 1-1 to 1-9). Pick a tuft of hair, comb and flatten it as close as possible to the scalp, starting at the top crown or center of the scalp and working outward (Figures 1-1 and 1-3). Work on one section of the hair at a time until all the hair is combed up, flattened, and close to the skull (Figures 1-1 to 1-9). If the hair is long, a few bobby pins should be used temporarily to hold the hair down in place; after the hair dries, the hair pins can be removed. Blow-dry the gelled hair to force it dry.

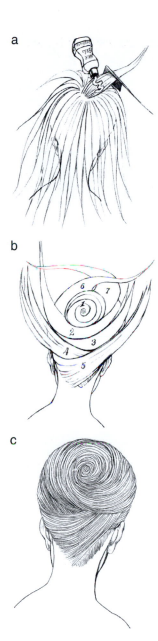

a

b

c

Figure 1-1 (a) Start from the top crown/center of the skull and work down. (b) Wrap sections of hair in an alternating directions to flatten the hair to the skull. (c) Completed, flattened hair.

Figure 1-2 Nina Blankenship, the model for flattening hair.

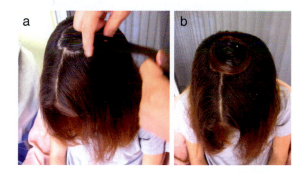

a   b

Figure 1-3 (a) Comb the first section of hair at the crown. (b) Spiral the section of hair around the center to flatten it.

Figure 1-4 (a) Start the second hair section next to the first spiral. (b) Comb this section of hair into a spiral, overlapping it slightly with the first flattened hair spiral. Repeat on opposite side.

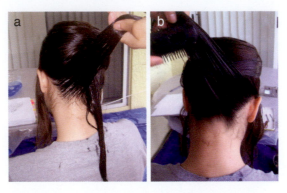

Figure 1-6 (a) The rest of the back portion of hair is divided into two sections. One of the sections is combed around the center spirals. (b) The other section is combed in the opposite direction.

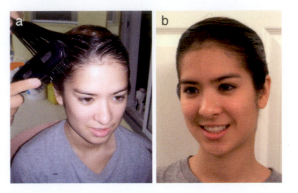

Figure 1-8 (a) The last tuft is combed in the opposite direction than the previous front tuft to complete flattening of the hair (notice the angled parting line in the front shows a smooth forehead). (b) The completed flattened hair — front.

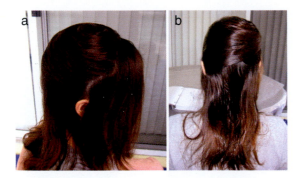

Figure 1-5 (a) The next section of hair is spiraled around the previous flattened spiral. (b) Another spiral on the opposite side of the previous one is combed and spiraled around the center. (Notice the pattern here of spiraling in alternating directions back and forth on opposite sides of the hair.)

Figure 1-7 (a) The completed back portion of the hair; a bobby pin may be needed temporarily to keep the hair in place. (b) There are two front sections left. One of the front sections is combed and spiraled toward the center spirals.

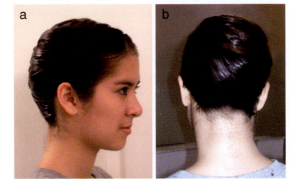

Figure 1-9 (a) The completed flattened hair — side. (b) The completed flattened hair — back.

Step Two: Putting on a Bald Cap

- Choose a large and deep bald cap to protect the hair.
- Put the bald cap on, stretching it close to the head, and then make trim marks on the edges of the cap with eyeliner pencil (Figure 1-10a).
- Trim the excess edge with scissors while the cap is on the head. Taking the bald cap off the head may ruin the flattened hair because the cap is stretched tightly over the head. Instead you should put your hand underneath the bald cap and then carefully cut it on the trimming line. Make sure the scissors do not touch the actor's face, ears, or hair while you trim. Then trace a natural hairline with the pencil (Figure 1-10b).
- Use spirit gum to glue down the edges of the cap. Start from the forehead and temple areas. Turn up the edge of the cap and brush the spirit gum about $\frac{3}{8}''$ to $\frac{1}{2}''$ from the very edge (Figure 1-11a), allow the glue to become tacky, and press down to the skin.
- Glue down the back cap edges. For a better result, the actor should keep his or her head in an upright position while you glue down the edges. (Figure 1-11b) This will reduce wrinkles from occurring in the neck area.

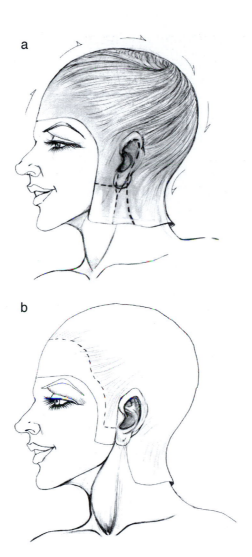

Figure 1-10 (a) Make trim marks on the bald cap. (b) Trim the edges of the cap and trace a natural hairline.

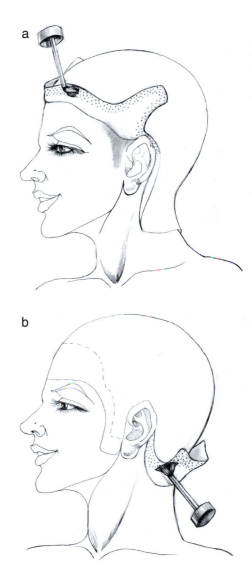

Figure 1-11 (a) Apply spirit gum to glue the frontal edges of the cap. (b) Keep the actor's head in an upright position while gluing down the cap's back edge.

Step Three: Preparations and Protections for the Actor before Casting

- Have the actor remove his or her contact lenses, if any, to avoid eye irritation.
- Prepare a pair of straws to be placed in the nostrils for the actor to breathe through.
- Cover the actor with a barber's smock and tape down the edge of the smock around the shoulders with masking tape.
- Apply an even coat of Vaseline all over the actor's face, ears, neck, shoulders, and facial hair (especially the eyelashes) and over the entire bald cap. For good and stable balance of the positive head mold, cast the shoulders as well. Comb any facial hair downward to prevent pulling the hair when you remove the negative casting mold from the face. Avoid applying too much Vaseline because it will destroy the results of the impressions of the face.
- Place cotton balls in both of the actor's ear canals to seal them and to prevent any liquid alginate from running in (Figure 1-12b). Add a proper amount of soft wax behind each ear for support and also to soften complex impressions

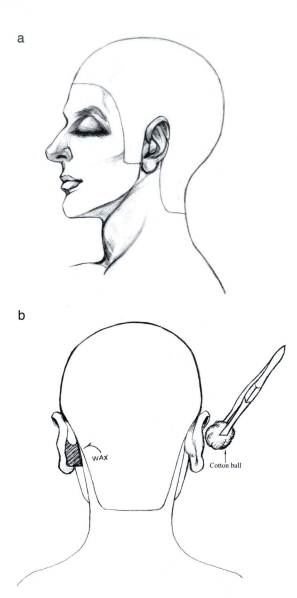

a

b

Figure 1-12 (a) Completed bald cap. (b) Stuff cotton balls into the ear canals, and add wax behind the ears.

and angular structures into more simplified forms (Figure 1-12b). The wax behind the ears will also facilitate easy removal of the casting mold from the actor's head.

- It is very important to explain every step of the process to the actor so he or she will be prepared and alerted. It will take at least 40 minutes for the whole process, from mixing the alginate to removing the casting mold from the face. When the alginate is poured on the face, the actor's face will feel cold. Even though there are two straws inserted into the nostrils, he or she will naturally be panicky about breathe. If the actor is too nervous and feels in danger, the alginate can be removed instantly. In this case, you will have to start over or you could use the plaster bandage method to finish the life casting.
- Give the actor a notebook and pen so her or she can write down what he or she needs while his or her face is being enclosed, or use simple sign language such as a thumbs up for "OK" and thumbs down for "not OK." From the very beginning to the very end of the casting procedure, DO NOT tell any jokes — jokes will cause the model to laugh or make any facial movements.

- After applying the plaster bandage over the alginate, wait for the plaster bandage to dry, but DO NOT ever leave the model alone in the room for safety reasons.
- Make sure the model is seated comfortably in an upright position, keeping his or her head and shoulders straight, so as not to distort the shape of the face and neck. If the actor is lying in a flat or backward position it will affect the fit of the prosthetic piece. Propping pillows behind the actor will provide some comfort.

Step Four: Mixing Alginate and Making a Negative Casting Mold

I used to use dental alginate with a 3-minute setting time before I started using the theatrical casting alginate with a 5-minute setting time. The longer setting time is better for casting a full head. I have always used nostril straws when life casting because this provides some reassurance to the actor because he or she can breathe under the creamy alginate. Most methods of life casting begin from the top of the forehead and work downward. I experimented with working the opposite way, working from the bottom up. This method allows me to make sure the alginate reaches all the

undercut corners that may easily be missed.

- Measure the appropriate amount of alginate and water (1 part : 1 part). Make sure to shake the alginate powder container up and down slowly to loosen or fluff up the powder in order to get an accurate measurement. Generally, $\frac{3}{4}$ lb is enough for a face casting. A whole-head casting requires about $2\frac{1}{2}$ to 3 lbs alginate. If warm water is used, the setting time will be faster; cold water slows down the setting time of the alginate. A cold or warm room temperature also affects the setting time in the same way.
- Use a large bowl for mixing the alginate. This will give you enough space for rapid mixing motions. Measure the powder first and then the water (Figure 1-13a). Pour the measured water over the alginate. Mix the alginate and water by hand or

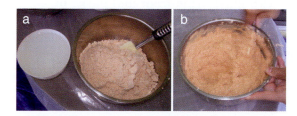

Figure 1-13 (a) Measure the alginate and water. (b) Mix the alginate.

spatula using quick circular movements and keep mixing (approximately 45–50 seconds) until the lumps disappear and the mixture has a creamy pastelike consistency (Figure 1-13b).

- Start working on the individual areas. You have to work very quickly. The coat doesn't need to be even, but it should cover the entire skin. Make sure the alginate reaches all the undercut corners that can easily be missed. Apply the alginate using a spatula by touching and leaving. Don't smear or stroke it back and forth; just let it flow naturally. Things flow more smoothly if two people are working together. I recommend that you work from the bottom up in the following order (Figure 1-14a).
  1. Apply the alginate under the chin.
  2. Apply it on the ears.
  3. Apply it above and below the mouth.
  4. Carefully insert breathing straws into the actor's nose and ask him or her to hold them.
  5. Apply the alginate around the nostril area and bottom of the nose and around the eye-socket area.
- Pour the rest of the alginate on top of the head (Figure 1-14b). Let it run down naturally and use your hand or a spatula to guide the running

a

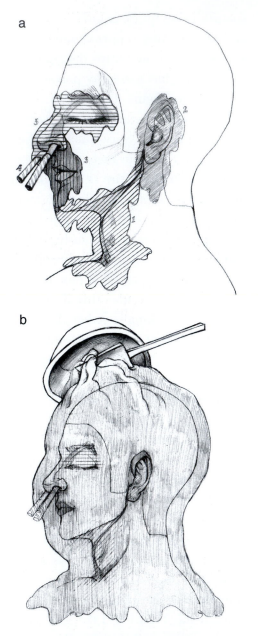

b

a

Figure 1-14 (a) Order of applying alginate. (b) Pour the remaining alginate over the entire head.

alginate over the entire face. The first layer of wet alginate will function as a guide so the second layer of alginate can run smoothly over the first.

- BEFORE the alginate sets (because once the alginate sets, it won't stick to any surface), QUICKLY place a few precut pieces of terry cloth on the surface of the wet alginate in places such as the forehead, nose bridge, chin, both cheeks, neck, and toward the edges of the casting mold. Press each piece of terry cloth into the surface of the wet alginate so that the underside of the terry cloth is embedded in the wet alginate (Figure 1-15a) (the top side of the terry cloth will be embedded in the plaster bandage strips in step five). The terry cloth functions as an adhesive between the alginate and the plaster bandage strips and keep them together.

- After the alginate has set, use an eyeliner pencil to divide the head in two halves (the front and back) by drawing a guideline from ear to ear across the top of the head down to the base of the neck; this is the dividing line for placing the plaster bandage strips.

a

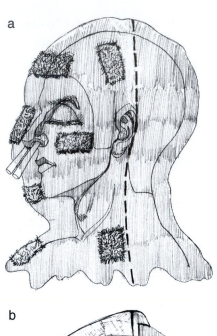

b

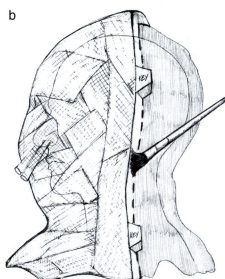

Figure 1-15 (a) First press pieces of terry cloth into the wet alginate; then draw a guideline on the casting alginate after it has set. (b) Apply plaster bandages to the front half of the head and build a wall with keys; then brush the wall with Vaseline.

Step Five: Applying Plaster Bandage over the Alginate Casting Mold

The alginate is soft and flexible even after it sets; therefore, it will not stay in shape by itself. Whether you cast a full head or just a face, several layers of plaster bandage strips must be applied on top of the alginate to create a rigid shell-like support system that is the shape of the casting mold. The front and back of the casting alginate must be covered with plaster bandage separately. Cover the front half first; then cover the back half.

- Cut the plaster bandage into strips of various lengths and widths ranging from 1″ to 20″. The small pieces will be used for the nose bridge and around the nostrils, and the large pieces will be used for the edge areas. Apply the plaster bandage strips on the front half of the mold first, usually starting from the edge to the center of the face.

- Dip the strip of plaster bandage in water and IMMEDIATELY take it out of the water and place it on top of the alginate (soaking the plaster bandage strip in water for too long and squeezing the excess water out will wash the powder out of the bandage); press it down so the strip hugs the planes of the alginate surface. Press and rub each layer of plaster bandage into the indentations on the surface and

overlap them. Also, alter the direction of the placement of each layer of the strips to reinforce the strength. Generally, three or four layers of strips are enough support for the alginate mold. The more layers you add, the stronger it will be.

- Reinforce the edges of the front plaster bandage shell by adding more layers of plaster bandage and building strength. The edge of the front shell must be at least ½″ thick all the way around. It needs to be sharp, smooth, and flat like building a wall. I have found that it is easier to build a short smooth wall if you mix a thicker paste of plaster of paris powder and apply it on top of the bandage.

- Create two keys on each side of the edge to lock the front and back shells together (Figure 1-15b). The wet plaster bandage will harden in approximately 15–20 minutes.

- Brush Vaseline on the short wall and a little bit on top of the wall to help release the mold (Figure 1-15b).

- Now make the back half of the head plaster shell. Repeat the same method of applying plaster bandage strips onto the back of the alginate casting mold. Because there is less detail in the back of head, the process will be much faster and easier than the front. Make sure the edge of the back shell meets well with the front shell (Figure 1-16a).

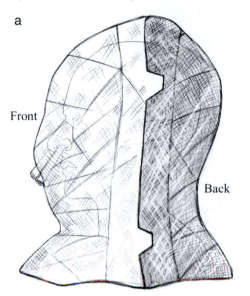

a

Front

Back

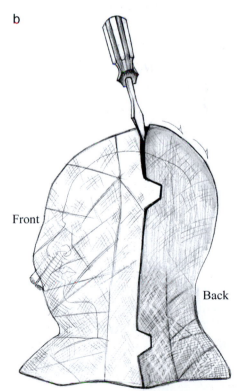

b

Front

Back

Figure 1-16 (a) Completed back plaster shell. (b) Remove the back plaster bandage shell.

Step Six: Removing the Casting Alginate Mold from the Head

- After the back plaster bandage shell hardens, use a screwdriver or butter knife as an aid to gently pry off the back plaster shell piece (Figure 1-16b) and remove the back half of the plaster shell from the alginate casting mold. DO NOT REMOVE the front half of the shell from the alginate casting mold!
- After removing the back half of the plaster bandage shell, the back of the alginate casting mold will be exposed again. GENTLY cut the center back of the alginate mold open from the top of the head to the bottom of the neck (Figure 1-17a) and also trim off the excess alginate at the very bottom of the casting mold with a butter knife or sculpting tool.
- Remove both the front plaster bandage shell and the whole alginate casting mold together at the same time (Figure 1-17b). Be careful not to accidentally separate the two molds. If you do, the detailed impressions on the face make it difficult to put separated molds exactly back in place. This will distort or deform the shape of the mold results so you may have to repeat the entire process again!

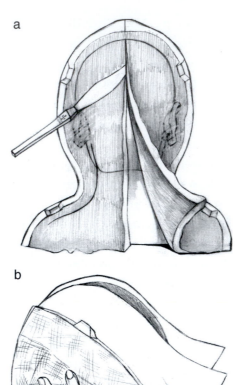

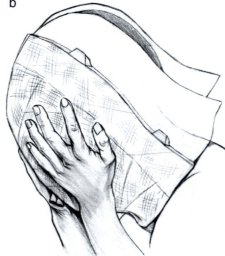

Figure 1-17 (a) Cut open the back alginate casting mold. (b) Remove the whole casting piece from the head.

- Ask the actor to lean forward and place his or her hands on the mold for support (Figure 1-17b), and then gently move his or her facial muscles underneath the mold to facilitate the separation of the skin from the inside of the mold. Tell the actor to sit forward and tilt his head down and to gently pull the negative casting mold down from the head. It will come off easily.

MAKING A FULL-HEAD POSITIVE MOLD FROM AN ALGINATE CASTING MOLD

The alginate will dry out soon, which will lead to a shrinkage problem. Therefore, a positive mold should be made immediately after the alginate life casting mold is off the actor's head or face. Only one positive mold can be made from a full-head negative mold.

PROCEDURE FOR MAKING A FULL-HEAD POSITIVE MOLD FROM AN ALGINATE MOLD

Materials Required:

- Modeling clay
- Spirit gum
- All-purpose spray adhesive
- Tape or ties (e.g., duct tape or a cord-like string)

- Box or container large and deep enough to hold the life casting mold
- Supporting materials (e.g., kitty litter, packing foam peanuts, or foam cubes)
- Vaseline
- Brushes for applying Vaseline and spirit gum
- Hair pins or clips
- Container for mixing
- Ultracal 30 (20 lbs)
- Water
- Mixing implement
- Long flat stick
- Butter knife or screwdriver
- Rubber hammer
- Sculpting tool

Ultracal 30 is gypsum cement. It works like plaster, but it is much heavier, harder, less porous, and more durable than plaster, with a light gray cement color. It is excellent for hot foam latex molds and teeth molds because of its strength and resistance to heat.

Step One: Closing the Front and Back Plaster Shells Together

- First, patch the two nostrils of the mold with modeling clay to prevent the leakage of the Ultracal 30 when you make the positive mold (Figure 1-18a).

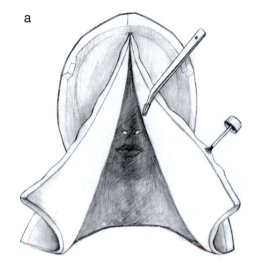

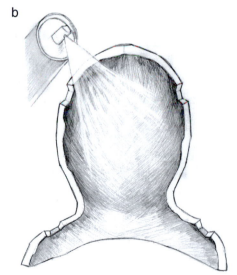

Figure 1-18 (a) Block the nostrils of the mold with clay, and apply spirit gum on the back cutting edge. (b) Spray glue on the inside of the plaster shell.

- Apply spirit gum on the back cut edges so they can nicely stay in place (Figure 1-18a).
- Apply a light coat of all-purpose spray adhesive on the inside surface of the back plaster bandage shell (Figure 1-18b), and then replace it on the back portion of the alginate casting mold where it was before. Making sure the keys match up exactly along the wall edges, press the back portion of the alginate casting piece from the inside to the plaster shell, making sure these two pieces properly coincide. Then tape or tie these front and back shells tightly together (Figure 1-19a).

Step Two: Positioning the Mold

- Prepare a box or container large and deep enough to hold the life casting mold. Put supporting materials such as kitty litter, packing foam nuggets, or foam cubes inside the box to stabilize the casting mold; the top of the skull on the mold is not a flat surface and will not stand by itself. Place the closed mold upside down in the box and stabilize it with the supporting materials (for this mask, I used packing peanuts) (Figure 1-19b).
- Brush Vaseline on any exposed plaster bandage mold around the opening edge.

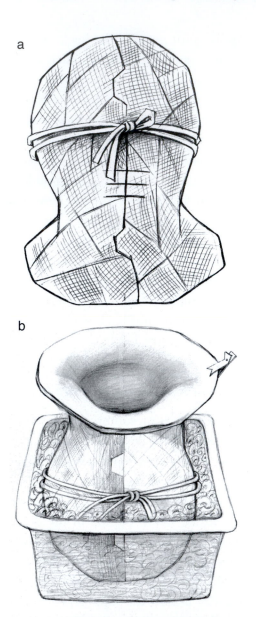

Figure 1-19 (a) Close the plaster molds together. (b) Place the closed mold upside-down in a box of packing foam nuggets; place a hair clip on the edge as necessary.

The Vaseline will ease the separation of the positive and negative molds later on. It is not necessary to grease the alginate part of the negative mold because once the alginate sets it won't stick to anything.

- If the plaster shell and alginate casting piece separate around the opening area, use hair pins or clips to clip them together before pouring in the Ultracal 30 (Figure 1-19b).

Step Three: Mixing the Ultracal 30

- Mixing Ultracal 30 and plaster of paris are basically the same procedure. Use a large container, and mix half of the total amount first because it is easier to manage. Pour water into the container first, and then sprinkle the Ultracal powder into the water. Do not stir while sprinkling; let the powder naturally absorb the water until it reaches $\frac{1}{8}''$ below the water level, and then stir with a spatula until it becomes a thin creamy paste.

Step Four: Pouring Ultracal 30 into the Casting Mold

Normally, the first coat of the plaster or Ultracal 30 should be brushed onto the negative mold to prevent any air bubbles from occurring. However, since the full-head casting mold is a deep-jar shape, it is impossible to brush the first coat of mix into the detailed impressions of the negative mold. The two shells are tied together, and it is not safe to move around the tied-together mold. Therefore, in this case, it is necessary to pour the mix into the casting mold to make a solid positive mold.

- Pour the Ultracal 30 mixture into the negative mold. Because of the depth of the mold, use a long flat stick as a guiding tool when pouring. Let the mixture flow down the guiding tool to the bottom center of the mold (Figure 1-20a). When the mixture reaches the bottom center, it will automatically spread around and push the air out of the mold. This is a way to inhibit air bubbles from forming underneath the mix. Pouring the mixture without a guiding tool will produce air bubbles on the positive mold.

- After the first mixture is poured in, mix the second container of Ultracal and pour it into the negative casting mold to fully fill it (Figure 1-20b).

- Wait overnight before opening the positive mold.

a

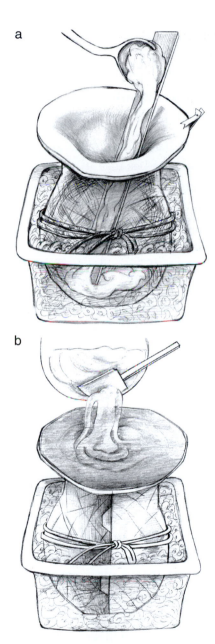

b

Figure 1-20 (a) Let the Ultracal 30 flow down the guiding tool into the mold. (b) Pour the second half of the Ultracal, fully filling the entire mold.

Step Five: Opening the Positive Mold

- Undo the tie or tape from the mold. Use a butter knife or screwdriver to pry off the back half of the plaster shell (Figure 1-21a). Do this just as you removed the casting mold from the actor's head when making the negative mold. You still must be careful working around the ears, but otherwise this time the back alginate piece can be ripped off.

- Use a rubber hammer to lightly knock the edges of the front shell loose. It should be gently pulled forward and downward; do not pull it up from the neck (pulling upward will destroy the features on the positive mold).

- If some craters appear on the surface of the positive mold (created by air bubbles), immediately patch them by mixing a little Ultracal 30 powder and smearing it into the crater. Dip your fingers in water and use them to flatten and smooth the surface. Do not put any Vaseline on the mold if you spot any craters that must be fixed. If there are any lumps copied from the alginate casting mold, use sculpting tools to carve them off.

- Let the positive mold dry. It may take a week to dry a solid mold (Figure 1-21b).

a

b

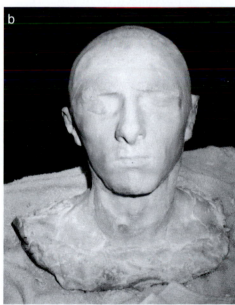

Figure 1-21 (a) After undoing the tie, pry off the back shell. (b) Photo of the completed full-head positive mold made from actor Tom McNelly, who played Dracula (the steps for making this particular mold were unfortunately not photographed).

SCULPTING WITH MODELING CLAY AND MAKING NEGATIVE MOLDS FROM THE MODELING CLAY SCULPTURE

Oil-based clay is the best material for sculpting because it will not dry out. The clay comes in small strips or large cubes of different colors. However, if you sculpt a large subject, your fingers may get sore. The clay can be softened with heating it; put the clay in a bowl and place the bowl in hot water or put the bowl on top of a heat radiator (if it's winter). Oil-based clay can be purchased from any art supply store or theatrical supply store (see Section Ten).

Prosthetic pieces can be made small or large, in several sections, or in a half or full mask. Taking drawing, art anatomy, and sculpture courses will help your understanding of the appearance and movements of the muscles so that you can effectively create them. Whether the prosthetic piece is small or big, the key is to make the edges super thin.

I did the necessary research for creating a 90-year-old Dracula face (Figure 1-22). The Dracula mask I made was a ³/₄ head mask: the full front face and two sides with the center back of the head left open and covered by an attached full wig.

Figure 1-22 Costume design for Dracula.

PROCEDURES FOR MODELING WITH CLAY AND A MAKING NEGATIVE MOLD

Materials Required:

- Oil-based clay
- Sculpting table (optional)
- Sculpting tools
- Old rough terry cloth, orange peel, or an old toothbrush
- Soft pointed brush and ink
- Clear plastic package covers or plastic milk jugs or water-based clay
- Vaseline or petroleum jelly or mold release
- Ruler
- Mixing bowl
- Ultracal 30 (about 15 lbs.)
- Water
- Spatula
- Screwdriver
- Clear lacquer

Step One: Positioning the Positive Mold

- Position the positive mold at eye level for modeling because it's easiest for checking proportions and the balance of the clay being added. Ideally, you should have a sculpting table to help in turning the mold and checking angles. If you don't have one, you'll have to move yourself around the modeling subject to view it from every angle and keep it in proportion and balance with the actor's body.

Step Two: Molding

- All the clay added to the positive mold should be skillfully and effectively managed. Too much clay will cause the sculpture to be too heavy. Use sculpting tools to create details such as wrinkles, bags, and sagging muscles. Taper down the edges where the clay will merge with the skin and blend them smoothly for a natural look. The thinner the edges of the prosthetic piece, the more realistic and natural it will appear on the actor's face. Thicker edges will produce a visible and noticeable line and will destroy the natural appearance.

- Use old rough terry cloth, orange peel, or an old tooth brush to create skin texture on the modeling clay, if desired (Figure 1-23).

Figure 1-23 Completed clay sculpture mold.

Step Three: Dividing the Modeling Clay Sculpture

To make a full-head foam mask, a full-head negative mold must be divided into sections to safely open the mold without breaking it. Dracula's mask was a $\frac{3}{4}$ full-head mask. The negative mold was divided into four sections because of the shape of the pointed ears: (1) the full front face with neck, (2–3) the two sides, and (4) the center top ($2\frac{1}{2}''$ square) of the head (Figure 1-24a). This worked well for this mask, but you may have different dividing positions depending on the mask shape.

- Draw the dividing lines as desired with a soft pointed brush and ink on the clay mold (Figure 1-24a). How you divide the mold and the number pieces to divide it into depend on the shape of the sculpture. Basically, simpler features should be divided into fewer pieces than the complicated ones. The negative mold for a full head can be divided from the center front to the center back of the head or from ear to ear across the top in two sections.

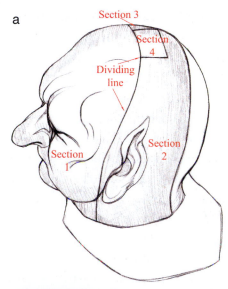

a

Section 3

Section 4

Dividing line

Section 1

Section 2

b

Figure 1-24 (a) Draw dividing lines on the sculpture. (b) Cut out dividers from thin plastic material.

Step Four: Creating and Inserting Divider Pieces and Adding Keys and a Clay Wall

- Plastic package cover pieces were used as dividers for the Dracula sculpture. Cut clear plastic package covers or plastic milk jugs into pieces about 2″ × 3–4″ in varied rectangular shapes (Figure 1-24b). (*Note:* Water-based clay can be also used as divider. Simply make a 2″ tall and ½″ wide clay wall-strip. The water-based clay is softer than oil-based clay; it easily conforms to the shape of the surface of the sculpture.)

- Insert the plastic pieces into the clay subject ON TOP of the dividing line (if you are using water-based clay, lay your clay wall NEXT to the dividing line). Overlap the pieces a little as you insert them until the desired section of the dividing fence is established. Finish one section at a time; repeat the process until all the sections are completed (Figure 1-25a). (The dividing line will be slightly visible on the hot foam prosthetic piece, but it will be covered by a wig.)

- Add a key by making a clay ball ⅝″ in diameter and cutting it in half with thread. Put each ball half on the top and bottom portion of the plastic

divider (Figure 1-25a). These two half balls will be used to lock the sections of the molds together. Be careful, do not make the keys too tall or deep or else they may become an obstacle when opening the molds.

- Build up a ½- to ⅝″-thick and 2″-tall clay wall around the edges of the sculpture. Use a rolling pin or a rolling-pin-shaped tool to roll the clay out flat and cut it into 2″-wide strips. Lay the wall 1″ away from the edges of the first section of the clay sculpture (Figures 1-25a and b).

Step Five: Taking Measurements and Applying Mold Release/Petroleum Jelly/Vaseline

- Apply mold release or Vaseline/petroleum jelly on any exposed surfaces of the Ultracal 30 mold (Figure 1-25b). This is very important. Any missed spot may be spoiled.

- Do not grease the surface of the clay when making a negative mold from it because Vaseline may destroy the texturing on the clay. In addition, oil-based clay will not stick to plaster, Ultracal 30, or the plastic divider materials.

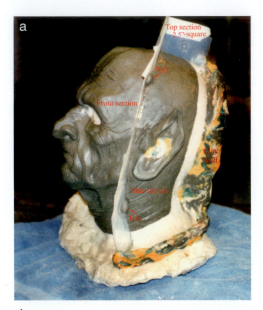

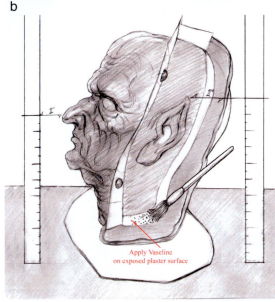

Figure 1-25 (a) Dividers, keys, and a clay wall are placed on the mold. (b) Apply Vaseline over any exposed Ultracal 30 surface, and measure the high points of the clay mold.

- The negative mold should be made at least 1″ thick in all places. It may be hard to tell when it reaches 1″ thick on high points such as the nose, so before pouring Ultracal 30 over the clay mold, it is wise to measure the high points, such as the tip of the nose, chin, and ears, to make sure the negative mold is 1″ inch thick over each high point. To measure the high point, place a ruler vertically on the table and measure up to the high point (in my example, the high points are the nose and ears), and record the measurement from the table's surface to the high point and mark the spot where the ruler is placed on the table. Then make another mark on the table 1″ away from the first mark. Use these marks as reference points to check the thickness of the Ultracal 30 after it has been poured on the mold and make sure these points are 1″ thick. To check other high points, such as the ear, use the same method (Figure 1-25b).

Step Six: Making the First Section of the Negative Mold

- Keep the positive mold in an upright position; this is the only way to make sectioned negative molds.

- Pour approximately 1 cup water into a mixing bowl. Sprinkle Ultracal powder into the water until it is ¼″ above the entire surface of the water and then stir until it becomes creamy paste (Figure 1-26a). This first coat of the Ultracal 30 mixture should not be too runny.

- Tap on the mixed Ultracal 30 with a brush from the bottom up (Figure 1-26b). Make sure there are no air bubbles, and try not to miss any spots. Avoid brushing the surface with the brush; just dip and gently tap with the brush until all textured details are well covered.

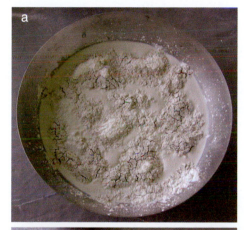

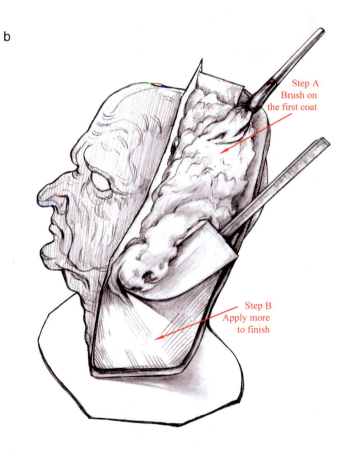

Step A
Brush on
the first coat

Step B
Apply more
to finish

Figure 1-26 (a) Mixing water and Ultracal 30. (b) Brush on the first layer of Ultracal 30 (Step A) and complete the section with the second layer (Step B).

- While you are waiting for the first coat to set, starting mixing the second and last coat. The second coat of Ultracal 30 should be thicker than the first coat. Again, pour water into the mixing bowl, and then sprinkle Ultracal 30 powder onto the water, letting the powder naturally absorb the water, until the powder reaches ½″ above the water. Then mix until the Ultracal 30 becomes a thicker creamy paste. Apply the paste all over the first coat of the negative mold with a spatula (Figure 1-26b) until it reaches the necessary thickness (use the measurements as reference).
- The surface of the Ultracal 30 will become warm and take about 15–20 minutes to harden. After it hardens, carefully remove the dividers piece by piece and clean out the clay from the keys if there is any clay stuck inside. DO NOT REMOVE the section.

Step Seven: Creating Pry Niches, Applying Vaseline to the Mold, and Making the Other Sections

- Make a few clay squares or rectangles that are ½″ and ⅛″ thick. Place them on the surface of the side plane of the plaster negative mold to create a few prying holes for later inserting a screwdriver as an aid for opening the

molds (Figure 1-27a). I recommend that you make three pry-niches: one on the top and one on each side of the negative mold.
- BEFORE CONTINUING on to the next section, do not forget a very important step — apply Vaseline to the side plane of the negative mold that was against the divider (apply Vaseline to all exposed Ultracal 30 surfaces).
- Repeat steps four to seven to complete the opposite side, front, and top negative molds. Complete each section one at a time in a continuous process.
- Mark several notches with markers across the edges where the front and back negative molds meet so that you can properly align them later when making the foam mask (Figure 1-27b).

Step Eight: Opening Molds

The average setup time of the Ultracal 30 is 25–35 minutes. The molds can be opened 40 minutes after the last section (the negative mold) is done.
- Insert a screwdriver into the prying niches, which should still be filled with soft clay, so the screwdriver should go in easily. Gently pry each section at the

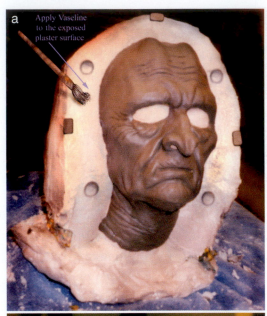

Figure 1-27 (a) Add pry niches on the mold, and apply Vaseline on the side plane of the plaster negative mold. (b) Completed negative mold of the entire head with marker notches.

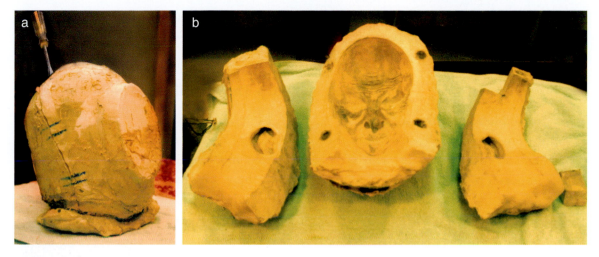

Figure 1-28 (a) Use a screwdriver to open the molds at the pry niches; (b) Opened and cleaned positive and negative molds.

PROCEDURE FOR MAKING A HOT FOAM LATEX MASK

The procedure for making hot foam is basically to follow the instructions that come with the kit.

Materials Required:

- Hot foam latex kit
- Soft brush for applying mold release
- Mixmaster or other blender
- Paper cups or plastic containers
- Oven
- Weight scale or gram scale
- Spoon
- Syringe or turkey baster
- Spatula
- Castor oil
- Hair dryer
- Scissors
- Wire or string
- Gloves or oven mitts
- Towels
- Knife
- Baby powder
- Screwdriver
- Wooden sculpting tool
- Brush for applying powder
- Black elastic strip (1″ wide × 2″)
- Snaps
- Needle and thread (some flesh-colored)
- Brown makeup eyeliner
- Full wig and loose hair

niches a little at a time to loosen the mold (Figure 1-28a). The direction of taking off the front negative mold pieces is downward and forward. In the example in Figure 1-28, the sides of the mold were taken off first and the front piece was taken off last.

- In most cases, the clay sticks to the negative mold when the positive mold is pulled off, so the clay should be cleaned out (Figure 1-28b). Use a sculpting tool or your finger to lift the edges of the clay and roll and lift inward so the clay doesn't smear and get stuck even more. Then use tweezers to pick up the small pieces and use your fingers for the large pieces. If you accidentally smear some, the best strategy for cleaning it off is to stick a piece of clay to the smeared clay and remove it.

- Allow the mold sections to dry a week, or put them in an oven at 200°F for faster drying. Be sure to dry them thoroughly — any moist or wet mold will produce a prosthetic piece of poor quality with lumps on the foam surface or with the skin of the foam piece separating from the other foam tissue layers underneath.

- After the mold sections are dry, spray two coats of clear lacquer as a sealer on the full-head positive mold ONLY to protect it from getting dirty and worn out. Do not spray any clear lacquer on any negative molds.

- Ventilating needle
- Liquid latex
- Rubber grease paints, aquacolors, or acrylic colors; or materials for airbrushing
- Watercolor brush

Step One: Applying Mold Release

- Mold release comes with the hot foam kit. Follow the instructions carefully to apply a coat of release with a soft brush on the inside of each negative mold section and everywhere on the positive head mold. Use a hair dryer for faster drying, if necessary.
- Apply two more coats of mold release on newly made positive and negative molds (including the side-walls and keys of the negatives) because the molds will absorb some of the release agent. It is difficult to reach the deep impressions (in this example, inside the ears) with a brush to apply creamlike release agent or with the spray-on release agent. The alternative to using mold release is to use caster oil. The solution is to pour some castor oil into the mold's ear canals and to rotate the mold in different directions so the castor oil runs into the crevices and corners that are hard to reach with a brush or spray. Then turn the negative

mold upside down so any extra castor oil drains out. It is not necessary to dry the oil, but you should not leave any oil puddles in the mold.
- Every duplication of the other prosthetic pieces requires a through application of mold release on both the positive and negative molds. This is very important.

Step Two: Weigh All Parts of the Hot Foam

- Follow the directions that come with the hot foam kit. Carefully and accurately weigh the hot foam material. Any careless mistakes in your measurements will produce a prosthetic piece of poor quality that will have to be redone.
- Follow the step-by-step mixing instructions carefully and accurately, and mix the parts together to produce a creamy foam paste. The higher the foam rises, the softer and more flexible the prosthetic pieces will be.
- Keep a clear and complete record of your procedure, including the amounts of each part, time it takes to blend, room temperature, baking time, and foam volume. If everything goes right or wrong, you'll have a record as a reference and can make the necessary adjustments. Following the kit

instructions well will lead to success.

Step Three: Filling the Molds

- Line the molds (coated with release agent) next to each other for quick and easy mold closing.
- If there are any deep impressions in the negative mold, such as inside the ear canal, use a syringe or turkey baster to inject the foam into the deep impressions. Then pour more foam into the mold with a spatula and spread the foam from the center out (Figure 1-29a); this will automatically drive the air out of the mold. You should work quickly!
- The amount of clay you added to sculpt the prosthetic piece will equal how much foam is needed to fill the gap between the positive and negative molds. Most of the time, adding a little bit more foam than needed is wise to make sure the foam covers all the areas in the negative mold. But adding too much foam will create a thick edge on the prosthetic piece.
- Quickly and carefully put the negative molds back on the positive mold (in this example, two side negative pieces were closed first, then the front piece), except for the top piece, matching the key

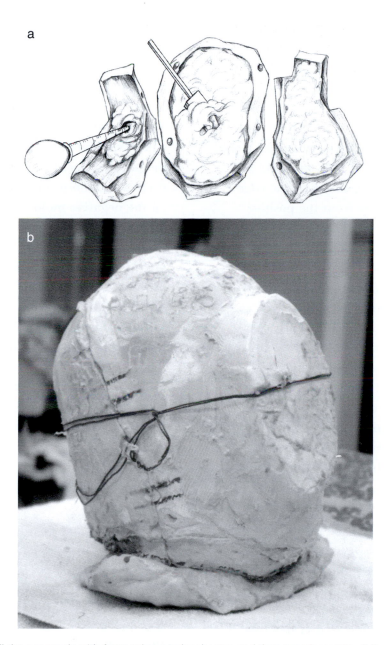

Figure 1-29 (a) Fill the ear canals with foam using a turkey baster, and then pour foam into all the negative molds with a spatula. (b) Tie the closed negative molds together.

marks on the edges where the molds meet. Firmly press the pieces of the negative molds to the positive mold; press hard. The excess foam will be driven out from the top opening, which was made for this. Then close the opening with the top piece. Tie all the negative molds to the positive mold with wire or string for reinforcement (Figure 1-29b). Let the foam set for 10–15 minutes until the foam stops rising, and then put it in the oven to cure.

- Keeping the mold in an upright position, put it in the oven to be cured. Bake it for 4 hours at 200°F. The curing time depends on the size of the prosthetic piece. Large pieces will take longer to bake. I recommend turning on the kitchen vent fans because of the odor during baking.

Lining up the notches and pressing the negative molds to the positive mold is how I experimented with making a ¾-head mask. It was quite a challenging process and worked well for the *Dracula* production. There are two ways to fill the foam latex into the negative mold: by pouring and by injecting. The pouring method works well on small prosthetic pieces such as individual facial features. Filling a mold by injecting is a common method for larger pieces. The foam can be injected into a closed mold with an injection gun. It is necessary to drill holes into the positive mold, one for injection and the other for venting air and allowing excess foam to run out in order to create a thin edge on the prosthetic piece. Dracula's mask is quite large, so it could have been done with the injection method. However, I chose a different way to make it because I didn't have an injection gun and I didn't want to drill holes into the positive mold.

Step Four: Opening the Mold and Removing the Hot Foam Prosthetic Piece from the Mold

- Once the foam is cured, press it with your fingers. The foam should bounce back; this shows that the foam is cured. If it does not bounce back, it needs to bake longer or it may have failed. The mold can be quite hot, so when you remove it from the oven wear a pair of gloves or oven mitts to protect your hands.

- Put the warm mold on a table and wrap it with several towels immediately so it can cool down gradually for about 30 minutes. A sudden drop in temperature may cause the mold to crack.

- After letting the mold cool for 30 minutes, unwrap the towels and try to open the mold. The mold should still be warm but not hot. It should be easier to open the molds when they are warm.

- Trim off the extra foam that escaped to the outside of the mold when you closed it. Use your fingers or a wooden sculpting tool to gently pull the edge of the foam away from the positive mold.

- Powder all the foam edges around the negative molds. The powder will prevent the thin edge of the foam from sticking to itself.

- Insert a screwdriver and gently pry loose the negative mold pieces (in the same way as shown in Figure 1-28a).

- After the negative mold loosens up, remove one side of the negative molds first and repeat the same steps to remove the other side of the negative mold, so you can remove the front piece. Hot foam is very flexible and durable. Pull slightly upward first and then pull downward. This will loosen, for example, the pointy ears of the foam from the negative mold. If the pointy ears of the negative mold are well covered with mold release, there will be no problem in separating the foam and mold.

- After both sides of the negative molds are removed, gently pry and loosen the center-face mold from the top edge, and slowly pull the front negative mold downward and forward to safely remove it. The foam piece will have the tendency to stick back to the negative mold side because of deeper and more complex impressions on the negative mold than on the positive mold. Use a brush and dust some loose powder between the foam and mold before separating them to prevent the foam from sticking back to the mold.

- If the negative molds are still warm, wrap them with towels again and let them gradually cool.

- Wash the whole mask in warm soapy water to clean the mold release from the foam. Gently pat the mask dry with a towel, and when it's half-dry, put it back on the positive mold to prevent shrinkage and to help keep its shape.

- Trim out the eye openings and slash the opening of the lips.

Step Five: Attaching an Elastic Strip and Snaps on the Foam Mask

- Glue and then sew a piece of 1″ wide × 2″ long black elastic strip horizontally onto each side of the back lower neck area of the foam mask. Glue down one end of each elastic piece on the wrong side to the back lower neck area with liquid latex. After it dries, sew it with large hand sewing stitches for reinforcement. These elastic strips are the closure for the mask (Figure 1-30a).

- Try it on the actor's head. Make marks on the elastic strips for where snaps will be sewn (Figure 1-30a). Avoid using Velcro for a closure; it will get caught in the actor's hair when you put the mask on or take it off.

The wig and mask will be handled as one piece; no adhesive will be used when the actor wears it. Because this mask was created from the actor's life casting mold, it fits perfectly on the actor's face. There are no restrictions on talking and the foam mask will naturally follow his facial movement. It works very well for quick makeup changes.

Step Six: Attaching a Full Wig to the Hot Foam Mask

- Mark a new hairline for the mask with a brown makeup eyeliner (it can be removed with makeup remover) (Figure 1-30b).

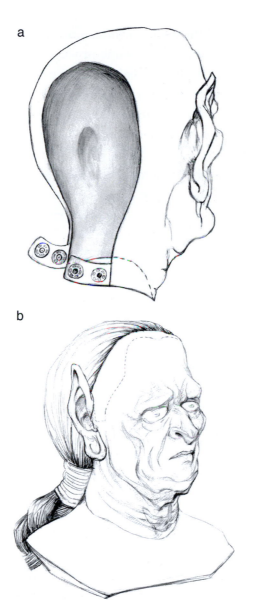

a

b

Figure 1-30 (a) Attach elastic and snaps to the foam mask. (b) Mark a new hairline, and attach the wig to the foam mask.

- To hide the wig hairline, position the wig about 1" away from the new hairline (Figure 1-30b). Attach the wig by hand with large sewing stitches and flesh-toned thread.

Step Seven: Inserting Hair and Facial Hair into the Foam Mask and Creating a New Hairline

- Insert a ventilating needle from the wrong side to the right side of the foam mask at the new hairline; picking one or two hairs with the needle's hook (Figure 1-31a).
- Pull about, ¼" of the hair to the wrong side of the foam mask, and then remove the needle without tying any knots (Figure 1-31b); just leave it as a loop. Avoid making big loops because bigger loops will be in the way for the next hair-inserting process. Bigger hair loops can be adjusted by pulling the hair back a little to the right side of the foam mask.
- The inserted hair will be temporarily held by the foam. Keep inserting hairs until you have a 1"- to 1½"-square group. Then apply some liquid latex over the hair loops and wait for the latex to half dry; then use your fingers to press the hair loops flat (Figure 1-31b). The latex will

a

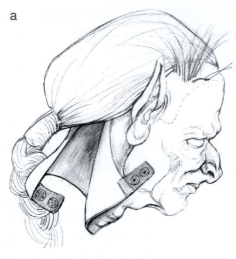

b

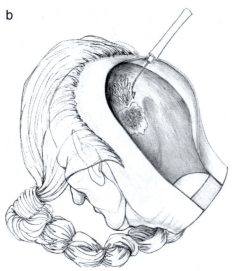

Figure 1-31 (a) Insert a ventilating needle from the wrong side of the mask to the right side of the mask, picking up the hair. (b) Pull hair to the wrong side of the mask and leave it in loops; later glue the hair loops down and flattened them to the mask with liquid latex.

secure the loops to the foam mask. Repeat the same process until all the new hairline areas are covered with hair. The inserted hair will cover the noticeable wig hairline to achieve a natural hairline look.

- Using the same method, insert some facial hair at the eyebrows, ears, and nostrils to achieve a characteristic appearance for, in this example, Dracula's mask.

As noted before, this foam mask was worn without any adhesive. The foam mask followed the actor's facial expressions perfectly, especially at the mouth when he was talking or laughing.

Step Eight: Painting the Hot Foam Mask

Hot foam or any other appliances can be painted with rubber grease paints, aquacolors, or acrylic colors. Rubber grease paints produce an opaque look, require powder, and may be rubbed off when the mask is handled during quick changes. Aquacolors are excellent for foam, but they are costly. Artist acrylic colors are economic with no rub-off problem, provide transparent natural skin coloration, and are powder free. Airbrushing the prosthetic pieces is

another other option. I used acrylic colors to paint Dracula's mask, using the watercolor painting techniques "wash" and "wet-on-wet."

- Mix a flesh-toned foundation with water and acrylic pigments on a color palette. Mix a plentiful amount of paint. Apply the paint over the foam mask with a large soft watercolor brush. The key to painting foam is to keep a transparent look; start out light and, if you need to go darker, add more layers of paint. Use a piece of excess hot foam trimmed from the foam edges to test the color first. Be careful — because foam absorbs acrylic pigments well, it is difficult to remove the paint if the surface of the foam is painted too dark.

- Mix a rouge color by adding a tint of red with the foundation color and apply it over the cheeks, lips, and a little all over the face, including the ears, to give the mask a harmonious healthy glow. Remember the key is to paint it from light to dark.

The completed Dracula mask is shown in Figures 1-32 to 1-33.

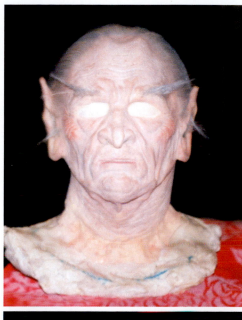

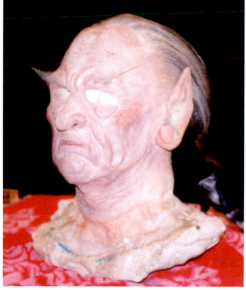

Figure 1-32 Completed wig and painted mask.

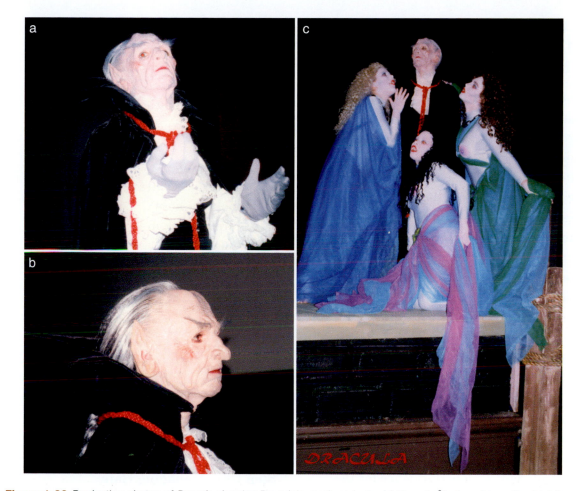

Figure 1-33 Production photos of *Dracula* showing Dracula's mask and wig. (a) Dracula ³/₄ view, (b) profile, (c) full-body. *Dracula played by Tom McNelly (middle). Three vampire wives played by (from left to right) Amber Hoff, Danika Eger, and Kerri Van Auken. Directed by Wesley Van Tassel. Scenic design by Randy B. Winder. Lighting design by Mark C. Zetterberg. Costume and makeup design by Tan Huaixiang. Central Washington University Department of Theatre Arts presentation.*

FACE LIFE CASTING AND MAKING A COLD FOAM PROSTHETIC PIECE

Making a cold foam prosthetic piece is similar to making a hot foam latex prosthetic piece. It requires a set of closed positive and negative molds. As an alternative to hot foam, cold foam is not as flexible and strong, but it is quick and easy to make. It sets within 25–30 minutes and no oven curing is required. It is not suitable for making large prosthetic pieces, but it is an excellent material for making small applications such as facial features for character makeup.

I experimented with cold foam when making Cyrano noses for the production *Cyrano de Bergerac* staged at the Department of Theatre Arts at Cornell University. A cold foam kit comes with all the required parts and instructions. Since making cold foam is a simple process, I made a new cold foam nose for each performance for the best natural look each time.

MAKING A FACE LIFE CASTING

PROCEDURE FOR FACE LIFE CASTING

Materials Required:

- 5-minute setting alginate
- Plaster bandage

- Plaster of paris or Ultracal 30
- Vaseline or petroleum jelly
- Comb
- Cotton balls
- Bald cap or plastic wrap
- Scotch tape
- Hair gel
- Spirit gum
- Large drinking straws (for breathing through the nose)
- A haircut mockup
- Scissors
- Terry cloth (about eight pieces, precut 1″ × 2″ or 2″ × 2″)
- Container for measuring alginate and water
- Container for water
- Mixing bowl
- Spatula
- Butter knife

Step One: Managing Hair

As mentioned in the instructions for full-head casting for a hot foam mask, put a bald cap on the actor's head to protect and manage the hair. Hair protection is much less complicated in face casting than full-head life casting. It requires you only to flatten all the hair and comb it back as close to the scalp as possible for both short and long hair.

- Apply hair gel to the front portion of the hair touching the skull (ear to ear across top of the head, not to the hair ends); make sure the hair gel reaches the hair roots and comb and flatten it to the skull as close as possible.
- If you want to save money on a bald cap, you may use a swimming cap or plastic wrap to cover the hair line area and ears. Covering the hair with plastic wrap is the most economical way.
- If you are using plastic wrap, cut a piece of plastic wrap large enough to cover the actor's entire front hair area. Lay it ½″ or ¾″ below the hairline all the way around the front hairline. Cut out another piece of plastic big enough to cover the back portion of the actor's hair (Figure 1-34a).

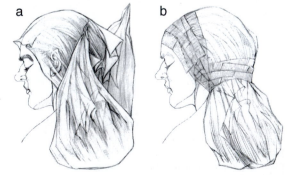

Figure 1-34 (a) Cover the actor's hair with plastic wrap. (b) Tape the plastic wrap down with scotch tape.

- Tape down the plastic wrap by placing pieces of tape next to each other, slightly overlapping them (Figure 1-34b).
- The other alternative is to use a cheap bald cap to cover long hair. Put a bald cap on the head, and trim down the edges of the cap as necessary (Figure 1-35). The ears can be covered with the cap. Because the cap is stretched to fit the head, the edges of the cap will naturally hug the head, so no glue is necessary.

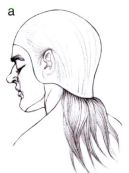
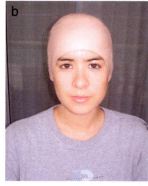

Figure 1-35 (a) Place the bald cap on the actor's head for face casting; (b) Nina Blankenship is the model for face casting. Her hair is covered with a latex cap. Her natural hairline is low and the bald cap is placed close to her eyebrows to protect her hair. If the actor has a higher hairline, the front edge of the bald cap should be farther back, exposing more of the forehead.

Step Two: Protecting the Face and Facial Hair

- Remove the actor's contact lenses (if any) to avoid eye irritation.
- Prepare a pair of straws for the actor to use to breath.
- Cover the actor with a barber smock.
- Apply an even coat of Vaseline all over the actor's face and neck, especially on the eyebrows, eyelashes, and beard. Comb the facial hair downward to prevent pulling on the hair when you remove the negative casting mold from the face. Avoid applying too much Vaseline because it can destroy the results of the impressions of the face and will make the face slippery so it will be difficult for the alginate to stay on the face. Also cast the neck in case you decide to make a prosthetic piece for the neck.
- Place cotton balls in both ears canals to prevent any liquid alginate from running in.
- Explain every step of the process to the actor so he or she is prepared and alerted. See the instructions for full-head life casting process for more details.

Step Three: Mixing Alginate

- Measure the appropriate amounts of 5-minute-setting alginate and water (1 : 1 ratio) (Figure 1-36a). Shake the alginate powder container up and down in slow motion before measuring it to loosen and fluff up the powder for more accurate measurements. Generally, $^3/_4$–1 lb is enough for face casting. Warmer water causes a faster setting time; colder water slows down the setting time of the alginate.
- Use a large bowl to mix the alginate so you will have enough space for rapid mixing motions. Pour the alginate powder into the bowl first and then the water. Mix the alginate and water with your hand or a large spatula in brisk motions and keep mixing (approximately 45–50 seconds) until the lumps disappear and the mixture becomes a smooth creamy paste (Figure 1-36b).

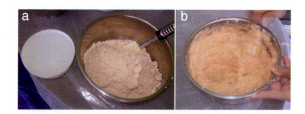

Figure 1-36 (a) Measuring the alginate. (b) Mixing the alginate.

- Start working on each individual area, working very quickly. I recommend working from the bottom up in the following order:
  1. Apply the alginate under the chin and neck (Figure 1-37a).
  2. Apply it above and below the mouth.
  3. Carefully insert the straws into the nose and ask the actor to hold them (Figure 1-37b).

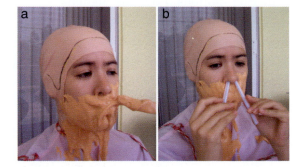

Figure 1-37 (a) Apply the alginate to the chin and neck. (b) Insert the straws into the actor's nostrils.

  4. Apply the alginate on the nose and around the nostrils (Figure 1-38a).
  5. Apply it around the eye-socket area (Figure 1-38b).

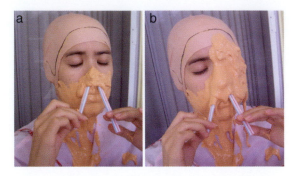

Figure 1-38 (a) Apply more alginate around the nose. (b) After one eye socket is covered, cover the other eye.

- Pour the rest of the alginate on the top of the actor's head so it runs down naturally. Use your hand or a spatula to guide the running alginate over the entire face (Figure 1-39a). The first layer of wet alginate is already on the face, so the second layer will easily flow over the first layer.
- Before the alginate sets (once the alginate sets, it won't stick to any surface), QUICKLY put a few pieces of precut terry cloth in various places on the surface of the wet alginate, such as the forehead, nose bridge, chin, both cheeks, neck, and the edges of the casting mold (Figure 1-39b). Press each piece of terry cloth into the surface of the wet alginate so the underside of the terry cloth is embedded into the wet alginate (the upper side of the terry cloth will be embedded into the plaster

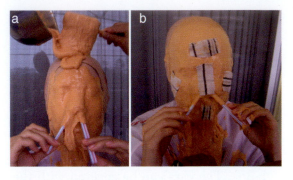

Figure 1-39 (a) Pour the rest of the alginate on the head and onto the face. (b) Press pieces of terry cloth into the wet alginate.

bandage strips applied in step four). The terry cloth will function as an adhesive between the alginate and the plaster bandage strips so they stay together.

Step Four: Applying Plaster Bandage over the Alginate Casting Mold

As I mentioned in the directions for full-head casting, alginate is soft and flexible even after it sets and will not retain its shape by itself. Several layers of plaster bandage strips must be applied on top of the alginate to create rigid shell-like support for the shape of the casting mold.

- Cut the plaster bandage into strips of various lengths and widths. The small pieces are used for the nose bridge and nostril areas around the straws, and the large pieces are used for the edges.

- Dip a strip of plaster bandage in water and IMMEDIATELY take it out of the water and press it down so the strip hugs the alginate surface. Soaking the plaster bandage strips in the water too long or squeezing the excess water out will wash the plaster powder out. Press and rub each layer of plaster bandage into the depressions of the surface and overlap the edges (Figure 1-40a). Also, alternate the direction of each layer of strips to reinforce the strength. Generally, three or four layers of strips should be enough support for the alginate mold, but the more layers of bandage strips added, the stronger the support. Strengthen the edges of the front plaster bandage shell with even more layers of plaster bandage. Allow 15 minutes for it to harden (Figure 1-40b).

Step Five: Removing the Face Casting Mold

- Trim off any unnecessary alginate edges around the plaster bandage shell (Figure 1-41a). Too much floppy and loose alginate edges will separate the alginate from the bandage shell.
- Now separate the alginate mold from the bald cap by gently pulling the bald cap down and back with your fingers and removing the mold. Make sure all the edges around the mold are separated from the bald cap underneath it (Figure 1-41b).
- Ask the actor to lean forward and put his or her hands on the mold, and then gently move his or her facial muscles to loosen it (Figure 1-42). At the same time, gently pull the mold down to separate the face from the inside of the mold. Keep the shell and alginate mold together while removing them.

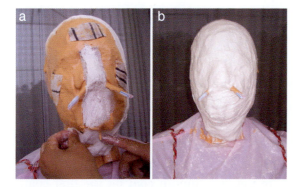

Figure 1-40 (a) Apply plaster bandages over the alginate casting mold. (b) Completed plaster bandage application.

Figure 1-41 (a) Trim the excess alginate edges. (b) Loosen the edges from the bald cap along the casting mold before removing the mold from the face.

Figure 1-42 Remove the face casting mold.

PROCEDURES FOR POURING A POSITIVE FACE MOLD INTO AN ALGINATE CASTING MOLD

The positive mold should immediately be poured into the alginate mold before the alginate can shrink. If you can't do this promptly, temporarily soak the alginate mold in water to prevent shrinkage.

The positive face mold can be made hollow or solid. A hollow positive mold reduces the weight and has space to insert a handle to help separate the positive and negative molds from each other. The demonstration next explains how to make a hollow positive mold.

Materials Required:

- Ultracal 30 or plaster of paris
- Mixing bowl
- Spatula
- Wooden or plastic handle (precut wooden or plastic rod 6–7 inches long)
- Modeling clay
- Box to support the mold
- Styrofoam peanuts or cat litter
- Screwdriver or butter knife
- Sculpting tools
- Soft-bristle brush
- Vaseline
- Sealer or clear acrylic spray

Step One: Preparations for Pouring the Ultracal 30 into the Alginate Mold

- Plug the nostrils on the alginate mold with modeling clay using tweezers or your fingers (Figure 1-43a).
- Put supporting material, such as cat litter, foam, or packing peanuts in a box to stabilize and support the mold. Then place and level the mold in the box with the alginate side facing up (Figure 1-43b).

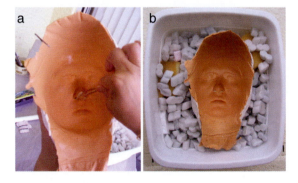

Figure 1-43 (a) Insert a piece of clay in each nostril with tweezers. (b) Place supporting material in the box to stabilize the alginate casting mold.

Step Two: Applying the First Coat of Ultracal 30 in the Alginate Casting Mold

- Pour a cup of water into a mixing bowl; don't make too much mix on the first coat because it may harden during the brushing process.

- Sprinkle Ultracal 30 powder on to the water. (You can also use plaster of paris; use the same methods of mixing and pouring and the same material proportions.) Do not stir until the powder reaches about $1/4''$ above the water; instead, let the powder absorb the water naturally (stirring early will cause lumps) (Figure 1-44a). After you stir, the mixture should be a suitable consistency for applying with a brush (Figure 1-44b).

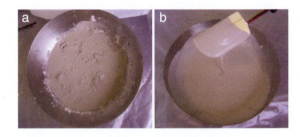

Figure 1-44 (a) Let the Ultracal 30 powder absorb the water; it is then ready to stir. (b) Stir the Ultracal 30 until the mixture is a creamy paste.

- Brush the first coat of Ultracal 30 onto the inside surface of the negative mold using tapping motions until the entire surface is covered (Figure 1-45a). There is no need to put the effort into trying to make a smooth coat on the first coat.
- After brushing on the first coat, pour the rest of the left over Ultracal 30 into

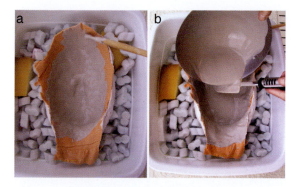

Figure 1-45 (a) Brush on the first coat of Ultracal 30. (b) Pour the rest of the Ultracal 30 into the mold, guiding it with the spatula.

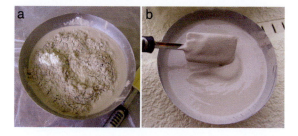

Figure 1-46 (a) For the second coat, let the Ultracal 30 powder absorb the water. (b) Stir until the mixture is a thicker, creamier paste than the first coat.

the mold, using the spatula to guide it (Figure 1-45b). It is not necessary to wait for the first coat to dry.

Step Three: Pouring the Second Coat of Ultracal 30 and Inserting a Handle for the Mold

- The second coat of Ultracal should be thicker than the first coat. Sprinkle the Ultracal 30 powder onto the water until it reaches about 1/2″ above the water level, letting the powder absorb the water (Figure 1-46a). Stir until the mixture becomes a thicker creamy paste (Figure 1-46b). Then pour the second mixture over the first coat. Spread it out with a spatula; avoid

touching the surface of the first coat (Figure 1-47a).

- A precut wooden or plastic rod 6–7 inches long will be used as a handle for the mold. Wrap the two ends of the rod with plastic bandage for better grip since the rod is slippery (Figure 1-47a). Place the handle in the middle of the mold in a vertical position after the second coat of Ultracal 30 has been

Figure 1-47 (a) Wrap the ends of the plastic handle with plaster bandage strips, and apply the second coat of Ultracal 30; (b) Place the handle in the middle of the mold and bind the ends of the handle to the Ultracal 30 with a couple of additional layers of plaster bandages.

applied. Then place a couple of additional layers of plaster bandages across the ends of the handle, binding it to the Ultracal 30 (Figure 1-47b). (For this step, as an alternative to plaster bandages, you can use burlap or cheesecloth strips dipped in mixed Ultracal 30.)

Step Four: Applying the Third Coat of Plaster to Complete the Positive Mold

- The third coat of Ultracal 30 is the final step in finishing up the mold. This coat should be a very thick but manageable paste. Apply the thick paste on top of the ends of the handle, making sure you leave enough space for a hand to grasp the middle of the rod (Figure 1-48a). Build up the sides of the mold until the mixture is level with the edge of the negative mold. Before it completely hardens, carve the date or any information you want to add into the mold (Figure 1-48b).

- Ultracal 30 paste becomes warm at first and then cools down; this takes 30–45 minutes. Plaster of paris, plaster bandage, and dental stone all have this same reaction. The mold can be opened once it has cooled down. You also can wait overnight to open the mold.

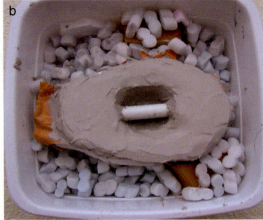

Figure 1-48 (a) Apply the third coat of Ultracal 30. (b) Completed poured positive mold.

- The newly made positive mold will take about a week to completely dry. Put the mold in an oven at 200°F for 4 hours if your need is to dry faster.

Step Five: Opening the Mold

- Gently loosen the edges all the way around between the alginate casting mold and the positive mold with a screwdriver or a butter knife (Figure 1-49).
- With one hand hold the handle of the positive mold and with the other hand pull the casting mold downward and then forward. Keep the alginate and the plaster bandage shell together if you are planning to duplicate more positive molds. You can duplicate three perfect positives from the same face life casting negative mold if you carefully separate the positive and negative molds each time. No waiting time is necessary between duplications. As mentioned earlier, soak the alginate casting mold in water between the pouring times to prevent shrinking.

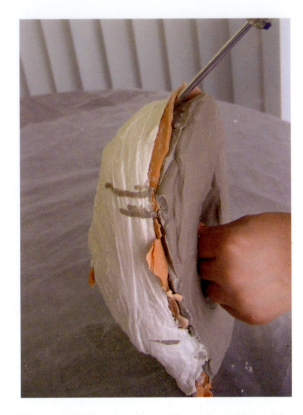

Figure 1-49 Separate the positive and negative molds.

- Carve the nostrils and clean the face up with sculpting tools, as necessary (Figure 1-50).
- After the mold is dry (Figure 1-51), spray on two coats of clear lacquer as a sealant to protect the mold from getting dirty and worn out.

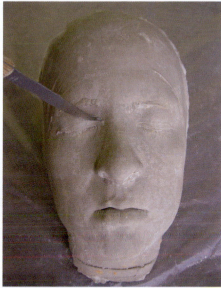

Figure 1-51 Completed positive mold.

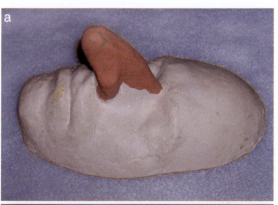

Step Six: Molding Individual Facial Features

Materials Required:

- Oil-based clay
- Sculpting tools
- Vaseline or petroleum jelly
- Brush for applying Vaseline
- Butter knife
- Rough terry cloth, orange peel, or stipple brush
- Rolling pin
- Soft cloth

When you mold a facial feature, its size should balance with other parts of the face unless you want to create an exaggerated or comical look.

- Start by building up the basic dimensions, body, and form of the features (Figure 1-52a). Do not work

Figure 1-52 (a) Build up the basic shape of the features with clay. (b) Completed Cyrano nose in clay.

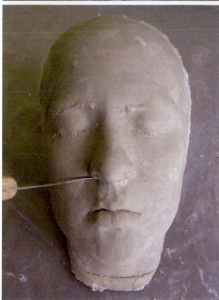

Figure 1-50 Use a sculpting tool to remove any lumps on the face and to carve and trim the nostrils.

on details at the beginning. Check the shape and symmetry from every angle; especially, look down on to the forehead toward the chin with the face of the mold facing away from you.

- Shape the facial features how you want them, and blend the clay edges into the plaster positive mold. Check the blended clay edge by running your finger cross it; if you feel a bumpy line, that means it needs more blending. Your clay creation is what the prosthetic piece will look like.
- Creating skin texture or depressions can be done with different objects, such as a rough terry cloth, orange peel, stipple brush, or sculpture tool, by pressing the object into the clay as desired (Figure 1-52b).

Step Seven: Creating a Boundary Line

- Place a roll of clay away from the edge of the clay nose (or other sculpted objects) to create a clayless boundary (a $\frac{1}{4}$"- to $\frac{3}{8}$"-wide gap) around the objects.
- Extend the roll of clay until it is $1\frac{1}{2}$–2" wide and $\frac{1}{4}$" thick. This provides a path for the excess foam from between the positive and negative molds when they are closed. It will also ease the separation of the molds and give any prosthetic piece a thinner edge.
- Once the clay pathway has been established, use a sculpting tool to neatly trim the clay around the plaster boundary line (Figure 1-53a).

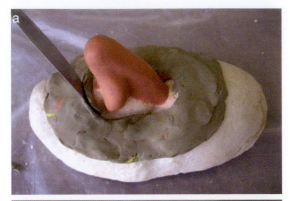

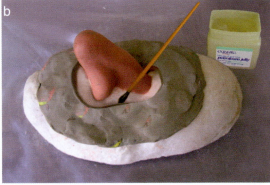

Figure 1-53 (a) Create a pathway and trim the clay. (b) Apply mold release or Vaseline.

Step Eight: Applying Mold Release and Building a Clay Wall

- Use a brush to apply a coat of Vaseline on the exposed plaster boundary line area to help release the positive and negative molds and prevent them from sticking together (Figure 1-53b).

- Build a clay wall around the clay nose for pouring the negative mold. Use a rolling pin to flatten the clay to a $\frac{1}{4}$- to $\frac{3}{8}$"-thick clay strip (Figure 1-54a); set the clay strip around the sculpture. The wall should be at least 1" taller than the tallest point (here the tip of the nose) and at least 1" away from the sculpted object all around (Figure 1-54b).

Figure 1-54 (a) Make the clay wall. (b) Build the clay wall around the nose sculpture.

Step Nine: Making a Negative Mold from the Individual Sculptured Object

- Mix enough plaster of paris to fully fill the mold. Pour water in the mixing bowl first, sprinkle the plaster powder onto the water without stirring until the powder reaches $\frac{1}{8}''$ above to the surface of the water. Then stir until the mixture becomes a creamy paste (Figure 1-55).

Figure 1-55 Mixing the plaster of paris for the negative mold of the individual object.

- Brush the first coat of plaster over the sculptured object (Figure 1-56a). Pour the rest of the plaster into the mold using a guiding tool. Start from one point and let the plaster naturally run in to drive out the air and slowly fill the mold (Figure 1-56b).
- When the plaster starts to get hard, draw an arrow on it to indicate where

Figure 1-56 (a) Brush the first coat of plaster over the mold. (b) Pour the rest of plaster into the mold. (c) Completely filled mold.

the top is. Allow it to set for couple of hours or overnight.

Step Ten: Opening the Mold

- Take down the clay wall (Figure 1-57a). Set the mold in an upright position, one hand holding the positive mold and the other hand holding the negative mold. Gently pull the negative mold down and forward

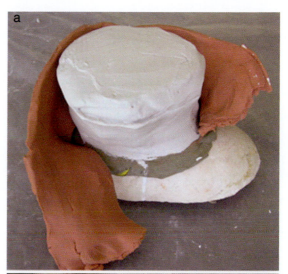

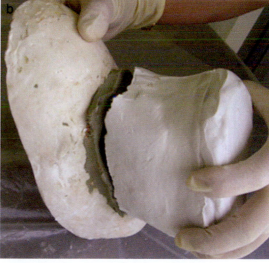

Figure 1-57 (a) Remove the clay wall. (b) Separate the positive and negative molds.

(Figure 1-57b). The negative mold will separate easily (Figure 1-58a).

- Clean off the clay stuck to the molds. Carefully lift and remove the large pieces of clay using a sculpting tool or your fingers (Figure 1-58b); remove the small pieces left inside of the negative mold with a large piece of clay. Small pieces of clay stuck to the positive mold can be removed with wooden sculpting tools and rubbed off using a piece of soft cloth and Vaseline.
- Let the negative mold dry for a few days (Figure 1-58c).

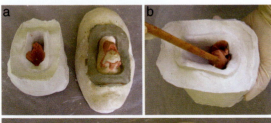
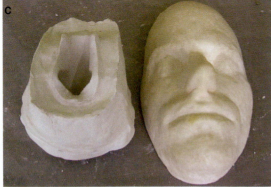

Figure 1-58 (a) Opened molds. (b) Clean the molds. (c) Completed positive and negative molds.

MAKING A COLD FOAM PROSTHETIC PIECE

Cold foam comes in a kit, which includes all the materials needed to make a prosthetic piece. Carefully following the instructions during every step is the key to success.

PROCEDURE FOR MAKING A COLD FOAM PROSTHETIC PIECE

Materials Required:

- Cold foam kit
- Mold release agent
- Acetone
- Cotton Q-tips
- Liquid latex
- Food coloring
- Baby powder and brush
- Weight scale (a postal scale will work)
- Set of positive and negative molds
- Plastic bowls or large cups (for mixing foam)
- Paper cups (for measuring)
- Plastic spoons
- Paper towels
- Apron
- Rubber gloves
- Pinking shears
- Spirit gum
- Spirit gum remover

Step One: Applying Mold Release

- Apply mold release agent on both positive and negative molds thoroughly, making sure all the corners of the negative mold are well covered with the release agent (Figure 1-59). Apply extra coats of release on a freshly made mold. Any missed spot will tear and destroy the prosthetic piece because the foam will stick to the spot. The drying time for the release agent varies depending on the type. The instructions that come with the cold foam package will explain every step. FOLLOW THEM

Figure 1-59 Spray the positive and negative molds with mold release.

EXACTLY. Challenge 90 Release is recommended on the package, but mold release spray (versatile, general purpose) was used in this example because the store did not have the other product at the time.

- Foam stuck to the negative mold is very difficult to clean, especially in places at the inside of the mold that are hard to reach. If the foam sticks, clean it off with acetone and cotton Q-tips.
- Pour a small amount of liquid latex into the negative mold (Figure 1-60a) and apply a thin coat of liquid latex that only reaches to the edges of the object being made (Figure 1-60b). The cold foam will be poured on top of the wet liquid latex and they will bind together, adding strength to the foam surface and preventing the foam from sticking to the inside of the negative mold (because latex doesn't stick to plaster surfaces). Latex dries transparent, so the color of the foam will show beneath it. The liquid latex takes several hours to dry.

Step Two: Weighing All Parts and Creating Flesh Color

- Soft foam 4100-3 A & B were used for this project. Weigh each part according to the ratio in the instructions using a weight scale; a postal scale was used for this project (Figure 1-61). The ratio is usually proportioned for a full mask. To make individual features such as a nose, scar, or chin, the ratio number can be divided by $\frac{1}{2}$, $\frac{1}{3}$, or $\frac{1}{4}$, depending on the size of the prosthetic piece being made.

- Put on a pair of rubber gloves and an apron for protection. The cold/soft foam is very sticky and hard to clean from the skin and clothes. Use cheap, one-time-use plastic containers to weigh and mix the foam. Paper towels will be needed to wipe your hands and the foam bottles. Cover the working area with newspaper or a plastic sheet. Work outdoors or in a well-ventilated area. I recommend wearing a mask.

Figure 1-60 (a) Pour liquid latex into the negative mold. (b) Apply a layer of liquid latex to the inside of the negative mold.

Figure 1-61 Two parts of cold/soft foam are weighed.

• Add flesh food coloring to the weighed foam Part B and mixing them together (Figure 1-62) is optional. The prosthetic pieces can also be colored with grease paint or aquacolor makeup pigments after being made. Precoloring the foam piece will make it easier to color later. I used food coloring because it is safe and inexpensive.

Figure 1-62 Add food coloring to Part B (white color) and mix.

• The number of food coloring drops used to produce flesh-toned prosthetic pieces is proportional to the amount of cold foam being used. The color proportion that most closely matched the actor's skin tone in this example is: 3 drops red + 3 drops yellow + 1 drop blue + 1 drop green. (The actor did not put much makeup on his face to keep a natural appearance.) I made one nose per performance, and there was no need to apply makeup on the cold foam nose because the color matched the actor's skin tone perfectly.

Step Three: Mixing the Foam Parts and Pouring the Cold Foam into the Mold

- After the food coloring is mixed, pour Part A into Part B and mix quickly (less than 10 seconds to make a nose) (Figures 1-63a and b). To make a full mask, I recommend using a mixer or blender; for a small prosthetic piece, hand-mixing is okay. A few seconds after Part A and B are poured together, the foam will rise in the container. This chemical reaction is toxic to breathe; work outdoors or in a well-ventilated room and also wear a mask during the process.
- Pour the mixed cold foam into the negative mold (Figure 1-63c) and quickly place the positive mold on top of it, pressing firmly until no more cold foam runs from the mold (Figure 1-64). Wait 5 or more hours for the latex to dry (if you are using latex). Wait 25–30 minutes without latex.

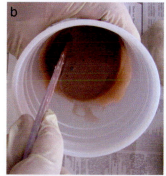
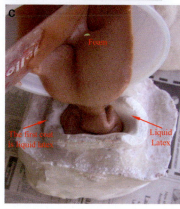

Figure 1-63 a and (b) Pour Part A into Part B and mix. (c) Pour foam into negative mold.

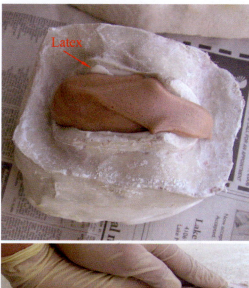

Figure 1-64 After filling the negative mold, place the positive mold on top and press.

Step Four: Opening the Mold

- Open the positive and negative molds carefully using your hands. With one hand, hold the positive mold in an upright standing position, loosen the foam edge from around the positive mold with the other hand; (Figure 1-65a). With two hands slowly separate the molds by pulling the negative mold downward and forward (Figure 1-65b).

- Most of the time, the foam piece will stick to the inside of the negative mold. Powder the foam with baby powder before lifting it and then carefully lift the excess foam that ran out of the molds when you pressed them together (Figure 1-66a). Sprinkle on more baby powder between the foam and the negative mold (Figure 1-66b) while pulling the foam out of the mold. Trim the prosthetic piece with pinking shears (Figure 1-67).

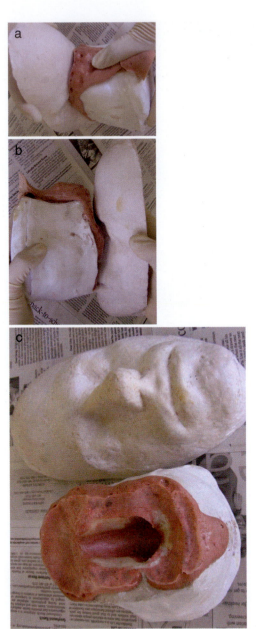

Figure 1-65 (a) Loosen the foam edge from the positive mold. (b) Open the mold. (c) Opened molds.

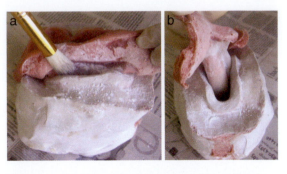

Figure 1-66 (a) Powdering the foam while peeling it away from the mold. (b) Remove foam from negative mold.

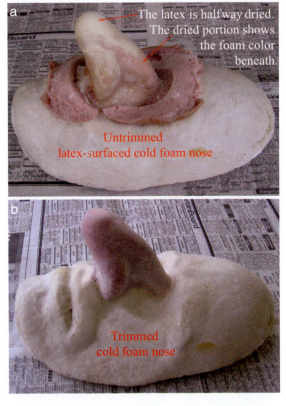

The latex is halfway dried. The dried portion shows the foam color beneath.

Untrimmed latex-surfaced cold foam nose

Trimmed cold foam nose

Figure 1-67 (a) Untrimmed latex-surfaced cold foam prosthetic piece. (b) Trimmed latex-surfaced cold foam prosthetic piece.

- To make a cold foam prosthetic piece without liquid latex, follow the same steps. Be sure to apply mold release thoroughly. Drying takes only about 25–30 minutes (instead of 5+ hours with latex), and then you can open the molds (Figure 1-68).

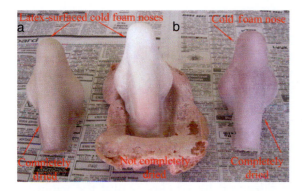

Figure 1-68 (a) Two latex-surfaced prosthetic pieces. (b) Cold foam-only prosthetic piece.

- Apply the prosthetic piece to the actor's face with spirit gum or adhesive. One prosthetic piece can last two to three performances if cleaned well. I recommend making one prosthetic piece per performance to easily portray a realistic, natural look.

The completed Cyrano de Bergerac makeup is shown in Figure 1-69.

Figure 1-69 Production photo of Cyrano de Bergerac with the actor wearing the nose made of cold foam. *Neera Rellan (L) as Roxane. Gabriel Barre (R) as Cyrano de Bergerac. Directed by David Feldshuh; Costume design by Judith Johnason. Cyrano nose made by Tan Huaixiang. Cornell University Theatre Arts Department presentation. Photo by Tim McKinney.*

MAKING GEL-FOAM AND LIQUID LATEX PROSTHETIC PIECES

Prosthetic pieces were used for the Wicked Witch in the *Wizard of Oz*, a University of Central Florida Conservatory Theater Production in summer 2005. Bill Brewer, a guest costume designer, designed costumes and makeup for the show (Figure 1-70). I helped to make the prosthetic pieces (the Witch's nose and chin). I was delighted to be working alongside an extraordinary costume designer.

Figure 1-70 Costume rendering for the Wicked Witch in the *Wizard of Oz*, by Bill Brewer, professor at University of South Florida, Tampa, Florida.

Equity actress, Carol Swarbrick, played the Wicked Witch. She had played the same role before and had earned an Ovation Award for her performance. She brought in her plaster positive face mold from her prior production. I followed Bill's design and made the Witch's nose and chin. Both gel-foam and liquid latex prosthetic pieces were used for the Wicked Witch. Gel-foam is economical, gelatin-like, translucent, flexible, extremely soft, easy to work with, and excellent when used in small quantities. The latex prosthetic piece can be made into a hollow shell so it's lightweight. It is soft but more rigid than gel-foam. It is easy to make and requires a negative mold only. Gel-foam requires both positive and negative molds just like hot and cold foam, so it's called a closed mold.

Carol Swarbrick played double roles in the *Wizard of Oz*: the Witch and Miss Gulch. There was very little time to switch between characters. This request for quick costume and makeup changes from one role to the other made the 3-D makeup change especially difficult. Taking off Miss Gulch's makeup and then gluing on the Witch nose and chin and putting on the Witch's makeup all had to be done rapidly. Before the glue could completely dry, the actress had to be on stage. The first prosthetic pieces used for the Witch

were made of gel-foam. Gel-foam is relatively heavy, so with sweat and facial movements, we had a hard time keeping the gel-foam prosthetic pieces on her face. The solution was to use a latex prosthetic piece instead; because it is much lighter, it worked much better. The examples here show procedures using both gel-foam and liquid latex.

PROCEDURES FOR MAKING MOLDS

Materials Required:

- Plaster of paris
- Vaseline
- Mixing bowl
- Spatula
- Oil-based clay
- Sculpting tools
- Marker or butter knife
- Two soft-bristle brushes (for applying Vaseline and plaster)
- Rubbing alcohol

Step One: Life Casting and Making a Plaster Positive Mold

- See the instructions for making full-head and face life castings, earlier in this chapter. An existing face mold was used in this case (provided by the actor herself) (Figure 1-71a).

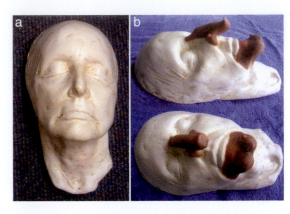

Figure 1-71 (a) Existing positive face mold. (b) Sculpt the Witch's nose and chin with molding clay.

Step Two: Sculpting Features with Oil-based Clay

- Using oil-based clay, sculpt the witch's nose and chin (Figure 1-71b). Make sure every edge of the nose and chin is well blended and smoothly merges with the surface of the face mold. The thinner you make the merging clay edges, the thinner the edges on the prosthetic piece will be.

Step Three: Creating a Boundary Line

- Create a $\frac{1}{4}$- to $\frac{3}{8}$"-wide exposed plaster mold surface boundary (clayless) around the sculpted objects (in this case, the chin and nose) by placing a roll of clay away from the edges of the clay nose and chin. In this example, the clay around the nose and chin is about 1–1½″ wide and ¼″ thick. As mentioned before, the reasons for doing this are (1) to make the separation of the negative and positive molds easier and (2) to allow the excess Gel-Foam between the positive and negative molds to be released when the two molds are closed together.

- Use a sculpting tool to neatly trim the clay around the boundary line near the sculpted object (Figure 1-72).

Plaster Mold Surface Boundary —
(Apply a coat of vaseline as mold release before pouring plaster on top of it)

— Clay Wall
(holds the plaster for making the negative mold)

Clay Boundary
(for easy release of negative and positive molds and fast release of excess gel-foam)

Figure 1-72 Trim the boundary lines and add a clay wall around the nose and chin.

- Carefully and evenly brush Vaseline on the exposed plaster surface in the boundary-line area to help release the positive and negative mold and prevent them from sticking together.
- Build a wall of clay around the sculpted nose and chin for pouring the negative mold. The wall should be at least 1″ taller than the tallest point of the sculpted object (Figure 1-72).

Step Four: Making a Negative Mold from the Clay Sculpture

The negative mold can be made from plaster of paris, dental stone, Ultracal 30, or the newer material, silicone. I have not experimented with the silicone materials yet. If you are interested in the silicone, you can get information about it from www.smooth-on.com. Plaster of paris is the cheapest material, so I chose it for this mold example.

- Mix the first coat of plaster of paris to be applied to the sculpted object (Figure 1-73). Do not mix too much or make the first coat too thick. Mix enough to fill about ⅓–½ of the negative mold. First pour water into the

Figure 1-73 Mixing the first coat of plaster of paris.

bowl, and then add plaster powder into the water until the powder is level with the water surface. Wait until all powder is absorbed by the water and then stir. If the mixture is stirred too early, lumps will form. After the mixture has been stirred, it should be creamy. If there are details and texture on the sculpture, make the first coat thinner.

- Use a soft-bristle brush to apply the creamy plaster to the surface of the entire sculpted object (Figure 1-74a). Do not use strokes. Apply the mixture using a tapping motion to avoid destroying the surface of the sculpted object and to make sure no air bubbles arise. This first coat of plaster should be roughly ¼–½″ thick or less and doesn't have to be even. Once the surfaces of the sculpture are covered with creamy plaster, pour the rest of the plaster on top of the first coat (Figure 1-74b).

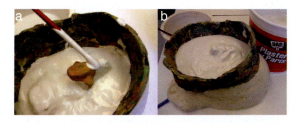

Figure 1-74 (a) Apply the creamy plaster with a soft brush to the sculpted objects. (b) Pour the leftover plaster on top of the first coat.

- Mix the second coat of plaster, thicker than the first coat. To make the thick plaster, add more plaster powder than water. Again, pour water into the bowl, but this time sprinkle powder in until it is a little above the water level and mix it. (Figure 1-75a)

Figure 1-75 (a) Mix thick plaster to finish filling the negative mold. (b) Filled negative mold.

- Pour the thicker plaster mix into the mold until it reaches the proper height

(1″ higher than the highest point — here the nose tip); any spot that's too thin may be easily broken. Then flatten the top surface of plaster negative mold before it hardens for stability when putting the positive mold on top of it (Figure 1-75b). Use a marker or butter knife to draw an arrow to indicate where the forehead is.

Step Five: Opening the Molds

- Wait for the plaster to harden and warm up before separating the molds. They will be easiest to separate when the plaster is warm.
- Take down the clay wall surrounding the negative mold, keeping the molds in an upright position. For a larger mold, work in pairs, with one person holding the positive mold and the other holding the negative mold. Gently loosen the negative mold and pull it down and forward. The two molds should open with no problem.
- After they are separated, clean the negative mold. If there is any clay stuck inside the negative mold, clean it with a sculpting tool. Gently lift up the clay and take it out a little at a time. Do not smear and rub the clay on the inside surface of the negative mold. Any smear will cause difficulty in taking the clay

out and can also destroy the texture on the surface of the negative mold.

- Clean the positive mold with soft materials like cotton balls or a piece of flannel fabric and a small amount of rubbing alcohol in a gentle rubbing motion.
- Allow the cleaned positive and negative molds to dry (Figure 1-76). You are

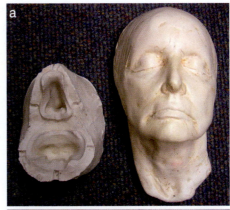

Figure 1-76 (a) Opened and cleaned mold. (b) Closed positive and negative molds.

then ready to make the Gel-Foam prosthetic pieces.

MAKING GEL-FOAM PROSTHETIC PIECES

PROCEDURES FOR MAKING GEL-FOAM PROSTHETIC PIECES

Materials Required:

- Positive face mold
- Negative prosthetic mold
- Gel-foam cubes
- Epoxy parafilm or silicone spray (mold release)
- Microwave
- Microwave-safe bowl for melting Gel-Foam
- Scissors
- Butter knife
- Freezer (optional)
- Ventilating lace for strengthening thin areas
- Baby powder
- Brush
- Pinking shears

Step One: Applying Mold Release

- Make four key marks at the top and bottom edges of the negative mold and positive mold so that they line up with each other when they are put together.

- Thoroughly spray mold release on both the positive and negative molds (spraying two or three coats of mold release to a set of newly made molds is recommended because the mold will absorb the first layer of release) (Figure 1-77).

Figure 1-77 Spray molds with mold release.

Step Two: Cooking the Gel-Foam

Gel-Foam comes in packages of six cubes. Six cubes should be enough to make a full-face prosthetic piece, but one big piece won't stay on the face because this material is much heavier than hot foam latex, cold foam latex, and latex prosthetic pieces. The number of cubes needed for an individual prosthetic piece depends on the size of the sculpted object. The cooking time will vary accordingly. One

cube of gel-foam was used for the Witch's nose and $1\frac{1}{4}$ cube was used for the chin.

- Cut the Gel-Foam cube into small pieces with scissors and put them in a microwave-safe bowl (Figure 1-78a).

Figure 1-78 (a) Cut a gel-foam cube into small pieces. (b) The gel-foam becomes gelatin-like after cooking in the microwave.

- Place the bowl with the gel-foam pieces into the microwave for 30–40 seconds to melt the gel-foam thoroughly to a gelatin-like consistency (Figure 1-78b). (According to the instructions that come with the gel-foam package, gel-foam should be heated in 1-minute intervals and mixed between heating cycles. Since the one cube used here is cut into small pieces, the heating time is reduced to 30 seconds for the nose and 40 seconds for the chin.)

Step Three: Pouring the Gel-Foam Gelatin into the Negative Mold

It is optional to lay a little piece of ventilating lace on a weak part of the gel-foam piece for enhanced strength. This will help prevent a weak part of the piece from ripping.

- Lay a piece of lace on the inside of the mold where it needs to be strengthened before pouring the gelatin into the mold (Figure 1-79a). The shape of the lace depends on how it can be laid flat inside the negative mold. To keep the lace in place, dip one corner of the lace into some gelatin and then place it where it is needed.

- Pour the gel-foam gelatin into the negative mold using a guiding tool (a butter knife was used for this example), starting from center point (Figures 1-79c, and 1-80). Continue pouring until the negative mold is full (Figure 1-80).

Step Four: Closing the Molds

- QUICKLY put the positive mold on top of the negative mold, matching the marks correctly, and press the molds firmly together; keep pressing for a minute until no more gelatin oozes out (Figure 1-81a). If you are

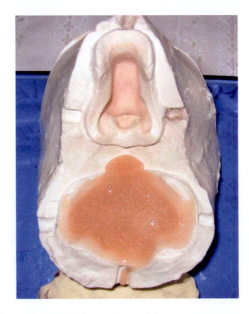

Figure 1-79 (a) Cut a piece of ventilating lace and place it in the negative mold. (b) Ventilating lace placed inside the negative mold. (c) Pour the gel-foam gelatin into the negative mold.

Figure 1-80 Filled negative mold.

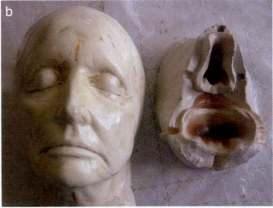

Figure 1-81 (a) Closed positive and negative molds. (b) Opened molds with the prosthetic piece inside the negative mold.

making a large prosthetic piece, you will require a few clamps to keep the molds firmly closed until they are completely set.

- Put the closed molds into the freezer for 10–15 minutes. The cold will help you peel the gel-foam piece from the inside of the negative mold.

I discovered the benefits of using the freezer by accident. One day I put the molds into a hair-dryer cabinet to avoid dust. Later, somebody turned the hair-dryer cabinet on a high temperature to set up wig curls without removing the molds from the cabinet. Therefore, the molds were cooked along with the wig. When I was ready to make more gel-foam prosthetic pieces, I discovered that the molds were cooking. I took the molds out of the cabinet and wrapped them with towels so they could gradually cool down because a sudden drop of temperature will cause the molds to crack. About an hour later, the mold was still warm, so I put the warm molds with the towels in the freezer to cool down for about 30 minutes. Later I made a Witch nose with a set of cold molds. When I opened the molds, I discovered it was much easier to remove the gel-foam this time than before. I tried making a gel-foam piece with cold molds again, and it was a success. This turned a negative experience into a positive one and was a pleasant surprise.

Step Five: Removing the Gel-Foam from the Negative Mold

- Loosen the edges of the gel-foam from the positive mold first, and then gently separate the positive and negative molds by pulling it with your hands. Most of the time, the gelatin will stick to the inside of the negative mold (Figure 1-81b). Trim off any excess the gel-foam connected to the edge of the prosthetic piece (Figure 1-82a) to reduce the risk of tearing the delicate edges while removing the prosthetic piece.
- You must powder the piece before peeling the gel-foam out of the mold; without powder, the edge of the gel-foam will fold over and stick to itself. Dust some baby powder or makeup powder on top of the gel-foam piece (Figure 1-82b). Carefully peel and powder as you go until the gel-foam is completely out of the mold (Figure 1-82c).
- Finally, trim the edge of the gel-foam prosthetic piece with pinking shears JUST BEFORE applying it to the actor's face (Figure 1-83). If you

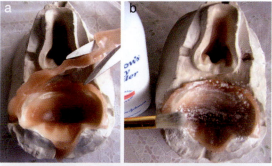

Figure 1-82 (a) Trim excess gelatin attached to the prosthetic piece. (b) Powder the prosthetic piece. (c) Powder the other side of the gel-foam as you peel it out of the mold.

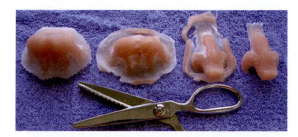

Figure 1-83 Prosthetic piece is trimmed with pinking-shears scissors.

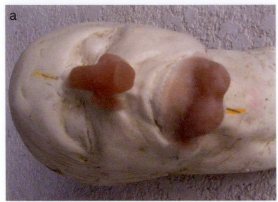

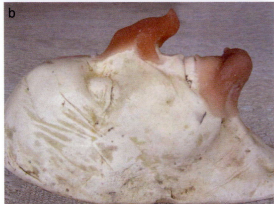

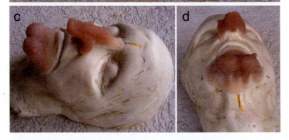

Figure 1-84 (a) Prosthetic pieces — front. (b) Prosthetic pieces — side. (c) Prosthetic pieces — ³/₄ view. (d) Prosthetic piece — bottom view.

trim it too early, the edge might start losing its shape and curving because of the thin edge, so trim it at most a couple hours before applying it to the face. Use pinking shears because a zigzag edge is less noticeable on the face (Figure 1-84). Repeat the same steps for making the witch's nose.

MAKING LIQUID LATEX PROSTHETIC PIECES

Latex prosthetic pieces can be made from either an open mold or a closed mold. When a prosthetic piece is made with closed positive and negative molds, the material (gel-foam, hot foam latex, or cold foam latex) poured will exactly fill the space between the two molds (where the sculpted clay object was) and produce a solid prosthetic piece. However, latex prosthetic pieces can be done with just one negative mold (also called an open mold). The latex piece made from an open mold will be hollow, flexible, and lightweight. The example that shows the process of making a latex prosthetic piece for the Wicked Witch in the *Wizard of Oz* follows.

PROCEDURES FOR MAKING A LATEX PROSTHETIC PIECE

Materials Required:

- Negative mold
- Liquid latex (clear)
- Food coloring pigments (optional)
- Sculpting tool or brush handle
- Baby powder
- Brushes

Step One: Pouring Liquid Latex into a Negative Mold

No mold release is needed for making a latex prosthetic piece. The latex won't stick to the negative mold.

- The liquid latex can be tinted with food coloring (food coloring is safe to put on the skin). Simply put a few drops of food coloring into the liquid latex and mix it to the desired color before pouring it into the negative mold (Figure 1-85). Be aware that when the latex dries, the color will be much darker than when it was wet.
- Pour a SMALL amount of liquid latex (enough for two or three coats) into the negative mold; too much liquid latex in the mold will be hard to manage

Figure 1-85 Tint the liquid latex with food coloring.

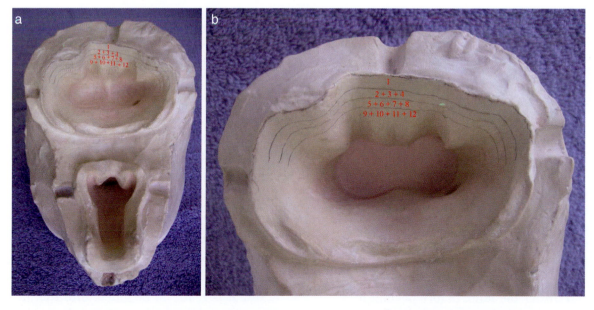

Figure 1-86 (a) Order of adding liquid latex layers. (b) Pour a small amount of liquid latex into the negative mold.

(Figure 1-86b). If you accidentally pour too much liquid latex into the mold, don't pour it out because this will create a thick edge where the latex was poured. Instead, suck it out with an eyedropper.

- Slowly turn the mold and allow the latex to run over the entire surface of the prosthetic piece area/negative mold. Use a sculpting tool or a brush handle to guide the liquid latex along the edges of the prosthetic piece without touching the surface of the mold (Figure 1-87a).

Diagrams in Figure 1-86 show how each layer of the liquid latex should be applied about $1/16''$ or $1/8''$ smaller in circumference than the previous one. This will produce a tapered edge and the outermost edge will be the thinnest part of the prosthetic piece. It is very important to have a thin edge in order for the prosthetic piece to look realistic. Clean the guiding tool between each coat.

- Pour more latex into the mold as necessary, until the latex is thick enough to hold the shape. Let the latex set for 2 minutes before adding the next layer. It is not necessary to wait for the latex to dry between each coat; running liquid latex over a wet latex surface will achieve a smooth finish. You can also dry each layer of liquid latex with a hair dryer; a dry or half-dry latex surface grabs more liquid latex than a wet surface.

- Continue turning the mold around and around until there is no liquid latex left in the negative mold; when you have enough layers, allow the latex to dry (Figure 1-87b). Do not leave any excess liquid latex at the bottom of the negative mold or else, after the liquid latex dries, it will add weight and create an uneven balance in the prosthetic piece. How thick you should

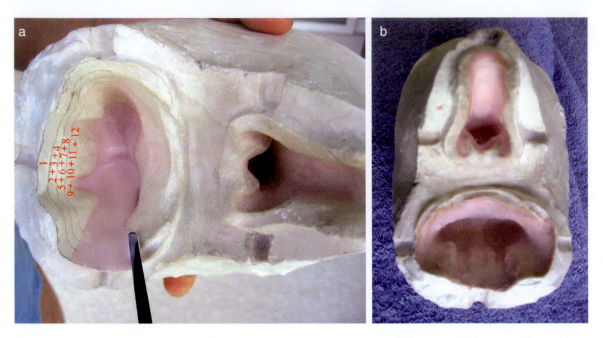

Figure 1-87 (a) Use a tool to guide the liquid latex over the edges of the prosthetic piece. (b) Completed latex piece left to dry.

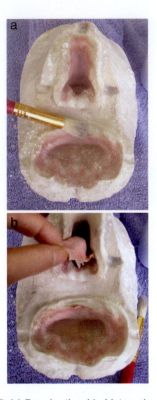

Figure 1-88 (a) Powder the dried latex piece before peeling it from the mold. (b) Gently peel and pull the latex piece from the negative mold.

make the prosthetic piece depends on the size of the piece. If you're making a scar or cut, usually three or four layers of latex will hold the shape. The Witch's nose and chin were made with about 12 layers of liquid latex. A dry or half-dry latex surface grabs more liquid latex than a wet surface, in that case, the number of layers of liquid latex should be reduced. The more coats of liquid latex added, the stiffer the prosthetic piece will be. The key is to keep the edge of the prosthetic paper-thin.

Step Two: Removing the Latex Prosthetic Piece

- Powder the latex before peeling it from the mold to prevent the edges from sticking to themselves (Figure 1-88a).
- Carefully peel the edge of the latex piece, powdering underneath it as you go (Figure 1-88b).
- Because the edges were carefully created from the beginning, it is not necessary to trim them (Figures 1-89 to 1-91). Now it is ready to be glued onto the face.

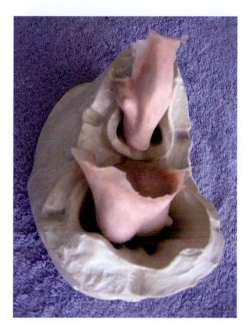

Figure 1-89 Latex prosthetic pieces removed from the mold.

Figure 1-91 (a) Left nose is made of gel-foam; two right noses are made of latex. (b) The two chins on the left are made of latex; the chin on the right is made of gel-foam.

Figure 1-92 Jeannie Haschube, a BFA design and technology student, applying the Witch makeup on the actress.

Figure 1-90 (a) Colored latex prosthetic pieces. (b) Uncolored latex prosthetic pieces (natural latex color).

Step Three: Applying the Prosthetic Pieces on the Actor's Face

A new set of prosthetic pieces was prepared for each performance for the *Wizard of Oz*. This is optional; the prosthetic piece can be used two or three times if they are carefully cleaned (Figure 1-92).

Applying Gel-Foam Prosthetic Pieces

- Apply Pros Aide adhesive glue on the inside of the entire gel-foam prosthetic piece and let it become tacky; then put it on the face. It can be done in an opposite way by applying the adhesive on the face, waiting for it to become tacky, and then gluing the prosthetic piece on the face. (When spirit gum was used for application, it ate away the edges of the gel-foam. Pros Aide works better.)

- Apply water-based makeup, aquacolor pigment, to the gel-foam prosthetic pieces and face.

- Add highlights and shadows to the edges of the prosthetic pieces as necessary to conceal them.
- Pros Aide remover is required to remove the Pros Aide glue.

Applying Latex Prosthetic Pieces

Applying latex prosthetic pieces to the face is different from applying gel-foam pieces. Latex pieces are shell-like. This means only the outer edge of the prosthetic piece can be attached to the face; the inner portion of the prosthetic piece will be hollow and away from the skin.

- Apply the glue only along the edges of the latex prosthetic piece (about $^3/_8''$ wide). Both spirit gum and Pros Aide glue worked for this application.
- Apply aquacolor makeup pigments to the face with damp sponges and brushes (this worked very well for this character).
- Spirit gum remover is required to remove the spirit gum. Pros Aide remover is required to remove the Pros Aide glue.

The completed Wicked Witch makeup is shown in Figure 1-93.

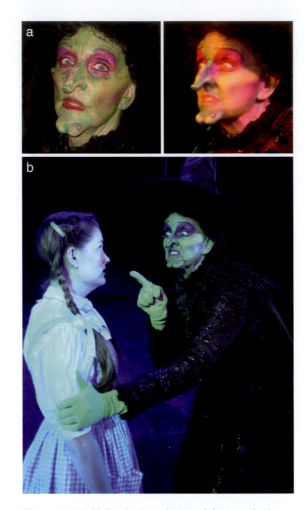

Figure 1-93 (a) Production photos of the prosthetic pieces on stage. (b) Production photo of the Witch (with prosthetic pieces) on stage. *Dorothy played by Gigi Vasser (left), a BFA music student. The Wicked Witch played by Carol Swarbrick (right). Directed by John Bell. Music directed by Jim Brown. Scenic design by Kyle Becker. Sound design by Martin Wootton. Lighting design by Eric Haugen. Costume design by Bill Brewer. University of Central Florida Conservatory Theatre presentation.*

Chapter 2   Teeth

Making false teeth is a part of my Advanced Makeup class. In this class, students are required to make two types of false teeth: a pair of fangs and a set of crooked teeth. After the class, some students made fangs for fun for Halloween parties. Making fangs involves directly building up on top of the positive teeth mold. Making a set of crooked teeth requires both a positive and negative mold to complete the process. Making vampire fangs for the production *Dracula* and crooked teeth for the musical *Big River* demonstrate executions of making false teeth. False teeth on stage are used for the special characters in the play. They can dramatically change the actor's physical appearance to support the character's disposition and mood and the theme of the play.

CREATING FANGS FOR VAMPIRES

Nine pairs of vampire fangs were needed for the production *Dracula*. During the execution of *Dracula*, I bought some cheap plastic Vampire fangs from a store and brought them to the production meeting. The director requested that all the vampires have more realistic-looking fangs. I don't believe that Dracula or vampires exist, so I asked the director, "Why do the fangs have to look real when vampires don't exist?" Then everyone started laughing, and they tried to convince me that Dracula and vampires do exist.

There are some beautiful fangs available on the market, but they are not made for quick changes on stage and are also quite expensive. The fangs purchased from stores are sold as a pair, and they need to be glued individually onto the actor's tooth. The glue must dry rapidly, so a quick change is impossible. All of this won't work for a stage production. To solve this dilemma, I developed fangs with a bridge that connects the two single fangs and can easily slip on and off the actor's teeth. It solved the quick-change problem and also achieved a realistic and dramatic change to the characters' appearance.

PROCEDURE FOR MAKING FANGS

The procedure for making a teeth mold is the same as that used by the dentist making an impression of his or her patients. The dentist can make molds to correct crooked teeth, but makeup artists also do this for creating character teeth for theatrical appearances. No matter which type of teeth you will make for a character, a life casting of teeth is required.

Materials Required:

- Dental trays — plastic impression plates for upper and lower teeth
- Dental alginate (3-minute setting)
- Dental stone or Ultracal 30
- Acrylic powder (ranges from very light to dark tones; choose one that matches the actor's real teeth)

- Dental Acrylic Monomer or Acrylic Liquid
- Dremel tool kit (includes tools for sanding, cutting, shaping, polishing; this is optional and requires practice before you use it on teeth)
- Fingernail files
- Container for mixing alginate and water
- Spatula
- Eye dropper
- Alcote separator or Vaseline
- Brush
- Butter knife
- Sculpting tools
- Hydrogen peroxide
- Container for hydrogen peroxide–water mixture
- Casting latex
- Oil-based clay
- Small sharp knife

Step One: Preparation

- Assemble your supplies (Figure 2-1a).
- Rinse a dental tray with clean water before putting it in the actor's mouth.
- Try the dental tray in the mouth for a proper fit (dental trays comes in large, medium, and three small sizes). When the actor bites down with his or her teeth, the teeth should not touch the walls and the bottom of the tray. The lips must also be pulled over the tray to

Figure 2-1 (a) Basic fang-making kit. (b) Measure the alginate powder and water for mixing.

get the entire gum line in the impression.

- Shake the container of alginate up and down slowly to loosen the powder and to obtain more accurate measurements. Follow the instructions on the alginate container to correctly measure the alginate and water proportions. Generally a 1:1 ratio of alginate and

water is standard. A measuring cup should be included with the alginate package. If there is none, you can use any cup and bowl as a measuring and mixing container since alginate is easily cleaned off.

Step Two: Making an Impression of the Teeth — Casting Teeth

- Measure one cup of alginate powder and pour it into the mixing bowl. Use the same cup to measure 1 cup of water and set that aside. A little cup (as shown in Figure 2-1b) of alginate is more than enough to fill the dental tray; overfilling the tray may cause the alginate to flow down the actor's throat.
- Pour the measured water into the alginate powder and mix with a small spatula or spoon until it becomes a smooth creamy paste (Figure 2-2a). Pour the creamy alginate paste into the dental tray and fully fill it (Figure 2-2b).
- Have the actor open his or her mouth wide and put the dental tray in the mouth. Be sure to pull the actor's upper lip forward and over the tray to cast the entire gum line and that he or she bites down and makes sure the alginate reaches the root of the gum all the way around. Alginate takes 3 minutes to set (Figure 2-3a).

Figure 2-2 (a) Mix the alginate. (b) Pour the alginate into the tray.

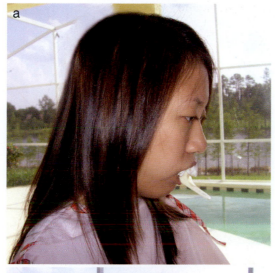

Figure 2-3 (a) Wait for the alginate in the dental tray to set. (b) Remove the tray from the mouth.

- Gently loosen the upper tray from every angle and then pull it downward to remove it from the mouth (Figure 2-3b). Pulling it down from the back of the hard palate will make removal easier if you're having a hard time taking it out.
- If the lower teeth need to be cast, just repeat the steps here, but turn the tray upside down before putting it in the actor's mouth. Pull upward instead of downward when removing the casting tray.

Figure 2-4 Completed upper teeth impression.

Step Three: Making a Positive Mold of the Teeth

Teeth have delicate structures and the positive molds are easily broken. It is better to use dental stone or Ultracal 30 to make the positive mold because they are much stronger than plaster of paris; however, they are still brittle. It is wise to make at least two positive molds from one negative mold if possible.

To avoid the shrinkage of the alginate casting mold, a positive mold should be poured into the negative mold immediately after the alginate casting mold is removed from the mouth. Temporarily setting the alginate casting mold in water will help prevent shrinkage, but it should not be soaked in water too long.

- Mix a cup of dental stone for the positive teeth mold. The mixing method and water to powder ratio ($1:2\frac{1}{2}$) is the same for both dental stone and Ultracal 30. Sprinkle the powder into the water until it is $\frac{1}{8}''$ above the level of the water, and then stir until it becomes a smooth creamy paste (Figure 2-5).
- Apply the first coat of dental stone paste to the alginate casting mold with a brush using tapping motions (Figure 2-6a). This ensures that no air bubbles will form beneath it.

Figure 2-5 (a) Sprinkle dental stone powder into the water. (b) Stir until the dental stone mixture becomes a creamy paste.

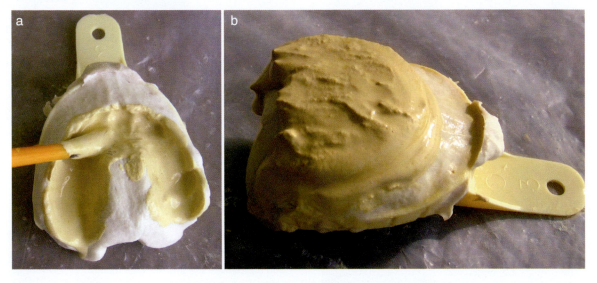

Figure 2-6 (a) Apply the first coat of dental stone with a brush. (b) Filled negative mold.

- Fill the negative mold slightly higher than the top of the negative mold and set it aside (Figure 2-6b).
- Wait a while until the mixed dental stone becomes much thicker. Then pour the rest of the dental stone onto a flat surface (Figure 2-7a). Build a cube-like dental-stone base the same width as the dental tray for the positive mold.
- Pick up the dental tray, turn it upside down, and place it on top of the dental-stone cube (Figure 2-7b). Gently press it down to bind them together. Do not put any release between them. The dental stone cube should stay in this shape when the casting mold is laid on top of it.
- The dental stone needs 30–45 minutes to completely set. It will become warm during the setting time. As soon as the dental stone becomes hard, trim off the excess dental stone around the dental tray with a butterknife (Figure 2-7c).

Step Four: Opening the Mold

Because the structures of the teeth are so delicate, I recommend waiting until the dental stone completely cools before separating the positive and negative molds.

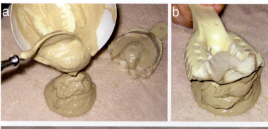
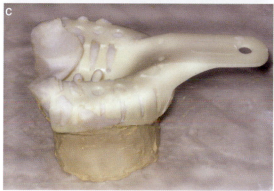
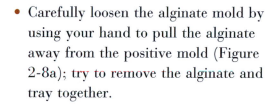

Figure 2-7 (a) Pour the rest of the dental stone onto a flat surface to form the base of the positive teeth mold. (b) Place the negative mold on top of the base. (c) Trim the base.

- Carefully loosen the alginate mold by using your hand to pull the alginate away from the positive mold (Figure 2-8a); try to remove the alginate and tray together.

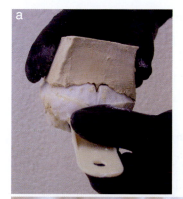

Figure 2-8 (a) Separate the positive and negative molds. (b) After the molds are separated, soak the negative alginate mold in water for the next duplication.

Step Five: Making a Second Positive Mold

If the alginate casting mold is still in good shape, you can make another positive mold, just in case the first one accidentally breaks. You can also later place the false teeth on the second positive mold as support to prevent shrinkage and maintain the shape of the teeth.

- Before you start making the next positive mold, put the alginate mold in water to avoid shrinkage while you prepare the materials (Figure 2-8b).
- Repeat steps three and four.

Step Six: Trimming the Positive Mold

- Trim the base with a butter knife when the mold is still damp and also trim off any excess dental stone above the gum line so it will not be an obstacle for modeling the false teeth later on (Figures 2-9 to 2-10). If you try to trim it when it's completely dry, it will be very difficult to cut.
- Clean the dental tray. This should be done before and after every use by soaking it in a mixture of equal amounts of hydrogen peroxide and water and then rinsing it clean with water.

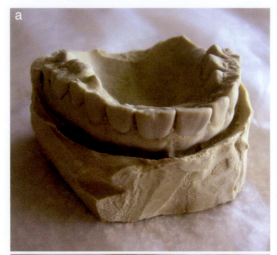

Figure 2-9 (a) Positive teeth mold before trimming. (b) Cut down the excess edge above the gum line with a butterknife.

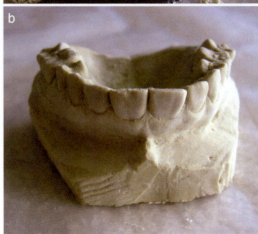

Figure 2-10 (a) Completed trimming of the edge of the right side. (b) Completed positive teeth mold — front.

Step Seven: Modeling Fangs with Acrylic

The fangs are made of acrylic powder and acrylic monomer directly built up and modeled on the positive mold. The acrylic powder comes in different shades. Depending on the purpose of the teeth being made, the shade can either match the natural shade of the actor's teeth or it can be yellow and repulsive.

The acrylic monomer dries quickly, but it is toxic. Always work in ventilated areas or outdoors and wear rubber gloves the whole time because the acrylic paste is sticky and hazardous when wet. The rubber gloves should be tight and snug around the fingers; otherwise, you will have difficulty molding the fangs with your finger tips.

- Apply mold release thoroughly over the entire positive mold. Both Vaseline and Alcote separator can be used. If you use Alcote separator, two coats should be applied; wait for each coat to dry before proceeding (Figure 2-11a) . I like using Vaseline because you don't need to wait for it to dry (Figure 2-11b) and it works very well as a release agent.
- Pour two equal-size mounds of acrylic powder (to help maintain equal-size fangs) on a piece of glass or plastic

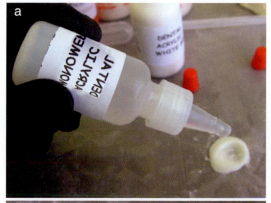

Figure 2-11 (a) Apply Alcote separator to the mold. (b) Or apply Vaseline to the mold.

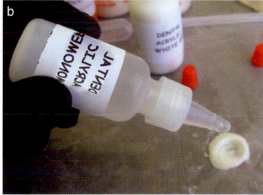

Figure 2-12 (a) Dig ditches in two mounds of acrylic powder in preparation for making fangs. (b) Drop acrylic monomer into the ditch.

surface, and dig a ditch at the center of each mound of powder to hold the acrylic monomer (Figure 2-12a).

- Place drops of acrylic monomer in the ditch (Figure 2-12b) until there is no more dry powder left and all the liquid has been absorbed. The acrylic monomer sometimes comes with a dropper in the lid. The acrylic powder will immediately absorb the liquid. Do

not mix too much powder at one time; mixing too much will be wasteful and hard to manage because it dries fast.

- Use a knife or your gloved fingertips to knead the acrylic like dough (Figure 2-13a). Place the dough directly on the canine tooth of the positive teeth mold and mold it with your fingertips to a fang shape (Figure 2-13b). Because the

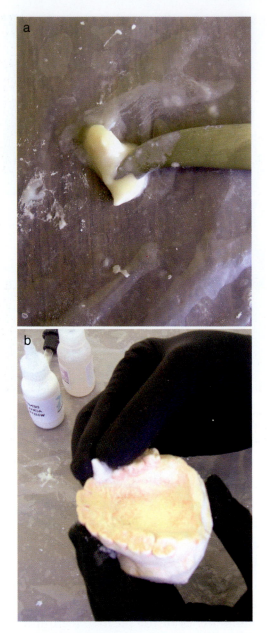

Figure 2-13 (a) Knead the acrylic like dough with a knife. (b) Mold a fang with your fingertips.

acrylic dough dries fast, put a few more drops of acrylic monomer on the dough while molding; this will help slow down the drying time and smooth the surface. Do not add too much acrylic dough at one time. Because the dough is sticky, it will be tough to remove any part of it if too much is added. If you have too little, it is easy to add more. First sprinkle on some acrylic powder and then drop one or two drops of acrylic monomer on top of the powder where it needs to be added (Figure 2-14). You can continually add layers until you are satisfied. The powder will naturally melt and bind to the acrylic fang that you are molding and the monomer will dry naturally smooth and shiny. This especially works well on details and edges.

- Mold the fangs with your fingertips until the front of the fang matches the shape of the real tooth on which it is built. The fang should perfectly cap the real tooth. The back portion of the fang will merge to a bridge later on.
- Mold each fang separately (the bridge will be molded next).
- After the two fangs are molded, flip the positive mold so the fangs are facing up.
- Start building a bridge on the positive mold between the two fangs at the

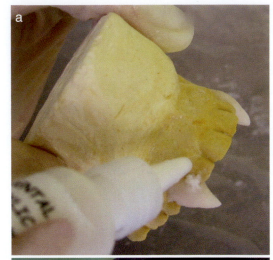

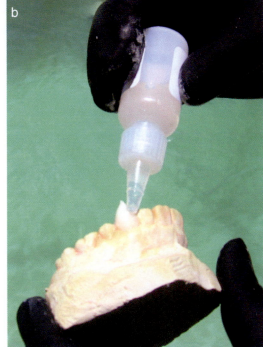

Figure 2-14 (a) If you need to, add acrylic powder to the fang cap. (b) Then drop liquid monomer on the powder to create a perfect smooth thin edge.

beginning of the hard palate (where the teeth meets the hard palate) by sprinkling acrylic powder on the mold (Figure 2-15a). Then put drops of acrylic monomer on the powder (Figure 2-15b). The acrylic powder will immediately absorb the liquid and create a nice shiny surface.

- Add more powder and monomer liquid on top of the first layer until the bridge achieves the appropriate shape and thickness. An ideal bridge is $\frac{1}{4}$–$\frac{3}{8}''$ wide and $\frac{1}{8}''$ thick with tapered edges. A bridge that is too thick will impede talking, whereas one that is too thin will be easily broken.

Step Eight: Removing the Fangs from the Positive Mold

- Acrylic takes 30–45 minutes to completely dry. After it is dry, use a pointed and flat sculpting tool to CAREFULLY AND GENTLY pry loose the edges around the fangs and bridge until they are completely loose from the positive mold (Figure 2-16). While doing this, always keep in mind the direction of the teeth underneath the fangs. If you apply an opposing force to the direction of growth, it may break the mold of the real teeth inside the fangs (Figure 2-17).

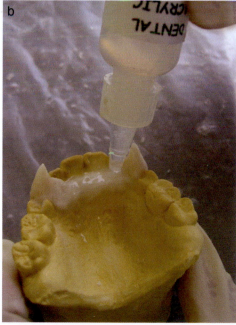

Figure 2-15 (a) Sprinkle acrylic powder between the two fangs to create a bridge. (b) Drip acrylic monomer onto the powder.

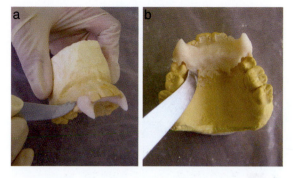

Figure 2-16 (a) Loosen and pry up the edge of the front of the fang with a pointed flat knife. (b) Loosen and pry up the edge of the bridge.

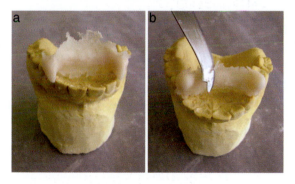

Figure 2-17 (a) Fangs removed from the positive mold (before being trimmed). (b) Trim off the excess edges with a knife.

Step Nine: Trimming and Polishing the Fangs

- Use a Dremel tool or hand tools to trim down any unnecessary edges (Figure 2-17b). Sand and polish the fangs (Figure 2-18). I felt safer sanding and

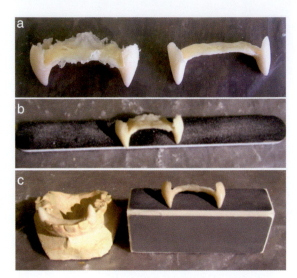

Figure 2-18 (a) Fangs before and after trimming and polishing. (b) Sand the fangs with a rough nail file or Dremel tool. (c) Polish the fangs with a four-sided nail file.

cutting it with hand tools like a knife and nail file. Because the fangs are so small, it is difficult to use electrical tools.

The completed fangs are shown in Figures 2-19 to 2-21. The fangs used in the production *Dracula* (Figures 2-22 to

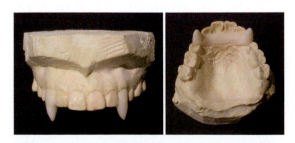

Figure 2-19 Completed fangs fitted on the positive mold.

Figure 2-20 Two sets of completed fangs fitted on the positive molds.

Figure 2-21 Yingtao Zhang modeling the fangs.

Figure 2-22 Costume design for *Dracula* — the vampire wives.

Figure 2-23 Fangs on Lucy and Dracula. Production photo of *Dracula. Lucy played by Jennifer Bennett, Dracula played by Tom McNelly. Directed by Wesley Van Tassel. Scenic design by Randy B. Winder. Lighting design by Mark C. Zetterberg. Costume and makeup design by Tan Huaixiang. Central Washington University Department of Theatre Arts presentation.*

2-24) were made the same way. The actors were able to slip the finished fangs on and off; no glue was needed. I thank Mary Ellen Musselman for helping me work on the fangs for *Dracula.*

Figure 2-24 Fangs used on stage for all the vampire wives (everyone is wearing fangs in this photo). Production photo of *Dracula. Vampire wives played by (from left to right) Amber Hoff, Kerri Van Auken, David Foubert, Becky Main, Danika Eger, and Yumi Fukushi; Dracula played by Tom McNelly. Directed by Wesley Van Tassel. Scenic design by Randy B. Winder. Lighting design by Mark C. Zetterberg. Costume and makeup design by Tan Huaixiang. Central Washington University Department of Theatre Arts presentation.*

MAKING CROOKED TEETH

To create crooked teeth, you need to physically change the look of all the front teeth to achieve an effective look; sometimes the lower teeth need to change as well. It is difficult and time consuming to build up details with acrylic directly on the positive teeth mold, as in making fangs. Using both a positive and negative mold is the best method for making false teeth.

PROCEDURE FOR MAKING CROOKED TEETH

Materials Required:

- Everything used for making fangs will be used for making crooked teeth
- Modeling clay
- Casting latex
- Old brush or foam sponge wedge
- Q-tips
- Tooth brown-out, black-out, or yellow-out
- Pink flesh-tone water-proof liquid acrylic ink
- Pink acrylic powder (optional)

Step One: Modeling Crooked Teeth with Clay

- Use oil-based modeling clay to model crooked teeth on top of the positive mold. The number of crooked teeth and how extreme they look depend on your design. The teeth can stop at the gum line or go over the gum line like dentures. Adding too much in the mouth can affect the actor's speech, so do not add too much.
- Using a sculpting tool, create the detailed structures of each tooth. Make sure the edges of the clay are blended smoothly with the natural gum line (Figure 2-25).

Step Two: Making a Negative/Casting Mold from the Crooked-Teeth Clay Sculpture

Alginate is an excellent material for making a negative casting mold. It replicates all the detailed impressions on any complex objects; however, it shrinks, allowing for only one duplicated set of crooked teeth. An alternative to the

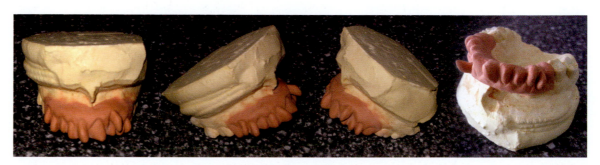

Figure 2-25 Several views of completed crooked teeth clay molds.

alginate is to use casting latex to make a negative mold, but it is much more time consuming. Five or more layers of dried casting latex becomes a rubbery and flexible material while still maintaining its shape. It is good for reproducing the product (false teeth) again and again.

- Apply a thick coat of casting latex to the positive clay mold with an old brush or a piece of foam sponge wedge. Let it dry and continue until you have applied at least five to six more coats (allow the mold to dry between coats). The thinner the latex, the more layers you need to add. For better results and accuracy, cover the entire positive mold with latex. (Figure 2-26). The completed latex negative mold will be flexible and strong and can be used for duplication.

- When the last coat of casting latex is completely dry, carefully separate the latex negative mold and the dental stone positive mold using both hands (Figure 2-27).
- Clean the clay from the negative and positive molds with cotton Q-tips and be ready to make acrylic teeth.

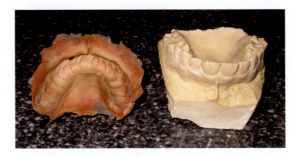

Figure 2-27 Separated latex negative mold and positive mold.

Step Three: Making Crooked Teeth with Acrylic Powder and Liquid Resin

- Thoroughly brush Vaseline on the positive teeth mold and set it aside.
- Drop a few drops of liquid resin into the latex negative mold in the crooked teeth cavities. Then squeeze a small amount of acrylic powder on the acrylic monomer (*liquid*) (about 1:1 in proportion). Let the powder naturally absorb the liquid. More liquid and more powder may be needed as you go until all the cavities are filled and there is a little extra floating around the gum line (Figure 2-28). Do not overfill; just estimate the amount of clay you used for sculpturing the crooked teeth and that should be how much powder and liquid are needed. Overfilling will create a thick gum line. Make sure no dry powder is buried inside of the tooth.

Figure 2-26 Create a crooked-teeth negative mold with layers of casting latex.

Figure 2-28 Fill in the latex negative mold with acrylic powder and monomer.

- Place the dental stone positive mold on top of the latex negative mold. Press the positive mold firmly for a minute while it fits in place (Figure 2-29). The positive mold will naturally push out the acrylic and fill the gap between the negative and positive molds.

Figure 2-29 Place the positive teeth mold on top of the latex negative mold and press firmly.

Step Four: Opening the Molds

The latex negative mold can be easily removed because latex is flexible. Pay special attention when separating the positive mold and the acrylic teeth. When the acrylic dries, it becomes hard and strong like real teeth. The positive mold will hug the acrylic teeth, so it is relatively hard to separate them. Any careless action can break the stone, even though mold release was applied, because the teeth on the positive mold are small and very delicate.

- Loosen up the edges of the acrylic teeth around the molds; employ the same method you used to remove the fangs from the positive mold earlier (Figure 2-16). Work with patience, attention, and care.

- If you break the acrylic teeth, gum line, or back bridge, you can piece them together by adding more powder and monomer liquid on top and around the break; it will look like new again. However, if you break the teeth or gum line on the stone positive mold, you can easily superglue the pieces together, but the mold won't last long and the shape of the teeth may get distorted.

Step Five: Trimming, Polishing, and Painting the Crooked Acrylic Teeth

- Trim the edges of the crooked teeth (use the same method as trimming and sanding fangs) with a sharp knife, fingernail cutter, or electric tool. Cut, sand, and polish the edges and the surface of the acrylic teeth with a fingernail filer so it's neat, thin, and smooth.

- Have the actor try the teeth on, and continue to adjust it by filing until it's comfortable. Then polish until it's smooth (Figure 2-30).

- Color or age the teeth with tooth brown-out, black-out, or yellow-out.

Figure 2-30 Completed unpainted acrylic crooked teeth — various views.

- Paint the gums a pink flesh-tone with water-proof liquid acrylic ink (Figure 2-31).

The completed crooked teeth are shown in Figures 2-32 to 2-34. Several sets of crooked teeth were used for village people in the musical *Big River*. There are no production photos available.

Figure 2-31 Paint the crooked teeth.

Figure 2-32 Completed and painted crooked teeth.

Figure 2-33 Yingtao Zhang, the model for the completed crooked teeth.

Figure 2-34 Yingtao Zhang modeling the crooked teeth.

Chapter 3   Wigs

ADDING A NATURAL HAIRLINE TO AN EXISTING WIG

When I designed costumes for the *Grapes of Wrath*, two full wigs were required: a gray-blonde wig with a low bun for Ma and a thin-haired half-bald brown wig for Jimmy Casey. Both actors were relatively younger than the characters in the play and had modern short hair styles without any gray hair. I used wigs to make both actors appear closer to the characters' ages. Purchasing a natural hairline wig was not practical because of the limited budget. The solution was to add a natural hairline to an existing wig for Ma and a half-bald wig for Jimmy Casey made from a bald cap.

PROCEDURE FOR ADDING A NATURAL HAIRLINE

Materials Required:

- Ventilating lace
- Ventilating needle
- Wig block
- Plastic wrap and Scotch tape
- Markers
- Needle and thread
- T-pins and headed pins
- Thin twill tape
- Wig stand
- Hair

Step One: Creating a Frontal Wig Hairline-Ventilating Pattern

- Cover the actor's forehead with plastic wrap to create a ventilating pattern (Figure 3-1a). Place Scotch tape in strips over the plastic wrap, slightly overlapping each tape strip to create a transparent plastic shell-like wrap (Figure 3-1b).
- Trace a solid line for the actor's natural hairline on the plastic shell wrap, and then draw a dotted line to make a new hairline that will be the ventilating hairline (Figure 3-1b). How high or low the new ventilating hairline is will be based on the shape of the actress's forehead and face. Keeping the hairline looking natural is the bottom line.

Step Two: Attaching Ventilating Lace to the Wig

- Remove the shell from the actor's head, trim off the excess plastic wrap, and then place the shell on the proper size wig block and pin it down (Figure 3-2a).
- Place a piece of ventilating lace on top of the plastic-wrap shell pattern. The ventilating lace should be much larger than the pattern to provide leeway when you manipulate it to fit over the actor's forehead. Make sure no wrinkles occur across the entire frontal area, and pin it temporarily for stability. Make a few darts on the top portion of the ventilating pattern to keep it wrinkle-free across the frontal area (Figure 3-2b), and then sew them by hand with matching thread. Each dart should be managed within the pattern;

67

a

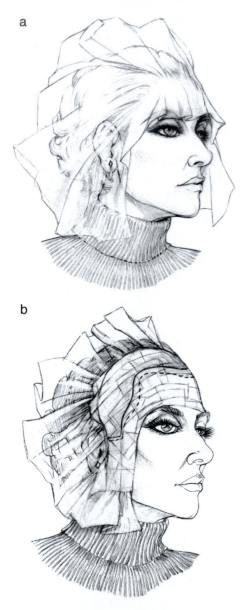

b

Figure 3-1 (a) Place a piece of plastic wrap over the actress's forehead. (b) Tape the entire forehead with Scotch tape; the actress's natural hairline and a new hairline for ventilating are marked on the plastic shell pattern.

a

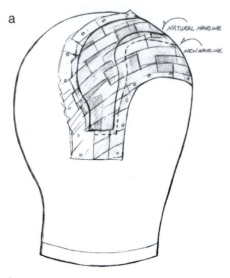

b

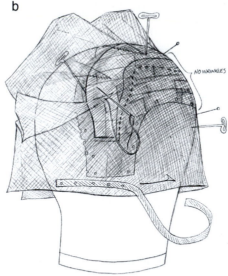

Figure 3-2 (a) Trim the ventilating shell pattern and place it on a wig block.; (b) Place the ventilating lace over the shell and create darts so that it fits over the shell.

these darts will be covered by the wig and hair tied over the ventilating lace.

- Wrap a piece of twill tape across the bottom of the lace, and pin it down. Place the existing wig on top of the ventilating lace about $\frac{1}{2}$–$\frac{3}{4}$" behind the traced natural hairline on the plastic shell. Use a needle and matching thread to sew the wig and the ventilating lace together with slanted hem stitches along the frontal wig edge (Figure 3-3a).

- After you finish sewing, remove the pins and carefully remove the wig and lace from the wig block. Then turn the wig inside out and place it back on the wig block. Trim the excess edge off the top edge of the lace about 1–$1\frac{1}{2}$" inch away from the edge of the wig (Figure 3-3b). Then sew the lace on to the wig (Figure 3-4).

Step Three: Ventilating the Hair

- After you finish sewing the lace on, turn the wig right side out and place it back on the wig block in the proper position, making sure it's wrinkle-free across the forehead but not stretched. Pin the outer edges of the wig down.

a

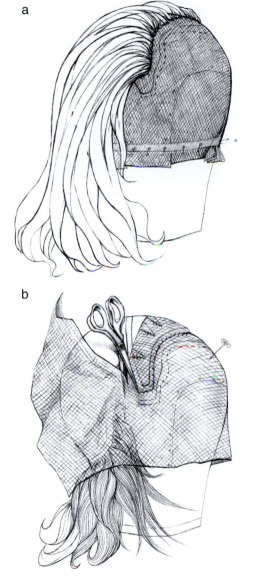

b

Figure 3-3 (a) Attach the existing wig to the ventilating lace. (b) Turn the wig inside out, and trim off the excess ventilating lace.

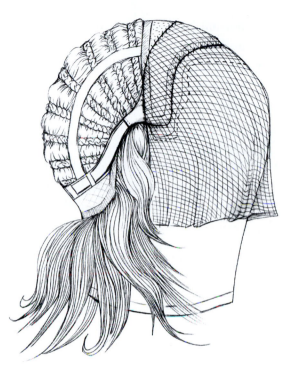

Figure 3-4 Sew the lace on to the wig.

• Place a piece of twill tape across the lower edge of the ventilating lace and pin it down. Because of the round-shaped wig block, a few darts will naturally appear at the bottom of the lace (Figure 3-5b).

• Choose the proper size ventilating needle, a small hook for catching less hair, and a large hook for catching more hair. Tie two to three strands of

a

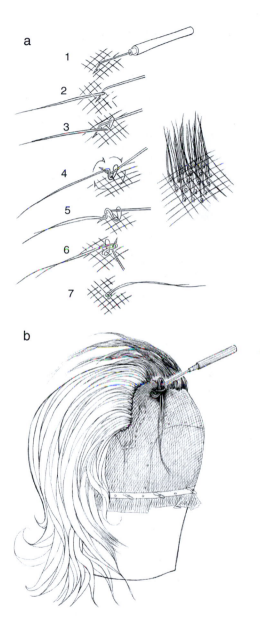

b

Figure 3-5 (a) Steps for tying hair on to the ventilating lace. (b) Ventilating hair, in process.

hair near the wig hairline to add thickness and cover the harsh line of the wig. Tie one or two hairs along the new frontal hairline to achieve a natural, fine-looking hairline.

- Ventilate the hair.
    1. Pull a small amount of hair, fold it over in half and pinch the hair between the thumb and index finger.
    2. Take the ventilating needle with the other hand with the NEEDLE POINT FACING YOU and insert it under and over the net thread (Figure 3-5) (a), catch two or three hairs and pull the hair underneath and through the net thread, keeping tension in both hands as they pull on the needle and hair in opposite directions (b). If your hands lose tension, the hair could slip off the needle hook.
    3. Once the hair has been pulled through and underneath the net, twist the needle with the hair wrapped around until the needle points upward (1–4) and keep on twisting the needle and hair until the needle points downward (5) and then pull the hair through the loop (6–7). BEFORE pulling all the hair out of the loop, tighten the knot with

tension in both hands on the hair and needle.

    4. Repeat steps 1–7 until the required net area is covered with hair. The direction of placing the hair depends on the direction of natural hair growth.

- If the character has gray or white hair, ventilate it into the new hairline. Tie the hair in a scattered, unparallel pattern. Continue to tie hair from the wig hairline toward the new hairline until the pattern is fully covered.
- Use a bright light source and a wig stand while ventilating hair on to the net. It is a time-consuming process, so take a break every once in a while.

The completed wig is shown in Figures 3-6 to 3-7.

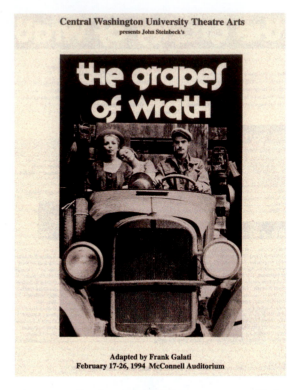

Figure 3-6 *The Grapes of Wrath* program cover; Ma is on the left.

Figure 3-7—Cont'd (c) *Ma played by Dude Hatten. Rose played by Leslie J. Webb, performance student. Grandma played by Milo Smith. Directed by Wesley Van Tassel. Scenic and Lighting design by Dutch Fritz. Costume design by Tan Huaixiang. Central Washington University, Theatre Arts Department presentation.*

Figure 3-7 Production photo of *The Grapes of Wrath* showing the wig, (a) side view, (b) front. *Ma played by Dude Hatten; Tom Joad played by Toby Dycus, performance major student.*

MAKING A HALF-BALD WIG

For this wig you need a high-quality plastic bald cap. It should be durable, stretchy, and large enough to conform to the actor's head. The plastic bald cap is extremely thin and translucent, and its edges can be blended into the skin with acetone or a gentle solvent (for *The Grapes of Wrath*, instead of using acetone, I used forehead wrinkle lines to disguise the edge of the bald cap; this worked well on stage). In order to conceal actor's dark hair, an opaque latex bald cap that is thick, strong, and effective in smashing down curly or full hair was used underneath the half bald wig (two layers of bold caps).

PROCEDURES FOR MAKING A HALF-BALD WIG

Material Required:

- Plastic bald cap
- Latex bald cap
- Ventilating needle
- Hair
- Pins and twill tape
- Wig block
- Hair gel
- Spirit gum
- Spirit gum remover
- Eyeliner
- PAX paints or greasepaint

Step One: Making the Bald Wig Hair Line

- Place the plastic bald cap on the actor's head. Use the actor's natural hairline as a reference for outlining a new half-bald hairline with eyeliner (Figure 3-8a). Then put the bald cap on a wig block (Figure 3-8b). The size of the block should be close to the actor's

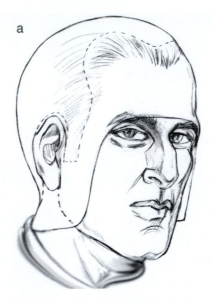

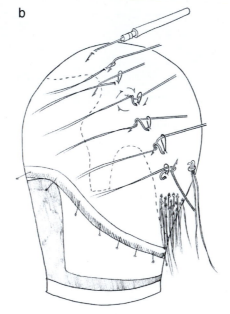

Figure 3-8 (a) Try the bald cap on the actor's head and mark a new hairline. (b) Place the bald cap on a wig block and ventilate the hair on the bald cap, following the steps.

head size. Pin a piece of twill tape on the lower portion of the cap. (Do not trim the excess edge off the bald cap until all the hair has been tied on the entire wig.)

Step Two: Ventilating the Hair

Start ventilating hair from the bottom back and work up toward the front hairline (Figure 3-8b). Because each top layer of tied hair will cover the layer below it, the bottom layers of hair will be hidden and they can be tied with three or four strands of hairs at a time and widely spaced; don't implement this 1″ from the hairline. This method speeds up the process. Since it is a half-bald wig, the hair tied to the wig should not be too thick.

- Ventilating hair on a bald cap uses the same process as on a net except that ventilating hair on a net is easier than on a bald cap because the net is an open-weave surface. The bald cap is a flat, smooth, and stretchy surface, so you have to push the needle into the bald cap.
  1. Carefully insert the ventilating needle into the bald cap and make sure the cap material that you hooked with the needle is about $1/16″$ wide and then pick one or two

strands of hair. You don't want the material you hooked to be too thick (because the resulting knot will be too big) or too thin (because the cap material will be vulnerable to ripping).

2. Gently pull the hair through the holes made by the needle and avoid tearing the latex cap.
3. Tie a knot.
4. Follow the direction of growth of the natural hair.

- As mentioned before, when you are about 1″ away from the front hairline, ventilate only one hair at a time to achieve a natural hairline finish.
- Trim the ventilated hair, while it's on the wig block, to the desired length and try it on the actor's head for a final check.
- Remove the half-bald wig from the wig block. Trim off the excess edges around the ears and back neck ½″ away from the hairline. The extra ½″ edge left on the cap will be glued down to the skin.

Step Three: Applying the Half-Bald Wig

- If the actor has dark-colored hair, two bald caps will be needed because the plastic cap is transparent. The first one will cover the actor's dark hair and can be cheap, opaque, or thick. A thick latex cap will help flatten the hair. I recommend using a flesh-toned bald cap. The edges of the first bald cap must be trimmed narrower than the edges of the wig cap (half-bald wig).
- Flatten the actor's hair with hair gel before putting on the first bald cap and use spirit gum to glue down all the edges. Even though this first layer is not visible, it still has to fit nicely and hug the head; otherwise, it will negatively affect the second cap — the half bald wig. (See Figures 1-10 to 1-12 for instructions on how to put on a bald cap.)
- Put the half-bald cap on the actor. In this example, the front edge of the half-bald wig was trimmed above the eyebrows in order to achieve a smooth bald forehead. Use spirit gum to glue all the edges of the cap to the actor's skin.
- PAX paints, greasepaints, or acrylic paints can be used on the bald cap to simulate the translucency of skin. In this example, grease makeup pigments thinned with caster oil were applied over the bald cap to match the actor's skin tone. Do not apply the paint too thickly or it will kill the translucent appearance of the skin; this is especially true for the half-bald wig. Apply a couple of wrinkles to the actor's forehead to hide the edges of the bald cap and add signs of age to the character.
- After every performance, use spirit gum remover to immediately remove the half-bald wig and to carefully clean the glued edge of the wig.

The completed half-bald wig is shown in Figure 3-9.

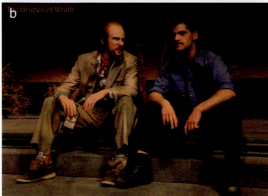

Figure 3-9 Production photos showing the half-bald wig in *The Grapes of Wrath* (a) front view, (b) ¾ view. *Jim Casey played by Craig Zagurski and Tom Joad played by Toby Dycus, performance major students. Directed by Wesley Van Tassel. Set and lighting design by R. Duth Fritz. Costume and wig design by Tan Huaixiang. Central Washington University Theatre Arts Department presentation.*

CREATING A JAPANESE WIG FROM SCRATCH

This traditional Japanese hairstyle female wig I constructed was used for character Katisha in the musical *Mikado*. This wig was built up on a wig base made of Fosshape. I have experimented with Fosshape since 1998. I first discovered this material when my millinery class visited the Creative Costuming Department at Walt Disney, and I thank Disney for introducing it to us. Because the humidity in Florida weakens the stiffness of buckram, Fosshape is used instead for making headdresses at Disney. Since then, I've used it in my classes and productions. Fosshape comes in two weights: 300 lightweight and 600 heavy duty. It looks like felt or nonwoven fabric, but unlike felt it can be heated or steamed to melt into the desired form and it can be sewn by hand or machine. Fosshape is an excellent material for headdresses or any craft construction.

PROCEDURE FOR CONSTRUCTING A JAPANESE WIG

Materials Required:

- 300 lightweight Fosshape
- Hat block
- Elastic

- Steamer and steamed iron
- Black spray paint
- Pieces of boning
- Hair wefts
- Needle and thread
- 2"-thick foam
- Fabric tacky glue
- Yarn
- Hair spray
- Hairbrush
- Scissors

Step One: Creating a Wig Base

- Cut a piece of Fosshape big enough to cover the hat block. Use elastic to tie the Fosshape to the hat block (Figure 3-10).

Figure 3-10 Tie a piece of Fosshape on a hat block with an elastic strap.

- Use both hands to pull the Fosshape down. Manipulate the material as best you can to get rid of the wrinkles along the elastic-tie area of the hat block

(Figure 3-11, left). The Fosshape is like felt and can easily be stretched.

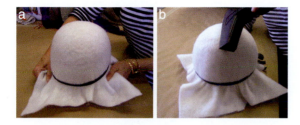

Figure 3-11 (a) Smooth the wrinkles by pulling and manipulating the material. (b) Steam the Fosshape from the top to bottom.

- Apply heat with the steamer over the Fosshape surface, and allow it to shrink around the shape of your object. Start steaming from the top and work your way down (Figure 3-11b). Use one hand to smooth out any wrinkles that appear on the fabric while you steam the bottom portion around the elastic area (two people working together is more effective: one person smoothes the fabric and the other steams it).
- Let the Fosshape harden. Once it hardens, it will be a shell-like cap. Make a 2 or 3″ slash in the lower back center portion of the base. Now it is ready to be separated from the head block.
- Insert pieces of boning between the hardened Fosshape cap and hat block

to help separate the wig base from the hat block (Figure 3-12a). Remove the cap from the hat block (Figure 3-12b).
- Cut out the upside-down U-shape (about 2″ or 3″ deep and 1¼″ or 1½″ wide) from the back of the wig base before fitting it to the actor's head (Figure 3-12c). Trim the fitted base according to the line marks made during the fitting.
- Then spray both the inside and outside of the base with the desired color using either shoe or craft spray paint.
- Sew a 1″ wide × 2″ long elastic strip at the bottom of the U-shaped area for better fit (Figure 3-12c).

Step Two: Attaching Hair Wefts to the Wig Base

- Sew two or three hair wefts together first in one place, and then sew it all the way around the bottom edge of the inside of the wig base with a sewing machine using zigzag stitches (Figure 3-13a). When you sew on top of the elastic area, stretch the elastic out to retain the stretchiness of the elastic after sewing. Hand-sew the wefts on to the wig base where the machine can't reach.
- Sew another row of hair wefts on to the outside (right side) of the cap,

a

b

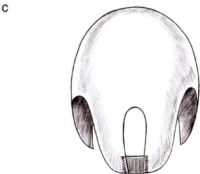

c

Figure 3-12 (a) Insert pieces of boning between the hardened Fosshape cap and hat block. (b) Fosshape cap wig base separated from the hat block. (c) Fit the Fosshape cap and cut it into a proper shape; sew a piece of elastic at the U-shaped bottom opening.

a

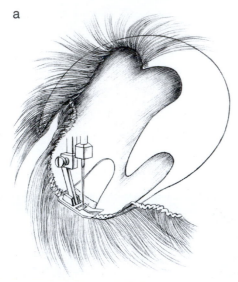

b

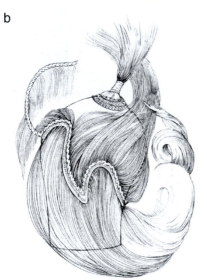

Figure 3-13 (a) Attach hair wefts to the inside edge of the wig base. (b) Attach the second row of hair wefts on the outside of the base cap above the first zigzag stitching line, and attach a tuft of hair weft to the top of the cap as a center root for securing the hair knot later.

above the first zigzag stitching line (Figure 3-13b).

- Sew a circle of hair wefts by hand around the top center of the wig base as a securing root where the rest of the hair will be gathered (Figure 3-13b). All the rest of the hair will be combed toward this root and secured (tied) at this root to become a long ponytail.
- Carve foam pieces into the proper shapes (based on the fullness and the style of the wig) with scissors (Figure 3-14a).
- Comb all the hair down. Attach the foam with fabric tacky glue on to the wig base next to the hair wefts where you need to add volume (Figure 3-14b).
- Cut a piece of foam to place in the center back opening into two pieces (Figure 3-15a). Place the two pieces on either side of the elastic band to allow room for the band to stretch.
- Divide the hair into four sections: a front section, two side sections, and a back section. Tie each section with black yarn. Comb each section individually over the foam toward the top root, and tie the hair near the root area (Figure 3-15b) (you may also tie them individually to the center root).
- Bundle all the ponytails together into one long ponytail (Figure 3-16a).

a

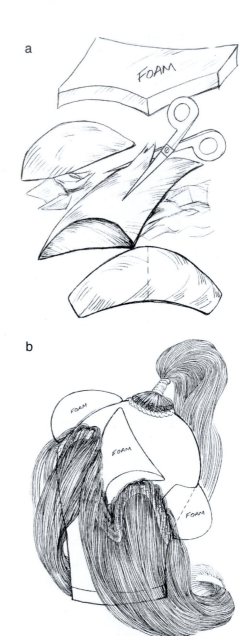

b

Figure 3-14 (a) Carve the foam pieces. (b) Glue the foam on to the wig base for volume.

a

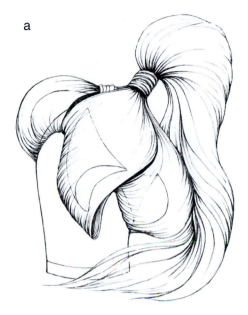

b

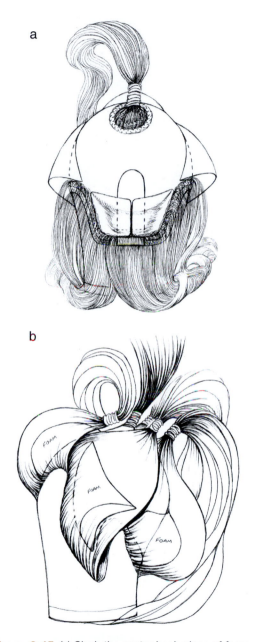

a

b

- Tie them into a knot by taking the ponytail and looping it and then tying the root of the loop to the main root of the ponytail and wrapping the rest of the ponytail around once or twice, depending on the hair length (Figure 3-16b). More wraps are more decorative.

- After wrapping the hair once or twice, fold the rest of the remaining ponytail once and place it inside the loop. Then secure it with a few coats of heavy-duty hairspray. It should look like half of a bow knot when you're done (Figure 3-17a). If the bow is too small or too large, change the number of wraps you made with the hair in the previous step.

This wig style is just one of the many Japanese hairstyles. You may create any hairstyle you want; each starts at the ponytail stage (Figures 3-18 to 3-19). The wig can then be decorated with flowers, combs, or chopsticks. The completed wig is shown in Figures 3-17b and 3-20.

Figure 3-15 (a) Slash the center back piece of foam into two pieces and place them on either side of the elastic. (b) Tie four sections of hair tufts to the center root.

Figure 3-16 (a) Tie all the hair at the center root to make a long ponytail. (b) Loop and secure the ponytail; wrap the remaining tail around twice and then tie a knot.

a

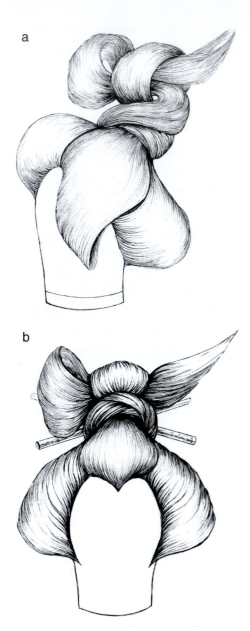

b

Figure 3-17 (a) Tie the hair into a bow knot.
(b) Completed Japanese-style wig.

a

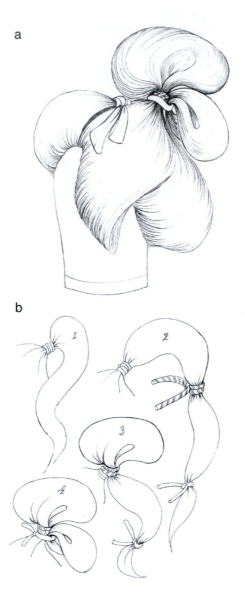

b

Figure 3-18 (a) Second Japanese hairstyle created from a ponytail. (b) Steps for tying the bow knot.

a

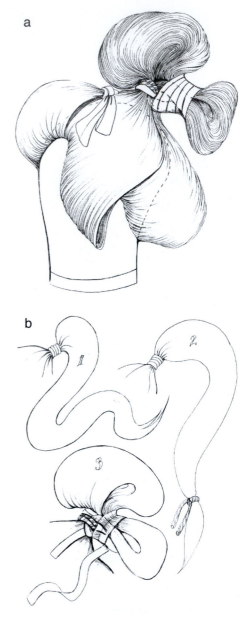

b

Figure 3-19 (a) Third Japanese hairstyle created from a ponytail. (b) Steps for tying the bow knot.

Figure 3-20 Production photo of the Japanese wig in *Mikado*. Katisha played by Anita Endsley. Ko-Ko played by Mark Catlett. Directed by John Bell. Scenic design by Joseph Rusnock. Lighting design by Adri Becker, graduate student. Costume design by Kristina Tollefson. Katisha's wig constructed by Tan Huaixiang. University of Central Florida Conservatory Theatre presentation.

Figure 3-21 Costume design for *Blithe Spirit*.

CREATING A WIG WITH YAK HAIR

In *Blithe Spirit*, when Madame Arcati, the spirit medium, puts on her wig, the wig helps present her spiritual/psychic power that conjures up the spirits and produces comical and animated moments for the audience. In the University of Central Florida production, the wig was carried in the character's hand bag and she put on the wig on top of another wig on stage in front of the audience (Figure 3-21). This required that the wig construction be durable and flexible. The inspiration for the wig's hairstyle was a sketch. Yak hair was chosen for this wig because it has volume for the braided hair style, is light in weight, and is long.

PROCEDURE FOR CONSTRUCTING A YAK HAIR WIG

Materials Required:

- An existing felt hat
- Hat block
- Piece of elastic (1″ wide)
- Packages of yak hair
- Beads
- String
- Crown (see Chapter 10)
- Needle and thread
- Extra-hold hair spray

Step One: Creating Hair Attachment on the Wig Cap

- Choose an old dark-colored felt hat (a felt hat can be stretched and reshaped).

Detach both the inside and outside hat bands. Place it on the proper-size hat block (Figure 3-22a) to create a deep-crowned wig cap (this wig has to fit on top of another wig, so the wig cap has to be deep) and spray the hat with water on both sides.

- Tie a piece of elastic at the brim to keep it in place, pull and manipulate the brim with both hands to force the brim to flatten until the most fullness of the brim disappears (Figure 3-22b).

- Cut an upside-down U-shaped opening at the bottom of the crown. Try the cap on the actor's head on top of the other wig, and flip up the extra cap edge (the amount depends on the fit) for reinforcement (Figure 3-23a).

- Attach a piece of 1″-wide piece of elastic to the opening (Figure 3-23a).

- Attach a crown (see Chapter 10 for instructions on creating a crown) to the outside of the cap with hand-sewn tacking stitches (Figure 3-23b).

- Sew a few shoelace strings on to the cap, spacing them out in different locations; they are for tying hair to the cap (Figure 3-24a).

- Tie tufts of yak hair on to the cap (Figure 3-24b). Tie each hair tuft 2″ below the tuft root with each string on the cap. The extra 2″ of hair will help

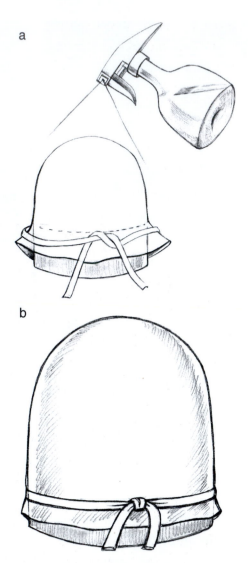

Figure 3-22 (a) Spray the felt hat with water; tie a piece of elastic at the brim. (b) Flatten the felt hat brim to make the crown deeper.

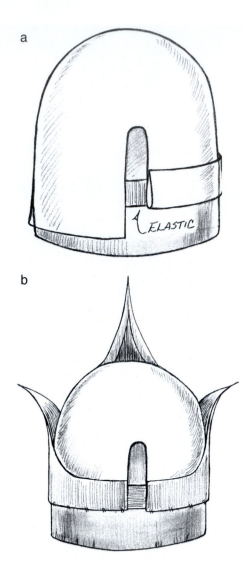

Figure 3-23 (a) Flip up the excess edge of the cap and add a piece of elastic at the upside-down U-shaped opening. (b) Attach a crown to the cap.

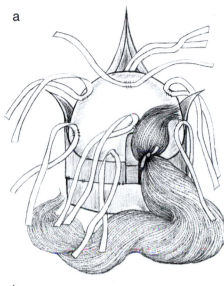

a

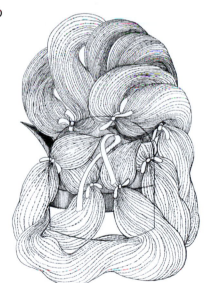

b

cover the surface of the cap and increase the hair volume.

- After all hair has been tied on to the cap, braid and twist the hair together to create the desired hairstyle. To make the center hair portion higher, braid the center front hair, form it into a loop, and tie it down (Figure 3-25).

- Sew a few strings of beads (Figure 3-26), and spray heavy-duty extra-hold hair spray all over the hair.

The completed wig is shown in Figures 3-26 and 3-27.

Figure 3-24 (a) Sew hair ties on to the cap for tying the hair. (b) Tie the hair tufts on to the cap.

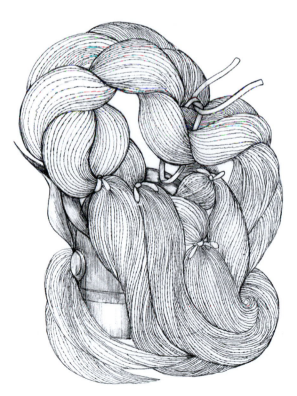

Figure 3-25 Braid the top portion hair and tie it down to the base to create a braided-hair loop.

Figure 3-26 Actor in the completed yak hair wig; some gold beads have been wrapped over the braids for decoration.

Figure 3-27 Production photo from *Blithe Spirit*. From left to right: Mrs. Bradman played by Ayla Harrison, Ruth played by Patrice Bell, Madame Arcati played by Charita Nakia, Charles played by Donté Bonner, and Mr. Bradman played by Michael Swichard. Directed by Jim Helsinger. Scenic design by Bert Scott. Lighting design by Jim Hart. Costume design by Tan Huaixiang. University of Central Florida Conservatory Theatre presentation.

DYEING WIGS

The director for *Blithe Spirit* requested a red color scheme for the spirit Elvira (Figure 3-28) and a green color scheme for the spirit Ruth (Figure 3-31) (the two ghosts in the play). Anything the characters wore on stage was to match their color schemes, so a red wig was used for Elvira and a green wig was used for Ruth. Both wigs were made of human hair and dyed with Rit dye. A light blonde wig was dyed red, and a medium brown wig was dyed green. Human hair absorbs dye much better than synthetic hair, and it is easy to style as well.

Figure 3-28 Costume design for Elvira in *Blithe Spirit*.

PROCEDURE FOR DYEING A HUMAN-HAIR WIG

Materials Required:

- Human-hair wig
- Red and green Rit dye
- Stove
- Product for highlighting hair
- Dye pot
- Spoon
- Scissors
- Decorated pearl beads
- Gloves and apron
- Hair curlers and hair pins

Step One: Dyeing the Wig

- Boil enough water in a pot for the wig to float in freely. Add the dye to the pot, and then put the stove on low.
- Wash the wig before dyeing, and squeeze out the excess water.
- If you want highlights, create them using with any hair highlighting product purchased from any beauty salon. The top of the brown wig had highlights put in it first; then it was dyed green.
- Cut off a little tuft of hair from the back of the pulled wig and put it in the dye bath to test the color.
- If you like the color, put the entire wig in the dye bath. Stir the water every 5 seconds until the wig reaches the desired color.
- Take the wig out of the water. Wash it with shampoo and conditioner, and rinse it.

Step Two: Styling the Wigs

Elvira's Wig

- Cut and style the wig. A 1920s bob hairstyle was used for the red wig.

Figure 3-29 Production photo of Elvira showing the wig close up, front.

- Attach decorations as needed.
The finished wig is shown in Figures 3-29 and 3-30.

Ruth's Wig

- Set curls on the green wig while it is wet.
- Style the wig after it dried. A 1930s style was used for the green wig.
- Attach decorations as needed.
    The finished wig is shown in parts b–d of Figure 3-31.

Figure 3-30 Production photo of Elvira showing the wig (a) back, (b) front.

Figure 3-31 (a) Costume design for Ruth in *Blithe Spirit*.

Continued

Figure 3-31—Cont'd (b) Production photo of Ruth showing the wig — front. *Ruth played by Patrice Lois Bell.*

Figure 3-31—Cont'd (c) Production photo of Ruth showing the wig with full costume — front. *Ruth played by Patrice Lois Bell.*

Figure 3-31—Cont'd (d) Production photo from *Blithe Spirit. Right to left: Ruth played by Patrice Lois Bell, Charles played by Donté Bonner, Elvira played by Lisa Bryant. Directed by Jim Helsinger. Scenic design by Bert Scott. Lighting design by Jim Hart. Costume design by Tan Huaixiang. University of Central Florida Conservatory Theatre presentation.*

CREATING HAIR EXTENSIONS

Nowadays, there are many wig products with a wide range of prices, lengths, and types available for theater, fashion, and everyday life. But recreating something from stock or creating a homemade product is always the first choice (especially when on a limited budget) because it is the most practical, inexpensive, and original. The following are examples demonstrating different methods of lengthening hair.

ADDING HAIR EXTENSIONS TO NATURAL HAIR

A long falling hair style was needed for Juliet in the production of Shakespeare's *Romeo and Juliet* for which I designed the costumes and makeup (Figure 3-32). Since the actress who played Juliet had blond short hair, hair extensions were attached to her own hair instead of her wearing a wig; this conveyed a more natural appearance for the character.

PROCEDURES FOR ADDING HAIR EXTENSIONS

Materials Required:

- Hair wefts in different lengths
- Wig clips (combs)
- Needle and thread
- Scissors
- Liquid latex or fabric tacky glue

Step One: Purchasing and Preparing the Hair Wefts

- Buy premade hair wefts with the proper colors and desired length. The wefts come in different lengths and colors. Choose the hair color that matches the actor's hair and measure the desired width (Figure 3-33a) and length of the hair extension before purchasing it. The width measurement of each row of weft will be different and will depend on the hairline shape. A set of four lengths of wefts (15″, 18″, 21″, and 23″) was purchased to create Juliet's hair style. Four rows of wefts were added on to the actress's hair. You can add more or fewer rows of hair wefts, depending on whether you want thick or thin hair.
- Secure two ends of each weft with glue, either liquid latex or fabric tacky glue (Figure 3-33b). A piece of hair weft is

Figure 3-32 Costume designs for *Romeo and Juliet*.

a

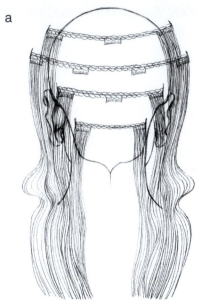

usually made with a weaving frame (the root of the hair is woven into threads) or sewn with a double-needle sewing machine (the roots of hair are fed under the sewing foot and double-stitched twice with a double needle to hold the hair together). If it is not secured, when it is cut, it will have a fuzzy end and some hair will fall off the cut end.

- Sew wig clips on to each measured weft with matching thread (Figure 3-33b). Sew at least three wig clips on to each weft and space them evenly. Four wig clips will be needed for a longer hair weft.

Step Two: Attaching the Hair Wefts

- Clip each weft on to the actress's hair using the attached wig clips. Start with the bottom row 2″ above the neck hair line (Figure 3-34). Comb the rest of the hair in back up toward the top of the head. Open each clip and insert it into the actress's hair, and then press it shut. Space each row of wefts about 2″ apart. Of course, if you prefer thicker, fuller hair, more rows will be needed.
- Carefully comb the actress's hair and wefts to blend them together.

The finished hair is shown in Figure 3-35.

b

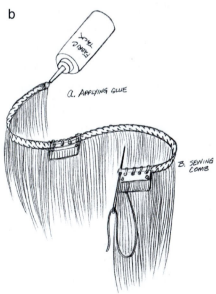

a. APPLYING GLUE

B. SEWING COMB

Figure 3-33 (a) Width measurements of each row of hair wefts. (b) Glue the ends of each hair weft, and then sew wig clips on to the hair weft.

Figure 3-34 Attach the hair wefts to the actress's hair.

Figure 3-35 Production photo of *Romeo and Juliet*. Romeo played by Keith Edie, performance student; Juliet played by Sara Hill, performance student. Directed by Brenda Hubbard. Set design by Tim Stapleton, Lighting design by Mark C. Zetterberg. Costume design by Tan Huaixiang. Central Washington University Department of Theatre Arts presentation.

CREATING HAIR EXTENSIONS AND ADDING THEM TO AN EXISTING WIG

In this example, a long-haired wig was created for the Enchantress in *Peer Gent*. This character's wig was made from an existing wig and hair in stock. It was a dyed light green. The foundation was a shoulder-length light-blonde wig; extensions were added to lengthen the wig to mid-thigh to suit the character's wildness.

PROCEDURE FOR CREATING HAIR EXTENSIONS

Materials Required:

- Medium-length blonde human-hair wig
- Tufts of blond hair at least 7″ long (the longer, the better)
- Organza fabric (white, off-white, or green in color; 1 yd)
- Water bottle
- Rubber bands
- Rit dye
- Clear glue or fabric tacky glue
- Wig block
- T-pins
- Dye pot
- Spoons
- Stove
- Gloves and apron
- Brush or comb
- Wig clips
- Pinking shears

Step One: Preparation and Dyeing the Hair, Fabric, and Wig

Choose a human hair wig, human hair lengths (7″-long tufts of human hair were used in creating this thigh-length wig because that was in stock; longer hair will give a better result but will cost more), and a piece of natural fiber organza fabric. For this wig, the hair was glued to the fabric strips and the fabric stripes were attached to the wig.

All the material should be dyed together in the same dye pot to get a matching color (for this wig, it was all dyed green). Human hair and natural fiber fabric absorb dye best (if you already have a piece of colored fabric that matches the desired hair color, this can be used instead of dyeing it).

- Divide the hair tufts into small sections, wet the tying root of the hair tuft with a water bottle for even colors when dyeing, and then tie the wet root with rubber bands to avoid tangling the hair (Figure 3-36a).
- Wet the wig, hair tufts, and organza fabric before dyeing them.
- Boil water, mix some Rit dye, and pour it into the water. Make sure there is enough water for everything to move freely in the water. Add the materials (Figure 3-36b) and stir every 5 seconds until the desired color is reached. Remove the materials, rinse, and dry.

Step Two: Gluing Hair to Fabric Strips and Attaching Them to the Wig

- Cut the dyed organza fabric into ¾″-wide strips of various lengths (18, 20, 22, or 25″). Cut the fabric with a

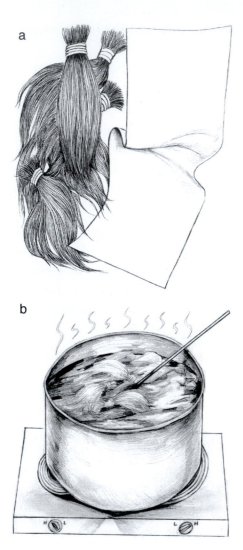

Figure 3-36 (a) Tie the hair into tufts; prepare the fabric for dying. (b) Dye the hair tufts, wig, and fabric together.

pair of pinking shears if the fabric unravels easily.

- Put a piece of newspaper or plastic sheet down to protect the surface you're working on.
- Pin the two ends of the strip on the flat surface; apply glue to the strip where the hair tuft will go. Start from the bottom of the strip and work your way up. Work on one section at a time.
- Cut the hair tuft at an angle; this angle will allow all the ends of hair to be glued to the strip. Place the tuft on the strip where you applied glue. Keep the hair flow in the same direction, and overlap each hair tuft 1–2″ until the desired length is reached. Then turn the strip over and glue more hair down in exactly the same places on the opposite side of the strip. Continue adding tufts on both sides of the strip (see Figure 3-37a).
- Sew the strips of hair on to the wig by hand or sewing machine. Spread the strips evenly in different alternative locations. The number of strips needed depends on how full the wig will be (Figure 3-37b; note that in order to clearly show where the strips will go, the figure shows the fabric strips without any hair on them).
- Sew a few wig clips on to the wig in the front and on the two temples areas to

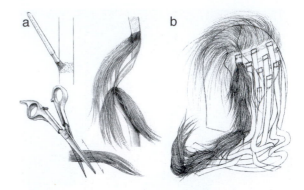

Figure 3-37 (a) Trim and glue the tufts of hair on to the fabric strip. (b) Attach the fabric strips to the wig (shown here without any hair on the strips for clarity only) — profile; do the same on the other side.

secure the wig to the head. It is now ready to put it on the actress's head.

The finished wig is shown in Figure 3-38.

Figure 3-38 (a) Production photo of *Peer Gent* showing wig with full costume.

Figure 3-38—Cont'd (b) Production photo of *Peer Gent* showing wig — right side. *Peer Gent played by Wei Xiaoping (left). Enchantress played by Zhang Xinxin (right).* (c) Production photo of *Peer Gent* showing wig. *Directed by Xu Xiaozhong, Bai Shiben, and Xu Min. Scenic design by Liu Yunsheng and Dai Dunsi. Lighting design by Mu Baisuo and Yu Haibuo. Costume design by Huo Qidi. Makeup and hair design by Tan Huaixiang. The Central Academy of Drama, Beijing, China, presentation.*

CREATING A BRAIDED PONY TAIL FROM AN EXISTING WIG

The wig for the character Lone in the Cornell University production of *Dance and Railroad* was a Qing Dynasty men's hairdo — a long braid or ponytail (Figure 3-39). About a 40″ length was added to a medium-length existing black wig from stock. A ventilated natural hairline was also added to this wig. The character was choreographed to swing the ponytail

Figure 3-39 Costume design for *Dance and Railroad.*

around in circles on stage to create a dramatic moment.

PROCEDURE FOR CREATING A BRAIDED PONYTAIL WIG

Materials Required:

- An existing wig
- Existing hair wefts
- Ventilating lace
- Ventilating needle
- Ventilating hair
- Thick black yarn
- Small black rubber bands
- Needle and thread
- Hairbrush

Step One: Adding a Natural Front Hairline

- Create a ventilating pattern for ventilating the hair to create a natural hairline (Figure 3-40). (See Figures 3-1 to 3-5 for the steps for creating a natural front hairline for a wig.)

Step Two: Creating Long Hair Wefts

- Pull whatever length hair wefts you have from stock. If a weft is not long enough, sew two ends of the short wefts together with a sewing machine to create a longer one. For thicker braids, put two or four wefts on top

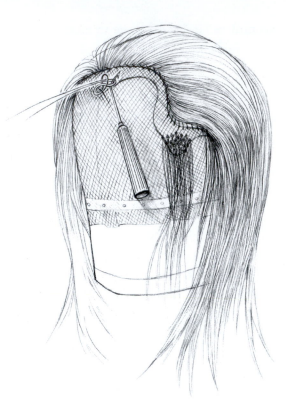

Figure 3-40 Ventilate a frontal natural hairline.

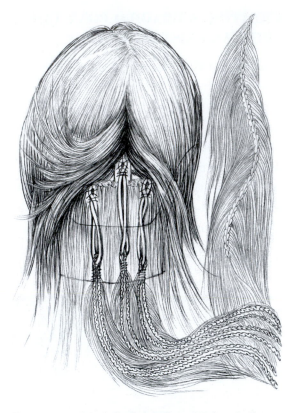

Figure 3-41 Attach the hair wefts extensions to the back of the wig.

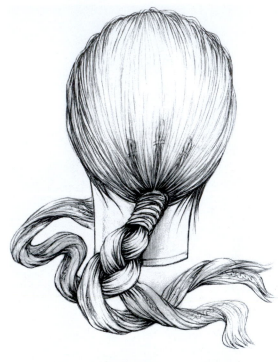

Figure 3-42 Braid the ponytail.

of each other and sew them with a sewing machine. You will need three of these if you intend to braid the hair.

- Then fold the long hair weft in half and tie it together with black rubber band ½″ below the loop. Do the same to the other two tufts if you intend to braid the hair.

- Cut a long piece of black yarn and fold it in half. Put the yarn fold through the hair weft loop and pull the other end of the yarn through its own loop (Figure 3-41). Go up 2 or 3″ on the yarn and tie another knot; trim off the extra yarn above the second knot. Sew the yarn connected to the hair weft to the wig with a needle and

thread (Figure 3-41). The yarn gives flexibility to the wig and makes the hair longer. If you sew the weft loop directly to the wig, it will be stiff and bulky.

- After the hair wefts are attached to the wig, comb the hair on the wig and braid the hair into a long braided ponytail (Figure 3-42). The wig as ready for the stage.

The finished wig is shown in Figures 3-43 to 3-44.

Figure 3-43 Actor Chris Sharp is in his production costume and the wig.

Figure 3-44 Production photos of ponytail wig in *The Dance and The Railroad*. (a) Chris Sharp played Lone. (b) *Lone (left)* played by Chris Sharp. *Ma (right)* played by Ricky T. Li. Directed and choreographed by Keith Grant. Scenic designed by Julia Gallager. Costume and makeup designed by Tan Huaixiang. Cornell University Department of Theatre Arts presentation.

CREATING A TRADITIONAL CHINESE HAIRSTYLE

An Asian hairstyle was used in Shakespeare's *Romeo and Juliet* staged at the Theatre Arts Department at Central Washington University (Figure 3-45). The director for this production requested that there be a couple of international guests attending the masked-party scene in Juliet's castle, so two Asian guests were added to the party scene. The costumes and hairstyles for these two Asian actresses had a Chinese traditional influence. Both actresses have natural black hair, so there was no need to make full wigs for them; instead hair attachments were added.

Figure 3-45 Costume design for *Romeo and Juliet*.

PROCEDURE FOR MAKING THE HAIR ATTACHMENT

Materials Required:

- Buckram (black)
- Black felt
- Yak hair
- Spray adhesive
- Sewing machine
- Needle and thread
- Fabric tacky glue
- Decorative flowers
- Wig comb
- Black horse hair (½″ wide)

Step One: Creating Patterns for the Hair Attachment

- Design patterns for the foundation and hair loop base of the hair attachment (Figure 3-46a).
- Cut the foundation from buckram, and sew a piece of millinery wire along the edge of it (Figure 3-46b).

Step Two: Covering the Buckram Foundation with Felt

- Spray adhesive on one side of the buckram foundation, and adhere it to a piece of felt that is a little bit bigger than the foundation itself. Then trim the edge of the felt around the foundation (Figure 3-47a).

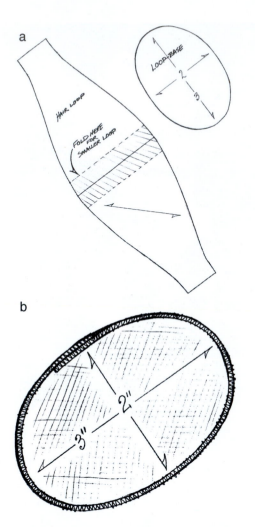

Figure 3-46 (a) Make patterns for the hair base and loop. (b) Attach millinery wire along the buckram foundation.

- Spray adhesive on the other side of the foundation, and place it on another piece of felt; this time leave a ¼″ seam allowance on the felt when you cut off the excess fabric (Figure 3-47b).

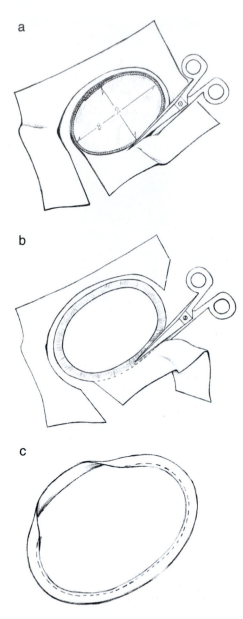

Figure 3-47 (a) Glue the foundation to felt; trim the excess fabric. (b) After attaching the second piece of felt, trim the excess leaving a seam allowance. (c) Machine stitch the foundation for a finished edge.

- Fold the ¼″ seam allowance up over the other side of the base, and top stitch it using the sewing machine for a finished edge (Figure 3-47c). It is now ready for attaching the hair loops.

Step Three: Creating Hair Loops

- Cut one layer of buckram from the hair loop pattern. Spray adhesive on one side of the buckram and glue it to a piece of felt a little bigger than the buckram. Leave a ¼″ seam allowance on to the felt when you cut off the excess fabric. Cut off the four corners of the felt (to reduce the bulk) (Figure 3-48a).
- Apply fabric tacky glue to the felt seam allowance and fold it over, gluing it to the buckram to finish off the edge (Figure 3-48b).
- Spray adhesive on the buckram side of the hair loop base (Figure 3-49a).
- Attach the yak hair on the sticky side of the hair loop base (Figure 3-49b). Repeat the same process to make the other two hair loops. The other two loops can be slightly shorter (by folding the middle of the pattern, see shaded area of Figure 3-46a).

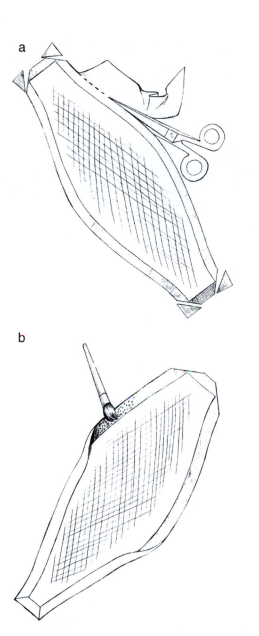

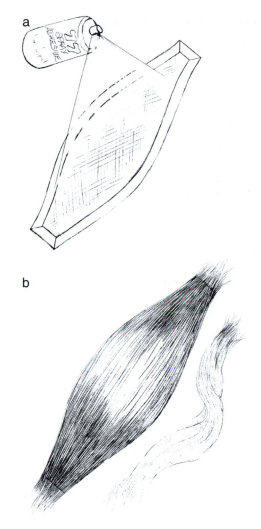

Figure 3-49 (a) Spray the hair loop base with spray adhesive. (b) Glue the yak hair to the hair loop base.

Figure 3-48 (a) After gluing the felt to the underside of the buckram hair loop piece, leave a seam allowance when trimming off the excess fabric and then trim the corners. (b) Apply glue to the seam allowance, and fold it over to finish the edge.

Step Four: Attaching the Hair Loops to the Base

- Sew the hair loops to the base by hand (Figure 3-50a). Use the same method to attach the other two hair loops.
- Sew a few pin loops on to the edge of the base to secure the hair attachment to the head (Figure 3-50b).
- Attach a few decorative flowers on to the base. Pin it on to actress's hair.

The completed hair attachments are shown in Figure 3-51.

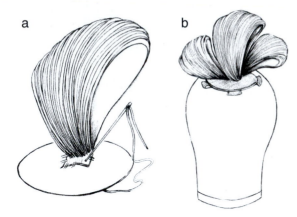

Figure 3-50 (a) Sew the hair loop to the base by hand. (b) Attach all hair loops and pin loops to the hair loop base.

Figure 3-51 Production photo showing the hair attachments in *Romeo and Juliet*. The two Asian dancers played by Pei Chen (left) and Yumi Fukushima (right). Directed by Brenda Hubbard. Scenic designed by Tim Stapleton. Lighting design by Mark C. Zetterberg. Costume and makeup design by Tan Huaixiang. Central Washington University Department of Theatre Arts presentation.

Figure 3-52 Costume design for *Pippin*.

ALTERING AN EXISTING WIG

A wig was needed for the character Bertha in the University of Central Florida production of the musical *Pippin*. Due to a budget shortage, an Irish-red wig pulled from stock was to be used for Berthe's wig, but it needed to be altered. Curly hair extensions that matched the wig were combined with the wig. Perhaps this was not the best way to construct the wig, but it was the most economical. If you have the budget, buying a long curly wig will be much easier and look natural and beautiful.

Mark Brotherton played King Charles as well as Grandma Berthe. This required a quick change of costume. A full feminine body suit was built for the actor. A wimple was designed to cover his muscular neck and was attached to Berthe's wig (Figure 3-52). The wig was attached to a wig base, and all these served as one piece for the quick change.

It worked marvelously for the performances.

PROCEDURES FOR ALTERING AN EXISTING WIG

Materials Required:

- Existing wig
- Curly matching hair extensions
- Wig base (made of Fosshape)
- Flesh-tone spray paint
- Matching color yarn
- Scissors
- Hair spray
- Hair tie strings
- Hair band
- Wimple (matching the costume)
- Needle and thread

Step One: Attaching the Existing Wig to a Wig Base

- Make a wig base for supporting the wig and the quick change. (See Figures 3-1 to 3-3 for the steps for making a wig base with Fosshape.) Spray-paint the wig base a flesh tone. Sew the existing wig to the base (Figure 3-53a).

Figure 3-53 (a) Attach the wig to a wig base. (b) Tie the hair tufts to the wig. (c) Tie the center tuft as a support (left) and connect the other extension tufts to the center tuft (right). (d) Wig with hair extensions.

Step Two: Attaching Extension Hair Tufts to the Existing Wig

- Divide hair extensions into tufts, and tie each hair tuft with matching yarn to the top of the wig for more fullness and volume (Figure 3-53b).
- Tie a hair tuft at the center top of the wig with yarn, and tie all the other attached tuft extensions to the center hair tuft to keep them in place. This center tuft is midpoint support for all the other tufts tied to it (Figure 3-53c). Trim hair if needed.
- Apply hair spray to secure the shape. The wig with hair extensions attached is shown in Figure 3-53d.

Step Three: Attaching a Hair Band and Wimple to the Wig

- First sew a hair band with tacking stitches to the wig at the front, sides, and back.
- Sew a wimple to the wig over the hair band at the back and sides of the wig.

The completed wig piece is shown in Figure 3-54.

Figure 3-54 Completed wig with hair band and wimple (a) front; (b) profile; (c) back. (d) Production photo of *Pippin* showing wig. *Berthe played by Mark Brotherton (center). Chorus players played by Chris Neiss (left) and Jason Whitehead (right), BFA student. Directed by John Bell, Scenic design by Joseph Rusnock, Lighting design by Eric Haugen. Sound design by Martin Wootton. Costume design by Tan Huaixiang. University of Central Florida Conservatory Theatre presentation.*

Chapter 4   Beards

MAKING A GOATEE

In the University of Central Florida production of *Pippin*, Mark Brotherton played double roles: King Charles and Grandma Bertha. The beard made a distinctive difference between these two roles. When the actor wore the beard, he portrayed a powerful king (Figure 4-1); beardless, he was a beautiful and kind grandmother.

PROCEDURE FOR MAKING A GOATEE

Materials Required:

- Fine flesh-toned ventilating lace
- Ventilating needle
- Beard block
- Poly stuffing or cotton balls
- Narrow twill tape
- T-pins
- Scotch tape
- Plastic wrap
- Hair (human or synthetic; naturally curly hair is preferred for beard making

Figure 4-1 Costume design for *Pippin*.

to create natural fullness and texture; a curly toupee hair piece or a curly wig can also be used for ventilating the beard)
- Scissors
- Colored marker
- Spirit gum or toupee tapes
- Spirit gum remover

Step One: Creating Goatee Pattern

- Place a piece of plastic wrap large enough to cover the actor's upper and lower jaw where a beard would grow. Mold and press the plastic wrap around the skin of the jaws.
- Overlap the ends of the plastic wrap at the center back of the actor's neck and place a few strips of Scotch tape down to hold it in place. The actor may assist in holding it down.
- Scotch tape the entire plastic wrap over the actor's jaws. Slightly overlap each Scotch tape strip next to each other against the plastic wrap (Figure 4-2).

97

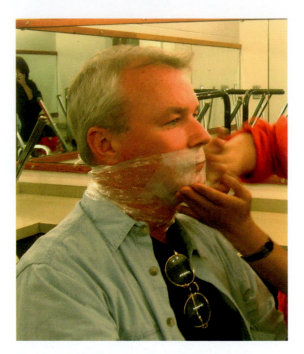

Figure 4-2 Place Scotch tape strips on top of the plastic wrap to create a beard shell.

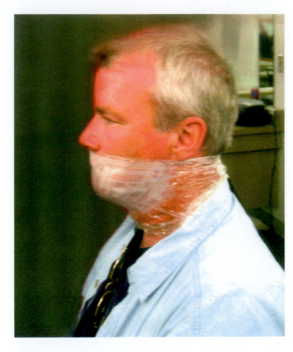

Figure 4-3 Completed and taped beard shell.

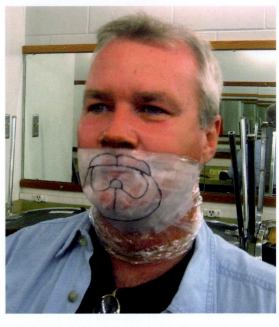

Figure 4-4 Outline the shape of the beard where the hair will be attached.

The finished form should resemble a shell (Figure 4-3).

- Outline the silhouette of the desired goatee with a marker to indicate where the hair will be ventilated (Figure 4-4). Since the plastic wrap and tape are transparent, you'll be able to see the actor's lips, chin, and jaw line. Now you've created a perfect goatee pattern for the actor.
- Remove the shell pattern from actor's face (Figure 4-5a).

Step Two: Putting the Beard Pattern on to a Beard Block

- Put the shell-like beard pattern on a beard block. If it does not fit well over the block, use poly stuffing or cotton balls to fill the spaces and gaps between the pattern and the block (Figure 4-5b) so there are no hollow areas (Figure 4-6a). The pattern should be smooth and not stretched. Then tape down the pattern on the beard block.

Step Three: Positioning Ventilating Lace over the Pattern and Ventilating the Hair

- Place a piece of ventilating lace on top of the beard pattern and temporarily pin it down (Figure 4-6b). It should be wrinkle-free across the front jaw line.

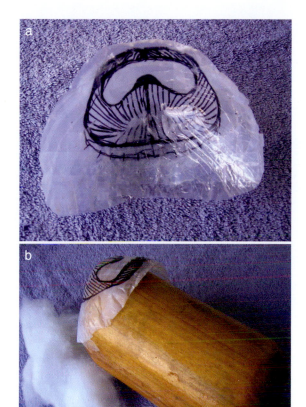

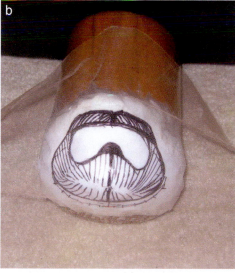

Figure 4-5 (a) Completed beard pattern removed from the actor's face. (b) Place the pattern on a beard block; fill any gaps between the pattern and block (like the one shown) with poly stuffing.

Figure 4-6 (a) Beard pattern piece stuffed with poly stuffing to fill the gap between the pattern and block. (b) Place a piece of ventilating lace on top of the beard pattern.

Make a few darts under the chin to fit the chin shape. Depending on the size of the individual's face, these darts may be deep or shallow. However, darts should always be placed under the chin area.

- Place a piece of narrow twill tape on top of the lace about $\frac{1}{2}$–$\frac{3}{8}$" away from the edges of the pattern, and then pin the twill tape and lace together to the beard block. Place the T-pins about $\frac{1}{2}$–$\frac{3}{4}$" apart (Figure 4-7a). The ventilating lace is netlike, so it won't hold pins, but the twill tape will help to stabilize the lace and pins in place.

- Tie hair on to the ventilating lace. Start from the darts underneath the chin area, tying a few hairs to the darts (Figure 4-7b) to secure them instead of sewing them with a needle and thread; the hair tied on the darts function as stitches. (The darts can be sewn with a needle and flesh-color thread as well.) Generally speaking, tie two or three hairs at the bottom of the beard, and tie one or two hairs at the top portion (near the hairline area) of the beard to portray a natural growing hairline (Figure 4-8a). (See Figure 3-5 for the steps for tying hair on to ventilating lace.)

- Add some highlights or shadows to the beard by mixing colors of hair.

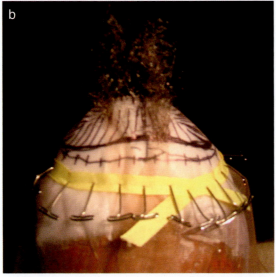

Figure 4-7 (a) Pin a piece of ventilating lace in place with a piece of twill tape and T-pins around the beard pattern. (b) Ventilate the hair, starting with the darts under the chin.

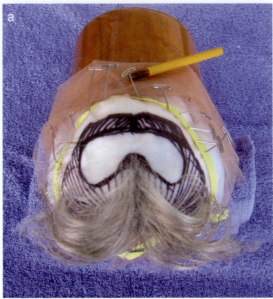

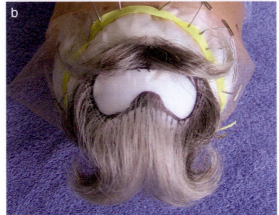

Figure 4-8 (a) Continue to ventilate the hair. (b) Completed and trimmed beard — highlights and shadows have been added.

Step Four: Trimming and Applying the Goatee

- Trim the beard hair. It's easier to trim the hair while it's on the beard block because the surrounding pins will keep the untrimmed beard in place.
- Trim the excess ventilating lace down to $\frac{1}{8}-\frac{1}{4}''$ away from the hairline.
- Use spirit gum to apply the beard to the actor's face. (Toupee tapes can also be used for fast changes, but they only work for a short time and allow fewer mouth movements).
- Clean the beard after each use with spirit gum remover. Comb or style the beard as necessary after each performance and pin it back on the beard block to maintain its shape.

The completed beard is shown in Figures 4-8b and 4-9.

Figure 4-9 Production photo of *Pippin* showing the beard. *King Charles played by Mark Brotherton. Directed by John Bell. Scenic design by Joseph Rusnock. Lighting design by Eric Haugen. Sound design by Martin Wootton. Costume design by Tan Huaixiang. University of Central Florida Conservatory Theatre presentation.*

MAKING A FULL BEARD

There are three wise kings in *The Butterfingers Angel*. In the University of Central Florida production, these three kings had dark, thick, curly beards in different styles (Figure 4-10). One actor who was playing a king had three different roles in the play, so we needed a

Figure 4-10 Costume design for *The Butterfingers Angel*.

full beard that could be put on and taken off without any adhesive for the quick changes on stage.

PROCEDURE FOR MAKING A FULL BEARD

Materials Required:

- Synthetic or human curly hair 8–10″ long

- Ventilating lace
- Ventilating needle
- Beard block
- Narrow twill tape
- T-pins
- Scotch tape
- Plastic wrap
- Hair spray
- ¼″-wide elastic
- Double-sided tape

Step One: Creating a Full Beard Pattern

- Making a full-beard pattern is the same as creating a goatee pattern but bigger. Place a large piece of plastic wrap on the actor up to the temples, and Scotch tape the entire upper and lower jaw to create a shell (Figure 4-11).
- Then outline on the beard pattern where the hair needs to be attached.

Step Two: Placing the Beard Pattern and Ventilating Lace on a Beard Block

- Remove the shell-like pattern from the actor's face, and trim off the unnecessary edges of the plastic wrap.
- Place the beard pattern on a beard block (Figure 4-12). Stuff any hollow areas between the pattern and the beard block with stuffing as necessary (see

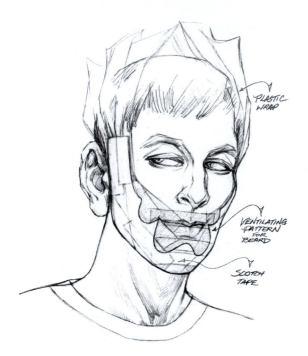

Figure 4-11 Create a full-beard pattern on the actor's face with plastic wrap and scotch tape.

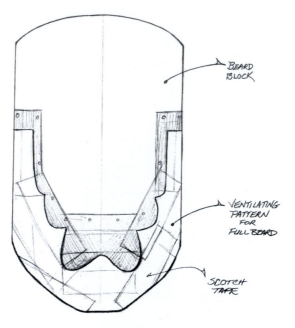

Figure 4-12 Place the beard pattern on the beard block.

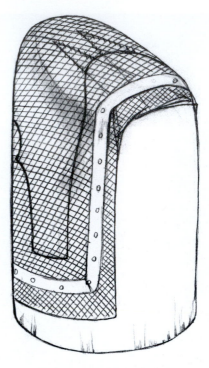

Figure 4-13 Pin the ventilating lace on the beard block.

Figures 4-5 to 4-6 for how to stuff the beard pattern).

- Place a piece of ventilating lace a little bit bigger than the beard pattern on the block. Lay a piece of twill tape on top of the ventilating lace ³⁄₄–1″ away from the outline of the beard pattern and stabilize it with many pins.

Step Three: Attaching Hair Wefts and Ventilating the Hair

The style of this full beard is based on the fashion of the ancient Assyrians — full, thick, long, curly, and square-shaped. In order to speed up completion of the beard, hair wefts were attached to emphasize thickness.

- Sew a few hair wefts on the ventilating lace with slanted stitches. Start from the bottom edge of the beard and work your way upward (Figure 4-14).
- Stop sewing the hair wefts about 1″ away from the hairline, and then start to ventilate the hair from there to the hairline. The dotted area in Figure 4-15 indicates the ventilation area.

- Tie two or three hairs at a time on to the net near the hair-weft areas; tie one or two hairs each time when you get close to the beard hairline. (See Figure 3-5a, for how to tie hair onto lace.)

Step Four: Trimming and Attaching the Beard

- Trim the beard to the suitable length and style, and try it on the actor's face.

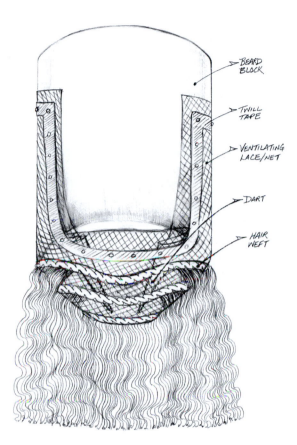

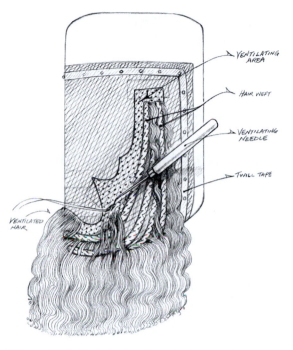

Figure 4-15 Attach hair wefts to the lace and ventilate the hair — profile.

Figure 4-16 Completed full beard.

Figure 4-14 Sew hair wefts on the ventilating lace — back view.

- Use hair spray to help the beard hold its shape.
- Measure off on the actor the length of the elastic needed for the beard — from ear to ear across the top of the head. Use a piece of elastic to attach the beard, instead of glue, for quick changes I recommend using clear elastic; dyeing white elastic to a flesh tone will also work.
- Sew the elastic on the side burns of the beard with a needle and thread.
- The beard is held on the face by the elastic strap. Place the two ends of the elastic just above the jaw line and secure with satin stitches or tacking stitches to support the weight of the beard (Figure 4-16). The upper portion of the elastic strap will be hidden under a hat. Use double-sided tape around corners, such as the chin and corners of the mouth for more security if necessary.

The completed beard is shown in Figures 4-16 and 4-17.

Figure 4-17 Production photo of *The Butterfingers Angel* showing the beard. *King (center) played by Todd Lawhorne, Harlot#1 (left) played by Jennifer SmitH, Harlot #2 (right) played by Rachel Fine, performance students. Directed by Mark Brotherton. Scenic design by Richard Dunham. Lighting design by Tom Begley. Costume design by Tan Huaixiang. University of Central Florida Conservatory Theatre presentation.*

MAKING A CHINESE OPERA BEARD

A Chinese opera beard was made for the character Ma in *The Dance and the Railroad* (Figure 4-18).

PROCEDURE FOR MAKING A CHINESE OPERA BEARD

Materials Required:

- Millinery wire
- Long synthetic or human hair

Figure 4-18 Costume design for Ma in *The Dance and the Railroad.*

- Scissors
- Needlepoint pliers with wire cutters
- Push pins or T-pins
- Hat or wig block
- Hair spray

Step One: Making a Wire Structure

- Cut a piece of millinery wire and drape the structure on the actor's face. Thick wire works better; doubled thin wire will work as well but you will have to wrap them together in parallel with thread before making the beard structure.
- Use the actor's face to measure and bend wire as you go. Start bending wire from the mouth area. Keep it symmetrical. The wire should not touch the upper jaw. Follow the actor's face frame and keep bending the wire until you achieve the proper shape. Secure the wire behind the actor's ears by forming the ends into hooks; these will hold the beard on the face (Figure 4-19).
- Trim off the extra wire. Bend the cut ends back toward the wire structure to round off the ends for smoothness and comfort (Figure 4-19).

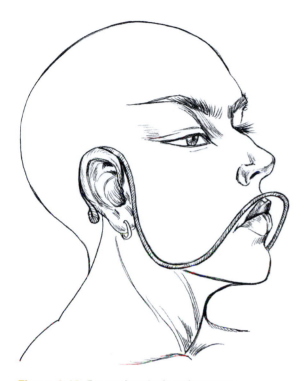

Figure 4-19 Create the wire beard structure.

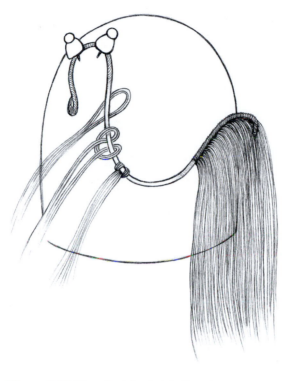

Figure 4-20 Steps for tying hair to the wire.

Figure 4-21 Completed Chinese Opera beard.

Step Two: Tying the Hair on to the Wire Structure

• Fold a small tuft of hair in half to form a loop. Put the loop underneath the wire and pull the loose hair with your fingers through this loop. Tighten it on the wire and allow the hair to hang (Figure 4-20). If you fold the hair off-center, you can extend the length of the hair if needed.

• The hair can be tied on the wire in three separate sections: the two sides and the center front. Or it can just be tied on as one big section, depending on the design.

Step Three: Trimming and Securing the Beard

• After tying the hair is finished, comb and trim it as necessary.

• Apply a little bit of hair gel over the hair knots tied on the wire to secure it. The beard is ready for stage.

The completed beard is shown in Figures 4-21 and 4-22.

Figure 4-22 Production photo of the beard in *The Dance and the Railroad*. *Ma* played by Ricky T. Li (right). Directed and choreographed by Keith Grant. Scenic design by Gallager Julia. Costume and makeup design by Tan Huaixiang. Cornell University Department of Theatre Arts presentation.

SECTION TWO *Masks*

Masks can be made from either closed molds or negative open molds that have been made from various materials. The main difference between making masks from positive versus negative molds is that a mask created on top of a positive mold can only be duplicated once because the positive mold (the clay sculpture) will often be destroyed when it is separated from the mask. Detailed impressions will diminish as more layers of materials are added to the mask. The advantage of making a mask from a positive sculptured mold is that you can create a mask that involves undercuts, crevices, and dramatic or extreme shapes (such as a large jaw), which are hard or impossible to create and separate from a negative mold. For example, the bird beak on the masks in Figures 7-1 to 7-7 will be difficult to copy from a negative mold because of the deepness of the beak and the slightly opened beak.

One advantage of making a mask from a negative mold is that it will capture the original impressions and details on the sculpture. In addition, the negative mold can be used to duplicate as many masks as needed. The disadvantage is you have to spend times making the plaster negative mold.

Chapter 5   Rubber Masks

MAKING LATEX MASKS WITH CLOSED MOLDS

A closed mold is a positive and a negative mold closed together to make a mask. The space between the two molds is filled with latex. The pig masks used for *Peer Gent* were made using this method. The mask is hollow in the thicker portions after the liquid latex dries (I don't know the reason why it does this, but that's how it dries). This reduces the weight of the mask and also provides flexibility. It is not necessary to add any foam strips or cubes to support such a latex mask because the mask is done with closed molds; it is a relatively solid piece and supports itself.

PROCEDURE FOR MAKING LATEX MASKS WITH CLOSED MOLDS

Materials Required:

- Clear liquid latex or casting latex
- Positive and negative plaster molds
- Oil-based clay
- Sculpting tools
- Ruler
- Vaseline
- Plaster of paris
- Soft-bristle brush
- Plastic sheet
- Mixing bowl
- Spatula
- Butter knife
- Baby powder
- Elastic
- Acrylic paints

Step One: Creating a Clay Sculpture and Preparing to Make the Negative Mold

- Build up the mask (in this example, a pig nose) on an existing positive face mold using oil-based clay (Figure 5-1b). The edges of the mask don't have to be thin but they should be neat and well-defined. Determine the highest point of the mask first and then balance the rest of the mask. When the basic proportions, height, and shape have been established, you may start working on details.
- Use sculpting tools to create detail and texture on the mask
- Place a ruler vertically on the table next to the mold and measure 1″ higher than the highest point of the sculpture (Figure 5-1c).
- Apply some clay over the eye sockets and lips to soften the impressions for easier separation of the molds (Figure 5-1c).
- Create a 2″-tall clay wall abut ¾ or 1″ away from the edge of the clay sculpture (Figure 5-1c).
- Apply an even coat of Vaseline on the exposed plaster mold as a release agent (Figure 5-1c). It is not necessary to apply Vaseline to the clay.

a

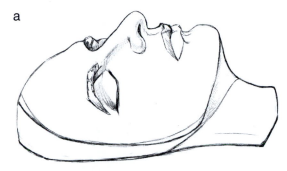

b

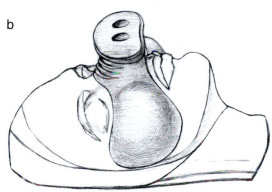

c

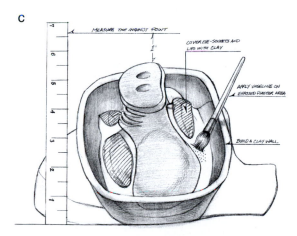

Figure 5-1 (a) Start with an existing positive face mold. (b) Build a pig nose on top of the existing positive mold with modeling clay. (c) Measure the highest point of the sculpture, cover the eye sockets and lips with clay, build a clay wall around the sculpture, and apply Vaseline to the exposed plaster surface.

Step Two: Making a Negative Plaster Mold from the Clay Sculpture

- Mix the plaster of paris. (See Figures 1-57 to 1-60 for how to mix plaster when making a negative mold from clay sculpture.)
- Brush on the first coat of plaster onto the sculpted mold with a soft-bristle brush (Figure 5-2a). Use the tap and release method until the entire mold surface is covered.
- Mix a thicker plaster paste to finish the negative mold. Build up the plaster around the sculpture until it reaches the required height (1″ above the highest point; in this case, the pig nose). Flatten the top of the plaster for stability when the mold is turned upside down. Carve an arrow at the top to indicate where the top is (Figure 5-2b).
- After the plaster starts to cool down, remove the clay wall. Make a few matching notches where the two molds meet on the front, sides, and back (Figure 5-2c).

Figure 5-2 (a) Apply the first coat of plaster to the entire clay sculpture. (b) Complete the plaster negative mold, flatten the top, and carve an arrow to indicate the top. (c) Remove the clay wall and make a few notches on the mold.

a

b

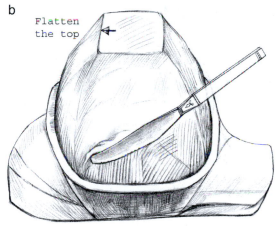

c

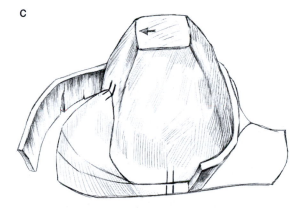

- Set the mold in an upright position, and pull the negative and positive molds in opposite directions to separate them (see Figure 5-3c). Because the eye sockets and lips were covered with clay, the molds can be easily opened. Clean both the positive and negative molds after you open them. Let the mold dry for several days.

Step Three: Making a Latex Mask

No mold release is required in making a latex mask or prosthetic pieces.

- Place the negative mold on the table (using a plastic sheet to protect the table) with the open side facing up.
- Slowly pour liquid latex into the negative mold to avoid creating air bubbles (Figure 5-3a). Fill about ⅘ of the negative mold.
- Set the positive mold on top of the negative mold, and make sure the notches match up (Figure 5-3b). The extra liquid latex will flow out when you place the positive mold on the negative mold. Just let it flow naturally; it will stop by itself.
- Let the latex dry. It will take at least one night. For faster drying, put the mold in a steamer (a large dye pot can be used as a steamer), and steam it for an hour. If you open the mold

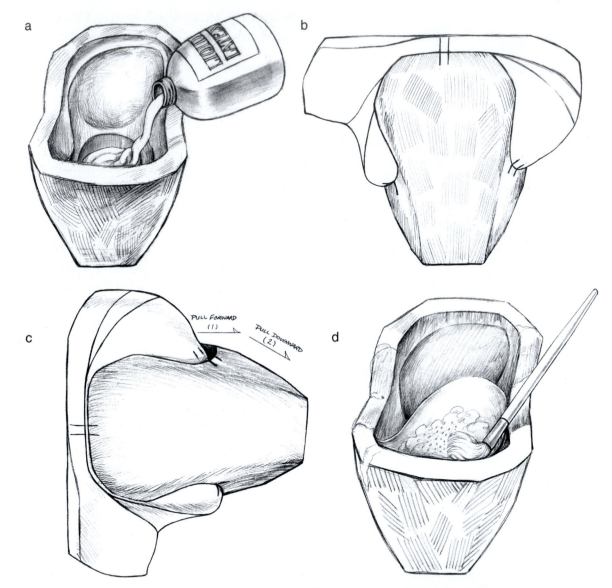

Figure 5-3 (a) Pour liquid latex into the negative mold. (b) Place the positive mold on top of the negative mold. (c) Open the molds. (d) Powder the latex prosthetic piece while pulling it out of the mold.

too early before it's dry, the wet latex mask will have holes and wrinkles.

- After the latex is dry, carefully open the molds (Figure 5-3c). Pull the mask from the negative mold, brushing baby powder on the latex while you pull it (Figure 5-3d). The powder will prevent the latex from sticking to itself.

- Glue an elastic strip (ends) on to the sides of the mask with liquid latex. Then apply more liquid latex over the ends of the elastic strip for added security. Because the latex mask is made with closed molds, it will be stiff enough to retain its shape by itself.

- Paint the mask with acrylic paint or spray paint as necessary.

The completed masks are shown in Figure 5-4. The pig masks shown here

Figure 5-4 (a) Production photo of the pig masks in *Peer Gent.* Sons of the Enchantress wore pig masks; their wigs were made of hemp-fibers (flax rope), dyed to purple and green then attached to wig bases. *Peer Gent played by Gong Xiaodong (bottom).* (b) Production photo of the pig masks in *Peer Gent. Peer Gent (front left) played by Wei Xiaoping. Enchantress (front right) played by Zhang Xinxin.* (c) Production photo of Enchantress. *Directed by Xu Xiaozhong Bai Shiben, and Xu Min. Scenic design by Liu Yunsheng and Dai Dunsi. Lighting design by Mu Baisuo and Yu Haibuo. Costume design by Huo Qidi. Makeup. and Hair design by Tan Huaixiang. Set and lighting design by Guo Qiang. The Central Academy of Drama, Beijing, China, presentation.*

were made of clear liquid latex, but it is more expensive than casting latex. Such masks can also be made of casting latex. I used liquid latex to make the pig masks (a total of nine) for the production *Peer Gent* because I got it free from a latex factory near the Central Academy of Drama, a well-known theater school in China. Because of the school's respected reputation, the factory offered the latex free.

MAKING RUBBER MASKS WITH AN OPEN NEGATIVE MOLD

Rubber masks are made of casting latex. This is an excellent material for making masks, especially duplications. Once the negative mold has been created, the process of duplicating masks is quick and easy. Since the casting latex is flexible, it's extremely easy to separate the mask from the mold when there are crevices, texture and details.

There were 13 masks needed for the University of Central Florida production of *Once on This Island* (Figure 5-5). I made two different negative molds from two different sculptures and then duplicated a total of 13 masks from those two negative molds.

Figure 5-5 Costume design for *Once on This Island*.

It is not necessary to do any life casting to make rubber masks if you have one or two positive face molds in stock. I used two positive molds because that's what I had in stock: one for male masks, the other for female masks. Because of the number of masks required for the production and the lack of workers, the masks had to be duplicated. Therefore, the masks were made a generic "one size fits all."

PROCEDURE FOR MAKING RUBBER MASKS

Materials Required:

- Existing positive molds
- Negative molds
- Oil-based clay
- Sculpting tools
- Vaseline
- Plaster of paris
- Mixing bowl
- Spoon and butter knife
- Spatula
- Casting latex
- 1"-thick foam strips
- Elastic
- Craft spray paint
- Crepe hair
- Clear liquid latex

Step One: Sculpting Masks with Clay and Making a Negative Mold from the Clay Sculpture

- Have the design and research ready for the project to be sculptured.
- On a positive mold, build up the highest point of the mask using clay and then balance off the rest of the face. When the basic proportions, height, and shape are established, work on refining the details.
- Make a negative mold from the clay sculpted mold (the same procedure as

in making latex masks; see Figures 5-1 to 5-2).

Step Two: Making a Casting Latex Mask from an Open Negative Mold

No release agent is needed for making rubber masks.

- Before you pour the latex into the mold, cut a few pieces of fitted foam strips to support and strengthen the latex mask (Figure 5-6b). Without any support, the latex will be spineless and floppy.
- Pour a small amount of casting latex into the negative mold. Slowly turn and rotate the mold so the latex runs over the entire surface of the mold and within the outer edge of the mask; make sure no air bubbles occur (Figure 5-7a).
- Add another coat of latex to the mold. Because casting latex is thicker than liquid latex, two even coats of latex will be enough to form the mask. Do not wait for the first coat to dry. Instead, continue running the second layer of latex on top of the first wet layer until it covers the entire surface. The more latex you add, the stiffer and heavier the mask will be.
- Before the latex dries, IMMEDIATELY insert the precut foam strips in place (Figure 5-8b). Emphasize the outer

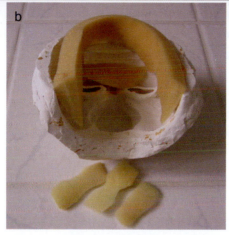

Figure 5-6 (a) Two completed negative molds made from the clay-sculptured molds.(b) Cut fitted foam strips to stiffen the latex mask.

edges, nose bridge, and cheeks with the foam pieces. (These foam strips will support, stiffen, and shape the mask.)
- Allow the latex to dry overnight.
- After the latex completely dries, pull the mask from the negative mold (Figure 5-8c). It will be very easy to remove because the latex won't stick to

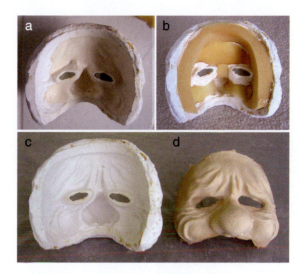

Figure 5-7 (a) Pour a small amount of casting latex into the mold and rotate the mask so that the latex covers the entire surface of the mold. (b) Insert the foam strips. (c) Dried latex mask removed from the mold.

the plaster surface. No powder is necessary for casting latex.
- There is no waiting time needed for the next duplication of the mask. Pour latex into the mold and repeat the same process.
- Trim the eye and nostril openings of the mask with scissors, if needed. It is ready to decorate.

Step Three: Painting and Decorating the Masks

- Sew a piece of elastic on the mask to fasten it to the actor's face.

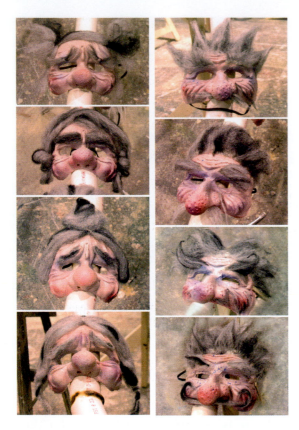

Figure 5-8 Left column: Completed female masks. Right column: Completed male masks.

of the latex. Clear liquid latex was used as glue because it dries transparent.

- Let the latex dry completely before you use the mask in a performance.

I used crepe hair for these masks because it is lightweight, is easy to style, and stays in shape well (a few cheap, full and long crepe hair beards were used for the masks). Black and white crepe hair was mixed together, and the hair styles were created by theater students.

The completed masks are shown in Figures 5-8 to 5-10. Frog, tree, and wind masks created in the same manner for the production are shown in Figures 5-11 to 5-17.

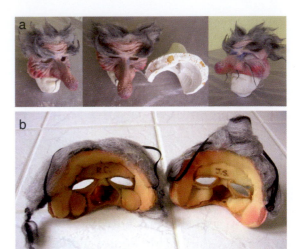

Figure 5-9 (a) Completed male mask. (b) Inserted foam strips that keep the masks in shapes — back of masks.

- Paint the masks with craft spray paints; add foundation, shadows, and highlights. Do not spray too much of each color; too much spray paint will cause the color to crack and chip off.
- To add hair, apply some clear liquid latex where the hair and facial hair will go, and then lay the crepe hair on top

Figure 5-10 Production photo of Gossipers masks on stage in *Once on This Island. Gossipers played by UCF theater students. Directed by Earls D. Weave. Scenic design by Vandy Wood. Lighting design by David Upton. Costume design by Tan Huaixiang. University of Central Florida Conservatory Theatre presentation.*

Figure 5-11 Costume design for the frog masks in *Once on This Island.*

Figure 5-12 Frog masks were also made from casting latex and produced using the same methods as the Gossipers masks. (a) Clay sculpture of frog head. (b) A negative mold was made from plaster and casting latex was poured into the negative mold.

Figure 5-13 Production photo of the frog masks in *Once on This Island.* The masks were painted by BFA design and technology student Shelby Fink. *University of Central Florida Conservatory Theatre presentation.*

Figure 5-14 Costume design for tree masks in *Once on This Island.*

Figure 5-15 Production photo of the tree masks in *Once on This Island.* The tree masks made by BFA design and technology student Lilly Helm. *University of Central Florida Conservatory Theatre presentation.*

Figure 5-16 Costume design for wind masks for *Once on This Island.*

Figure 5-17 Production photo of the wind masks in *Once on This Island*. Masks were made by Tramaine Berryhill, BFA design and technology student. *University of Central Florida Conservatory Theatre presentation.*

Chapter 6   Varaform and Wonderflex Masks

MAKING A VARAFORM MASK WITH A POSITIVE MOLD

In Act I, Scene 3 of *Pippin*, the main character has a fantasy scene with women strangers. In the University of Central Florida production, all eight players wore half masks to disguise themselves (Figures 6-1 to 6-2).

I chose heavyweight Varaform for the eight masks. Varaform is an open-weave material with a mesh and fishnet nature; it was suitable for my design. The Varaform is made of cotton fibers coated with a high-density thermoplastic resin that is naturally white; it comes in sheets or strips of different sizes. I used a sheet that was 45 × 60 cm. This was just enough to make two half masks. Varaform is lightweight, durable, and easy to work with. This material is great for molding detailed curves and different shapes, and it also sticks to itself with the application of heat. Varaform can be heated and cooled repeatedly, and it can be molded as many times as you want. It

Figure 6-1 Costume design for *Pippin* — male players.

can also be painted with all kinds of paint pigments or sprays.

The mesh masks were made in generic sizes and then sculpted and built over existing plaster positive face molds, which

I had in stock. No mold release was required. I made the male masks broad and bold and the female masks more delicate and small. To create a smooth and strong edge, I rolled the edges of the

118

Figure 6-2 Costume design for *Pippin* — female players.

- Wide cooking pot
- Scissors
- Spoon
- Marker for drawing lines
- Elastic straps
- Black craft spray or shoe spray
- Clear waterproof spray/clear Acrylic spray
- Narrow gold and silver ribbons
- Colorful chiffon fabric scarves

Step One: Molding the Basic Shape of the Mask on a Face Positive Mold

- Cut the Varaform to the size needed for the mask (Figure 6-3a). (It can be cut on the bias or cut following the grain.)
- Heat water in a wide, open cooking pot until it's hot (70–160°C). The pot should be wide enough so that you can place the piece of varaform in the water without folding it (folding will cause it to stick together).
- Immerse the Varaform in hot water (Figure 6-3b). The higher the temperature of the water, the faster the Varaform will soften. After a few seconds, the Varaform will become moldable and soft. Take it out of the hot water, drain it a little, lay it on top of the plaster face mold, and start to mold the mask (Figure 6-3c). You should move quickly.

Varaform up to form rolled or self-binding edges.

Strength and design can be created in the mask by folding (about ¼–½″) the material in a horizontal or vertical direction as desired. In this case, I folded the material horizontally to create eyebrows. More folds, such as wrinkles, were added for designs purposes. Consequently, the masks held together quite well through all the 4-week run

performances, including dress rehearsals.

PROCEDURE FOR MAKING THE VARAFORM MASKS

Materials Required:

- Varaform
- A plaster positive face mold
- A stove or an electronic cooking pot
- Hot water

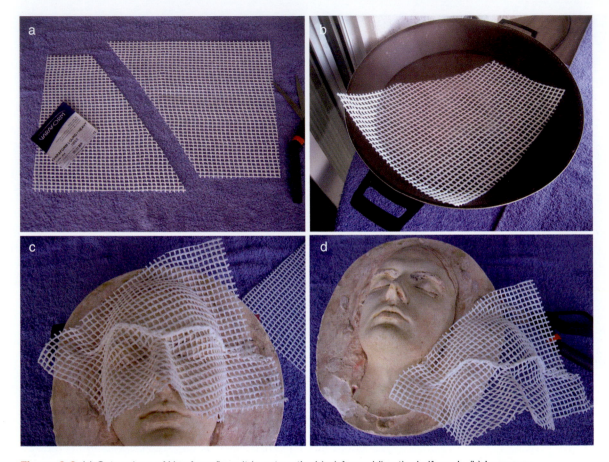

can reheat and soften the Varaform so it can be molded as many times as you need. You must BE VERY CAREFUL when using the heat gun; sometimes high heat will melt and damage the Varaform and create a big hole. Once the Varaform mask cools on the face mold, it will harden, retaining the molded shape. Remove it from the mold for next steps. (Figure 6-3d).

Figure 6-3 (a) Cut a piece of Varaform (here it is cut on the bias) for molding the half mask. (b) Immerse the Varaform in hot water. (c) Mold the Varaform over the positive face mold; create eyebrows by folding. (d) Remove the cooled Varaform from the face mold.

- Push and mold the Varaform to the indentations and structures of the face. Quickly make folds around the forehead area for eyebrows or wrinkles (if you want to add any). Some folds can be made at the nose bridge and temples to add strength to the mask.

- In approximately 1–2 minutes, the varaform will become hard. Dipping it back in hot water or using a heat gun

Step Two: Adding Decorative Folds and Cutting the Edges

- Create more folds in the mask for decoration by dipping parts of the shaped Varaform piece back in the hot water and folding. In this case, the forehead was redipped in the hot water and a second row of folds were created (Figures 6-4a–b).
- Trim the outer edge of the mask, leaving about a ½–¾″ seam allowance (to roll back later for a nice, finished edge; a wide edge will create a thick rolling edge on the mask; a narrower edge will create a thinner rolling edge) (Figures 6-4c–d). I recommend cutting it while the Varaform is cold; when it's warm, the Varaform sticks to the scissors.

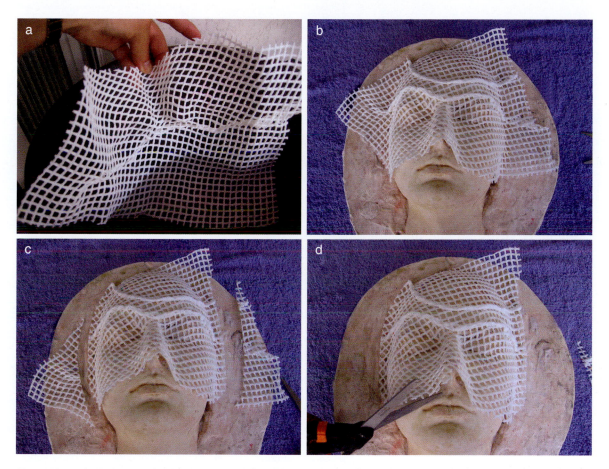

Figure 6-4 (a) Dip only the forehead portion of the shaped Varaform in the hot water. (b) Create the second row of folds. (c) Trim the side edges of the mask. (d) Trim the bottom edge of the mask.

Step Three: Molding the Outer Edges of the Mask

- Dip the bottom side of the trimmed edge (only the seam allowance part) in hot water (Figure 6-5a).
- Quickly set the mask back on the face mold and roll the soft edge back to produce a rolled edge (Figure 6-5b).
- Dip one side-edge seam allowance of the mask (work on one side at a time) in hot water. Put it back on the positive mold, and roll the edge toward the center to create a rolled edge (Figures 6-5c–d). Repeat on the other side to finish the edges (Figure 6-6a).

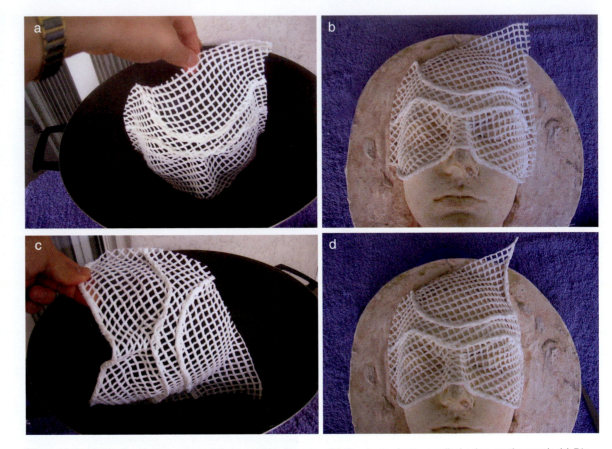

Figure 6-5 (a) Dip the bottom edge of the mask in hot water. (b) Create the bottom rolled edge on the mask. (c) Dip one side of trimmed edges in hot water. (d) Create a rolling edge on that side.

Step Four: Creating Eye Openings

- After all the outer edges are completed, mark where the eyes will be (Figure 6-6b) and cut the eyes open. Trim only a little bit of the center out to leave seam allowance (Figure 6-6c) so you can roll the edges back.
- Heat only the eye-opening part with hot water by pouring spoonfuls of hot water directly on the eye opening to soften it (Figure 6-6d). A heat gun will work for this as well.
- Roll the soft edge back to create a rolled edge around the eye opening (Figure 6-7a). (The more you roll the edge back, the bigger the eyes will be.)
- Repeat the process for the other eye (Figures 6-7b–c).
- Since the eye openings aren't big, there won't be much extra edge for rolling. If you want to strengthen them, add an extra strip of varaform along the eye opening edge. The varaform sticks together when heated.

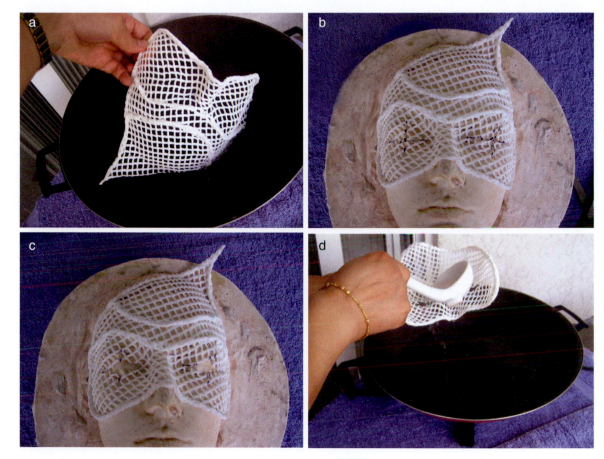

Figure 6-6 (a) Dip the other side edge of the mask in hot water to finish the side edge. (b) Mark the placement of the eyes. (c) Trim the eye openings leaving a seam allowance. (d) Heat one eye with hot water.

Step Five: Decorating the Masks

- Attach elastic on both sides of the mask.
- Paint the mask. Varaform withstands any type of paint. Black shoe spray was used for these masks. The inside of the mask was kept white and sprayed with a clear waterproof spray/Clear Acrylic spray because we did want to get any stains on the actors' face when they sweated.
- Decorate the mask. There are many ways to decorate masks. They can be painted with specific colors or decorated with feathers, ribbons, or jewelry. In the *Pippin* production, "the black leather and gold-silver look" was the color

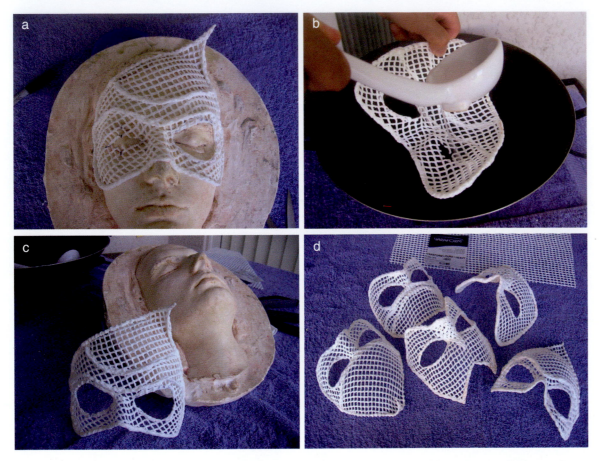

Figure 6-7 (a) Roll back the edge of the first eye opening. (b) Heat the other eye. (c) Completed eye openings. (d) Completed unpainted masks.

Figure 6-8 Completely painted and decorated mask.

Figure 6-9 A group of painted and decorated masks.

scheme incorporated into the leather teddy costumes. Narrow silver and gold ribbons were woven through the open-weave masks, which provided highlights and contrast.

• Insert colorful chiffon scarves into the masks, functioning as decoration and tie the masks to actor's faces.

The completed and decorated masks are shown in Figures 6-8 to 6-10. I thank our guest designer on the *Wizard of Oz*, Bill Brewer, University of South Florida, who created the tasteful bows that were used to tie the chiffon scarves to the masks. They were artistic and beautiful.

Figure 6-10 (a) Production photo for *Pippin* showing the masks. Players: *Steven Gatewood (left), Andrea Dunn (right), Jason Whitehead (top middle), Tiara Young (bottom middle)*. (b) Production photo for *Pippin* showing the masks with full costumes. *Players (from left to right): Steven Gatewood, Andrea Dunn, Tiara Young, Jason Whitehead, Justin Sargent (middle, playing Pippin), Michael Navarro, Denver Clark, Christopher Pearson Niess. Directed by John Bell. Set design by Joseph Rusnock. Lighting design by Eric Haugen. Sound design by Martin Wootton. Costume design by Tan Huaixiang. University of Central Florida Conservative Theatre presentation.*

MAKING WONDERFLEX MASKS WITH A POSITIVE MOLD

In Catherine's bedroom scene in the *Pippin* production, two more masks were used, made from a material called Wonderflex. These masks were inspired by leather masks with eyelashes on them.

MAKING THE FIRST WONDERFLEX MASK

PROCEDURE FOR MAKING WONDERFLEX MASKS

Materials Required:

- Wonderflex
- A plaster positive face mold
- Hot water (on a stove or an electronic cooking bowl)
- Heat gun
- Scissors
- Marker or pencil
- Black shoe spray
- Metallic paint
- $\frac{1}{2}$″-wide elastic strap fitted to the head (holds mask in place)

Step One: Outlining and Cutting the Wonderflex

- Cut a piece of Wonderflex large enough to make a half mask.

- Outline the openings of the eyes with eyelashes on the upper eyelids (Figure 6-11a). Leave a little seam allowance at the bottom of the eyelid to create a small rolling edge on the bottom eyelid.
- Cut out the eye openings (Figure 6-11b). It's easier to cut this when the piece is flat.
- Slash the center of the forehead from the top of the forehead to above the eyebrows to create designs on the forehead (Figure 6-11c).

Step Two: Molding the Wonderflex into a Shape

- Put the entire piece of Wonderflex in hot water for about 30 seconds until it becomes soft and moldable (Figure 6-12a).
- Take the soft wonderflex out and lay it on top of the positive mold. You have about 2 minutes to mold it before it becomes hard again. Make sure the eye openings are at the correct positions. Quickly shape it from the center out. Press and mold the Wonderflex into the indentations, and form the basic shape of the mask. Make a horizontal fold across the middle of the nose bridge, and make several folds on one side of the forehead (Figure 6-12b). (The number of folds needed is based on the

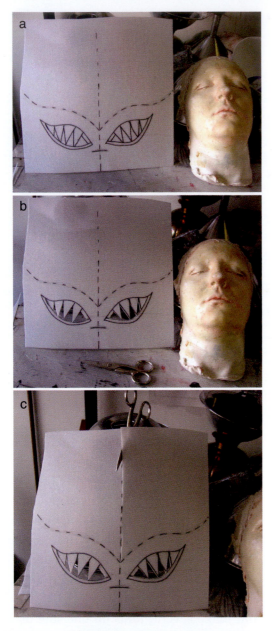

Figure 6-11 (a) Outline eyes with eyelashes on the Wonderflex. (b) Cut out the eyes with scissors. (c) Slash the center of the forehead.

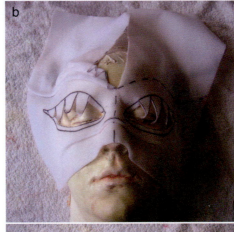

Figure 6-12 (a) Immerse the Wonderflex in hot water. (b) Mold the Wonderflex over the positive mold, creating with folds across the nose bridge and forehead. (c) Complete the folds on both sides of the forehead.

design and the size of the material). By this time, the unpleated side of the forehead will have cooled and become hard. Like Varaform, Wonderflex can be dipped in hot water many times, but do not leave it in the hot water for more than 30 seconds at a time.

- Dip the unpleated side of the forehead in hot water (keep the pot of water on low heat). When the Wonderflex is soft, makes symmetrical folds on the other side of the forehead (Figure 6-12c).

Step Three: Working on the Outer Edges and Eye Openings

- Slash the extra edges at the top of the forehead (Figure 6-13a) to prepare it for being molded into a decorative style.
- Trim the outer edges of the mask (Figure 6-13a). Leave some seam allowance to fold back. There are three reasons for rolling the edge of the Wonderflex mask: to add strength to the edge of the mask, to create a nice finished edge, and to prevent rough edges from scratching the actor's face.
- Wonderflex is thicker and stronger than Varaform, so it will be more difficult to roll the edge. Fold the edge back $\frac{1}{8}$–$\frac{1}{4}$" instead rolling it (Figure 6-13b the bottom edge of the mask). Work one edge at a time. Start by dipping the

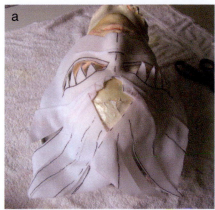

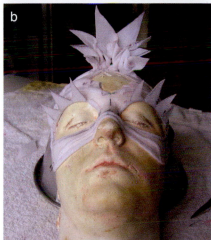

Figure 6-13 (a) Trim the outer edges of the mask, and slash the top of the forehead. (b) Mold the slashes into a leaflike shapes. (c) Spray the mask black.

bottom of the edge in hot water. Put it on the face mold and quickly fold the edges back once to achieve a finished and smooth edge.

- Dip the slashed upper forehead in hot water. Put it back on the face mold and quickly shape each individual slashed piece into a design or style. The leaflike decoration was naturally created with the slashed pieces by rolling and twisting the slashed pieces together (Figure 6-13b).

- Use a heat gun when you work on the eye openings. Bend the lashes up in the desired position, and fold the edge of the lower eyelids down for a soft, smooth finish. The heat gun helps when you are working on details such as eyelashes.

- Use a heat gun to reinforce all the folded and overlapped edges of the slashed pieces. It will help the folded edges stick together tightly and neatly.

- You may also sand the rough edges with sandpaper so it's comfortable to wear, if necessary.

Step Four: Decorating the Mask

- Spray the mask black (Figure 6-13c), and highlight it with metallic paint.

- Add an elastic strap for wearing the mask.

The completed mask is shown in Figures 6-14a–b.

MAKING THE SECOND WONDERFLEX MASK

The construction of the silver and black Wonderflex mask in Figure 6-14c was done basically the same way as the first mask, except that the forehead slashes were folded and braided together.

- Follow the steps for creating the first Wonderflex mask until after you slash the forehead and heat the forehead slashes in step three.

- First, fold each slashed piece in half toward the wrong side of the mask, and press them together while the Wonderflex is soft.

- Then trim the end of each folded piece to a tapered point.

- After all slashes are trimmed, braid them together to form a design.

- Use a heat gun on the overlapping areas so they stick together.

- Decorate the mask.

The completed mask is shown in Figure 6-14c.

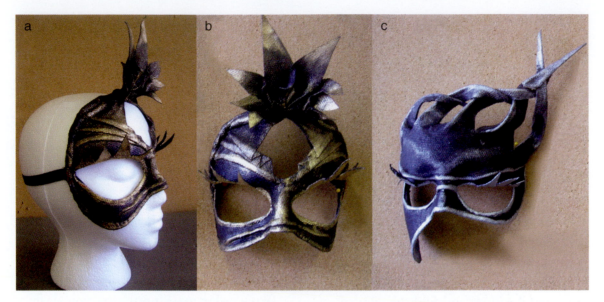

Figure 6-14 (a–b) Completed Wonderflex mask. (c) Completed second Wonderflex mask.

Chapter 7   Mixed-Materials Masks

MAKING A BUCKRAM AND PAPER MASK FROM A POSITIVE MOLD

Masks were needed for the character Pikok/Shaman in production *The Walker in the Snow*. The shaman is considered as a supernatural being and functions as a healer and advocator for the "other world" in Eskimo society. Animal masks are in the shaman's enactment of myths, stories, and ceremonial presentations. Three masks were made for the production: a sea gull and two raven masks. All three were molded directly on the clay sculptured positive molds. The example described here is the sea gull mask (Figure 7-1). Real Eskimo masks are made of wood and feathers. However, buckram, paper, and wallpaper paste were used for making those masks; as a result, the masks were lightweight, durable, and inexpensive.

Figure 7-1 Costume design for *The Walker in the Snow*.

PROCEDURE FOR MAKING A MASK FROM A POSITIVE MOLD

Materials Required:

- An existing positive mold
- Oil-based clay
- Vaseline
- Sculpting tools
- Freezer
- Wallpaper paste or Elmer's glue
- Buckram
- 1"-thick foam piece
- Millinery wire
- Fabric tacky glue
- Felt strip and felt for lining mask
- Spray adhesive
- Torn paper (newspaper, paper toweling, or brown pattern paper)
- Brush and acrylic paints
- Craft spray paints
- Scissors
- Awl

129

- Sharp knife
- Plastic zip-lock bag
- Container for water
- Container for glue

Step One: Sculpting the Mask with Clay

- Find an existing positive face mold (Figure 7-2a). If you don't have one, you may need to make a life casting (see Chapter1 for the process of face life casting).
- Use oil-based clay to sculpt the mask on a face positive mold. After finishing the sculpture, brush a light, even coat of Vaseline over the surface the clay sculpture as a release for the mask (Figure 7-2b).

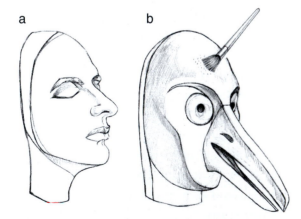

Figure 7-2 (a) Existing positive face mold. (b) Sculpt the mask on the existing mold with clay; then apply a coat of Vaseline to the entire surface of the sculpture.

Step Two: Applying Buckram to the Clay Sculpture

- Put the clay mold inside the freezer for 30 minutes to harden it. Hardening the clay prevents the buckram from distorting the shapes and details on the clay structure when the buckram is applied to it.
- Cut the buckram on the bias into pieces of various sizes for more flexibility. The small pieces will be used around the eyes and nose; the large pieces will be used on the forehead and cheeks.
- Dip the buckram pieces in water, and take them out and put them in a plastic zip-lock bag for 2 minutes. After 2 minutes, the buckram pieces will become soft and sticky.
- Press each piece down into the impressions on the mold using your fingers or a sculpting tool, overlapping the edges of each piece and smearing them with your fingers to smooth them. Two layers of buckram are enough to form a foundation for the mask, but add an extra layer around the outer edge; alter the direction of the pieces when you apply the next layer of buckram to strengthen the mask (Figure 7-3a).

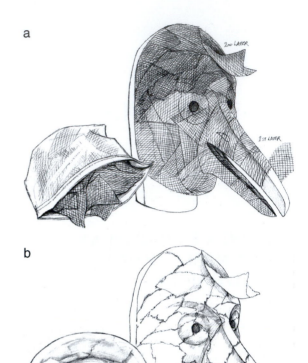

Figure 7-3 (a) Apply buckram pieces to the clay sculpture in different directions. (b) Soak torn pieces of paper in glue and apply them over the buckram.

- Work around the eyes and nostrils. If you cover those areas, you can cut them open by using a sharp knife.
- Allow the buckram to dry.

Step Three: Applying Paper over the Buckram

- Tear paper into pieces of various sizes (paper towels were used for this mask), and soak them in the wall paste or Elmer's glue (1:1 ratio of glue and water). Tearing the paper creates feathery edges that will diminish the overlap lines created with the paper strips.
- Apply two or three layers of paper in alternative directions on top of the buckram to create a smooth surface mask (Figure 7-3b).
- After it completely dries, carefully remove the mask from the positive mold. Trim the edge of the mask neatly, and finish the edge by wrapping two more layers of paper along the outer edge for reinforcement (Figure 7-4).

Step Four: Creating Decorations for the Mask

- Make decorative pieces, such as bird feet and legs, from 1"-thick foam. Cut the foam into the desired shapes,

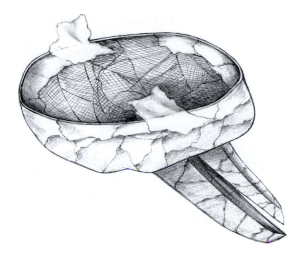

Figure 7-4 After you remove the dried mask from the clay positive mold, finish the outer edge by wrapping more layers of paper along the outer edge of the mask.

and carve the details with scissors (Figure 7-5a).
- Cut 7"-long pieces of millinery wire and fold them in half. Apply fabric tacky glue to the end with the fold, and insert the glued end into the foam feet (Figure 7-5a).
- Attach the bird feet and legs to the mask. Use an awl to poke a hole where the bird's foot and leg will go, and insert the doubled wires into the awl hole from the right side of the mask to

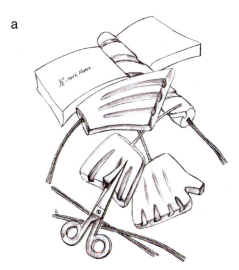

a

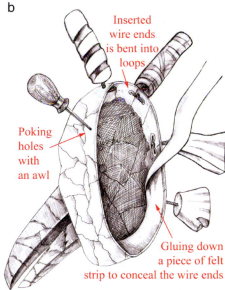

b

Inserted wire ends is bent into loops

Poking holes with an awl

Gluing down a piece of felt strip to conceal the wire ends

Figure 7-5 (a) Create decorations from foam and millinery wire. (b) Poke holes with an awl, insert the wires of the bird feet and legs into the mask, and bend the wire ends into loops; then glue down a felt strip over the wires along the outer edge of the inside mask.

the wrong side. Then bend the ends of the wire into a loop or open circle and flatten them to the inner surface of the mask (Figure 7-5b).

- Conceal and secure the wires by gluing a felt strip piece over the wires along the outer edge of the mask with fabric tack glue (Figure 7-5b).
- Carefully trim the eye openings, nostrils, and outer edges of the mask with a sharp knife.
- Line the mask with felt if desired, using spray adhesive.
- Spray-paint the mask and foam feet with craft paint. Highlight, shadow, and accent it with acrylic paints.

All three shaman masks were made using this method. The completed masks are shown in Figures 7-6 to 7-7. (Figure 7-13 shows another kind of buckram mask.)

Figure 7-6 Masks used in production the *Walker in the Snow*. All three masks were made using the same method.

Figure 7-7 Production photo of *Walker in the Snow* showing the mask. *Pikok played by Robert Herderson. Fantasia played by Annette Johnson. Directed by Lynda Linford. Scenic design by Sid Perkes. Lighting design by Steve Twede. Costume design by Tan Huaixiang. Utah State University Department of Theatre, presentation.*

MAKING A MASK FROM INSTANT PAPIER-MÂCHÉ

There are more materials that can be used for making masks. Economical materials such as fabric, instant papier-mâché, traditional papier-mâché, or buckram and sculpture coat can also be used for making masks on either positive or negative molds.

The mask described next is made of Instant Paper-Mâché molded in a negative mold. Instant Papier- Mâché can be purchased from art supply or craft stores; instructions are included in the package. The papier-mâché can be handled like clay; you can use it to build and mold images on positive and negative molds. It is nontoxic, fast, easy to mix, lightweight, strong, and durable, and it can be used for casting and modeling. When it's wet, it's soft and moldable; once it dries, it is hard and lightweight.

PROCEDURE FOR MAKING AN INSTANT PAPIER- MÂCHÉ MASK

Materials Required:

- Negative mold
- A package of Instant Papier-Mâché (comes in white or gray)
- Sculpting tools
- Mixing bowl
- Water
- Spatula
- Brush and Vaseline
- Butter knife
- Acrylic paints and Right-Step clear varnish

Step One: Preparation

- Create a negative mold (Figure 7-8a). See Figures 5-1 to 5-3 for how to create

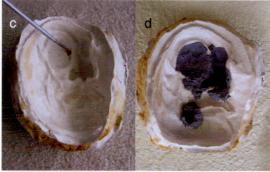
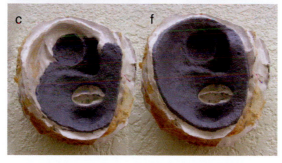

Figure 7-8 (a) Set a negative mold aside and put the Instant Papier-Mâché in a mixing bowl. (b) Mix the papier-mâché. (c) Apply Vaseline to the inside of the negative mold. (d) Start molding the papier-mâché from the lowest point in the mold and work your way out. (e) Keep an even coat of papier-mâché while pressing and smearing the papier-mâché around the mold. (f) Completed filled mold.

a mask with clay and how to make a negative mold from it.

- Mix the Instant Papier- Mâché (Figure 7-8b). According to the package instruction, the mixing ratio is 32 oz water : 1 lb Instant Papier-Mâché. Knead it until it is firm like clay with no dry spots. If the mixture is too soft, add more dry Mâché; if it's too dry, sprinkle it with some water. One pound of Instant Papier-Mâché is enough to make four standard-sized masks.

Step Two: Applying the Papier-Mâché to the Mold

- With a brush, apply an even coat of Vaseline as a release to the entire inside surface of the negative mold (Figure 7-8c).
- Apply the papier-mâché over the negative mold. Start from the lowest areas or center first and work your way out to the edge of the negative mold (Figure 7-8d). The purpose of this is not to fill the negative mold up but to create an even layer on the entire surface of the negative mold like a shell. Take a small amount of papier-mâché, press it into the impressions and keep the coat of papier-mâché an even thickness on the entire surface of the

mold (Figure 7-8e). Mold the outer edge neatly (Figure 7-8f).

Step Three: Removing the Mask from the Negative Mold and Painting the Mask

- Let the papier-mâché dry for 1 or 2 days or force-dry it using a hairdryer.
- After the papier-mâché is completed dried, use a butter knife to carefully loosen the edge around the mask and remove it from the negative mold (Figure 7-9a).
- The mask can be sanded with sandpaper for a smooth texture. The papier-mâché mask in this example was not sanded to keep the natural rough texture (Figure 7-9b).
- Paint the mask with acrylic pigments mixed with Right-Step clear varnish. Paint the shadows on the mask first and then the highlights (Figures 7-9c–d).

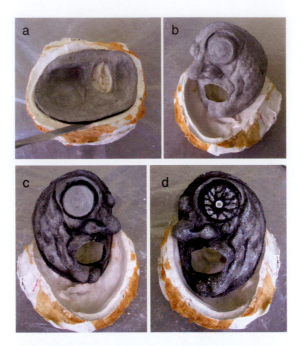

Figure 7-9 (a) Pry mask from the mold using butter knife. (b) Dried unpainted papier-mâché mask after being removed from the mold. (c) Apply the shadows to the papier-mâché mask. (d) Apply the highlights to the papier-mâché mask.

MAKING A MASK FROM LAMINATED FABRIC

I remember that every summer my grandmother laminated three or four layers of fabric strips soaked in wheat starch to make stiff fabric sheets. Then she would put her shoe patterns on it and cut them out to make shoes for her bound little gold-lily feet. I now understand that those laminated fabric strips functioned to support and add sturdiness and durability to the shoes. This memory of my grandmother inspired me to make masks using fabric strips.

When the fabric is cut on the bias into small strips, it will be easy to lay it in the negative mold, like papier-mâché. But here you are dealing with fabric, which is more durable and colorful than paper.

PROCEDURES FOR MAKING A LAMINATED FABRIC MASK

Materials Required:

- Fabric strips (any leftover fabric corners from making costumes will work for the mask)
- ½ cup of wheat flour or wallpaper paste
- Stove
- Cooking bowl for making the wheat starch
- Scissors
- Spatula
- Negative mold
- Vaseline and brush
- Acrylic paints and Right-Step clear varnish
- Elmer's glue

Step One: Preparation

- Cut the fabric on bias in the preferred shapes and sizes that will fit in the mold (Figure 7-10a).
- Put a cup of water in a heat-proof cooking bowl and place it on the

stove. Sprinkle and stir wheat flour into the cool water while it's heating (similar to making gravy; but the result is thicker than gravy). When the water boils, turn off the stove and let simmer for 1 minute. Continue stirring until the mixture becomes a creamy paste (Figure 7-10b). (Wallpaper paste can be used instead of preparing the wheat flour.)

Step Two: Laminating Fabric Strips

- Apply an even coat of Vaseline to the entire surface of the inside negative mold (Figure 7-10e).
- Soak the fabric strips in starch (Figure 7-10c). Take the strips out of the starch and place them on a plate and use a spatula to scrape off the excess starch (Figure 7-10d).
- Lay any specific design pieces that you want to show in the mold first (Figure 7-10f).
- Laminate or apply more layers of fabric strips to the entire mold (Figure 7-11a). The openings for the eyes, nostrils, and mouth can be left uncovered, or you can cover them and cut them open later with a sharp knife. Three or four layers of fabric strips will be enough for the mask. As when you applied the

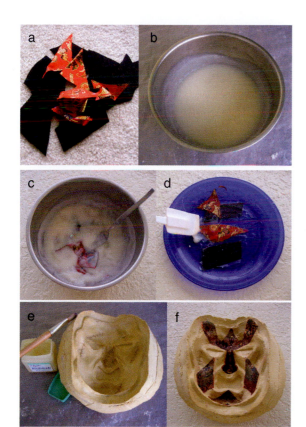

Figure 7-10 (a) Cut the fabric into a variety of sizes and shapes. (b) Cook the wheat flour starch. (c) Soak the fabric strips in the starch. (d) Scrape the excess starch off the fabric strips. (e) Coat the negative mold with Vaseline. (f) Lay the design pieces in the negative mold first.

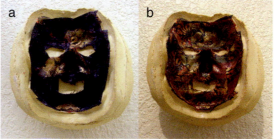

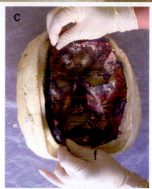

Figure 7-11 (a) Apply more layers of fabric strips. (b) Laminate the last layer of fabric strips. (c) Remove the dried mask from the mold. (d) The completed mask.

buckram strips in an earlier mask, alter the direction of each layer to reinforce the mask.

- Let the mask dry for 1–2 days or force-dry it by heating it.
- Loosen the outer edges of the mask, and then carefully pull it from the negative mold (Figures 7-11c–d).

Step Three: Trimming and Painting the Mask

- Trim the outer edges and the openings of the eyes, nostrils, and lips with a small scissors or sharp knife.
- Check to make sure there are no starch stains. Dried starch will leave stains on the dark-colored fabric. The red fabric used for the mask in this example is silk, note that there are no starch stains on the red fabric strips (Figure 7-12a).
- Apply a coat of Elmer's glue to the black fabric areas only for reinforcement (Figure 7-12a).
- After the glue dries, paint the mask (the black areas) with acrylic colors mixed with varnish (Figure 7-12b). In this mask, the red-colored fabric strips is kept its natural color.

The completed mask is shown in Figure 7-12d. Compare it to a buckram mask made from the same mold (Figure 7-13).

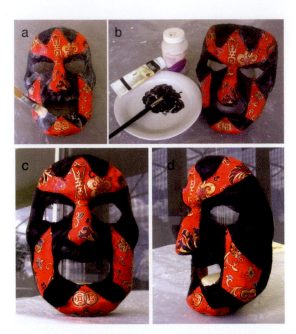

Figure 7-12 (a) Apply a coat of Elmer's glue to the black fabric. (b) Paint the mask with acrylic colors and varnish. (c–d) Completed laminated fabric mask — front and profile.

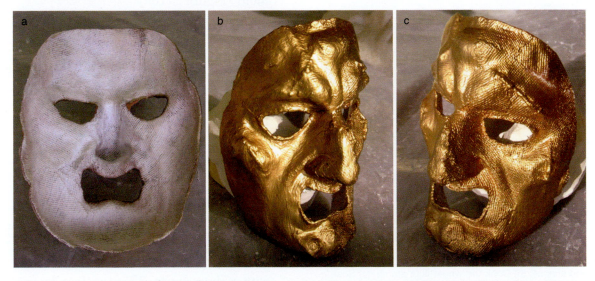

Figure 7-13 A buckram mask painted with sculpture coat made from the same negative mold. The surface of the sculpture coat was sprayed with gold spray paint. (a) Inside of the mask, displaying the buckram. (b) The left side of the buckram mask was painted with three layers of sculpture coat for a smooth finish. (c) The right side of the buckram mask was painted with one coat of sculpture coat for a textured surface.

Chapter 8   Variety Hats

MAKING A TOP HAT

Making a top hat is always the first project in my millinery class because it covers most of the principal techniques of hat construction from patterning, cutting, and wiring to attaching the lid, sideband, and brim together to line the hat.

A top hat can be in any style with a straight, tapered up/down, or curved sideband and a flat or curved brim. Each hat style has a similar construction procedure. The top hat described here has a tapered down sideband crown that dips down in the front and back.

PROCEDURE FOR MAKING A TOP HAT

Materials Required:

- Pattern paper
- Buckram
- Mold or ring block for brim
- Plastic bag
- Plastic wrap
- Push pins
- Marker
- Millinery wire
- Interfacing or flannel
- Spray adhesive
- Hat-covering fabric
- Hat-lining fabric
- Scissors
- Sewing machine
- Needle board
- Iron
- Needle and thread (Hy-Mark thread)
- Fabric tacky clear glue
- Fabric scraps or paper towels
- Trim fabric and ribbons

Step One: Creating the Patterns

- Determine the hat circumference. The head circumference is a major measurement for this. A simple formula to determine this is: Hat circumference = Head circumference measurement + $\frac{1}{2}$–$\frac{3}{4}$″ (ease for fabric seam allowance) + Overlapping seam allowance. The height of the sideband depends on the design (from 1 to 12″ tall).

- The crown is usually developed first, and then the lid and brim are developed from the crown. The top hat crown pattern can be developed from a straight-edge rectangle or a curved rectangle cut from a hollow circle (Figure 8-1). A crown made from a

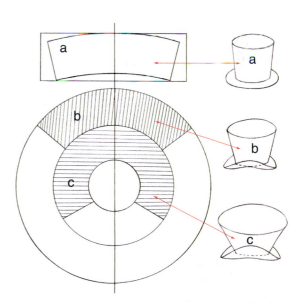

Figure 8-1 Examples of crown patterns: (a) A crown that tapers down is developed from a rectangle with shallow curves; (b) a crown that tapers down even more is developed from a large circle; (c) a crown that tapers extremely is developed from a smaller circle

137

straight-edge rectangle creates a straight crown; the curved rectangle creates a crown that tapers up or down. Thus, a top-hat crown is developed from a smaller circle (i.e., one with greater curve) will be extremely tapered; a crown developed from a larger circle (imagine this large circle to be the same size as your cutting table) will be less tapered. It will create a natural styled top hat.

- Decide on the brim. The brim shape can be flat, curved, even, or uneven. Bending the wire trim on the edge of the brim will curve the brim to a small degree. A brim with a deeper curve has to be shaped over a mold or block (the shape of the mold or block determines what shape the brim will be). Curved brims in this demo are created over a ring block (can be purchased from craft stores).

- Cut a piece of buckram larger than the ring block. Wet the buckram, and seal it in a plastic bag for 2 minutes. It will become soft and easy to mold into shapes.

- Cover the ring block and the work table with plastic wrap because wet buckram is sticky.

- Lay the wet buckram flat on the table and place the ring block on top (Figure 8-2a). Bring two opposite

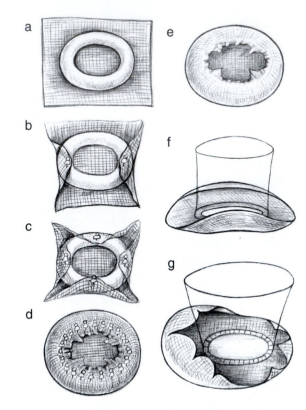

Figure 8-2 Examples of creating curved brims from a ring block: (a) Place the ring block on the wet buckram. (b) Pin the opposite edges of the buckram to the ring block. (c) Pin the next two other opposite edges to the ring block. (d) Pin all the wet buckram edges around the ring block. (e) Remove the dried buckram from the ring block. (f) Cut an even, curved brim from the curved buckram. (g) Create an uneven brim from the curved buckram.

edges toward each other to the center of the ring block; pull the material tight, and push-pin it down to the top of the ring block (Figure 8-2b). Repeat the same steps working on two opposite edges at a time until all the edges are pinned to the top of the block (Figures 8-2c–d). Let the buckram dry for 24 hours or heat it for faster drying.

- After the buckram is completely dry, remove all the push pins and the curved buckram from the ring block (Figure 8-2e). Outline the brim as desired on this curved buckram and cut it out (Figure 8-2f or 8-2g).

- The top hat in this example is developed from a large circle. Additional two inward curves made at the bottom that dip $\frac{5}{8}''$ deep on either side of the crown (Figure 8-3a) will create a dip at the front and back brim to create a naturally curved brim (instead of using a curved brim blocked on a ring showing in Figure 8-2). The greater the inward curves, the greater the dipped brim will be.

- Transfer the crown shape from a paper pattern to a piece of buckram with a marker and cut it out (Figures 8-3b–c).

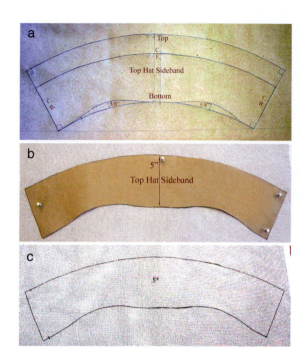

Figure 8-3 (a) A tapered down top-hat crown (or sideband) pattern (5″ and 7″ tall) with two ⅝″ dips. (b) Place the paper pattern (here the 5″-tall pattern) on top of buckram. (c) Transfer the pattern to buckram.

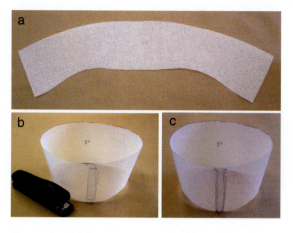

Figure 8-4 (a) Cut out the crown. (b) Overlap the seam allowances and temporarily staple them together. (c) Sew the seam allowances together on a sewing machine.

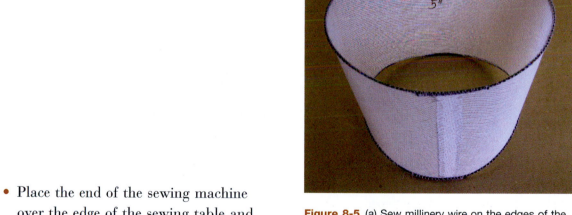

Figure 8-5 (a) Sew millinery wire on the edges of the crown. (b) Wired crown.

Step Two: Closing the Center Back of the Crown/Sideband and Wiring the Edges

• Cut out the buckram crown piece (Figure 8-4a). Overlap the center back seam allowances and temporarily staple them together (Figure 8-4b). Then sew them together using a sewing machine (Figure 8-4c).

• Place the end of the sewing machine over the edge of the sewing table and place the buckram crown around the end of the sewing machine (Figure 8-5a); sew a piece of millinery wire along the top and bottom crown edges (Figure 8-5b).

Step Three: Creating the Lid and Brim

- Shape the top wire on the crown into a perfect circle, and shape the bottom (with the dip curves) wire into an oval so that it properly rests on the head.
- Place the top edge of the crown upside down onto a piece of buckram to make the lid; stabilize it by placing a few push pins along the wired edge (Figure 8-6a).
- Trace the circle INSIDE the crown with a marker (because the lid will fit inside the circle of the crown). Remove the crown and add a ³⁄₄″ seam allowance around the traced circle (Figures 8-6b–c).
- To make the brim, place the crown's bottom wire on top of another piece of buckram and push-pin it down at the front and back (Figure 8-7a). No pins can be added to the sides of the crown because the arced inward curve won't attach to the flat table surface.
- Trace the head opening of the brim on the inside of the oval with a marker, keeping the marker straight when tracing the arced inward curves (Figures 8-7a–b).
- Remove the crown from the brim buckram and create a ³⁄₄″ seam allowance around the head opening

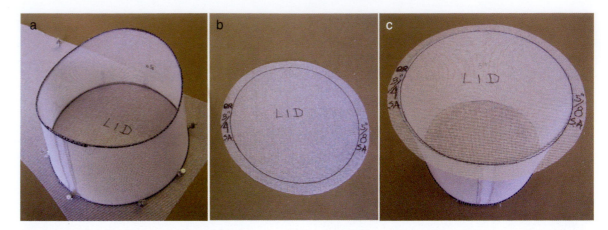

Figure 8-6 (a) Pin the crown onto buckram. (b–c) Add a ³⁄₄″ seam allowance around the edge of the lid.

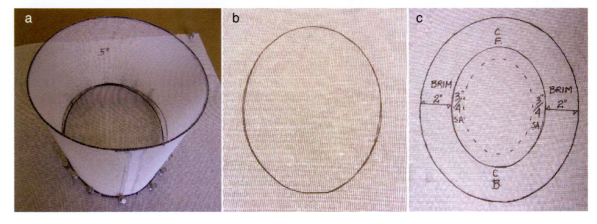

Figure 8-7 (a) Pin the crown onto the brim buckram on a table; trace the head opening on to the brim buckram. (b) The traced head opening. (c) Add the seam allowance to the head opening; add the brim line.

from the tracing line toward the center of the oval (Figure 8-7c).

- The width of the brim in this example extends 2″ out from the tracing line. Mark the outer edge of the brim (Figure 8-7c), and trim off the excess buckram (Figure 8-8a).
- Clip the head opening seam allowance all the way around the tracing line (Figure 8-8a), and bend the seam

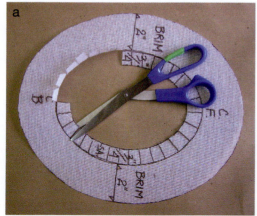

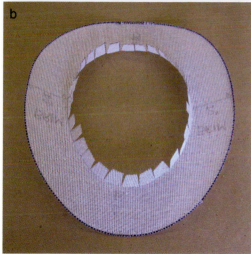

Figure 8-8 (a) Trim off the excess buckram; clip the seam allowance. (b) Bend up the seam allowance, and wire the brim's outer edge.

allowance clips up (Figure 8-8b) before covering with fabric.

- Wire the outer edge of the brim with machine-sewn zigzag stitches (Figure 8-8b).

Step Four: Smoothing the Buckram Surface

- A layer of plain flannel or soft knit woven interfacing fabric can be glued over the buckram to smooth out the buckram's rough surface. If a lightweight fabric is used for the hat, flannel should be used as interfacing fabric. Since a heavy fabric is used for this example, a fine knit woven fabric is used here. Cut the interfacing fabric 1″ wider than the pattern pieces all the way around (Figure 8-9a).

- Flatten the bent-up seam allowance, apply an even coat of spray adhesive to the surface of the brim, and place the glued side over the interfacing fabric (Figure 8-9b). (The bent-up seam allowance on the buckram marks where the crown will sit.)

- Evenly spray a coat of adhesive over the other buckram hat pieces and glue down the interfacing fabric (Figure 8-9b).

- Trim off the excess fabric. Glue the seam allowances down (Figure 8-9c).

Step Five: Covering the Buckram Pieces with Fabric

- Place the paper crown pattern, the buckram lid, and brim on the top hat fabric and cut out pieces at least 1″

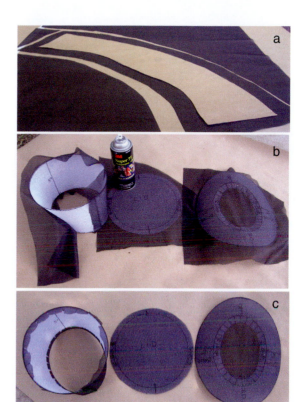

Figure 8-9 (a) Cut the interfacing fabric. (b) Glue the interfacing fabric to the buckram pieces. (c) Trim the excess fabric, and glue the seam allowance of the interfacing fabric to the inside of the crown.

larger than the pattern pieces (Figure 8-10a). Cut 1 piece of fabric for the lid, 1 piece for the crown, and 2 pieces for the brim (to cover both the top and bottom brims). Long-piled velvet is used for this hat.

- Wrap the crown fabric over the buckram crown, and pin the seam

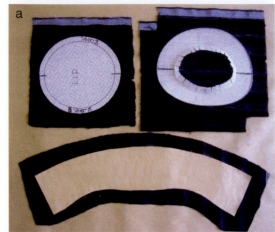

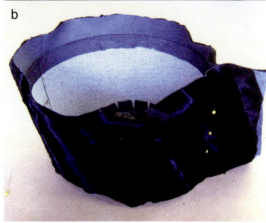

Figure 8-10 (a) Cut the fabric hat pieces 1″ larger than the pattern piece. (b) Fit the crown fabric over the buckram crown.

allowance together. Normally the right side of the fabric faces the inside, but in Figure 8-10b the right side of the fabric faces the outside to make it is easier to match the stripes up at the center seam.

- Remove the fitted fabric with the pins still attached from the crown. Turn the wrong side of the fabric out (inside out), and make chalk marks along the pinned seam line (Figure 8-11a).
- Remove the pins (Figure 8-11b) and draw two continuous lines using the marks. This is the stitching line (Figure 8-11c). Match the sides together, pin them (Figure 8-11c), and machine sew them together.
- Trim the seam allowance to $\frac{3}{8}$″, and press it open over a needle board (Figure 8-12b) (the board prevents the pile from being crushed during pressing). Turn the right side of the fabric out; it will look like a tube.
- Fit the tubular crown fabric over the buckram crown, and glue down the fabric seam allowances with fabric tacky glue (no glue is needed on the rest of the crown) (Figure 8-13). Do not apply too much glue or it will be difficult to pull a needle through when you attach the crown to the lid and brim.
- Now take the brim piece. Spray an even coat of adhesive on one side of the buckram brim and place the glued side on fabric (Figures 8-14a–b). Trim the excess fabric hanging from the brim's outer and inner circles (Figure 8-14c).

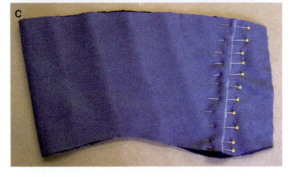

Figure 8-11 (a) Make chalk marks along the pin line. (b) Remove the pins. (c) Draw a continuous stitching line drawn along the dotted lines, and pin the seam allowances together.

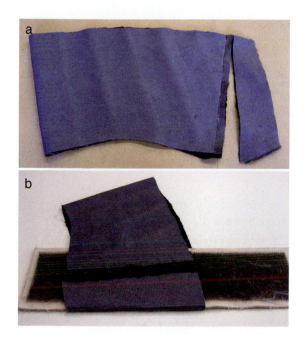

Figure 8-12 (a) Trim the seam allowance. (b) Press open the seam allowance over a needle board.

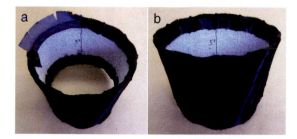

Figure 8-13 (a) Fit the hat fabric over the crown, and glue down the seam allowance. (b) Completed crown.

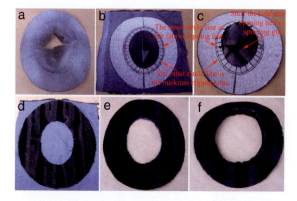

Figure 8-14 (a) Spray one side of the buckram brim with adhesive. (b) Glue one side of the brim to the first piece of brim fabric. (c) Trim the excess fabric, clip the seam allowance, and stuff the center of the circle with fabric scraps. (d) Glue the other side of buckram brim to the second piece of brim fabric. (e) Trim the excess fabric, and clip the seam allowance. (f) Bend up the clipped seam allowance.

- Follow the clipping cuts that you made earlier on the buckram to clip the fabric seam allowance that you just glued. The clips on the fabric must be $\frac{1}{8}$–$\frac{1}{4}''$ shorter than the buckram clips. Note that in Figures 8-14b–c two circles positioned closely together have been drawn at the head-opening seam allowance. The outer circle is the actual head opening and the stop line for buckram clipping; the inner circle is the stop line for fabric clipping. Deeper fabric clips will be exposed and are hard to cover up with lining, and this will make the hat look sloppy. Buckram is stiff so it's not easy to bend the seam

allowance; this is why the buckram clips must be deeper than fabric clips.

- Turn the brim over, and stuff the center opening with fabric scraps or paper towels (Figure 8-14c) before spraying the adhesive to avoid getting it on the fabric that you just glued to the opposite side.
- Glue the uncovered side of the buckram brim to the second brim fabric piece (Figure 8-14d).
- Trim the excess fabrics around both the inner and outer circles (Figure 8-14e). Machine zigzag large stitches through all the layers of material along the outer brim edge before trimming it.
- Clip the fabric seam allowance (Figure 8-14e). (The sides of fabric are glued and clipped one at a time.)
- Bend the originally bent buckram layer up 90 degrees along the head-opening line (the outer traced circle) (Figure 8-14f). This upright seam allowance will join to the crown.
- Now take the lid piece. Using the buckram lid as a pattern to cut out the lid lining (see step eight), Spray adhesive over the buckram lid and glue it to the fabric. Trim and clip the fabric lid seam allowance in the same way as the head-opening seam allowance on the brim fabric (Figure 8-15).

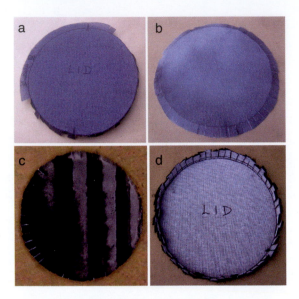

Figure 8-15 (a) Bend down the buckram lid seam allowance. (b) Flatten the seam allowance, and spray adhesive on the surface. (c) Glue the fabric to the buckram lid, and clip the seam allowance. (d) Bend up the seam allowance 90 degrees.

Step Six: Trimming the Outer Edge of the Brim

Various trims that possess ease and stretch can be used to finish the brim edge; grosgrain woven ribbons, bias-cut fabric trim, or self-binding finish are some examples. The most common trimming method involves folding the trim almost in half so that one half is slightly bigger than the other (similar to the way that bias tape purchased from the store is folded). The brim's edge is inserted into the fold of the strip with the strip's wider half along the bottom edge of the brim and the narrower half on top. The placement of the trim ensures that the entire bottom trim will be fully stitched while sewing along the narrower top half. The method of brim trimming in my example here is to trim the hat brim with a single unfolded bias strip. It is supposedly easier to manage.

- Cut a 2″-wide single-bias strip (cut the strip wider and longer than needed and trim off the excess later) from black satin fabric.
- Fold one end of the strip over crosswise $\frac{1}{2}$″. Place the right side of the strip along the brim's edge; stitch it beginning at the center back of the brim (Figure 8-16a). (The sewn width of the trim in this example is $\frac{1}{4}$″.) Pins are not necessary unless you are not comfortable sewing without pinning; just carefully manipulate and pull the trim as needed to keep it in place while sewing. Overlap the ends about $\frac{3}{4}$″, and trim off the excess fabric.
- Pull the nonstitched edge of the strip to the other side of the brim, and pin along the nonstitched strip edge (Figures 8-16b–c). Turn the brim over and machine stitch directly over the seam line (often called "stitching in the ditch"). Or, alternatively, both the upper and lower edges on the trim can be top-stitched as desired.

- After the stitching is finished, turn the brim over and NEATLY and CAREFULLY trim off the excess seam allowance on the strip down to the stitching line (do not cut the fabric while trimming) (Figures 8-16d–e). Because the trim is cut on bias, it won't ravel.

Step Seven: Putting the Hat Parts Together

- Attach the crown to the brim by placing the bottom of the crown over the brim's bent-up seam allowance, matching the center fronts and backs of the brim and crown together (Figure 8-17a).
- Apply a small amount of fabric tacky glue to only the upper part (the tips) of the seam allowance at the front and back, and glue and pin the seam allowance to the inside of the crown.
- After the glue on the front and back dries, glue the sides of the seam allowance, again applying glue to only the upper part of the seam allowance. Due to the deepened curves previously made on the sides of the crown, the seam allowance on the sides of the head opening needs to be pushed up until the bottom of the seam allowance attaches to the wire edge on the bottom

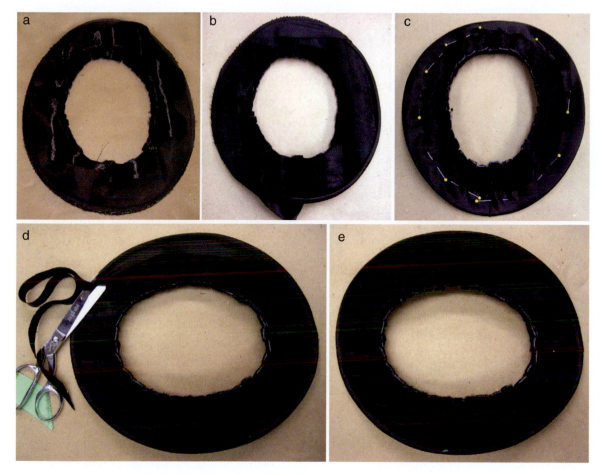

Figure 8-16 (a) Sew one edge of the bias strip on to edge of the brim. (b) Turn the unsewn edge of the bias strip to the other side of the brim. (c) Pin this edge of the strip in place. (d) Trim off the excess seam allowance after you finish stitching. (e) Completed trimmed brim edge.

8-18a–b), and push the seam allowance against the crown to make sure it fits properly all the way around. It should fit perfectly if the seam allowance is correctly bent. If it doesn't fit, retrace the shape of the lid or double-check the seam allowance bending line and make corrections until it fits properly.

- Once the lid is in place, apply fabric tacky glue all the way around the tips (only) of the lid seam allowance and press the tips to the upper crown edge. Before the glue completely dries, make sure the lid surface is leveled with the edge of the crown; adjust the lid position as needed.

- Hand-sew the lid fabric to the crown fabric with ¼" (or smaller) tunnel stitches (sometimes called ladder stitches) (Figure 8-18c). Tunnel stitches alternatively travel through the folding edge of the lid and crown fabric so the stitches are completely hidden. A thin curved needle will work best due to the round shape of the hat, but a straight needle will work as well.

The assembled pieces are shown in Figure 8-18d.

of the crown. Then glue them in place. Pin the stiff seam allowance in place before the glue dries. The fabric tacky glue is used to temporarily stabilize the seam allowance in place (Figure 8-17b).

- Hand-sew the seam allowance in place using doubled Hy-Mark thread (Figure 8-17c).

- Attach the lid to the crown. Place the top of the crown around the bent-up lid seam allowance on the lid (Figures

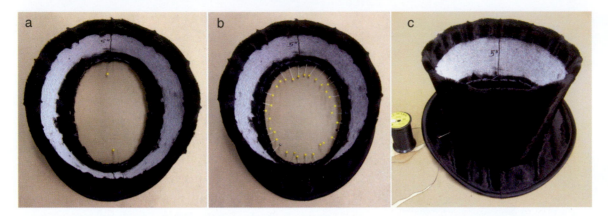

Figure 8-17 (a) Place the crown around the head-opening seam allowance in the brim, and pin the center front and center back seam allowances in place. (b) Glue the head-opening seam allowance (apply the glue only to the tip seam allowance), and pin it in place. (c) Hand-sew the brim to the crown.

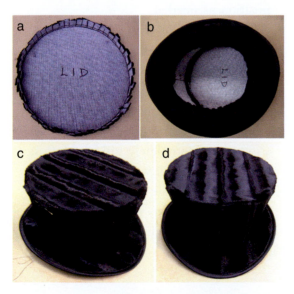

Figure 8-18 (a) Bend up the lid seam allowance (see Figure 8-15). (b) Insert the lid seam allowance into the crown top, and glue it to the edge of the crown. (c) Stitch the lid and crown together by hand with tunnel stitches. (d) Completed lid and brim sewn to the crown.

Step Eight: Lining the Hat

Garment-lining fabric is often used to line a hat, but other fabrics can also be used, such as felt, flannel, fine cotton, or any nonslippery fabric. If heavy or bulky fabric is used, be sure to add extra space when you make the head opening.

- Make the lid lining. Trace the buckram lid as a pattern for the lid lining, or turn the hat upside down and trace the crown's upper edge, subtracting $\frac{1}{4}''$ all the way around the circle because the inside of the crown is smaller than the outside of the crown (Figure 8-19a).
- Make the crown lining. Use your paper crown pattern to cut the lining fabric on the bias. Add a 1″ seam allowance on

all edges except the crown's top edge (Figure 8-19a).

- Fit the crown lining by wrapping the lining fabric around the outside of the crown and pinning the seam allowance so that it meets in the center back (Figure 8-19b).
- Remove the lining (with pins intact) from the crown, lay it flat on the table, and draw a new stitching line $\frac{1}{4}''$ in from the pinned line, that is, toward the center front (since the inside of the hat is smaller than the outside) (Figure 8-19c).
- Pin the new seam allowance together and machine stitch it. Trim the seam allowance down to $\frac{3}{8}''$, and press it open (Figures 8-19d–e).
- Sew the lid lining and crown lining together. Make four equally spaced marks with chalk on the seam allowances of the lid lining and on the crown lining's top edge (Figure 8-20a).
- Match the four marks made on the seam allowances, pin the pieces together (Figures 8-20b–c), and machine stitch them together with a $\frac{1}{4}''$ seam allowance (Figure 8-20d).
- Fold the seam allowance on the stitching line toward the head opening, and press (Figure 8-20e).
- Apply fabric tacky glue to the entire inside surface of the lid, especially

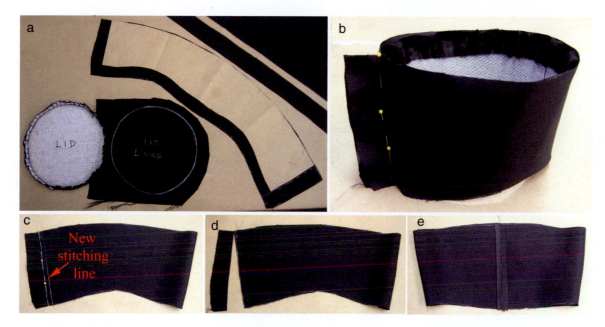

Figure 8-19 (a) Cut out the fabric lining. (b) Fit the crown lining fabric over the crown, and pin it. (c) Draw a new stitching line on the fabric. (d) Stitch the seam and trim off the excess seam allowance. (e) Press the seam open.

Figure 8-20 (a) Make four chalk marks on the seam allowance of the lid lining and crown lining. (b) Match the four marks, and pin. (c) Place more pins between the four marks, pinning the linings together. (d) Stitch the lid and crown linings together. (e) Press the seam allowance up toward the head opening.

along the bent edge and seam allowance (Figure 8-21a). Use a flat object to smear the glue to an even coat.

- Place the lining inside the hat with the right side facing out, match the center fronts and backs, and glue and press the lid lining to the lid surface. Glue the fabric lid seam allowance to the buckram lid seam allowance especially well (Figure 8-21b).

- Apply more glue on the entire crown, staying 1″ away from the head-opening stitch line, and use a flat object to even out the glue. Do not apply too much glue in one spot; you do not want it to soak through the fabric. Smooth out the crown lining fabric from the lid toward the head opening. The lining seam allowance will stick out of the inner crown (Figure 8-21c).

- Fold the raw edge of the lining seam allowance under to the wrong side of the lining so it is ⅛″ below the bent line of the brim's head-opening seam allowance. Pin all the way around the fold (Figure 8-21d).

- Sew the lining edge by hand using tunnel stitches or slanted hemming stitches (Figure 8-21e).

   The completed hat is shown in Figure 8-22.

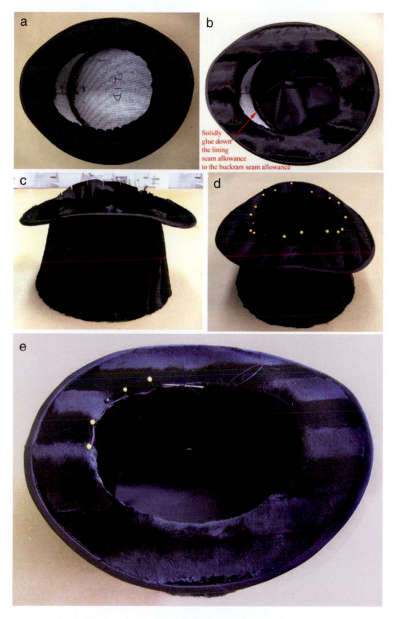

Figure 8-21 (a) Apply glue to the inside of the buckram lid. (b) Place the lining inside the crown, and glue the lining to the buckram lid seam allowance. (c) Glue the crown lining to the inner buckram crown. (d) Fold the lining seam allowance under, and pin it in place. (e) Hand-sew the lining using tunnel stitches.

Figure 8-22 Completed top hat.

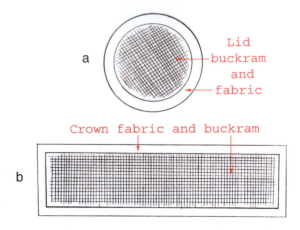

Figure 8-23 (a) Cut out the lid pieces from buckram and fabric. (b) Cut out the crown (side) pieces from buckram and fabric on bias.

MAKING A BRIMLESS HAT

A brimless hat is much simpler to make than a brimmed hat. I made a brimless hat for *Romeo and Juliet*.

PROCEDURE FOR MAKING A BRIMLESS HAT

Materials Required:

- Pattern paper
- Buckram
- Millinery wire
- Padding for lid
- Hat fabric
- Trim
- Foam cord
- Fabric tacky glue
- Spray adhesive

- Sewing machine
- Needle and thread
- Scissors

Step One: Creating a Pattern and Cutting the Hat Materials

- Create patterns for the crown and lid. The crown pattern for this hat is developed from a straight rectangular shape; the lid is a simple circular shape.
- Cut out pieces for the lid and crown from buckram and the hat fabric (Figure 8-23).

Step Two: Putting the Hat Together

- Sew the center back seam of the buckram crown together by hand (Figure 8-24a).

- Wire the crown's top and bottom edges using a sewing machine, as in the top hat (Figure 8-24b).
- Cut a $5/8''$-diameter foam cord in half lengthwise. Glue the flat cut surface of one of the halves all the way around the buckram crown's top edge with fabric tacky glue (Figures 8-24c–d).
- Wrap the crown hat fabric (with the right side facing the buckram crown) over the buckram crown and pin the seam allowance together.
- Remove the hat fabric from the buckram crown, and machine stitch the pinned stitching line. Trim off the excess seam allowance, and press the seam open. Turn it right side out. It will look like a tube.

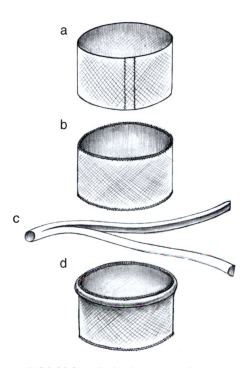

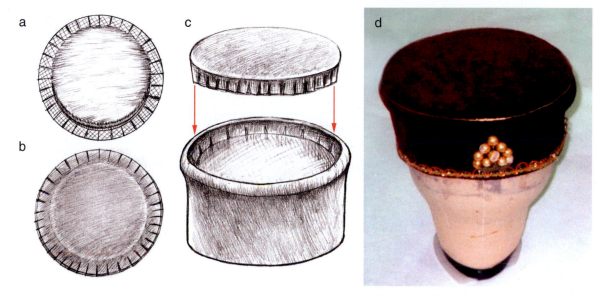

Figure 8-25 (a) Pad the buckram lid with a thin layer of poly padding. (b) Glue the hat-fabric to the padded buckram lid; trim and clip the seam allowance. (c) Bend down the seam allowance, and insert it into the crown. (d) Completed hat.

Figure 8-24 (a) Sew the buckram crown's center back seam together. (b) Sew millinery wire to the edges of the buckram crown. (c) Cut a piece of foam cord in half lengthwise. (d) Glue one piece of the foam cord to the top of the buckram crown.

- Spray adhesive over the entire outside surface of the buckram crown, and insert it into the fabric tube. Pull and smooth the fabric, and wrap the upper and lower seam allowances to the crown's inside (Figure 8-25c, crown); glue them with fabric tacky glue.

- Spray adhesive over the buckram lid and cover it (only on the lid, no padding on the seam allowance area) with a thin layer of poly padding to create extra dimension (Figure 8-25a). Spray adhesive on the padding, and glue the lid hat fabric to it (Figure 8-25b).

- Trim, clip, and bend the lid seam allowance 90 degrees up (Figures 8-25b–c), as in the top hat lid.

- Insert the lid into the crown's top edge (Figure 8-25c), and glue the tips of the seam allowance to the crown.

- Hand-sew the lid and crown together using tunnel stitches.

- Attach trims to the hat with glue or hand-sewing.

- See Figures 8-19 to 8-21 for instructions on how to line the hat.

The completed hat is shown in Figures 8-25d and 8-26.

Figure 8-26 Production photo of *Romeo and Juliet* showing the brimless hat. *From left to right: Capulet played by Jeremy Sonney, Lady Capulet played by Colleen Smet, and Paris played by Tom McNelly. Directed by Brenda Hubbard. Scenic design by Tim Stapleton. Lighting design by Mark C. Zetterberg. Costume design by Tan Huaixiang. Central Washington University, Department of Theatre Arts presentation.*

MAKING A ROUND CROWN AND BIG-BRIMMED HAT

A hat with a round crown is the most common style used for both men and women. It can be made of felt, buckram, or Fosshape, with a shallow or deep crown molded over a round hat block or object.

Fosshape is used on the wide-brimmed hat in this example, created for *Once on This Island* (Figure 8-27). Fosshape can be draped over a mold and formed into the molded shape with a steam iron or

Figure 8-27 Costume design for *Once on This Island*.

clothing steamer; if laid on a flat surface, it will become a flat sheet under the heat. The degree of stiffness is determined by the amount of heat, time, and pressure applied to the Fosshape.

PROCEDURE FOR MAKING A ROUND CROWN HAT

Materials Required:

- Fosshape #300 (or #600)
- Hat block
- Elastic string
- Push pins
- Scissors
- Millinery wire
- Iron and steamer
- Hat fabric
- Trims

Step One: Creating the Crown

- Cut a piece of Fosshape large enough to cover half the hat block. #300 Fosshape will provide lightweight support; #600 Fosshape will provide heavier and stiffer support.
- Place the Fosshape over a hat block, and tie it at the bottom with elastic string. Use both hands to pull the Fosshape down. Manipulate the material as best you can to get rid of

the wrinkles along the elastic-tied area (Figure 8-28a).

- Steam the Fosshape from top to bottom; manipulate and stretch the Fosshape while you steam it to smooth out any wrinkles that appear around the tied area (Figure 8-28b).
- The Fosshape will become semi-hard from the steaming. For an even harder and stiffer crown, provide more heat with a steam iron and press. If you do this, put a piece of thin muslin under the iron or else the Fosshape will make the iron sticky. Beware: Excess ironing can make the Fosshape too stiff and tough to sew.
- After the entire base becomes hard, it will be a shell-like cap. Trim the excess material at the bottom of the crown. Since the crown is shallow, it will easily separate from the hat block.
- Fit the crown on the head, and trim it to a desired shape (Figure 8-28c).

Step Two: Creating Brim

- Draft the brim on a piece of pattern paper to determine the size and shape. The example here has two triangular-shaped flat brims.
- Cut a piece of Fosshape for the brim. The Fosshape will shrink when heat and steam are applied, so cut this piece

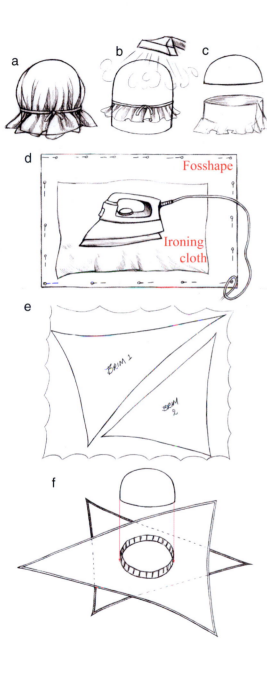

Figure 8-28 (a) Tie the Fosshape over a hat block. (b) Steam the Fosshape. (c) Cut the round crown. (d) Pin the Fosshape brim material to the ironing table, and iron it. (e) Outline the brims on the hardened flat Fosshape piece. (f) Add millinery wire to the brims and cover them with fabric; clip the head-opening seam allowance, and bend it up.

about 4″ larger around all edges than the actual size needed for the brim.

- Place the Fosshape on a flat surface. Insert straight pins around the edges of the Fosshape, closely spaced, to prevent the edges from wrinkling when the Fosshape is being ironed for an even, smooth, and flat Fosshape brim. Iron and steam the Fosshape on the flat surface (Figure 8-28d). A steam pressing machine is the ideal equipment to create a flat piece of Fosshape. If there isn't one available, use a steamer or steam iron, using a pressing cloth under the iron to prevent the iron from becoming sticky. Steam or iron the Fosshape from the center out, and continue to iron the surface several times until the desired hardness of the brim is attained.
- After the Fosshape is hardened and flattened, mark the pattern on the Fosshape and cut out the brim (Figure 8-28e).

- Wire the edges of the brim, and clip the head-opening seam allowance (Figure 8-28f). It is not always necessary to wire Fosshape because Fosshape stays in shape and doesn't stretch. Nonwired brims display a natural bounce (Figure 8-29); wired brims maintain a firm shape. It depends on what you want to achieve.

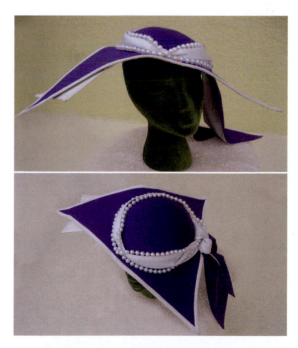

Figure 8-29 A shallow crowned hat made of Fosshape with a nonwired brim. It shows a natural draped look.

Step Three: Putting the Hat Together

- Spray adhesive on each Fosshape piece, and cover them with hat fabric. Trim the brim edges with bias-cut fabric strips. (See Figures 8-14 to 8-15 for instructions on how to cover a hat with fabric and how to trim the brim edges with bias-cut strips.)

- Attach the brim to the round crown, in the same way as the top hat. Insert the head-opening seam allowance of the brim inside the crown, pin the pieces together, and sew them together by hand.

- Lining the inside of the round crown is similar to lining a top hat. Create a lid and bias-cut crown pattern, and use them to cut out the lining fabric. Sew the lining pieces together, and attach the lining to inside of the hat crown. (See Figures 8-19 to 8-21 for instructions on how to line a hat.)

The completed hat is shown in Figures 8-30 to 8-31.

Figure 8-30 Completed wide brimmed hat.

Figure 8-31 Production photo of the round crown hat in *Once on This Island. Andrea played by Patrice Lois Bell; Daniel played by Edward Davis. Directed by Earl D. Weaver. Scenic design by Vandy Wood. Lighting design by Dave Upton. Costume design by Tan Huaixiang. University of Central Florida Conservatory Theatre presentation.*

ALTERING AN EXISTING FELT HAT TO A 1920s HAT

Felt hats can be dyed, darted, seamed, reshaped, and reconstructed. The example here is an existing generic felt hat altered to a stylized 1920s woman's hat for *Death of a Salesman* (Figure 8-32).

Figure 8-32 Costume design for *Death of a Salesman*.

PROCEDURE FOR ALTERING A FELT HAT TO A PERIOD HAT

Material Required:

- A felt hat
- Chalk
- Scissors
- Needle
- Thread
- Head block
- Trim

Step One: Outline the Changes on the Existing Hat

- Pull a felt hat from stock, and put it on the proper-size hat block.
- Based on the design, make marks on the hat to indicate a new brim-attaching line and slashing line (Figure 8-33a).
- Follow the slashing line and slash the brim from the center front to the center back (halfway around the hat). As you're cutting the brim, make a dip at the side crown (cut slightly deeper here than at the center front and back crown) (Figure 8-33a).

Step Two: Reconstructing the Hat

- Place a decorative hatband over the crown and hand-sew it.

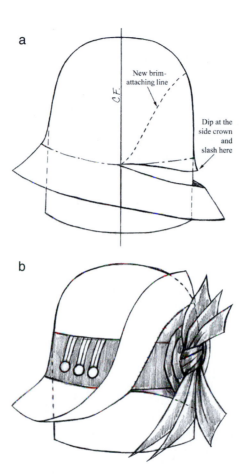

Figure 8-33 (a) Mark the changes and slash the lines on the hat; cut the slash with the side crown dipped down a little. (b) Completed alteration.

- Pull the slashed part of the brim up to the brim-attaching line you made in step one, and hand-sew it down, matching thread right on the brim-attaching line.

  The completed hat is shown in Figures 8-33b and 8-34.

Figure 8-34 Production photo of the hat in *Death of a Salesman*. Miss Francis played by Patrice Lois Bell. Hat altered by Dvorah Neubauer, BFA design and technology major student. Directed by Donald Seay. Scenic and lighting design by Richard Harmon. Costume design by Tan Huaixiang. University of Central Florida Conservatory Theatre presentation.

BLOCKING A FELT HAT

Felt is a nonwoven material without a straight grain like fabric has. It can be stretched in any direction when moistened. After felt dries, it will hold the shape that it has been molded into, but sizing is needed to maintain it. The more expensive and dense the felt, the less sizing it requires to hold its shape. Felt purchased from a fabric store or Wal-Mart won't work for blocking hats because it is made of synthetic fibers that aren't dense enough to retain a shape; it is, however, very suitable for lining armor, headdresses, or other craft work.

A shallow crown with a wide floppy brim is called a hat body; it is made from wool felt and comes in various colors. It can be purchased from any millinery supply store (see Section Ten). It costs $8.50 a piece (in 2007) plus shipping, a good price and quality for theatrical use. The felt hat example made for *The Boy Friend* is a hat body (Figure 8-35a).

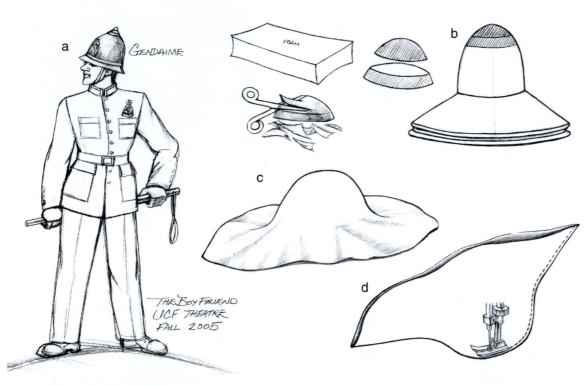

Figure 8-35 (a) Costume design for *The Boy Friend*. (b) Trim the foam padding with scissors and tape it to the hat block to create a pointed hat block. (c) Take a hat body purchased from millinery store. (d) Top-stitch the center folding line of the felt hat body to create a ribbed edge on the hat.

PROCEDURE FOR BLOCKING A FELT HAT

Materials Required:

- Wool felt hat body
- Hat crown/block
- Foam piece
- Fabric tacky glue
- Plastic wrap
- Brim block
- Cooking pot or dye vat
- Water
- Stove
- Washing machine
- Towel
- Two pieces of 28"-long elastic
- Hat sizing
- Sewing machine
- Pattern paper
- Lining fabric
- Chalk
- Iron
- Scissors
- Decorations

Step One: Preparation

- In this example, the design of the hat is pointed. Tape foam on top of the hat block with masking tape to create the point. Use scissors to trim a piece of thick foam to the desired shape (Figure 8-35b). If the foam is not thick enough, glue several layers of foam together. Cover the hat block with plastic wrap for protection.

- Create a ribbed edge down the purchased hat body. To do this, fold the felt hat body in half and top stitch the fold edge with a $\frac{1}{8}''$ seam allowance (Figures 8-35c–d).

Step Two: Blocking the Hat

- Boil water in a large dye pot or dye vat, turn the stove to simmer, and immerse the felt body in the hot water for 10 minutes until the water completely soaks through the dense felt (Figure 8-36a). Any dry spot on the felt will be hard to stretch and manipulate, so make sure the hat body is completely covered with water. It is not necessary to stir constantly; too much stirring may destroy the texture of the felt.

- Spin the excess water off the hat body in the washing machine until the hat body is half dry. Use a towel to blot the water, but don't press down too hard or wrinkles will appear on the felt body.

- After removing the excess water, thoroughly spray a coat of hat sizing on the INSIDE crown of the wet hat body and spray less on the brim (Figure 8-36b). Sizing leaves noticeable stains on the hat surface.

- Place the felt body on the hat block, and tie elastic around the bottom of the crown to hold it on the block (Figure 8-36c).

- Using both hands, pull and stretch the felt down and smooth out any wrinkles that appear on the crown and brim (Figure 8-36d).

- Then use the second piece of elastic to tie the brim edge down to the brim groove (there is a groove built into

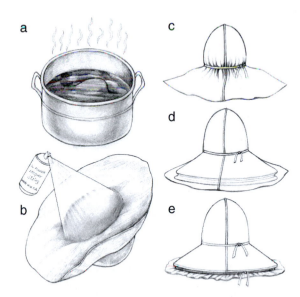

Figure 8-36 (a) Soak the hat body in hot water. (b) Spray sizing on the inside of the crown. (c) Tie the hat body on the hat block. (d) Smooth out the wrinkles around the bottom of the crown. (e) Tie the brim of the hat body to the brim block, and smooth out the wrinkles on the brim.

the brim block for tying elastic). Smooth out any wrinkles that appear around the elastic-tied area (Figure 8-36e).

- Allow the felt to dry completely (24 hours) before removing it from the block.

Step Three: Edging the Hat

To edge the brim, you may either self-bind the edge (fold the same brim-covering fabric over the edge of the brim and stitch) or trim the edge with grosgrain ribbon or a bias strip. Trimming the edge with ribbon does not require a seam allowance on the brim, but self-binding the edge does. A self-bound edge is used in this example.

- After the hat is completely dried, mark the width of the brim with a piece of chalk, and then trim the extra felt off.

- Turn the outer edge back toward the crown about $\frac{1}{4}$–$\frac{3}{8}''$ and top-stitch it down using a sewing machine (Figure 8-37).

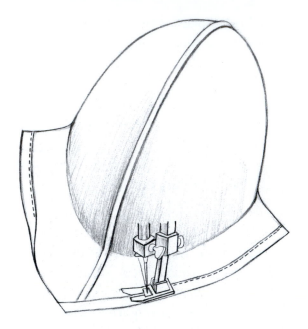

Figure 8-37 Stitch the self-bound edge.

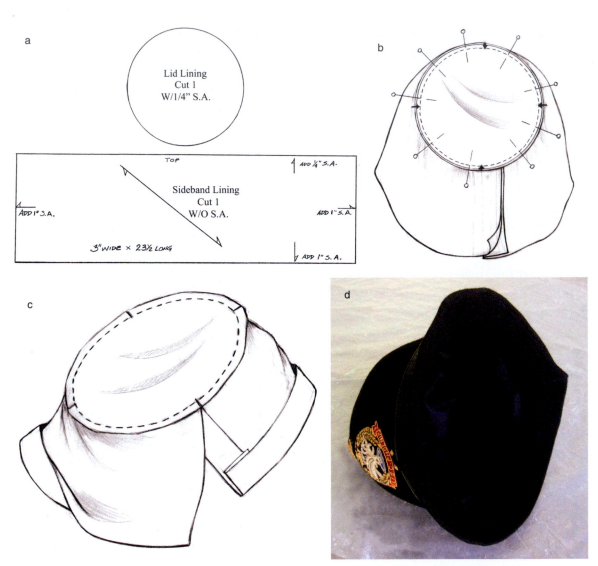

Figure 8-38 (a) Create the crown lining pattern. (b) Pin the top lid and sideband, and sew them together with an overlapped back seam allowance on the sideband. (c) Fold up the 1″ bottom sideband seam allowance. (d) Completed hat showing lining.

Step Four: Lining and Decorating the Hat

A crown lining is added to the hat to absorb sweat and to establish a better fit because the pointed crown is too deep to properly fit on the head.

- Create the lining pattern. The lining in this example consists of two pieces: a top (an 8″-diameter circle) and crown (a 3″-wide bias strip) (Figure 8-38a).

- Cut the lining fabric, adding a $\frac{1}{4}''$ seam allowance at the top of the crown and 1″ on each side and bottom of the crown. Make four equally spaced marks around the edge of the circle. Also divide the crown strip into four equal sections (don't include the 1″ seam allowance on each side of the crown).
- Match the four marks on the circle to the four marks on the crown strip, overlap the two 1″ seam allowances on the crown strip (Figure 8-38b), and pin them together. Then sew the pieces together with a $\frac{1}{4}''$ seam allowance. Leave the center back seam open for adjusting the hat.
- Fold the 1″ seam allowance (bottom hem) of the crown up, and iron it flat (Figure 8-38c).
- Top stitch the crown lining to the inside around the head opening. The stitches that show on the outside of the crown will be covered by a hat band or trim.
- Attach a hat band and decorations to the hat.

The completed hat is shown in Figures 8-38d and 8-39 to 8-40.

Figure 8-39 Completed policeman's felt hat.

Figure 8-40 Production photo of the policeman hat in *The Boy Friend*. Gendarme played by Colin Bryson. Directed by Kate Ingram. Musical Director, Jim Brown. Choreographer, Judy Siegfried. Scenic design by Kyle Becker. Lighting design by Neal Kerr. Sound Design by Martin Wootton. Costume design by Tan Huaixiang. University of Central Florida Conservatory Theatre presentation.

MAKING A WIRE-FRAMED HAT

A wire-framed hat can be made in many styles. The finished hat will be lightweight, transparent, beautiful, strong, and easy to bend into shapes. The wire hat here was made for Gwen in *The Importance of Being Earnest* (Figure 8-41). The front brim of the hat was made shorter than the back to achieve an asymmetrical look and to avoid shadowing the actress's face.

Figure 8-41 Costume design for Gwen in *The Importance of Being Earnest*.

PROCEDURE FOR MAKING A WIRE-FRAMED HAT

Materials Required:

- Millinery wire
- Tie wire
- Needle-nosed pliers with wire cutters
- Head block
- T-pins and push pins
- Stiff formed hat with a shallow crown from stock
- Lace fabric
- Sewing machine
- Needle and thread
- Scissors

Step One: Developing a Pattern

- Design and determine the size and shape of the hat, and develop a pattern for cutting the wire. Make marks that indicate the location of the joints (intersection of wires) of each wire piece (Figure 8-42a). (In this example, the head opening is set off center to avoid shadowing the face. The middle rows of wire can also be reduced to three rows.)
- Use an existing 1950s shallow-crowned hat as a base (Figure 8-42b). The wired frame will be attached to this hat. (If you don't want to use an existing hat, you may make a base from wire as

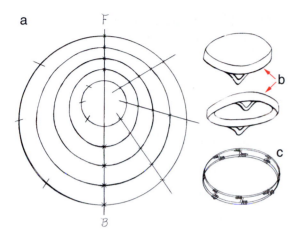

a

F

B

Figure 8-42 (a) Complete the pattern for cutting the wire. (b) Pull a shallow crown hat from stock. (c) Completely constructed wired ring crown.

well.) Sew two bobby-pin horsehair loops on to the shallow crown to secure the hat to the actor's head.

- Make a wire ring crown that will later be fitted over the shallow crown hat. Cut two pieces of wire, equal in length, and join the ends to form two rings. Join the ends by overlapping them $1\frac{1}{2}$–2″ and tying them together.

- Cut a few short wire pieces, and bend each wire into a Z shape with needle-nosed pliers. Then vertically insert the Z-shaped wire between the two wire rings, and tie it on to the rings. The two wire rings will be parallel when joined together (Figure 8-42c).

Step Two: Constructing the Wire-Framed Hat Brim

- Pin your pattern to a cutting table, and, following the pattern, cut wire pieces, adding $1\frac{1}{2}$–2″ to each wire piece for overlapping (Figure 8-43a).

- Join the wire rings together first; then join the vertical wires. The ends of the vertical wire pieces should be bent so that each entire vertical wire becomes an elongated Z shape; this is so they

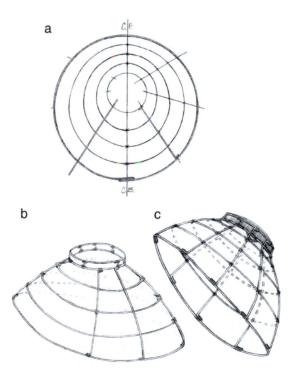

Figure 8-43 (a) Following the pattern, cut the wire pieces. (b) Join the wire pieces together. (c) Completed wire frame.

can be joined with the rings. Attach the top end of each vertical wire to the ring crown made earlier, and attach the bottom end to the outer wire ring; then tie all the other intersections of wires with tie wire (Figures 8-43b–c).

Step Three: Covering the Wire Frame with Fabric

- Choose fabric suitable for the wire fame. The fabric should be lightweight and sheer with nice patterns, such as a lace material. (The figures here have been simplified, so the fabric doesn't show a pattern.)

- Dye the fabric to match the costume if necessary. (The fabric used for the example was dyed lavender to match the costume.)

- Sew the fabric into a tube on the sewing machine using a French seam; this tube will be fitted over the outer ring (the largest wire ring of the brim). The length of this tube is the original width of the fabric.

1. With the WRONG sides of the fabric together, sew the edges of the fabric with a $\frac{1}{4}$″ seam allowance. Trim off half ($\frac{1}{8}$″) of the seam allowance, and press the remaining seam allowance toward one side (Figure 8-44a).

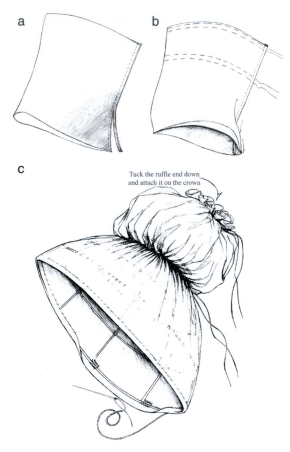

a

b

c

Tuck the ruffle end down
and attach it on the crown

Figure 8-44 (a) Stitch the hat fabric into a tube, wrong sides together, and trim off the seam allowance. (b) With the right sides together, stitch the second part of the French seam; sew two sets of gathering stitches on the fabric. (c) Stitch the bottom hem by hand, and gather the material.

2. Turn the tube inside out (the right sides of the fabric is facing each other), and fold on the stitching line and iron the seam flat. Stitch another seam at this edge with a ⅛″ seam allowance (Figure 8-44b).

- Sew two sets of two parallel gathering stitching lines (Figure 8-44b). First sew a set of double parallel gathering stitching lines on the tube where the crown meets the brim. Then sew the second set of double parallel gathering stitching lines at the very top of the tube. (Sewing just one row of gathering stitches will also work, but double rows make it easier to control the fullness of the gathered fabric.)

- Place the fabric tube over the wire frame, pull it from the top down until it reaches the bottom widest wire. Hand-sew the bottom hem with matching thread (Figure 8-44c). (Because the style of the brim in this example drapes down, the hat fabric is placed over the outer part of the wire frame. If you are making a turned-up brim, cover the underside of the wire with fabric where needed. If you choose to cover both sides of the wire, it will also work, but you'll lose the beauty of the transparent look of the fabric.)

- Pull the parallel gathering threads tight to fit over the bottom of the ring crown, and then tie the gathering thread in a knot (Figure 8-44c). Sew a few tacking stitches to secure it in place.

- Pull the other parallel gathering threads at the very top end of the tube, gathering all the fullness of the fabric together, and tie the threads in a knot. Then tuck this bundle of gathered fabric on to the top of the crown (Figure 8-44c).

Step Four: Decorating the Hat

- There are so many ways to decorate this hat. The key to decorating a wire-framed hat is to keep it lightweight and balanced. Artificial flowers were sewn on this hat.

- Spray a touch of color (if necessary) to tone down the flowers and gain a more harmonious look to the hat.

   The completed hat is shown in Figures 8-45 to 8-46.

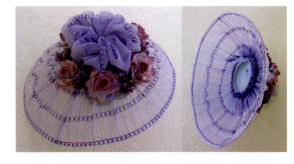

Figure 8-45 Completed wire-framed hat.

Figure 8-46 (a) Production photo of the hat with full costume in *The Importance of Being Earnest*. (b) Production photo of the hat (back view). (c) Production photo of the hat (side view). (d) Production photo of the hat. *From left to right: Cecily played by Jessica Matthews; Lady Bracknell played by Shane Serena; Merriman played by Gianfranco Ferri; John Worthing played by Chris Taylor; Gwen played by Mindy Shepherd-Anders. Directed by Jim Helsinger. Scenic design by Paul Lartonoix. Lighting design by Eric Haugen. Costume design by Tan Huaixiang. University of Central Florida Conservatory Theatre presentation.*

Chapter 9 Straw and Horsehair Hats

MAKING A STRAW BONNET

The bonnet in this example was made used for Mary in the production *Tom Sawyer* (Figure 9-1).

Figure 9-1 Costume Design for Mary in *Tom Sawyer*.

PROCEDURE FOR MAKING A BONNET

Materials Required:

- Straw wefts or a straw hat
- Pattern paper
- Sewing machine
- Scissors
- Container for water
- Needle and thread
- Fabric, lace trim, and ribbon
- Wig comb

Step One: Preparing Pattern and Straw Braids

- Make a pattern for both a straw brim (Figure 9-2c) and fabric cap.
- Undo the straw-hat braids (Figure 9-2a), and soak the braids in cold water for 30 minutes to straighten them (Figure 9-2b). Then drain the water, and let them dry. If you purchase the straw braids, they will not be as curly, so you won't need to soak them in water. You may simply steam or iron them instead.

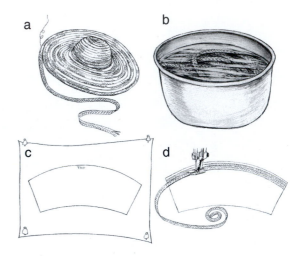

Figure 9-2 (a) Undo the braids of a straw hat. (b) Soak the straw braids in water. (c) Create a bonnet pattern. (d) Sew the straw braids to the pattern.

- Place a braid horizontally on the paper pattern $\frac{1}{2}''$ in from the outer edge of the pattern, and sew it with a sewing machine with large straight stitches (Figure 9-2d). Stop both ends of the braids $\frac{1}{4}''$ from the outer edges of the pattern to reduce bulkiness around the edge. Overlap each braid $\frac{1}{8}''$ when you connect them while sewing. Continue until the entire pattern is covered with braids. Tear the paper pattern off after the sewing is done.

- Finish off the outer edges on the brim by attaching two continuous braids to both sides of the brim (Figure 9-3a).

a

b Attach to Fabric Cap

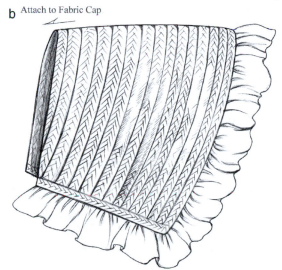

Figure 9-3 (a) Sew two continuous braids on both sides of the brim. (b) Attach the ruffle trim to the brim.

- Attach a ruffle of lace fabric trim to the front edge of the brim (Figure 9-3b).

Step Two: Creating the Fabric Cap and Attaching it to the Straw Brim

- Cut the fabric according to the paper cap pattern to make a mobcap. Sew two parallel gathering stitches along the circular edge of the fabric (Figure 9-4a).

- Sew a piece of lace material on the right (outside) side of the cap at the center back (Figure 9-4a).
- Pull the gathering threads to gather the fabric cap until it fits over the straw brim (Figures 9-4b–c). Sew the fabric cap to the straw brim.
- Sew a wig comb inside the bonnet, and attach lace and ribbon to complete the bonnet.

  The completed bonnet is shown in Figure 9-5.

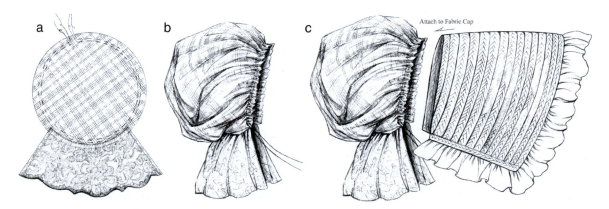

Figure 9-4 (a) Attach lace to the cap, and sew gathering stitches along the circular edge. (b) Gather the edge of the fabric cap. (c) Fit the fabric cap and straw brim together.

Figure 9-5 (a) Completed bonnet. (b) Production photo of Mary wearing the bonnet in *Tom Sawyer. Directed by Brenda Hubbard. Scenic design by Mark C. Zetterberg. Lighting Design by Dutch Fritz. Costume design by Tan Huaixiang. Central Washington University Theatre Arts Department presentation.*

Figure 9-6 Costume design for *Look Homeward, Angel*.

ALTERING HORSEHAIR HATS

Horsehair hats are made of many horsehair braids sewn together; they come in a variety of colors. They are lightweight, durable, voluminous, and extremely flexible.

USING TWO HORSEHAIR HATS

The hat that was made for *Look Homeward Angel* (Figure 9-6) used two horsehair hats: one as a base and the other unwound into braids. Adding more horsehair braids to the base in an asymmetrical fashion achieves a new style. The new-style horsehair hat in the demo was created by Dvorah Neubauer, a BFA design and technology student.

PROCEDURE FOR ALTERING A HORSEHAIR HAT 1

Materials Required:

- Two horsehair hats
- Pattern paper
- Seam ripper
- Scissors
- Sewing machine and thread
- Millinery wire
- Artificial flowers
- Needle and thread
- Hat block or wig block

Step One: Creating a Pointed Brim

- Pull from stock or purchase two horsehair hats in the same color. Undo the braids on one hat. The other hat is your base hat.

- Sew a piece of millinery wire to the base hat away from the edge of the brim. Bend both sides of the brim up to create a Napoleon bicorn hat (Figures 9-7a–b).

- Drape the pattern of the new style you would like to create over the base hat. Outline the positions of each braid on the pattern (Figure 9-7c).
- Following the pattern, sew horsehair braids on to the pattern, overlapping each braid $\frac{1}{8}''$ until the entire pattern is covered and then remove the paper pattern (Figure 9-7d).
- Attach this new piece to the back of the base hat with machine stitches (Figure 9-7e).
- Sew a piece of wire to the new piece to add strength to the hat (Figure 9-7e).
- Tack half the front brim down to the crown to lower the front brim (Figure 9-7f).

Step Two: Decorating the Hat

- Attach artificial flowers on to the hat to complete it (Figure 9-8).

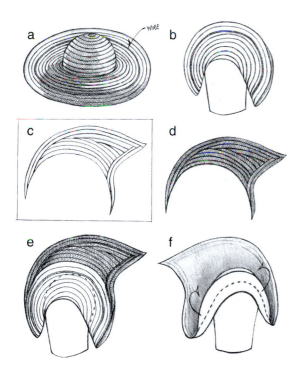

Figure 9-7 (a) Sew millinery wire on the brim of the base hat away from the edge. (b) Bend the base hat into a Napoleon-hat style. (c) Draw a pattern on a piece of pattern paper. (d) Sew the horsehair braids on to the pattern shape. (e) Attach the new piece to the back side of the brim, and sew a wire to the new piece for support. (f) Tack the front brim down to crown (dotted line represents the edge of the brim after it is folded in).

Figure 9-8 Completed hat.

ENLARGING A HORSEHAIR HAT

In this example, a nylon horsehair hat was made for *Amadeus* by adding width to the brim of an existing hat (Figure 9-9). The hat was still lightweight. Flowers in this example were made from scratch.

Figure 9-9 Costume design for *Amadeus* (hat is marked with arrow).

PROCEDURE FOR ALTERING A HORSEHAIR HAT 2

Materials Required:

- Three nylon horsehair hats
- Millinery wire
- Sewing machine
- Serger
- Scissors
- Needle and thread
- Fabric and ribbons

Step One: Creating a Large Brim

- Obtain three nylon horsehair hats.
- Undo two of the hats into braids/wefts (Figure 9-10a). The third hat is your base.
- Machine-sew the braids/wefts in rows on to the base hat to enlarge its brim (Figure 9-10b).

  Overlap each braid ⅛″ and continue to sew the wefts until the brim is the desired size.
- Sew three or four rows of millinery wire around the brim with machine zigzag stitches to support and control the brim (Figure 9-10b). Overlap the end of the each wire about 1½–2″. Cross-wires can be added for reinforcement if needed.

Step Two: Shaping and Decorating the Hat

- Turn one side of the brim upward. The rows of wires will support the brim's shape.
- Make some fabric flowers and ribbons, and attach them to the hat for decoration.
  1. Cut fabric into bias strips, fold each strip in half lengthwise, and round

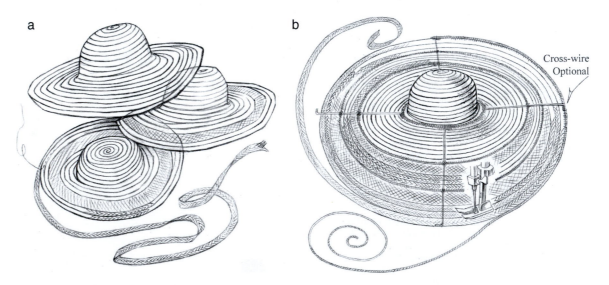

Figure 9-10 (a) Undo the horsehair braids from two of the hats. (b) Sew the braids to the base hat to create a large-brimmed hat; wire the brim to stabilize its shape.

off the two ends with scissors (Figure 9-11a).

2. Slightly gather the seam allowance, and serge it. Then roll the material to create roses (Figure 9-11b); secure each rose with tacking stitches in the seam allowance.

The completed hat is shown in Figure 9-12.

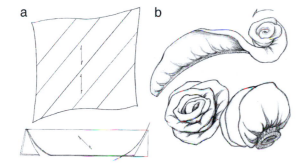

Figure 9-11 (a) Cut the fabric into bias strips; fold the strips and round off the ends. (b) Create fabric roses.

Figure 9-12 Production photo of *Amadeus*. *Amadeus* played by *Kareem Bandealy*; *Constanze* played by *Catherine Johnson*. Directed by *Donald Seay*. Scenic and lighting design by *Joseph Rusnock*. Costume design by *Tan Huaixiang*. University of Central Florida Conservatory Theatre presentation.

Chapter 10   Crowns

MAKING AN EGYPTIAN CROWN

The Egyptian crown in this example was created for Lord Edgar, an Egyptian priest, in *The Mystery of Irma Vep* (Figure 10-1). The shape of the crown was based on the blue war crown worn by Egyptian Pharaohs and made from molded Fosshape.

PROCEDURE FOR MAKING AN EGYPTIAN CROWN

Materials Required:

- Fosshape #300 or #600
- Mold for creating the crown (a tailor's ham and sofa-cushion foam were used for this crown)
- Steam iron
- Scissors
- Push or straight pins
- Sewing machine
- Needle and thread
- Outer fabric
- Lining fabric (e.g., felt)

Figure 10-1 Costume design for *The Mystery of Irma Vep*.

- Fabric tacky glue
- Trim and decorations

Step One: Creating the Foundation for the Crown

- Make a foundation for the crown from Fosshape, following the instructions for creating a wig base (see Chapter 3).

Step Two: Creating the Mold for the Crown

A large tailor's ham is used for the basic shape of the Egyptian crown; the ham's surface is round and hard enough to mold the Fosshape over.

- Cut a curved foam strip from sofa-cushion foam (this foam is firm and flexible), and fit it around the tailor's ham to make the crown deeper; glue the ends of the foam (Figures 10-2a–c). Secure the strip around the ham with masking tape (Figure 10-2d).

Step Three: Molding the Crown

- Cut a piece of Fosshape 4″ larger then the tailor's ham. Drape the Fosshape over the ham, smooth out the wrinkles, and pin edges of the Fosshape to the table away from the bottom of the ham (Figure 10-3a). (The Fosshape will shrink when is heated, and the pins will keep the Fosshape in place.)
- Steam the Fosshape on the ham from the center down, manipulating the Fosshape so there are no wrinkles at the bottom and the flatten surface around the bottom crown (Figures 10-3a–b).
- After this first shell-like structure is complete, repeat the same steps to make another shell.

Step Four: Covering and Decorating the Crown

- Fit the two shells over the crown foundation before covering them with fabric.
- Spray each shell with glue, and cover it with fabric. (This example used dyed Egyptian design fabric highlighted with gold glitter paint.)

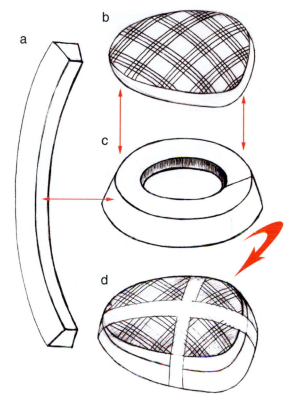

Figure 10-2 (a) Cut a curved strip of sofa-cushion foam. (b) Take a tailor's ham. (c) Glue the ends of the foam strip ends together to form a ring around the tailor's ham; this adds height to the ham. (d) Tape the tailor's ham and foam strip together to form the mold for the Egyptian crown.

- After the two shells are covered with fabric, sew their edges together.
- Place the shell-crown over the foundation, and sew the bottom to the foundation.
- Trim the crown with gold trim for a nice finish. You can attach a rubber

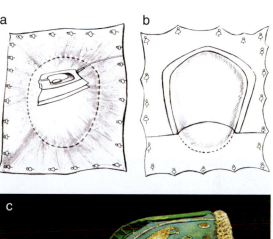

Figure 10-3 (a) Drape a piece of Fosshape over the mold and pin its edges to the table; iron and steam the Fosshape. (b) The crown shape outlined in the hardened Fosshape. (c) Completed crown.

snake to the center front of the crown as a decoration.

The completed Egyptian crown is shown in Figures 10-3c and 10-4 to 10-5. Another crown made using this technique is shown in Figure 10-6.

Figure 10-4 Completed Egyptian crown.

Figure 10-5 Production photo of the crown in *The Mystery of Irma Vap*. *Orlando Civic Theatre presentation (photo from the Orlando Repertory Theatre's collection).*

Figure 10-6 Oversized Fosshape crown made for *Until You Have Faces*.

MAKING MEDIEVAL EUROPEAN CROWNS

Crowns can be made from Fosshape, Wonderflex, or buckram. Fosshape is hardened with steaming and ironing. Wonderflex is softened with hot water and then shaped into the desired form. Buckram is ready to use; simply cut it into the desired form.

The crowns here were made for *The Lion in Winter* (Figure 10-7). The shapes and colors of the crowns were designed to reflect the statuses and personalities of the characters in the play.

Figure 10-7 Costume designs for *The Lion in Winter*.

PROCEDURE FOR CREATING A EUROPEAN CROWN

Materials Required:

- Pattern paper
- Pencil
- Buckram
- Scissors
- Knife
- Millinery wire
- Sewing machine
- Needle and thread
- Gold and silver leaf
- Gold trims (cords)
- Jewels
- Liquid shoe dye (for shadows)
- Paint brush
- Clear fabric tacky glue

Step One: Creating the Patterns and Cutting Out the Buckram

- Outline a crown on a piece of pattern paper with pencil.
- Then trace the crown pattern on a piece of buckram, and cut it out. Because of the detailed shapes on the crowns, you may need to use a knife.

Step Two: Assembling the Pieces

- Overlap the center back seam of the crown, and sew it together by hand.
- Wire both top and bottom edges of the crown with millinery wire. The bottom edges can be sewn with a sewing machine; however, due to the shaped edges on the crown, the top edges has to be hand sewn using buttonhole stitches and double threads.

Step Three: Covering the Crown

- Cover the buckram surface. Various materials can be used: fabric, spray paint, acrylic paint, paper, or gold or silver leaf. (The crowns in Figure 10-8 were covered with gold and silver leaf.)
- Decorate the crown with cord and flat trims and jewels. This adds a 3-D texture.
- Add shadows and highlights using liquid brown and black shoe dyes mixed together. This emphasizes the contours and details of the crowns and gives the crown a metal look.
- You can line the back of the crown with felt.

The competed crowns are shown in Figures 10-8 to 10-9. Two other crowns in this style are shown in Figure 10-10.

Figure 10-8 Crowns made for *The Lion in Winter*.

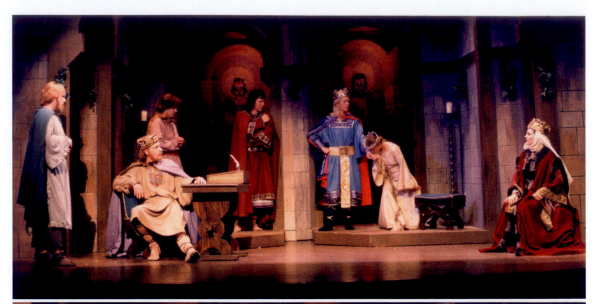

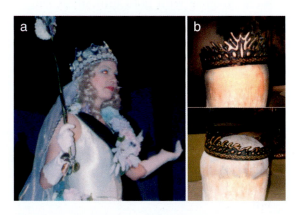

Figure 10-10 (a) Crown made of buckram and covered with fabric and trims for *Elves and Shoemaker*. (b) Crown made of Fosshape with hot glue 3-D form designs for *Till We Have Faces*.

Figure 10-9 Production photos showing crowns in *The Lion in Winter*. *Directed by W. Vosco Call. Scenic design by Sid Perkes. Lighting design by Kim Brandt. Costume design by Tan Huaixiang. Utah State University and Old Lyric Repertory Company presentation.*

Chapter 11   Turbans and Hoods

MAKING A ROUND TURBAN

An Eastern-style turban was made for one of the three wise kings in *The Butterfingers Angel* (Figure 11-1). It was padded instead of wrapped.

PROCEDURES FOR MAKING A ROUND TURBAN

Materials Required:

- An existing hat (an old hat with a brim)
- Hat block
- Foam strip
- Poly stuffing
- Fabric (matching the costume)
- Sewing machine
- Hy-Mark thread
- Chalk
- Needle and thread
- Scissors
- Decorative pearls
- Plastic needlepoint canvas

Step One: Creating a Foundation for the Turban

- Obtain a used and stiff hat of the proper size. Pull down the inside headband attached to the inside of the hat (Figure 11-2a). This headband will become the turban headband, but first it needs to be reinforced.

Figure 11-1 Costume design for *The Butterfingers Angel*.

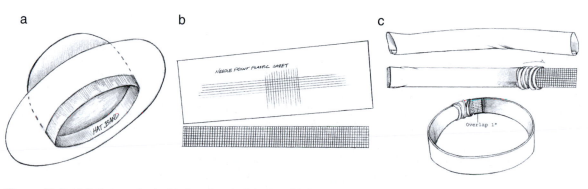

Figure 11-2 (a) Pull down the inside headband of the hat. (b) Cut a strip of plastic needlepoint canvas to reinforce the headband. (c) Sew the fabric into a tube, cover the plastic strip with fabric, overlap the ends to form a ring, and sew them together.

- Cut a strip of plastic needlepoint canvas the same length as the headband and $1/2''$ wider (Figure 11-2b). (The plastic strip is used on the headband because it won't stretch when it becomes wet from sweat and it supports the turban. Other waterproof materials such as Fosshape or Wonderflex will also work for this purpose.)
- Cut a piece of contrasting fabric the size of the plastic strip plus a $1/2''$ seam allowance on all edges. Fold the fabric lengthwise, right sides together, and machine stitch it into a tube (do not stitch the ends) (Figure 11-2c); then turn it inside out.
- Insert the plastic strip into the fabric tube; overlap the two ends of the plastic strip and fabric and hand-sew them together to form a ring (Figure 11-2c).

Step Two: Attaching the Fabric to the Foundation

- Cut a piece of turban fabric longer than the circumference of the finished turban (because the fabric will be gathered). For example, if the circumference at the widest part on the turban is 44″, the fabric should be at least 50″ long. Cut the fabric so that its width is the same as the height of the turban. The width of the fabric in this example is 16″. The

length and width of the fabric depend on the design and size of the finished turban.
- Machine stitch two parallel gathered stitch lines (large stitches) at the both top and bottom of the turban fabric (Figure 11-3a). If the turban fabric is heavy and bulky, zigzag stitch over a strong thread, such as Hy-Mark, to be used as a gathering thread. To do this, place the strong thread $1/8''$ above the

actual seam line, and use a large zigzag stitch over the thread to hold it in place. Sew the other zigzag stitching line above the first one.
- Machine stitch the center back seam of the fabric together with a $1/2''$ seam allowance, and then turn it inside out (Figure 11-3b). This turban fabric is now a tube. Make a little notch at the center front in the seam allowance to later match up with the foundation.

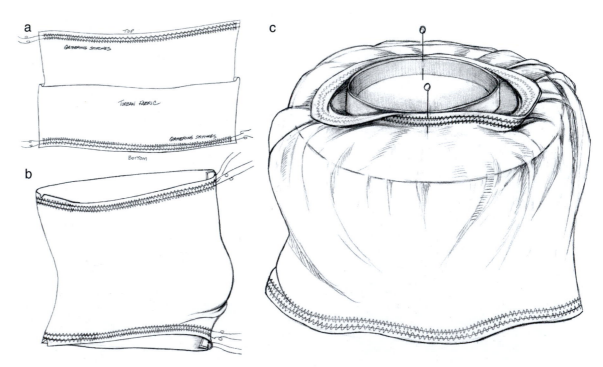

Figure 11-3 (a) Stitch two rows of gathering stitches at the top and bottom of the turban fabric. (b) Sew the center back seam of the turban fabric, and turn the fabric tube inside out. (c) Pin the fabric tube and turban foundation together at the center fronts and backs.

- Make two marks with chalk at the center front and back of the headband on the turban foundation, and place the foundation inside one end of the fabric tube, matching one chalk mark with the notch made previously on the tube and the other chalk mark with the seam.
- Pin these two spots down (where you matched the fronts and backs) (Figure 11-3c).
- Tie one end of the inserted strong gathering threads (Hy-Mark) in a knot, and pull the other end to gather the fabric until the fabric fits perfectly over the headband (do this to only ONE set of parallel zigzag stitches) (Figure 11-4a). The center pin will help distribute the fabric equally around the headband. Then place more pins around the headband to secure the fabric, and machine zigzag stitch the fabric tube and the foundation together around the entire middle of the headband circumference (Figure 11-4a).
- Place the plastic headband covered with contrasting fabric over the foundation headband and fabric, and hand-sew attach them together using vertical hem stitches and matching thread (Figure 11-4b). Also, sew a few tacking stitches around the edge of the headband.

Step Three: Padding the Turban

- Place the turban foundation (with the fabric tube attached to it) on a hat block, letting the fabric hang.
- Pad and stuff the turban. First, place a relatively large foam strip around the crown of the foundation on top of the brim to add solid volume. Then use poly stuffing to stuff the rest of the space on top of the foam until you get the desired shape (Figure 11-5a). The original brim of the hat will function as support for the padding. The amount of stuffing you use depends on the style of the hat.
- After the padding and stuffing are complete, pull the fabric tube over the padding.
- Tie a knot on one end of the other set of parallel zigzag stitches. Pull the two parallel threads to gather the fabric tube until it fits around the padding, and tie a knot to secure it. Make sure the gathers are evenly spread over the padding and then hand sew it down (Figure 11-5b).

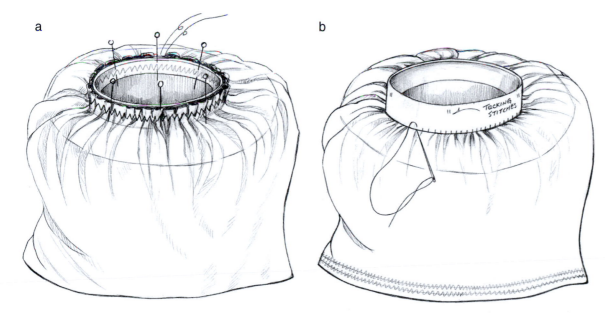

a   b

Figure 11-4 (a) Gather the fabric tube so that is fits the headband; sew it to the headband. (b) Hand-sew the fabric-covered plastic headband to the foundation headband.

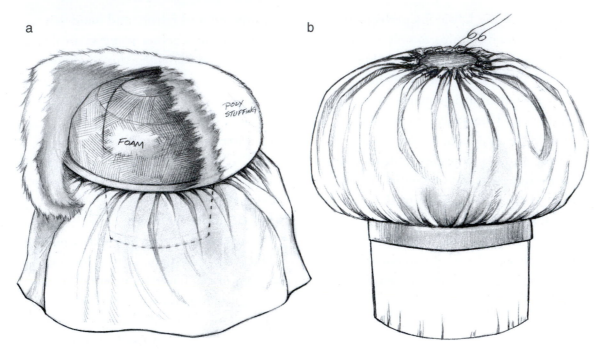

Figure 11-5 (a) Pad the turban with foam and poly stuffing. (b) Gather the top end of the turban fabric over the stuffing, and stitch it down.

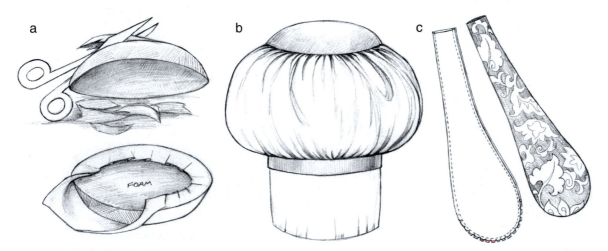

Figure 11-6 (a) Carve the foam into a dome shape, and cover it with fabric. (b) Attach the dome top to the turban body. (c) Notch the seam allowance of the lappets, and turn them right side out.

Step Four: Finishing the Turban

The dome-shaped top of the turban is created by carving a piece of 1″-thick foam or stuffing the turban with poly stuffing (foam was used for this turban). The dome shape is then covered with fabric that contrasts with the turban fabric.

- Carve the dome shape from foam (Figure 11-6a).
- Cover the foam with fabric by wrapping the fabric around the foam and gluing the seam allowance to the bottom of the foam (Figure 11-6a).
- Attach the dome on top of the turban with hand-sewn slip stitches (invisible stitches) (Figure 11-6b).
- Make two lappets with contrasting fabrics on either side: on one side use the turban fabric and on the other side use fabric that contrasts with the turban fabric. Place the right sides of the fabrics together, and sew them together with a ¼″ seam allowance. Make a few notches around the curve of the seam allowance to reduce the bulkiness of the inward seam allowance (Figure 11-6c).
- Turn the lappets right side (Figure 11-6c) out and press it.
- Attach the two lappets on the inside of the headband, positioning them behind

the actor's ears (placement will depend on the design style).

- Finally, sew some pearls on the turban to decorate it.

The completed turban is shown in Figures 11-7 and 11-8.

Figure 11-7 Completed round turban.

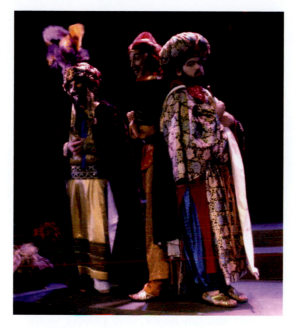

Figure 11-8 Production photo of the turban in *The Butterfingers Angel*. Three Kings played by (from left to right) Daniel Robbins, Jordan Reeves, and Matt Burdelsky. Directed by Mark Brotherton. Scenic design by Richard Dunham. Lighting design by Tom Begley. Costume design by Tan Huaixiang. University of Central Florida Conservatory Theatre presentation.

MAKING A WRAPPED HARD-BODY TURBAN

A hard-body turban is made with turban fabric wrapped over a turban base. This base is an excellent way to support and maintain the shape of a wrapped or draped turban. The actor handles the turban like a hat and so it is easy to put on and take off. The base can also be used for any headdress or wig. It can be blocked with either buckram or Fosshape by pulling, manipulating, stretching, and smoothing the material to form a base over a hat block. For the wrapped hard-body turban in *Merchant of Venice* (Figure 11-9), buckram was used.

In this example, the turban base is lined with felt, an excellent fabric for this purpose. Felt is not slippery, absorbs better than other fabrics, and provides a cushion for the actor's head. Hat, headdress, and wig bases can all be lined with felt.

Figure 11-9 Costume design for *Merchant of Venice*.

There are two methods for lining the base: (1) by making the lining in pieces and seaming the pieces together to fit inside the base (see Figure 8-31 for instructions on making a seamed lining) and (2) by blocking a piece of felt over a hat block and fitting it inside the base. Because felt has no grain, it is easy to pull and stretch over a hat block to smooth out wrinkles when it is damp. After it dries, it retains the shape and can be attached to the inside of the base. If the headdress is going to be lined with felt, ½″ extra needs to be added to the headdress circumference because the bulkiness of the felt will slightly reduce its finished circumference.

PROCEDURE FOR MAKING A WRAPPED HARD-BODY TURBAN

Materials Required:

- Hat block (two are best, one smaller than the other)
- Plastic wrap or foil
- Buckram
- Piece of elastic about ½ × 24″ (to tie the buckram on the hat block)
- Scissors
- Felt for lining
- Water in a spray bottle
- Large zip-lock plastic bag (to seal the wet buckram)

- Container for water
- Push pins
- Piece of 1 × 2″ elastic strip (for the back opening of the base)
- Millinery wire
- Sewing machine
- Needle and thread
- Clear fabric tacky glue
- Spray adhesive
- Steamer or iron
- Corset boning
- Fabric

Step One: Creating the Turban Base

- Cover the hat block with plastic wrap or foil for protection.
- Cut a 22 × 22″ square piece of buckram (a deeper crown will need a larger square). For solid support, use two layers of one-ply buckram or one layer of two-ply buckram.
- Wet the entire buckram piece thoroughly under the faucet, or soak it in a bowl of water. Then put it in a large zip-lock bag and wait 2 minutes (Figure 11-10a).
- After 2 minutes, the stiff buckram will become soft, flexible, and ready to block over a hat block (this method is used to block a hat crown as well). Drape the soft buckram over the hat block, and tie a piece of elastic around the bottom

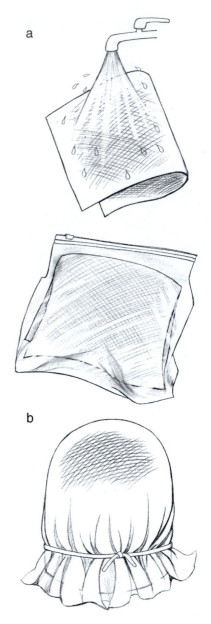

Figure 11-10 (a) Seal the wet buckram in a zip-lock bag. (b) Tie the buckram to the hat block.

of the buckram to secure it (Figure 11-10b).

- Pull and manipulate the buckram to smooth out the wrinkles around the elastic string. Buckram is a loosely woven material, so it will easily smooth out. Insert push pins, placed close together, just under the elastic to hold the stretched buckram. Trim off the excess buckram below the push pins (Figure 11-11a), and let it dry overnight.

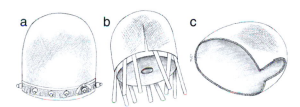

Figure 11-11 (a) Block and pin the buckram; trim off the excess edge. (b) Cut a slash and insert boning pieces between the dried buckram base and the hat block to separate them. (c) Cut the back opening of the base in a U-shape; wire the bottom edge of the base.

- When the buckram is dry, it will be stiff like a shell. The glue sizing already present on the buckram will also cause it to stick to the hat block. Slash the center of the bottom edge $2\frac{1}{2}''$ up, and insert a bundle of boning to aid in the release of the buckram turban base from the hat block (Figure 11-11b).

- Cut the back slash into an upside-down U-shaped opening (Figure 11-11c). Try the turban base on the actor's head.
- Wire the edge of the turban base by hand using buttonhole stitches (also called blanket stitches) or by machine using zigzag stitches (Figure 11-11c).

Step Two: Lining the Turban Base

- Cut a $22 \times 22''$ square of felt. Use a spray bottle to dampen the felt thoroughly (but not so it is dripping wet) with water (Figure 11-12a).
- If possible, take a hat block one size smaller than the hat block you used for the buckram base (because the lining circumference is smaller than the circumference of the outer base). Place the damp felt on the hat block and tie a piece of elastic around the bottom edge. Steam it from the top down, at the same time pulling, stretching, and manipulating the edge of the felt below the elastic string until the wrinkles disappear (Figure 11-12b). Insert push pins below the elastic, trim off the excess edge below the pins, and let the felt dry.

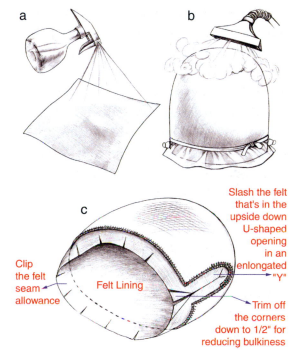

Slash the felt that's in the upside down U-shaped opening in an enlongated "Y"

Clip the felt seam allowance

Felt Lining

Trim off the corners down to 1/2" for reducing bulkiness

Figure 11-12 (a) Dampen the felt with water. (b) Block the felt lining over a hat block while steaming it. (c) Glue the felt lining on to the buckram base and clip the lining seam allowance; cut an elongated Y in the felt U-opening and trim off the corners below the U-opening.

- The dry felt will be soft. Carefully remove it from the block.
- Apply an even coat of spray adhesive to the inside surface of the buckram base. Place the felt crown inside the buckram base. Press and smooth it from the center out, until the felt is evenly glued to the entire base (Figure 11-12c).

- Trim off the excess felt, leaving a 1″ seam allowance around the edge of the buckram base.
- Clip ½″ of the 1″ seam allowance to help flatten it when you later glue it down over the base (Figure 11-12c).
- Slash the upside-down U-opening in the felt into an elongated Y. Trim the two corners below the U-opening to reduce bulkiness (Figure 11-12c).
- Wrap the 1″ seam allowance over the edge of the base and glue it down with fabric tacky glue. Figure 11-13a shows how to fold the seam allowance around the corners.
- Sew the 1 × 2″ piece of elastic to the bottom of the U-shaped opening as a size adjustor (Figure 11-13b).

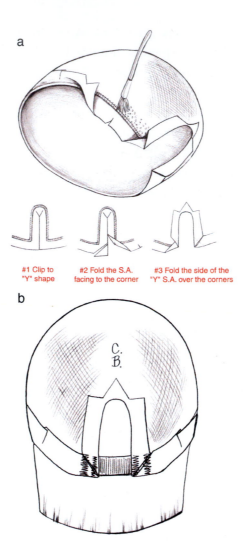

#1 Clip to "Y" shape   #2 Fold the S.A. facing to the corner   #3 Fold the side of the "Y" S.A. over the corners

Figure 11-13 (a) Fold the felt lining seam allowance up, and glue it to the buckram base. (b) Sew elastic across the bottom of the U-opening.

Step Three: Wrapping a Turban over the Buckram Base

The turban base is wrapped with a long strip of fabric (sewn into a tube), which can be pulled from stock or purchased. In this example, striped fabric cut on the bias was used.

- Cut the fabric into bias strips (Figure 11-14a), and piece all the strips together into one long continuous strip of the desired length. Fold this long strip in half lengthwise with the right sides of the fabric together (wrong sides facing out).
- Cut one end of the fabric strip into the desired decorative shape; cut the other end into a pointed shape (Figure 11-14b).
- Pin the edges of the fabric strip together, and sew them with a ¼″ seam allowance, leaving the middle 4″ unstitched (so that later you can turn the strip right side out). The fabric strip is now a long tube (Figure 11-14b).
- Baste a gathering line on the decorative end of the fabric tube. Pull the thread to gather it.
- Place the gathered end (the decorative end) of the fabric tube 4″ above the turban base's center front edge, and sew a tacking stitch affixing the gathering line to the base. Pull the rest of the fabric tube across the top of the turban

a

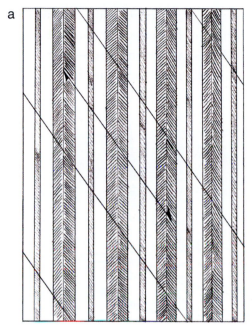

b

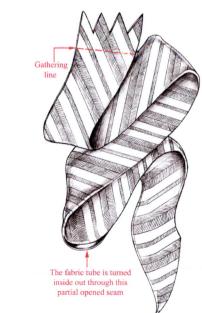

Gathering
line

The fabric tube is turned
inside out through this
partial opened seam

Figure 11-14 (a) Cut the turban fabric into bias strips. (b) Sew the bias strips into a long tube with a decorative end and a pointed end.

base toward the center back, and tack it down at the top edge of the buckram base's U-shaped opening (Figure 11-15).

- Crisscross the fabric tube at the front of the turban base, and bring it to the back. Keep the fabric tube about $\frac{1}{2}$–1″ below the edge of the buckram base when you wrap it over the bottom of the turban base. Alter the wrapping direction for each wrap; overlap each wrap in a crisscross fashion from the bottom up (in the front) (Figure 11-16). Longer tubes create more layers of crisscross than shorter tubes. Continue wrapping the fabric and crisscrossing it at the front until the desired shape is achieved.
- When you near the end of the fabric tube, pull the pointed end through the last layer of wrapping, and let it stand on top of the turban as decoration (Figure 11-17). Secure it to the turban base with hand-sewn tacking stitches.
- Make tacking stitches between the overlapping layers (hide the stitches in the folds) to secure the wraps and

a

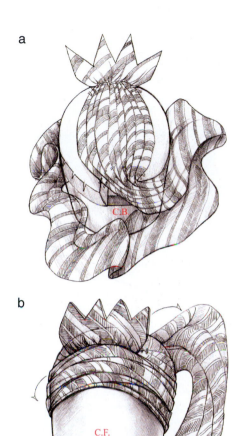

CB

b

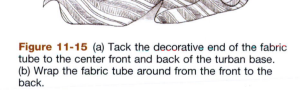

C.F.

Figure 11-15 (a) Tack the decorative end of the fabric tube to the center front and back of the turban base. (b) Wrap the fabric tube around from the front to the back.

a

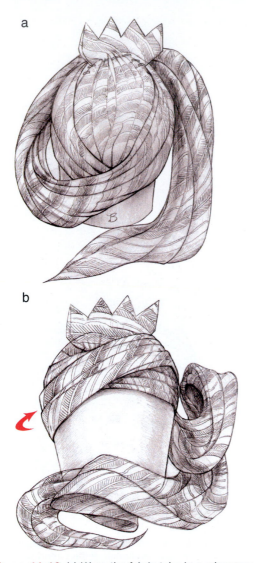

b

Figure 11-16 (a) Wrap the fabric tube in a crisscross fashion back to front. (b) Wrap the fabric tube across the front at an angle to achieve the crisscross style.

a

Alter the direction of each wrap to create a criss-cross fashion at center front

b

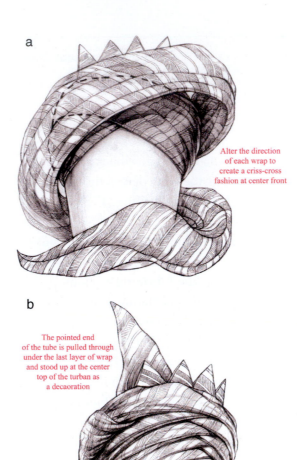

The pointed end of the tube is pulled through under the last layer of wrap and stood up at the center top of the turban as a decaoration

Criss-cross Front

Figure 11-17 (a) Continue to wrap the fabric tube in alternative crisscrosses until all the fabric is wrapped. (b) Pull the pointed end of the tube through the last wrap, and let it stand on top of the turban, following the design.

prevent them from coming undone during performances (Figure 11-18).

• Add decorations such as jewels, pins, and feathers to complete the turban.

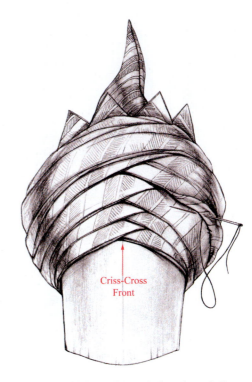

Criss-Cross Front

Figure 11-18 Make tacking stitches through the wrapped layers for security.

Figure 11-19 Production photo of turban in *Merchant of Venice. The Prince of Morocco played by Marvin Denman. Directed by Wesley Van Tassel. Scenic and Lighting design by Mark Zetterburg. Costume design by Tan Huaixiang. Central Washington University Theatre Arts Department presentation.*

with a single triangle-shaped piece of velour fabric attached to an elastic headband without any seams and an edged finish. Velour is a great material for one-size-fits-all turbans. First, the raw edges of the fabric don't need to be finished because the fabric will curve back, forming a natural rolled edge without fraying. Second, the material's four-way stretch easily adjusts to fit over any head size.

PROCEDURE FOR MAKING A SOFT-BODY TURBAN

Materials Required:

- Stretchy velour fabric
- Decorative Trim
- Scissors
- Sewing machine
- Needle and thread
- Hat block
- 1"-wide elastic strip

Step One: Making a Turban Pattern, and Cutting Out the Fabric

Adjustability is the key for one-size-fits-all turbans. This turban tries to achieve simplicity and elegance. An organic triangle-shaped turban pattern was developed. A scarf-like draping was created on the turban pattern; this

MAKING A SOFT-BODY TURBAN

There were 11 characters who wore turbans in the ball scene in the production *Once on This Island*. It was challenging making all these turbans because of limited workers and construction time.

Furthermore, those turbans required quick costume changes. One-size-fits-all stretch turbans were developed. Each turban was wrapped to itself without a hard foundation; hence, these are called soft-body turbans.

Stretchy velour fabric was used for the 11 turbans. Each turban was wrapped

Figure 11-20 Costume designs for *Once on This Island*.

draping scarf functions as a decoration as well as a size adjuster. The pattern is about 84″ wide (triangle base) and 40″ long (triangle height).

- Lay the pattern on the bias of the velour fabric. Cut it out (Figure 11-21). Velour fabric comes 60″ wide; the pattern is cut on the bias to fit the full length of the pattern on the material (the piece may be a little off the true bias line).

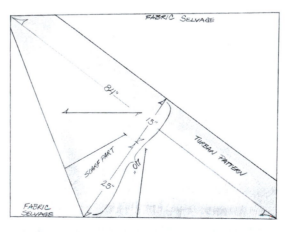

Figure 11-21 Lay the turban pattern on the fabric for cutting.

Step Two: Sewing the Trim and an Elastic Strip to the Turban Fabric

- Fold 2″ of the fabric's front edge to the wrong side of the fabric and pin it in place with straight pins (Figure 11-22a).
- Turn the fabric over to the right side; lay a piece of decorative trim (the length should fit from ear to ear) ½″ away from the front edge of turban fabric, and pin it down (Figure 11-22b). Sew it in the middle with machine tacking stitches every 3″. The back of the turban will be wrapped, so the untrimmed portion won't be seen.
- Cut a 1–24″ elastic strip to secure the turban to the actor's head.

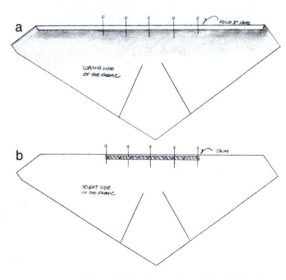

Figure 11-22 (a) Fold the front edge of the fabric to the wrong side of the fabric. (b) Pin the trim on the right side of the front turban fabric.

- Lay the turban fabric on a flat table with the wrong side facing up. Pin the middle of the elastic strip ¾″ away from the front edge of the turban fabric (Figure 11-23a).

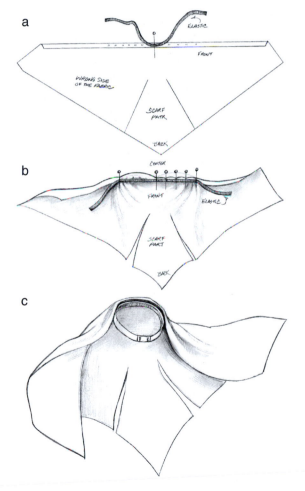

- Bring each end of the elastic strip to each side. Pull each side of the elastic strip ¾″ tighter than the fabric beneath it to achieve full elasticity from the strip. Distribute the tightness of the elastic equally with the fabric underneath it, and pin the stretched elastic strip along the edge of the turban fabric (Figure 11-23b). Sew only the portion of the elastic strip that equals the length of the trim (elastic is sewn on the wrong side and the trim is sewn on the right side); the rest will hang loose on both sides for adjustments; sew it with machine tacking stitches every 2½″. The unattached elastic strip left at each end will overlap each other from 1 to 2″, forming an elastic headband. Sew it together with machine tacking stitches (Figure 11-23c).

Step Three: Wrapping the Turban

- Place the elastic headband with attached turban fabric over a large hat block, which will provide ease on the elastic. Because an irregular shape exists on the side ends of the fabric, loosely roll the fabric in each end into a long tube for easy management and neatness (Figure 11-24a). The excess fabric on the side ends is kept because it adds fullness and volume to the turban.

Figure 11-23 (a) Pin the elastic strip to the center of the wrong side of the turban fabric. (b) Add more pins to the elastic strip. (c) Overlap the ends of the elastic strip to form a ring, and stitch them together.

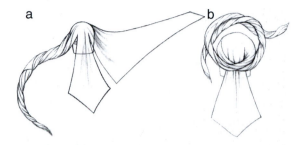

Figure 11-24 (a) Roll the side ends of the turban fabric into tubes. (b) Wrap the fabric tubes, crossing them in the back and front.

- After rolling the two side ends into tubes, cross the two fabric tubes at the center back over the draping scarf; then bring them up toward the center front, and cross them again (Figure 11-24b). Continue to bring them toward the center back and tie them in a square knot in the back (Figure 11-25).

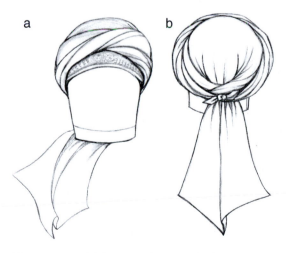

Figure 11-25 (a) Completed wrapped turban — front. (b) Tie the two ends of the fabric tubes in a knot at the back of the turban.

Step Four: Securing the Wrapped Fabric Tube with the Turban Crown

- Hand sew tacking stitches through the front and two sides of the wrapped materials to the crown to provide some stability. Leave the back of the wrapped fabric free so that you can make any adjustments that may be needed because of the actor's head size and hair style, but sew the knot and wrapped/crossed fabric in the back together. Pull the top of the scarf up to increase the turban size, and pull the scarf down to decrease the size.

The completed turbans are shown in Figure 11-26.

Figure 11-26 Production photos showing soft-body turban in *Once on This Island*. (b) *Storytellers, back row from left to right played by*: Jamie Phipps, Rita Coleman, and Erika Hallback. Patrice Lois Bell, middle front, played Andrea. Directed by Earl Weavor. Scenic design by Vandy Woods. Lighting design by David Upton. Costume design by Tan Huaixiang. University of Central Florida Conservatory Theatre presentation.

MAKING MEDIEVAL CHAPERON HOODS

In *Robin Hood*, all the characters needed headdresses, most of them medieval chaperon hoods (Figure 11-27). Making the chaperon hoods became a class assignment in my Costume Construction class, each student being required to make a medieval chaperon for this production. Each chaperon has a long liripipe/tail and a draped shoulder cape with decorative edges in a dagged (intricate), scalloped, or leaf-shaped pattern. They were made from rough textured drapery and colorful contrasting fabrics and were completely lined. The students did a great job making them.

ROBIN HOOD

LITTLE JOHN

WILL SCARLET

ALLEN O'DALE

MOTHER MEG

ROBIN HOOD
CWU THEATRE ARTS DEPARTMENT

Figure 11-27 Costume design for *Robin Hood*.

PROCEDURE FOR MAKING CHAPERON HOODS

Materials Required:

- Loosely woven rough-textured fabrics (outer material)
- Heavy knit fabric (drapes well) in contrasting colors (lining material)
- Pattern paper
- Scissors
- Sewing machine
- Fabric markers or chalk

Step One: Creating Patterns for the Chaperon Hoods

- Make a pattern for the chaperon hoods. The hood size and shape is determined by the following head and neck measurements: from the center top of the head down to the front neck base and back neck base, the head and neck circumferences, and from shoulder to shoulder across the front and back. The hood should be loose-fitting. The pattern shown in Figure 11-28 is one

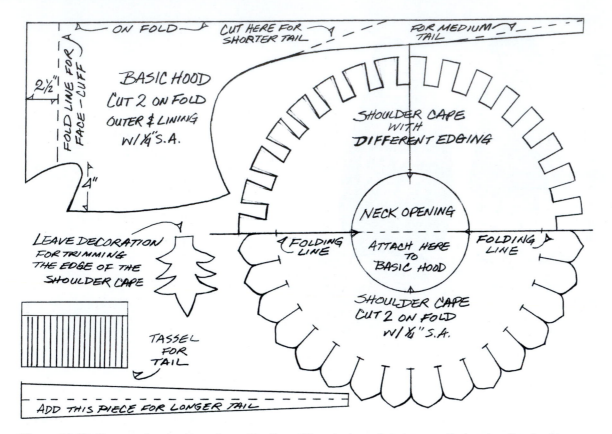

ON FOLD

CUT HERE FOR SHORTER TAIL

FOR MEDIUM TAIL

2½"

FOLD LINE FOR FACE - CUFF

BASIC HOOD
CUT 2 ON FOLD
OUTER & LINING
W/¼" S.A.

4"

SHOULDER CAPE
WITH
DIFFERENT EDGING

NECK OPENING

ATTACH HERE
TO
BASIC HOOD

FOLDING LINE

FOLDING LINE

LEAVE DECORATION
FOR TRIMMING
THE EDGE OF THE
SHOULDER CAPE

SHOULDER CAPE
CUT 2 ON FOLD
W/¼" S.A.

TASSEL
FOR
TAIL

ADD THIS PIECE FOR LONGER TAIL

Figure 11-28 Chaperon-hood pattern pieces. The three different edges of choices are displayed on the shoulder cape pattern; use only one edge in any chaperon hood (mirror the preferred choice to get the whole pattern).

size fits all and is developed in two parts: the basic hood with tail and the shoulder cape with decorative edge. Add a ¼" seam allowance to the pattern pieces.

- Lay the outer layer and lining fabrics on top of each other and place each pattern piece on top of the fabrics (Figure 11-29), pinning it down. Cut out the fabric.

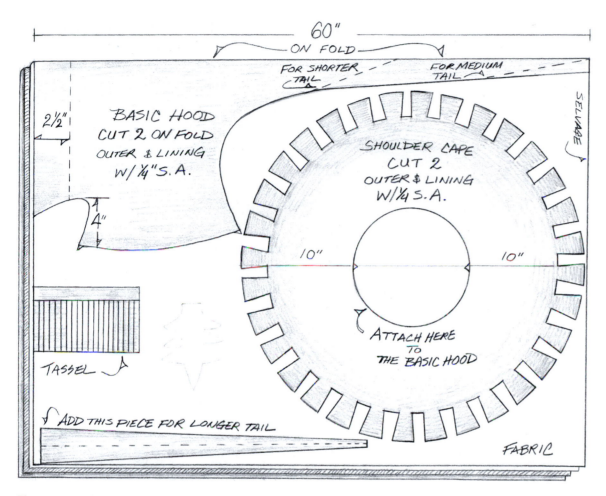

60"

ON FOLD

FOR SHORTER
TAIL

FOR MEDIUM
TAIL

SELVAGE

2½"

BASIC HOOD
CUT 2 ON FOLD
OUTER & LINING
W/¼" S.A.

4"

SHOULDER CAPE
CUT 2
OUTER & LINING
W/¼ S.A.

10"

10"

ATTACH HERE
TO
THE BASIC HOOD

TASSEL

ADD THIS PIECE FOR LONGER TAIL

FABRIC

Figure 11-29 Lay the pattern pieces on top of the fabrics.

a

BASIC HOOD

#1 SEW CENTER
SEAM

TAIL

LINING FABRIC
OUTER FABRIC

b

BASIC
HOOD
LINING

#2 PRESS THE
SEAM ALLOWANCE
TOWARD
ONE SIDE

Figure 11-30 (a) Sew the front open seam of the hood together. (b) Press the seam flat toward one side.

Step Two: Sewing Hood Fabric Pieces Together

- With the right sides of the fabrics together, pin the front open seam of the hood outer layer and lining together and machine stitch them (with ¼″ seam allowance) (Figure 11-30a).
- Open the fabric and press the seam allowance flat toward one side (Figure 11-30b).

- Fold both the outer and lining hood fabrics in half with the right sides of the fabrics together. Match and pin the center seam first; then pin the rest of the seam allowances together, except the neck base seams. Machine stitch the seam allowances (Figure 11-31a). Fold the seam allowance directly on the stitching line toward one side and press it with an iron. You may choose to cut

the back portion of the lining tail off to reduce the bulk when you later stuff the lining tail into the outer tail (Figure 11-31a).

- Trim off the front opening seam corner (Figure 11-31a).
- Turn the outer hood fabric right side out from the neck opening, and pull it over the lining piece. Insert the lining tail into the hood tail. Press all the seams flat. Machine zigzag stitch the bottom neck-base seams of the outer fabric and lining together (Figure 11-31b).
- Slash some of both the lining and outer fabrics into strips, and bundle them together to create a tassel. Stitch the tassel to the end of the tail (Figure 11-31b).

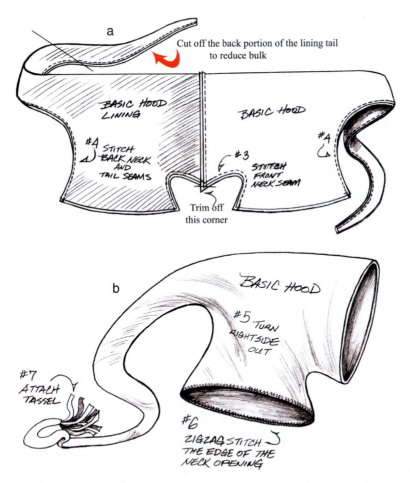

Figure 11-31 (a) Fold the hood piece in half, and sew the front, back, and side seams together; trim the corner. (b) Turn the outer fabric right side out and over the lining fabric; machine zigzag stitch the neck base seam, and attach the fabric tassel to the tail.

Step Three: Sewing the Shoulder Cape Together and Attaching the Shoulder Cape to the Hood

- With the right sides of the lining and shoulder cape fabrics together, pin the outer seams together and machine stitch them. Clip the inside corners, and trim the outside corners of each scalloped seam (Figure 11-32a).
- As in step two, press all the seams and turn the cape piece right side out. Fold directly on the stitching line and press the seam flat.

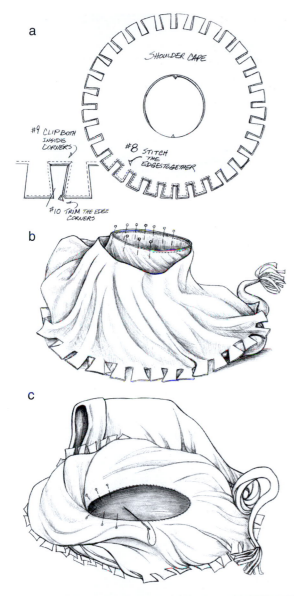

a

SHOULDER CAPE

#9 CLIP BOTH INSIDE CORNERS

#8 STITCH THE EDGES TOGETHER

#10 TRIM THE EDGE CORNERS

b

c

Figure 11-32 (a) Stitch the outer edge of the shoulder cape seam; clip the corners. (b) Sew the outer layer of shoulder cape to the hood neck seam. (c) Hand sew the lining of the shoulder cape to the hood.

- Insert the zigzag-stitched neck seam of the hood into the shoulder cape opening from the outer-fabric side (the right sides of the outer fabrics should be together). Let the shoulder cape lining hang free; you want to sew only the OUTER layer of the cape to the hood. Match the notches on the OUTER layer fabric cape with the front and back seams of the hood, pin them, and machine stitch them together (Figure 11-32b). Press the seam allowance toward the cape side.

- Pin the entire lining seam allowance on top of the seam joining the hood and outer layer of the cape (the seam you just made), and hand sew it with slanted hem stitches (Figure 11-32c). Press the seam flat.

The completed hoods are shown in Figures 11-33 to 11-34.

Figure 11-33 Completed chaperon hoods, made by Central Washington University Theatre Department students.

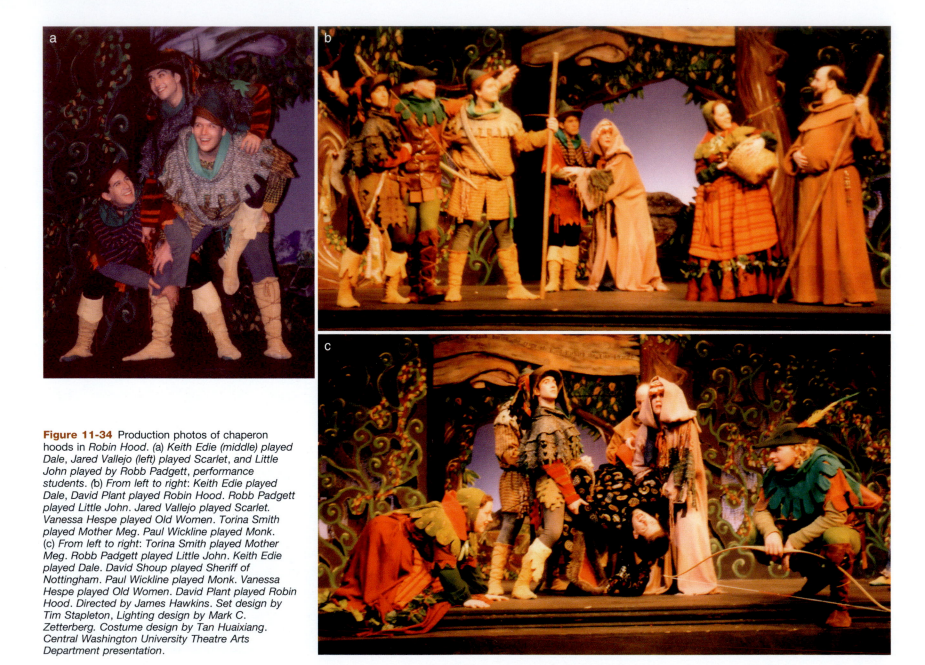

Figure 11-34 Production photos of chaperon hoods in *Robin Hood*. (a) Keith Edie (middle) played Dale, Jared Vallejo (left) played Scarlet, and Little John played by Robb Padgett, performance students. (b) From left to right: Keith Edie played Dale, David Plant played Robin Hood. Robb Padgett played Little John. Jared Vallejo played Scarlet. Vanessa Hespe played Old Women. Torina Smith played Mother Meg. Paul Wickline played Monk. (c) From left to right: Torina Smith played Mother Meg. Robb Padgett played Little John. Keith Edie played Dale. David Shoup played Sheriff of Nottingham. Paul Wickline played Monk. Vanessa Hespe played Old Women. David Plant played Robin Hood. Directed by James Hawkins. Set design by Tim Stapleton, Lighting design by Mark C. Zetterberg. Costume design by Tan Huaixiang. Central Washington University Theatre Arts Department presentation.

Chapter 12   Headdresses

MAKING EXOTIC HEADDRESSES

The musical production *Once on This Island* tells the mythical tale of a beautiful peasant girl (Ti Moune) who saves the life of a young Mulatto aristocrat (Daniel) after his car crashes near her rural village. Ti Moune pledges her own life to the god of Death in order to keep the boy alive; when he survives, Ti Moune becomes convinced that the powerful gods of her island have destined her to share his life. Against the warnings of her beloved parents, Ti Moune sets off on a journey to find Daniel and convince him that he must marry her; she becomes his mistress and he falls in love with her. But at a magnificent ball where she is presented to island society, Ti Moune learns that Daniel's parents have already arranged for their son's marriage to a girl from his own class. In despair and goaded on by the god of Death, Ti Moune tries to kill Daniel, but at the last moment her love for him triumphs. Ti Moune fulfills her promise to the gods, proving the power of love by giving her life in exchange for Daniel's. At the end of the play, Ti Moune becomes a tree.

From the director's notes:
One man. Two drums. He calls the community, and they respond. Some talk of the day's events. Some share gossip heard on the road. Some simply dance to his musical beat that speaks to their souls. All of them have stories. But the gods only hear the prayers of one small girl.

The way Ti Moune and her people pray to their gods Asaka (Earth), Erzulie (Love), Papa Ge (Death), and Agwe (Water) is emotional: the hopes and dreams of childhood, the barriers of class and race, the power of love and nature, the resignation of death, and the resurrection of life in the face of seemingly insurmountable obstacles.

I studied the visual elements of Caribbean culture, from Haitian paintings to festival costumes and masks, trying to imagine what the costumes might eventually look like on stage. Based on my research, the following concepts were established.

The costumes for *Once on This Island* portrayed Caribbean-influenced tropical patterns and colors in styles that appeared to be homemade by the characters. I used colorful and flavorful costumes that harmonized with Caribbean rhythms and culture by emphasizing texture, colors, primitive styles, simple forms, and movement.

The costumes for four gods and a tree focused on mystical and exaggerated silhouette forms. The gods' headdresses were especially larger than life to symbolize spiritual power of sending Ti Moune on a journey of love. Asaka's (god of Earth) costume was associated with the globe and its resources; Erzulie's (god of Love) costume was connected with the heart (Figure 12-1). Papa Ge's (god of Death) costume used a skull and dagger with red and black colors to symbolize blood and death; Agwe's (god of Water)

Figure 12-1 Costume design for the gods of Earth and Love in *Once on This Island*.

costume had aqua blue water waves to symbolize water (Figure 12-2). A tropical banyan tree with endless roots was used for Ti Mouue.

This section discusses the construction of three of the headdresses used for *Once on This Island*. These headdresses were class projects created by theater design students in my millinery class. Those students did excellent work, and I am very proud of them.

PROCEDURES FOR MAKING THE HEADDRESSES

Materials Required:

- Fosshape #300
- Hat blocks
- Steamer and iron
- Corset boning
- Scissors, thread, and needles
- Sewing machine
- Elastic

- Fleece and stretch velour fabrics
- Spray adhesive #77
- Fabric tacky glue
- Copper wire
- Foam cord (⅞″ thick)
- Premade curved wooden block (god of Water headdress)
- Screwdriver and screws
- Drill
- Pattern paper
- Premade wooden board support
- Rubber skull
- Acrylic paints and craft spray paints
- Large air-filled rubber ball
- Miscellaneous decorative craft stuff (e.g., artificial leaves and miniature animals)

Step One: Making the Headdress Support Base

Each headdress is attached to a support base made of Fosshape. As mentioned earlier, Fosshape is a better alternative than buckram because no wire is needed around the edges of the base and it is also waterproof.

- Cut a piece of Fosshape large enough to cover the entire hat block. Fosshape #300 requires two layers; #600 Fosshape requires only one layer to create a good stiff base. Place the Fosshape over the hat block, and tie it

Figure 12-2 Costume design for the gods of Water and Death in *Once on This Island.*

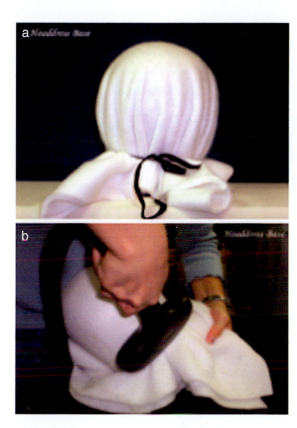

Figure 12-3 (a) Tie the Fosshape over a hat block. (b) Steam and smooth the Fosshape.

down at the very bottom with elastic string (Figure 12-3a).

• Steam the Fosshape from the top to bottom while manipulating the Fosshape with your hands to smooth out the wrinkles that appear around the bottom of the base (Figure 12-3b).

• The steaming will make the Fosshape semi-hard. To make an even harder and stiffer shell base, next use a steam iron to iron the Fosshape. Put a piece of thin muslin under the iron while you iron so that the Fosshape doesn't make the iron sticky

(Figure 12-4a). Be careful — too much ironing can cause the Fosshape to become too hard to sew.

- After the entire base becomes hard, trim off the excess material at the bottom of the base (Figure 12-4b).

- Slash the back center of the base halfway open to make it easier to release it from the hat block. Pull the base and hat block in opposite directions. Insert some corset boning to aid in separating the base from the hat block (Figure 12-5).

- Fit the base on the actor's head, and trim it to the desired shape (Figures 12-6b and 12-7).

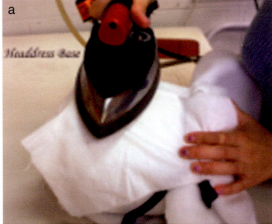

Figure 12-4 (a) Iron the steamed Fosshape on the hat block. (b) Trim the base.

Figure 12-5 Insert corset boning and separate the base from the hat block.

Figure 12-6 (a) The creators of the gods of Water and Earth headdresses. (b) Fit the base on the actor's head.

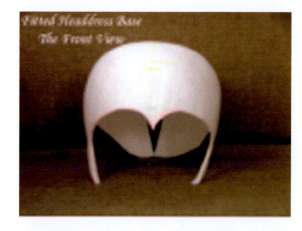

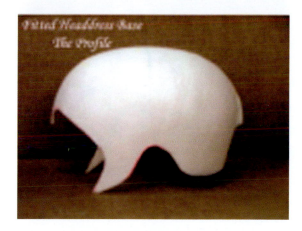

Figure 12-7 Completed trimmed base.

Step Two: Covering the Base with Fabrics

- Use spray adhesive #77 to glue the covering fabrics to both sides of the base (in these examples, the fabrics used for covering both sides of each

base matched the gods' costumes) (Figure 12-8). Glue down the edges of the fabric with fabric tacky glue.

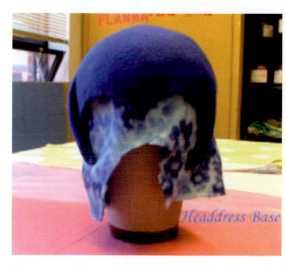

Figure 12-8 Cover the base with fabric on both sides.

Step Three: Constructing the Headdresses

God of Water Headdress

- Cover the headdress base with the appropriate fabrics.
- After the base is covered with fabrics, attach a curved wooden block (made by Nichole Getz, a BFA design and technology major student) on top of the base and secure it with screws (Figure 12-9a). Drill some holes in the wooden block for inserting the wires that form water waves later on.

Figure 12-9 (a) Secure a curved wooden block to the center top of the base so that you have a place to insert the water-wave wire pieces. (b) Insert a wire into each foam cords, and cover the foam cords with fleece fabric strips.

- Create the water waves. Cut pieces of copper wire, foam cords, and fabric strips (in this example, we used fleece, which is easy to use because it's stretchy and easy to manage). Insert a wire into each foam cord, and then cover it with fabric strips by wrapping the strips around and around. Secure the end of the fabric with fabric tacky glue (Figure 12-9b). The copper wire will support the shape of the wave.

- Put glue on one end of the wire in each water wave, and then insert that end into a hole in the wooden block. Then bend all the pieces in a water-wave design (Figure 12-10). (The creator added plastic water bubbles that hung from the waves.)

The completed headdress is shown in Figures 12-11 to 12-13.

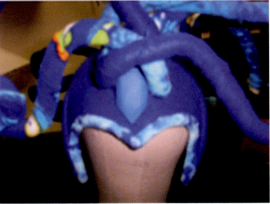

Figure 12-10 Insert the water-wave wires into the wooden block, and bend the water waves.

Figure 12-11 Completed god of Water headdress. *Created by Nichole Getz, a BFA design and technology major student at the University of Central Florida Conservatory Theatre. Water God played by Eric Ulloa, musical performance major student.*

Figure 12-12 Production photo of the god of Water in *Once on This Island*, close-up. *Water God played by Eric Ulloa, musical performance major student.*

Figure 12-13 Production photo of the god of Water in *Once on This Island*. *Water God played by Eric Ulloa, front row players Wes Miller; Desmond Newson, and Robert Dupont. Directed by Earl D. Weaver. Music/vocal direction by Jim Brown. Choreography by Brian Vernon. Scenic design by Vandy Wood. Lighting design by Dave Upton. Costume design by Tan Huaixiang. University of Central Florida Conservatory Theatre presentation.*

God of Death Headdress

- Cover the headdress base with the appropriate fabrics (Figure 12-14).
- Make patterns for the 3-D frame part of the headdress. (In this example, the frame shape was meant to symbolize daggers.)
- Cut a piece of Fosshape 4″ bigger than the pattern all the way around (because the Fosshape will shrink when heated), and iron it into a flat sheet with a steam iron on the highest temperature.

Figure 12-14 The headdress base, fitted and covered with fabric. The base is worn here by Keiko Kasai, BFA design and technology major student at the University of Central Florida Conservatory Theatre and one of the creators of the god of Death headdress.

Figure 12-15 Cut out the hardened Fosshape frame, following the headdress pattern.

Figure 12-16 Skull and wooden board attached to the headdress base (a) side;

- Following the headdress pattern, cut out the Fosshape frame (Figure 12-15).
- Run wire through the Fosshape frame to add strength and support, and secure it with zigzag stitches.
- Next, spray the frame on both sides with silver spray paint.
- Attach a wooden board on top of the base with screws, and attach the skull to the top of the wooden board with glue (Figure 12-16).

- Attach the Fosshape frame to the base with glue and hand sew it to secure it.
- Paint highlights and shadows on the frame to give the illusion of bloody daggers. Hang red strips of fabric on the back of the headdress for running blood.

The completed headdress is shown in Figures 12-17 to 12-19.

Figure 12-18 Completed god of Death headdress, worn by Tramaine Berryhil, a BFA design and technology student at the University of Central Florida Conservatory Theatre and one of its creators.

Figure 12-16—Cont'd (b) front.

Figure 12-17 Completed headdress — profile.

Figure 12-19 Production photo of the god of Death headdress in *Once on This Island. Death God played by Wesley Holiday, musical performance student. University of Central Florida Conservatory Theatre presentation.*

God of Earth Headdress

The god of Earth's headdress was designed to symbolize the globe.

- Cover the headdress base with the appropriate fabric.
- Use a large air-filled rubber ball as a mold for the globe. Cut a piece of Fosshape large enough to wrap around the ball. Steam and iron it until it forms

Figure 12-20 Steam the Fosshape over the ball to create a globe shape.

a ball-shaped shell with the ends open around the rubber ball, using your hands to smooth out any wrinkles (Figures 12-20 to 12-21).

Figure 12-21 Shape the Fosshape around the rubber ball, leaving the ends open.

- After the Fosshape is formed around the rubber ball, release the air from the ball and remove it from the Fosshape shell (Figure 12-22).

Figure 12-22 Deflate and remove the ball from the Fosshape shell. Emily Strickland, a BFA design and technology student at the University of Central Florida Conservatory Theatre.

- Draw the headdress design on the Fosshape and cut the globe into the proper shape (Figure 12-23a).
- Attach the globe to the headdress base with glue and hand sew it to secure it (Figure 12-23b).
- Paint the globe with oceans and continents using craft spray paints and acrylic paints. Fill the inside of the globe with mountains, trees, and animals. (The mountain in this example is a piece of foam covered with green moss.)

The completed headdress is shown in Figures 12-24 to 12-25.

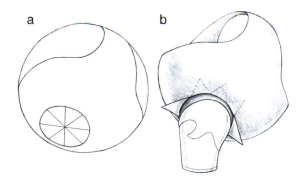

Figure 12-23 (a) Outline the design on the Fosshape, and cut the Fosshape globe so it is the proper shape and fits over the base. (b) Attach the globe to the base.

Figure 12-24 (a) Production photo of *Once on This Island* showing the god of Earth headdress — front. *Mimi Jimenez played the Earth God.* (b) Completed globe headdress — side.

Figure 12-25 Production photo of the four gods in *Once on This Island*. Left to right: Earth God played by Mimi Jimenez, Love God played by Miriam King, Death God played by Wesley Todd Holidays, Water God played by Eric Ulloa. Directed by Earl D. Weaver. Music/vocal direction by Jim Brown. Choreography by Brian Vernon. Scenic design by Vandy Wood. Lighting design by Dave Upton. Costume design by Tan Huaixiang. University of Central Florida Conservatory Theatre presentation.

MAKING A HORN HEADDRESS

The horn headdress made for the King in *Big River* (Figure 12-26) has one eye in the middle of the face and two horns on the head. Unusual materials were used for this headdress to achieve its dramatic appearance. Nevertheless, the materials

Figure 12-26 Costume design for *Big River*.

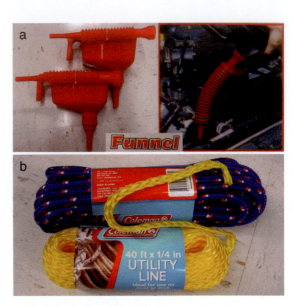

Figure 12-27 (a) Plastic funnel noses. (b) Utility cords.

were cheap and the headdress was quickly put together.

PROCEDURE FOR MAKING THE HORN HEADDRESS

Materials Required:

- Head block
- Three funnel noses (the kind used to add oil to cars) (Figure 12-27a)

- Nylon utility lines/cords (yellow and blue) for creating hair (Figure 12-27b)
- String
- Baseball cap
- Curved needle and thread

Step One: Preparation

- Pull from stock a used baseball cap whose colors will harmonize with the horn colors. Detach the visor.

- Put the baseball cap on a head block.
- Obtain the funnel nose parts and utility lines/cords.

Step Two: Attaching Stuff to the Baseball Cap

- The three funnel noses are used for the horns (Figure 12-28a).
  1. Leave one as is (long).
  2. Bend one.
  3. Cut one in half (1 in Figure 12-28a) and trim the edge inward (2 in Figure 12-28a). The inward curve helps you to fit it on to another funnel.

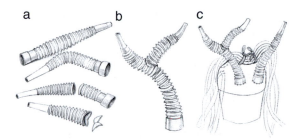

a b c

Figure 12-28 (a) The three funnels; cut the third funnel and trim the edge to an inward curve (1 and 2 in figure). (b) Attach the short funnel nose to the long one. (c) Attach the funnel noses and utility cords to the cap.

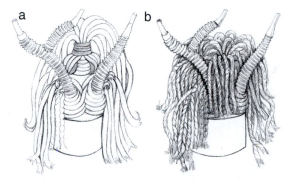

a b

Figure 12-29 (a) Tie the utility cords in a pony tail; wrap the horns and tie knots on the side. (b) Completed horn headdress.

Figure 12-31 The Chrysler Building.

- Attach the short nose to the long nose by hand using a curved needle and vertical hem stitches (Figure 12-28b).
- Hand sew the plastic horns on the baseball cap (Figure 12-28c).
- Sew two pieces of string on top of the baseball cap, and use them to tie a bundle of utility cords (blue and yellow mixed) on the cap. Hand sew some more single or double cords, and space them out on the baseball cap (Figure 12-28c).
- With another string, tie the bundle of cords on the hat in a pony tail. Wrap more utility cords around the roots of the horns, and tie knots on the sides (Figure 12-29a).
- Arrange and trim the cords to the desired length and shape.

The completed headdress is shown in Figure 12-29b and 12-30.

Figure 12-30 Production photos of the horn headdress in *Big River*. King played by Mark Brotherton. Directed by Donald Seay. Scenic design by Joseph Rusnock. Lighting design by Richard Dunham. Costume design by Tan Huaixiang. University of Central Florida Conservatory Theatre presentation.

MAKING A "CHRYSLER BUILDING" HEADDRESS

The headdress made for Julie in *Lend Me a Tenor* was based on the Chrysler Building in New York City (Figure 12-31).

PROCEDURE FOR MAKING THE CHRYSLER BUILDING HEADDRESS

Materials Required:

- Shiny confetti dot fabric
- Car-roof foam
- Sewing machine
- Needle and thread
- Hat block
- Decorative jewels
- Buckram
- Black fabric
- Millinery wire
- Fabric tacky glue

Step One: Creating the Foundation

- Research on the headdress, and make a pattern (Figure 12-32a).

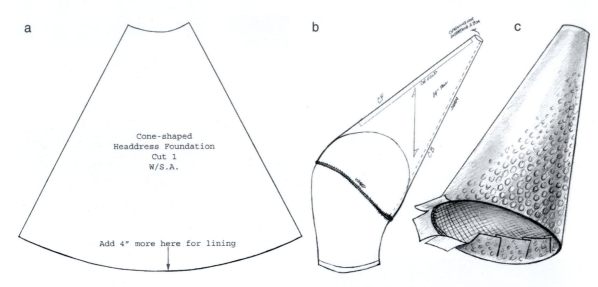

Figure 12-32 (a) Create a cone-shaped pattern (used for cutting the buckram and fabric). (b) Sew and wire the cone-shaped buckram base. (c) Cover the cone-shaped buckram with the cone-shaped fabric, gluing the top and bottom hems.

- Create a 14″-tall cone-shaped foundation from one layer of buckram (the Chrysler petal pieces will be attached to this). Cut out the buckram following your pattern, and hand sew the center seam together, leaving openings at the top and bottom (Figure 12-32b).
- Wire the edge of the buckram, securing the millinery wire with machine zigzag stitches (Figure 12-32b).
- Cut out black fabric following the cone pattern, and sew the center back seam together with a sewing machine. Pull the black cone over the buckram foundation. Glue the top and bottom hems with fabric tacky glue (Figure 12-32c).

Step Two: Creating Chrysler Petals

The headdress has three pairs of Chrysler petals in different sizes. The inner pair of petals (#3) is the largest, and the outer pair (#1) is the smallest (Figure 12-33a.). The bottom edge of pair #2 recedes about $\frac{1}{8}$″, and the bottom edge of pair #3 recedes about $\frac{1}{4}$″ to reduce the bulk at the bottom edge of the headdress. Each petal will be stuffed with one layer of foam for support and covered with black fabric on one side and silver on the other. Alternating black and silver confetti dot fabric was used on the petals to gain contrast. For example, if the outside of a petal is silver, then the inside is black. The outside of the middle pair (#2) is black to create contrast between the silver used for pairs #1 and #3.

- Follow the patterns, and cut one black and one silver piece of confetti dot fabric with a $\frac{1}{4}$″ seam allowance for each Chrysler petal (remember that you are making two petals of each size).
- With the right sides of the black and silver fabrics together, machine stitch around the edge of each petal with a $\frac{1}{4}$″ seam allowance. Leave a 3″ opening at the bottom of each petal so you can turn it right side out later (Figure 12-33b).
- Trim off the corners to reduce bulk (Figure 12-33b).
- Following the pattern, cut two pieces of foam for each pair of petals (one for each petal). No seam

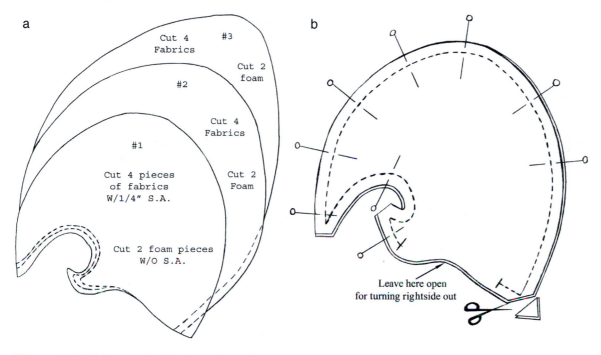

Figure 12-33 (a) Patterns for the three sizes of Chrysler petals. (b) Sew the fabrics for each Chrysler petal together.

allowance is needed on the foam (Figure 12-34a).

- Turn each petal right side out through the opening that you left in the seam, and insert the correct-size foam piece inside through the opening (Figure 12-34b). Manipulate all the corners of the foam piece so they are in their proper positions. Each foam piece should fit snugly and neatly inside its fabric pocket.

- After the foam is in place, close the opening by folding the seam allowances inside and machine stitching them shut using a zigzag stitch (Figure 12-34c). Finish all six Chrysler petals in this way.

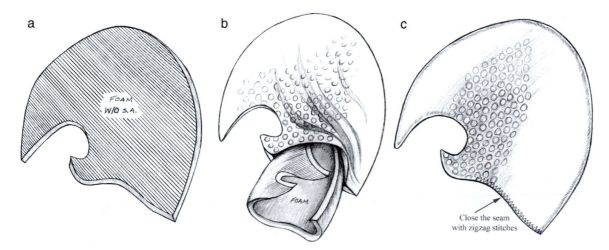

Figure 12-34 (a) Cut out a foam piece. (b) Insert the foam piece into the fabric petal through the opening of the seam. (c) Machine stitch the opening in the petal closed using zigzag stitches.

- Cut out a few black elongated triangles, and glue the triangles on the side of each Chrysler petal that will face out with fabric tacky glue (Figure 12-35a). Decorate all six Chrysler petals in this way.
- Machine sew the bottom edges of one set of petals #2 and #3 together with zigzag stitches. Be sure to place petal #3 about ⅛″ away from the edge of #2 to reduce bulk (Figure 12-35b). Sew the other set of petals #2 and #3 (for the opposite side of the headdress) so they are a mirror image of the first set.

Step Three: Attaching Chrysler Petals to the Foundation

- Attach petals #2 and #3 to the cone foundation. Do this by placing the center and side curved tips/points of each petal below the wire edge of the cone foundation and attaching it to the foundation by sewing two rows of large zigzag machine stitches just above the foundation's wire edge (Figure 12-36a).
- Cut three 7″-long pieces of millinery wire. Fold each wire in half and bend the ends into small circles to protect people from their sharpness. Hand sew the wires to the tips/points of the petals #2 and #3. The wire will help keep the corners in their places.
- Then attach the front pair of petals (#1) to the foundation. Do this by, first, overlapping and machine stitching (zigzag stitch) the center front points together (Figure 12-36b). Next, place the front petals on top of petals #2 and #3, pin the edges ⅛″ below petals #2 and #3, and hand sew the petals, using slanted hem stitch, from the inside (Figure 12-36c). No stitches should show on the outside.

Step Four: Lining the Headdress

- Draw the cone-shaped pattern on to a piece of black fabric, adding 5″ to the bottom (to line the front and side points). Cut it out.
- Sew the center seam of the fabric together. Apply fabric tacky glue to the INSIDE of the buckram foundation, and glue the cone-shaped lining inside the foundation.
- Trim the bottom of the lining piece to ½″ (as a seam allowance) below the

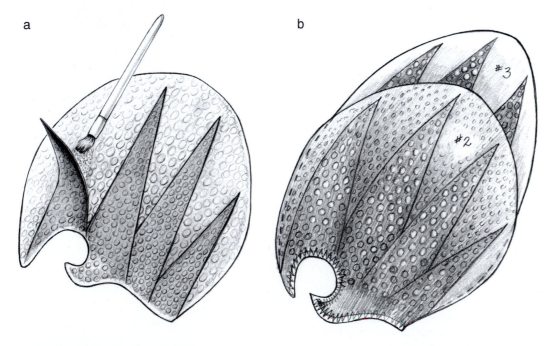

a   b

Figure 12-35 (a) Glue black triangles on the Chrysler petal. (b) Sew on set of petals #2 and #3 together at the bottom with zigzag stitches.

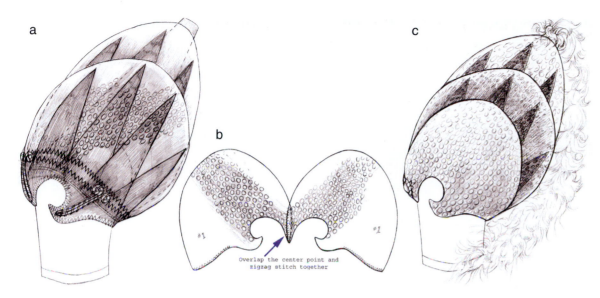

Figure 12-36 (a) Attach petals #2 and #3 to the foundation with two rows of zigzag stitches, then hand sew wires to the points/tips of the petals. (b) Sew the front center points of petals #1 together. (c) Attach the petal #1 pair to the foundation.

entire edge (Figure 12-37a). Finish the hem with hand-sewn slanted hem stitches.

Step Five: Decorating the Headdress

- Sew jewelry or a pin at the center front, and stick a boa inside the pointed top of the foundation to complete the headdress.

The completed headdress is shown in Figures 12-37 to 12-38. (No production photos are available for this headdress.)

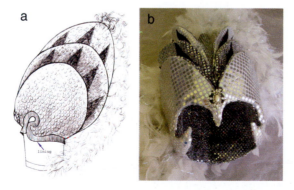

Figure 12-37 (a) Glue the lining to inside of the foundation, and trim the seam allowance. (b) Completed headdress showing the lining.

Figure 12-38 Completed Chrysler headdress (a) front and (b) profile views.

Continued

Figure 12-38—Cont'd Completed Chrysler headdress (c) side and back views.

MAKING A PEASANT HEADDRESS

The Peasant's headdress in *The Frog Prince* (Figure 12-39) was made of things that would grow in a village and its mountains since that's where the Peasant is from. The design scheme goal was colorful and fruity.

PROCEDURE FOR MAKING THE PEASANT HEADDRESS

Materials Required:

- Artificial fruit
- Artificial leaves
- Twig wreath/ring
- Felt

- Tie wire
- Wire cutters
- Long-haired wig
- Wig block
- Pins

Figure 12-39 Costume design for the Peasant in *The Frog Prince*.

Step One: Preparation

- Pull from stock or purchase materials such as artificial fruit, leaves, and a twig wreath.
- Obtain a long-haired wig, put it on a wig block, and pin the bottom edges down.

Step Two: Putting It All Together

- Create a twig wreath/ring that fits over the wig (Figure 12-40a). (If you can buy a suitable-sized wreath, you don't have to make it.)
- Arrange the artificial fruit and leaves on the twig wreath, and attach them with tie wire (Figure 12-40b).

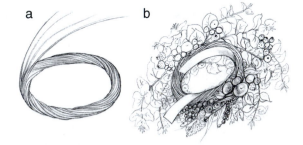

Figure 12-40 (a) Create a twig wreath/ring. (b) Attach the fruit and leaves, and glue a felt strip on the inside of the wreath.

• Glue a piece of felt on the inside of the wreath (Figure 12-40b) so that the headdress is comfortable to wear and to prevent the actor's hair from getting caught.

The completed headdress is shown in Figures 12-41 to 12-42.

Figure 12-41 Completed headdress.

Figure 12-42 Production photo of Peasant with Woman and the headdress in *The Frog Prince. Sophie Ahsen played the Peasant. Directed by Ken Westerman. Scenic and Lighting design by Julie Gallager. Costume design by Tan Huaixiang. Cornell University Department of Theatre Arts presentation.*

MAKING A MEDIEVAL CAUL HEADDRESS

A medieval women's headdress was created for *Robin Hood* (Figure 12-43). It is wire-framed, covered with mesh fabric, and decorated with pearls.

PROCEDURE FOR MAKING CAUL HEADDRESS

Materials Required:

• Millinery wire and tie wire
• Buckram
• Short fur material (to cover headband, other fabrics may be used as well)
• Fabric tacky glue
• Gold net fabric
• Pearls
• Needle and thread
• Chiffon fabric for scarf

Step One: Making the Headband

• Cut out a piece of buckram to make a headband (as support); it should be $1\frac{1}{4}''$ wide and 1″ longer than the actor's head circumference.
• Overlap the short ends of the buckram 1″, and hand sew it together with slanted stitches. Wire both top and

LADY MERLE   SHERIFF OF NOTINGHAM   SHERIFF'S WIFE   MOTHER MEG

OLD WIDOW

ROBIN HOOD

CWU THEATRE ARTS DEPARTMENT

Figure 12-43 Costume design for *Robin Hood*.

bottom edges and then cover it with fabric (Figure 12-44a).

- Cover the headband with fur fabric (or another fabric type). To do this, cut a piece of fur fabric large enough to wrap around and cover both sides of the buckram headband, and glue it around the headband (Figure 12-44a).

Step Two: Making the Wire Frames

- Each caul in this headdress is constructed from a wire frame (there

Figure 12-44 (a) Sew the buckram headband together, wired it, and cover it with fur fabric. (b) Make two wire rings; place the bent supporting wire between the rings, and attach the wire to the rings with cross-wires. (c) Cover the wire frame with mesh fabric, and decorate the fabric with pearls.

are two; one sits on either side of the head). Cut four pieces (about 15″ to 18″ long, two for each caul) of millinery wire of equal length. Overlap each wire 1″ to form a ring, and tie the ends together with tie wire.

- Cut two pieces of wire (about 26″ to 30″ long, one for each ring frame) to become the central supports. Bend one of the supporting wires into a zigzag shape, (each zigzag is about 2″ or 3″ tall and wide) and fit it between two rings to form a frame. Tie the supporting wire to the rings at each bend (Figure 12-44b). Repeat to form the second wire frame.

Step Three: Covering the Wire Frame with Fabric

- In this example, gold net/mesh fabric was used to cover the wire frame. Cut a piece of fabric large enough to cover the wire frame like a drum (Figure 12-44c). Fold the edges to the inside of the wire frame, and glue them with clear tack glue or sew it by hand. No darts or seams are needed when wrapping the fabric over the wire frame because the net is a loosely woven fabric and can easily to be pulled and manipulated.

- Repeat the same process to make the second caul.
- Hand sew pearls to the outside of the gold net fabric (Figure 12-44c).

Step Four: Attaching the Cauls and Scarf to the Headband

- Hand sew one caul to each side of the headband.

- Attach a veil at the back of the headband.

  The completed headdress is shown in Figure 12-45.

Figure 12-45 Production photos of *Robin Hood* showing the caul headdress. (a) Front view. *Abra Stanley played Lady Merle.* (b) Side view. *From left to right: Abra Stanley played Lady Merle. Torina Smith played Mother Meg. Paul Wickline played Chef. Jared Vallejo played Guard. David Shoup played Sheriff of Nottingham.*

Continued

Figure 12-45—Cont'd (c) Production photo of the caul headdress in *Robin Hood*. Abra Stanley (front) played Lady Merle. Back row from left to right: Torina Smith played Mother Meg. David Plant played Robin Hood. Elisa Taylor played Maid Marion. Vanessa Hespe played Sheriff's Wife. David Shoup played Sheriff of Nottingham. Keith Edie played King Richard. Tom McNelly played Casper. Directed by James Hawkins. Scenic design by Tim Stapleton, Lighting design by Mark C. Zetterberg. Costume design by Tan Huaixiang. Central Washington University Theatre Arts Department presentation.

MAKING A RENAISSANCE ROUNDELET HEADDRESS

The Prince's headdress for *Romeo and Juliet* was finished with velveteen and gold lace fabrics. It was supported with foam cord (poly stuffing can also be used).

PROCEDURE FOR MAKING THE ROUNDELET HEADDRESS

Materials Required:

- Hat block
- Maroon-colored velvet
- Gold trim
- Sewing machine
- Needle and thread
- Foam cord (2½″ in circumference) or poly stuffing
- Scissors
- Knife or saw
- Fabric tacky glue
- Needle board
- Iron

Step One: Creating a Padded Roll

A piece of 2½″-circumference foam cord is the perfect size for making a roundelet headdress. If the available foam cord is too thin, layers of poly stuffing can be padded over the foam cord to get the desired shape. Or you can use poly stuffing by itself to create a padded roll.

- Measure the actor's head circumference, and choose the proper size hat block accordingly.
- Cut a piece of foam cord 2½″ longer than the actual headdress size to allow for an overlapping seam allowance.
- Next, prepare the foam cord to hook together tightly by cutting out a knob on one end of the foam and an insertion for the knob on the other end of the foam roll with a long knife or saw (Figure 12-46a).
- Cut a bias strip of velvet fabric long and wide enough to cover the foam cord

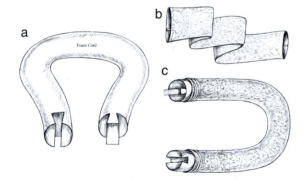

Figure 12-46 (a) Notch the ends of the foam cord to fit like a puzzle. (b) Sew the velvet into a tube, and turn it right side out. (c) Pull the velvet tube over the foam cord.

plus an added seam allowance. With the right side of the velvet strip together, stitch it into a tube; turn it right side out (Figure 12-46b). Then pull the velvet tube over the foam roll (Figure 12-46c). Pull the velvet back in order so that you can hook the foam cord into a circle (Figure 12-47a).

- Glue the hooked foam ends together with fabric tacky glue (12-47a), being careful not to get glue on the velvet.
- After the glue dries, pull both ends of the velvet over the foam cord join,

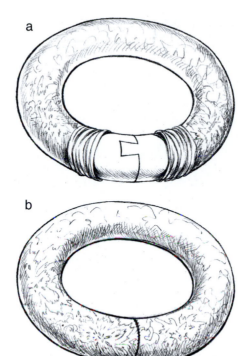

Figure 12-47 (a) Hook together and glue the ends of the foam cord. (b) Overlap the ends of the velvet and stitch them together.

overlap the seam allowance, and hand-stitch them together with matching thread (Figure 12-47b).

Step Two: Creating Patterns, Cutting the Velvet, and Sewing It Together

Roundelet headdress drapery can be shaped in a circle, rectangle, or square.

Velvet or velveteen is the best fabric for making a roundelet headdress and liripipe/tail. It looks rich and was the fashion of the period. The center of the drapery can be cut out or left uncut.

A circle-shaped velvet drapery was used for this example (Figure 12-48). Since both sides of the drapery fabric will be seen, it should be lined with the same velvet fabric or with a fabric of contrasting color.

- Cut two 45″-diameter (these can be smaller or bigger) circles with decorative shapes along the circumference from velvet fabric, following the pattern. Cut one circle out as a whole circle, and for the other one, cut in two half circles, adding ½″ seam allowances at the stitching edges.
- With right sides together, pin the seam allowances of the two half circles together along the diameter. Machine stitch along the edge, leaving a 5″ opening in the middle (Figures 12-48a

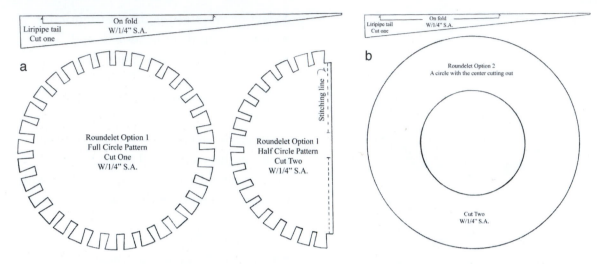

Figure 12-48 (a) Roundelet headdress drapery pattern option 1, full circle. (b) Roundelet headdress drapery pattern option 2, circle with center cut out.

sew the decorative outer edges of the circles together (Figure 12-49b). Trim each outer corner and clip each inner corner of the seam allowance to reduce bulk (Figure 12-49b).

- Turn the stitched circle right side out through the opening in the seam line for the two half circles; hand-stitch the opening shut (Figure 12-49c).
- Trim the outer decorative edge of the drapery with gold trim (Figure 12-49c).

Step Three: Attaching the Liripipe/Tail and Circular Drapery to the Padded Roll

Roundelet Headdress Drapery Pattern Option 1

- Cut the liripipe/tail from the same velvet, on the bias or following the grain. With the right side of the velvet together, sew the side seam allowance together so that the material is a tube. Turn it right side out (Figure 12-50a).
- Place the padded roll over a hat block. Hand sew the liripipe/tail to the head opening on the side of the padded roll (Figure 12-50b). Remove it from the hat block.

and 12-49a) so you can later turn the piece right side out (if you leave an opening on the decorative outer edge of the circle when you stitch it later, you will find it hard to close). Place the

right side of the velvet on top of a needle board to press the seam allowance open (Figure 12-49b).
- Place the joined half circles on top of the whole circle, pin them together, and

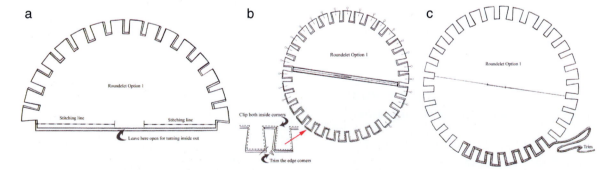

Figure 12-49 (a) Stitch the two half circles together, leaving a center opening (so you can turn it right side out later). (b) Press the seam joining the two half circles open; pin the joined half circles to the full circle of fabric, and stitch them together; clip all the corners of the decorative edge. (c) Turn the drapery right side out and stitch the opening closed; add gold trim to the decorative edge.

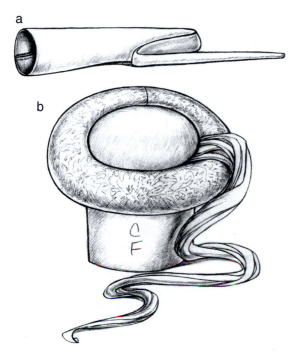

Figure 12-50 (a) Stitch together the liripipe/tail. (b) Attach the liripipe/tail to the side of the padded roll.

- Center the circular drapery over the hat block, and pin it at the top (Figure 12-51a).
- Place the padded roll upside down on top of the drapery, and pin the padded roll and drapery together all the way around the head opening (do not pin them to the hat block) (Figure 12-51b).
- Remove the pinned roll and drapery from the hat block, and sew them together by hand along the pins (Figure 12-52a).

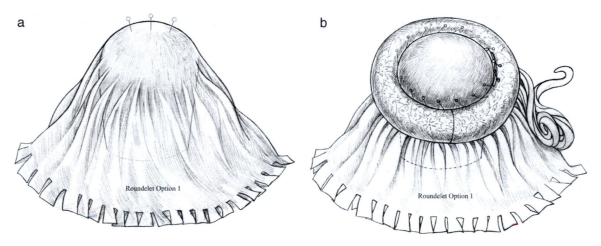

Figure 12-51 (a) Center the drapery over the hat block and pin it. (b) Place the padded roll upside down over the drapery; pin them together.

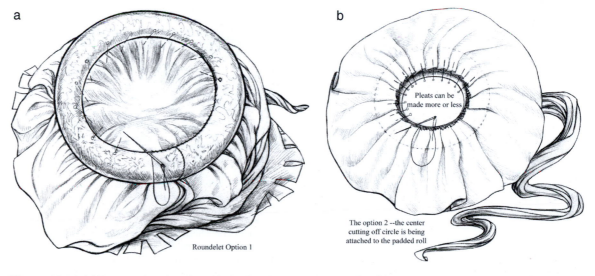

Figure 12-52 (a) Remove the pinned padded roll and drapery from the hat block, and sew them together. (b) Method of attachment for drapery option 2.

Roundelet Headdress Drapery Pattern Option 2

The construction of the drapery for option 2 is similar to option 1. The construction of the padded roll and the contraction and attachment of the liripipe/tail are the same.

- To attach the drapery to the padded roll, pin the edge of the drapery's center cut-out circle to the hat opening of the padded roll, with or without pleats.
- Place the headdress on top of the hat block with the drapery on top of the padded roll. Arrange and tack the drapery in the desired position (Figure 12-52b).

The completed headdress is shown in Figures 12-53 to 12-54.

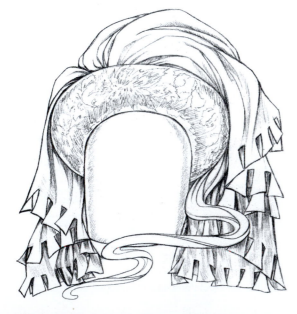

Figure 12-53 Completed roundelet headdress.

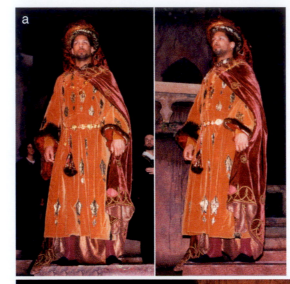

Figure 12-54 (a) Production photo of the roundelet in Romeo and Juliet. *Prince played by Harris Smith.*
(b) Production photo of the roundelet in *Romeo and Juliet. Prince played by Harris Smith. From left to right. Back Row: David Whatley played Peter. Colleen Smet played Lady Capulet. Jeremy Sonney played Capulet. Front Row: David Plant played Tybalt. David Shoup played Benvolio. Simon Burzynski played Balthasar. Ryan Horner played Gregory. Sabrina Mansfield played Citizen. David Foubert played Montague. Kevin F. Coiley played Citizen. Letty Drew played Citizen. Harris Smith played Prince of Verona. Torina Smith played Lady Montague. Jared Vallejo played Citizen. Craig Zagurski played Mercutio. James Austin played Abram.*

Figure 12-54—Cont'd (c) Production photo of the roundelet in *Romeo and Juliet. From left to right: Paris played by Tom McNelly, Prince played by Harris Smith, Juliet played by Sara Hill, Romeo played by Keith Edie, Friar Laurence played by Robb Padgett, Montague played by David Foubert, Lady Montague played by Torina Smith. Directed by Brenda Hubbard. Scenic design by Tim Stapleton. Lighting design by Mark C. Zetterberg. Costume design by Tan Huaixiang. Central Washington University Department of Theatre Arts presentation.*

MAKING A ROLLER HEADDRESS

The six roller-headdresses in *Grease* (Figure 12-55) have two parts, a headdress base and hair rollers. The headdress bases were altered from premade cape net hats (top-hat style) purchased from a theatrical supply store. Cape net is a lightweight, open-weave material that contains sizing. It becomes completely pliable when wet and retains its blocked shape after it dries. The

Figure 12-55 Costume design for *Grease*. (Rollers were vertically arranged on the finished headdress)

lightweight rollers were created with 3″-wide silver sequence trim.

PROCEDURE FOR MAKING A ROLLER HEADDRESS

Materials Required:

- Premade cape net hat (top-hat style; purchased)
- Water in a spray bottle
- Hat block
- Push pins
- Craft spray paints
- Foam cord ($1\frac{1}{4}″$ diameter)
- Sharp cutting knife
- 1″-wide elastic
- Millinery wire
- 3″-wide silver sequence trim
- Fabric tacky glue

Step One: Creating a Foundation

- Place the cape net hat on a hat block, and spray it evenly with water to moisten it (Figure 12-56a).
- Pull the cape net and stretch it down, forming it to the hat block (Figure 12-56b). Make sure the bottom edges are evenly level after you pull it down.

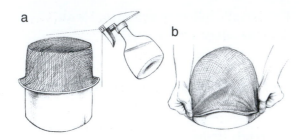

Figure 12-56 (a) Spray water on the cape net. (b) Pull down on the cape net, stretching it to create a headdress base/foundation.

- Place push pins along the very bottom of the hat, and let it dry.
- Spray-paint the cape net foundation medium gray (Figure 12-57a).

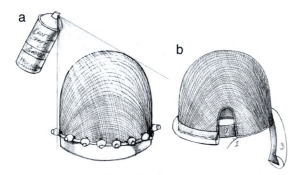

Figure 12-57 (a) After the cape net hat is formed to the hat block and pinned, spray-paint it gray. (b) Wire the bottom edge, and attach elastic to the base; glue the foam cord to the base.

- After the paint dries, cut an upside-down U shape $1\frac{1}{2}''$ wide and $2\frac{1}{2}''$ tall in the center back, and sew millinery wire along the bottom edge of the foundation (Figure 12-57b).
- Sew a strip of elastic along the bottom of the U-shaped opening (Figure 12-57b) so that the size of the foundation is adjustable.
- Cut a piece of $1\frac{1}{4}''$-diameter foam cord the same length as the bottom circumference of the foundation. Slash the middle of the cord $\frac{2}{3}$ of the diameter down with a sharp cutting knife. Apply fabric tacky glue to the inside of the slashed surface, and insert the bottom edge of the headdress base into the slashed foam cord (Figure 12-57b). The gray foam cord provides a nice finished edge on the headdress.

Step Two: Creating Rollers

- I used 3"-wide silver sequence trim to simulate metal hair rollers. Cut the trim into $3 \times 3\frac{1}{2}''$ pieces. Overlap each one $\frac{1}{2}''$ to form a tube or roller, and glue it with fabric tacky glue (Figure 12-58a).

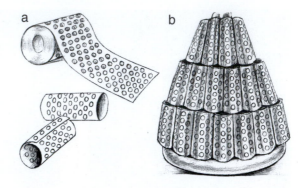

Figure 12-58 (a) Create the rollers. (b) Attach the rollers to the headdress base vertically.

You need 25–30 rollers for each headdress.

- Attach all the rollers to the foundation vertically with fabric tacky glue (Figure 12-58b). (Note that the original costume design in Figure 12-55 shows the rollers attached to the headdress base horizontally.)

The completed headdress is shown in Figure 12-59.

Figure 12-59 (a) Production photo of hair roller headdresses in *Grease. Tricia Thiel played Marty. Brandy Black played Sandy. Leslie J. Webb played Frenchy. Kerri L. Van Auken played Parry. Kyra McGough played Cha Cha. Directed by Brenda Hubbard.* (b) *Back Row, left to right: Dominica Myers played Jan, Roger Shoup played Teen Angel, and Jennifer Fox played Rizzo. Front Row, left to right: Kerri L. Van Auken played Parry, Kyra McGough played Cha Cha, Tricia Thiel played Marty, and Brandy Black played Sandy. Directed by Brenda Hubbard. Lighting and scenic design by Mark C. Zetterberg. Costume design by Tan Huaixiang. Central Washington University Theatre Arts Department presentation.*

MAKING A CARMEN MIRANDA–STYLE FRUIT HEADDRESS

The fruit headdress made for *Lend Me a Tenor* was based on the exotic and glamorous headdresses worn by Carmen Miranda, a well-known actress and singer in the1930s–1950s. The character in this production does not partake in much movement, so no turban base was attached to the headdress. Instead, the headdress was secured on the actress's head by tying it under her chin using two wide ribbons. The headdress was on stage for only a brief moment but achieved an outrageous theatrical moment.

PROCEDURE FOR MAKING THE FRUIT HEADDRESS

Materials Required:

- 3 shell-shaped baskets of different sizes (small, medium, and large)
- Hot glue gun and glue sticks
- Artificial fruits and flowers
- Tie wire
- Hat/wig block
- Piece of ½″ foam to pad the inside of the basket for comfort
- Wide ribbon to tie the basket to the head

Step One: Creating a Foundation

• Purchase a set of three shell-shaped baskets in different sizes (small, medium, and large) (Figure 12-60a).

Figure 12-60 (a) Shell-shaped baskets. (b) Attach the two smaller baskets to the large basket to create a foundation.

• Glue a piece of foam on the inside of the large shell basket at the top; hand sew a piece of wide ribbon to the foam and basket with tacking stitches (see Figures 12-62b). The position of the ribbon will depend on how it fits on the actor.

• Place the large shell basket over a wig block, and tie the ribbon to secure it on the block.

• Attach the small basket, upright, to one side of the large basket with thin tie wire, and then use hot glue to reinforce it. Attach the medium basket on to the large basket in the desired position in the same way (Figure 12-60b).

Step Two: Decorating the Headdress

• Attach fruit and flowers with a hot glue gun (Figure 12-61). I recommend you also sew them on, if you have time.

Figure 12-61 Attach the fruit and flowers.

The completed headdress is shown in Figure 12-62. (No production photos are available for this headdress.)

Figure 12-62 Completed fruit headdress (a) front and side views; (b) back and bottom views.

Figure 12-63 Costume design for *The Dance and the Railroad*.

MAKING A CHINESE OPERA HEADDRESS

The opera headdress created for the production of *The Dance and the Railroad* (Figure 12-63) was not made using the traditional Chinese methods and materials. It was made using a method I made up.

PROCEDURE FOR MAKING A CHINESE OPERA HEADDRESS

Materials Required:

- Pattern paper
- Headdress fabric
- Headdress lining
- Buckram
- Steel springs

- Wire cutters
- Millinery wire
- Needle and thread
- Fabric tacky glue
- Marker
- Acrylic paints
- Pearls
- Red fringe
- 1½″ and 2″ red pompoms
- Spray adhesive
- Hat block
- Tailor's chalk
- Craft spray paint
- Hot glue gun and glue sticks

Step One: Creating the Pattern

- Create a cone-shaped opera headdress foundation pattern (Figure 12-64a) by draping it over a hat block.
- Try the paper pattern on the head to check the size, height, and angle.

Step Two: Constructing the Buckram Crown

- Cut a piece of buckram following the pattern (if you are using one-ply buckram, you will need two layers; if you are using two-ply buckram, you will need one layer).

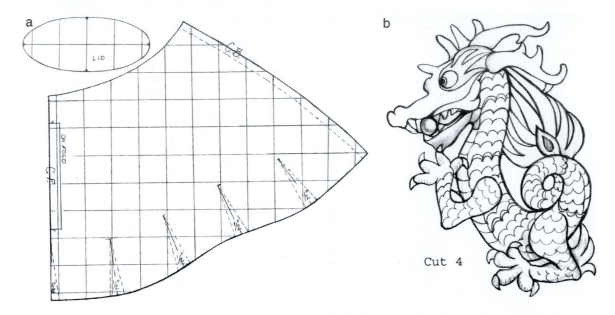

Figure 12-64 (a) Cone-shaped foundation pattern — crown and lid. (b) Dragon decoration for the opera headdress.

- Slash the darts, overlap each one ¼″ at the dart bottom (Figure 12-65a), and machine stitch the dart using zigzag stitches.
- Temporarily staple the center back seam allowance together, and hand sew the seam with slanted hem stitches. Then wire both the top and bottom edges of the cone-shaped crown, and machine stitch the wire on to the crown using zigzag stitches (Figure 12-65b).

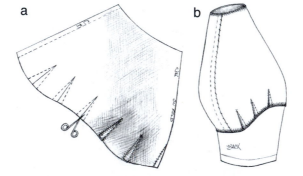

Figure 12-65 (a) Slash and overlap the darts and zigzag stitch them together. (b) Sew the center back seam together, and wire the crown at both the top and bottom edges.

Step Three: Constructing the Buckram Lid

- Cut out a piece of buckram following the lid pattern, adding a ½″ seam allowance.
- Shape the top wire of the buckram crown to match the shape of the lid, and turn it upside down on the lid. Trace the outline of the top of the crown on the buckram with a marker to ensure a perfect fit (Figure 12-66a).
- Clip the buckram-lid seam allowance up to the tracing line around the entire oval shape (Figure 12-66b).

Step Four: Covering the Buckram Foundation with Fabric

- Cut out a piece of fabric for the lid following the pattern.
- Spray adhesive on the buckram lid, glue it to the fabric, and trim off the excess fabric (Figures 12-66b–c). Reclip the lid, following the clips made in the buckram but stopping halfway to the traced line (Figure 12-66c).
- Attach the lid to the top of the cone-shaped crown with fabric tacky glue (Figure 12-66d).

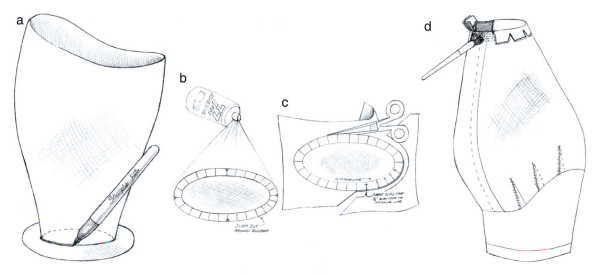

Figure 12-66 (a) Trace the shape of the top of the buckram crown on the lid. (b) Clip the buckram lid; spray it with adhesive. (c) Glue fabric to the lid; trim off the excess fabric. (d) Glue the lid on to the crown.

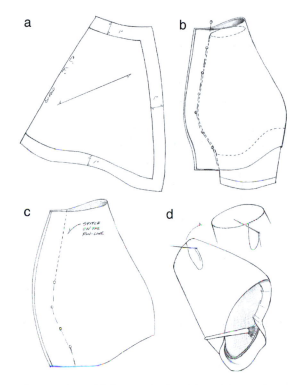

Figure 12-67 (a) Cut out the headdress fabric with a 1″ seam allowance. (b) Fit the fabric over the buckram crown, and pin it. (c) Following the pin line, sew the fabric into a tube. (d) Fit the fabric over the buckram crown; stitch the top edge and glue the bottom edge of the fabric to inside of the headdress.

- Cut out, on the bias, a piece of fabric following the cone-shaped crown pattern and adding a 1″ seam allowance on all edges of the pattern (Figure 12-67a). Cut two notches at the center of the fabric on the top and bottom.
- Wrap the fabric over the cone-shaped buckram crown, with the outside of the fabric facing in (it'll be turned right side out later). Pin the center top and bottom of the fabric to the center top and bottom of the buckram. Bring the fabric around to the center back of the buckram crown, and place pins along the back seam from the top to the bottom so that there is a perfect fit (Figure 12-67b). Remove it from the buckram crown (if the fabric is cut on bias, it will be easily removed and put back to the crown).
- Machine sew the back seam of the fabric on the pin line, removing each pin as you go (Figure 12-67c); trim the seam allowance to $\frac{1}{2}$″. Press the seam allowance open, and turn the fabric right side out. The fabric is now a tube.
- Pull the fabric tube over the buckram foundation. Fold under the $\frac{1}{2}$″ top seam allowance, and hand sew it down along the edge of the lid using slanted hem stitches (Figure 12-67d).
- Now fold the fabric over to the inside of the bottom edge of the buckram crown, and glue it down (Figure 12-67d).

Step Five: Lining the Headdress with Felt

- Cut out the lid pattern on felt.
- Make four marks (marking the front, back, and centers of the two sides) on the lid lining.
- Cut out the crown pattern on felt, adding a 1″ seam allowance on all edges of the pattern. Cut two notches,

marking the center, at the top and bottom.

- In the same way as for the covering material in step four, wrap the felt around the crown. Pin the center top and bottom of the felt to the center top and bottom of the crown. Bring the felt around the crown, and place pins along the back seam so that it is a perfect fit.
- Remove the felt from the crown with the pins in place, and lay it on the table. Draw a stitching line $\frac{1}{4}''$ in from the pin line (you make the lining smaller in this way because the lining must fit inside the crown) (Figure 12-68a).

- Machine sew the back seam; the felt crown lining is now a tube. Trim the seam allowance to $\frac{1}{2}''$.
- Trim the top seam allowance to $\frac{1}{4}''$. Make four marks (marking the front, back, and the centers of the two sides) on the top edge of the crown lining. Match the marks on the lid lining to the marks on the crown lining, and pin them together. Machine sew them together with a $\frac{1}{4}''$ seam allowance (Figure 12-68b).
- Glue the lining to the inside of the headdress with fabric tacky glue and hand sew the lining hem using slanted hem stitches. (Figure 12-68c).

Step Five: Decorating the Headdress with Pearls and Pom-Poms

- Sew pearl trim along the bottom edge of the headdress, and mark the positions of the steel springs (which will attach the pom-poms) with tailor chalk (Figures 12-69a and c).
- Hand sew each steel spring on to the crown; glue pearl strings around the root of each spring. Then glue pom-poms on top of each spring with fabric tacky glue (Figure 12-69b).

Step Six: Creating and Attaching a Decorative Dragon

- A pair of dragons is needed to decorate the Chinese opera headdress. Cut out two layers of buckram following the dragon pattern (Figure 12-64b) (Fosshape or Wonderflex can also be used) for each dragon.
- Cut a piece of wire the length of the dragon plus 2″ and then double the whole length. Fold it in half.

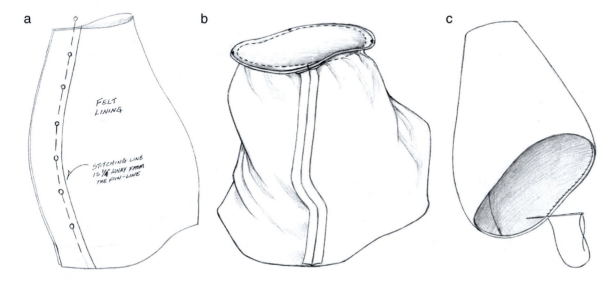

a

FELT
LINING

STITCHING LINE
IS $\frac{1}{4}''$ AWAY FROM
THE PIN-LINE

b

c

Figure 12-68 (a) Draw a new stitching line on the felt, $\frac{1}{4}''$ in from the pin line. (b) Sew the lid lining to the crown lining. (c) Glue the lining to the inside of the headdress and stitch the hem.

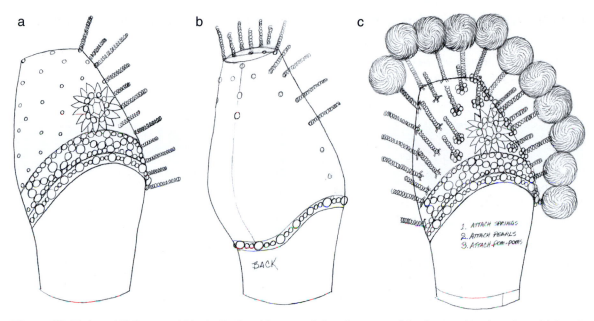

Figure 12-69 (a and b) Sew pearl trim to the headdress; mark the placement of the front and back springs. (c) Attach the springs, pearl strings, and pom-poms.

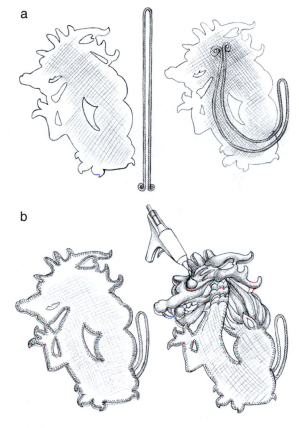

Figure 12-70 (a) After cutting out the dragon, sew the folded wire on to one piece. (b) Sew the second piece on; add scales to the dragon with hot glue.

- Bend the two ends of the wire into small loops (Figure 12-70a) to hide the sharp ends and secure the wire.
- Place the folded wire on one of the dragon buckram pieces and bend it into a curve (Figure 12-70a). Machine or hand stitch the folded wire using a zigzag stitch to the center of the dragon buckram piece, leaving the extra 2″ of the folded wire hanging out to the side (so it will be attached to the headdress)

(Figure 12-70a). Lay the other buckram piece on top, and machine stitch them together around the edge (Figure 12-70b). The inserted wire will provide support to the dragon.
- Spray the buckram with a foundation color (in this example, blue) using craft spray paint.
- Use hot glue to create decorations such as dragon scales (Figure 12-70b), and paint them with acrylic paint.

- Hand sew the wire that's sticking out the side of the dragon to the side of the headdress (Figure 12-71).
- Hand sew red fringe to the bottom back of the headdress, and attach two long tassels to the bottom of the dragons to complete the headdress (Figure 12-71).

The completed headdress is shown in Figures 12-71 to 12-73. The actor wore a plastic mask to complete the final look of the character. A red foundation was sprayed on the mask, and the eyes, eyebrows, and forehead wrinkles were outlined in Chinese Opera face painting fashion.

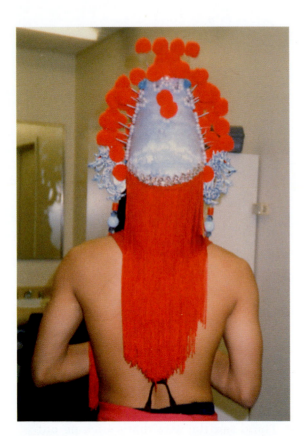

Figure 12-71 The back of the completed headdress, showing the dragons, red fringe, and tassels.

Figure 12-72 Completed Chinese Opera headdress — front. Ricky T. Li in the headdress played Ma.

Figure 12-73 Production photo of *The Dance and the Railroad* showing the Chinese opera headdress. *Ricky T. Li played Ma. Directed and Choreographed by Keith Grant. Scenic and lighting design by Julie Gallager. Costume Design by Tan Huaixang. Cornell University Theatre Arts Department presentation.*

Chapter 13   Rubber Outfit

Casting latex is often used to make rubber masks, but it may be used to make costume outfits. It has unique qualities that fabrics cannot compete with. Once the casting latex has set, it becomes very durable, flexible, stretchy, waterproof, dyeable, paintable, and stitchable.

MAKING A CROCODILE COSTUME

I made a crocodile outfit for *Peter Pan* (Figure 13-1) before moving to Florida. After moving to Florida, I was eager to visit the park where the crocodiles lived even though the crocodile costume had been done. When I saw many crocodiles sleeping on the bank with their mouths open, I appreciated their natural beauty. I was proud to have made the crocodile outfit.

The crocodile costume was made of casting latex and consisted of four separate sections: head, body, tail, and limbs. Each section was molded and sculpted with clay to imitate the

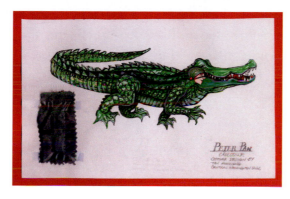

Figure 13-1 Costume design for the crocodile in *Peter Pan*.

crocodile's scaly skin. Each clay sculpture was then made into negative molds with plaster of paris, and casting latex was poured into these negative molds to produce scaled rubber sheets. The scaled rubber sheet was glued to a $\frac{1}{2}''$ foam sheet for support. When the actor was inside this crocodile costume, moving, talking, and acting, the crocodile effectively came to life on stage.

PROCEDURE FOR MAKING THE RUBBER OUTFIT

Materials Required:

- Pattern paper
- Plaster of paris
- Oil-based modeling clay
- Sculpting tools
- Sculpting table or hat block
- Aluminum wire
- 2 mirror balls (for crocodile eyes)
- Plastic bags
- T-pins or wire ties
- Wire screening (cut into strips)
- Wig stand
- 2 mixing bowls
- Spatula
- Butter knife
- Screwdriver
- Casting latex
- Foam strips
- Baby powder
- Rit dye
- Stove or Dye Vat
- Washing machine or large garbage can (if dye vat is not available)

231

- Headdress foundation (made from buckram or Fosshape)
- Leather glue-barge
- Heavy-duty zipper
- Industrial or heavy-duty sewing machine
- Canvas
- 2″-thick sofa cushion foam
- 2″-thick Styrofoam
- Black duct tape
- Velcro
- ½″-thick foam sheet
- All-purpose spray adhesive
- Knit fabric
- Fabric tacky clear glue
- Red chiffon fabric
- Acrylic paint
- Paint brushes
- Clear acrylic spray

Step One: Creating Patterns

The pattern for the crocodile outfit was based on measurements of the actor's body. The rubber outfit was lined with ½″-thick foam, which increases volume of the human body as well as supporting the floppy rubber sheet of the crocodile skin.

The finished rubber outfit looked like a fat long-john pajama suit, except the legs were seamed to the torso and a long tail was added.

- Draw patterns for the torso front (cut 2), torso back (cut 1), arm (cut 2), leg (cut 2), and tail (cut 1). A mock-up may be needed for a trial fitting of the outfit so that corrections can be made to the pattern.
- Lay each pattern piece on a ½″-thick foam sheet, and cut it out with scissors.
- Spray glue on the side of the foam piece that will face the actor's body (Figure 13-2a). Glue it to the knit

fabric. The knit fabric functions as lining and eases stitching to the foam (i. e., prevents ripping the foam from stitching).

- Machine sew the front and back torso pieces together by sewing the side, shoulder, and crotch seams (Figure 13-2b). Do not sew the arm and leg parts together yet. Sew a heavy-duty zipper in the center front opening to open/close the outfit.

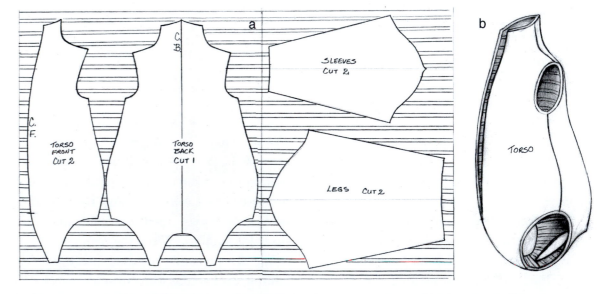

Figure 13-2 (a) Glue the foam pieces to a piece of knit fabric. (b) Sew the front and back torso together.

Step Two: Creating the Crocodile Tail

The crocodile tail was built as an individual piece separate from the rest of the outfit, and attached to the actor's waist with a belt. The support for the tail was constructed from canvas and foam cubes. The swing motion created for the tail was based on a wooden snake toy. The tail could swing and wag when the crocodile crawled and walked along.

- Cut out the patterns for the belt and tail from canvas (Figures 13-3a–b). Keep the tail piece folded.

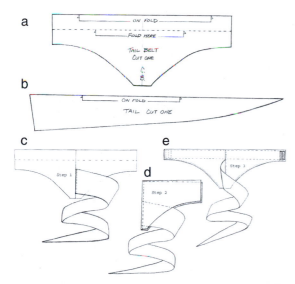

Figure 13-3 (a) Pattern for belt. (b) Pattern for tail. (c) Top-stitch the tail to the center line of the belt. (d) Fold the left side of the belt over the tail piece, and stitch over the center folding edge of the belt. (e) Open the belt, and top-stitch along the center seam line you just made.

- Place the root of the tail at the center line of the belt and top-stitch over the tail seam allowance at the very edge (Figure 13-3c).
- Fold the left side of the belt over the tail piece, so the tail piece is sandwiched in the belt piece, and stitch over the center folding edge of the belt with $1/2''$ seam allowance (Figure 13-3d).
- Unfold the belt and top-stitch along the center seam line you just made, catching all the layers of the seam allowance for reinforcement (Figure 13-3e).
- Based on the width and length of the tapered elongated tail, cut sofa foam (2–3″ thick) into rectangles of different sizes (in reference to the tapered tail shape).
- Glue each foam rectangle to the tail canvas using fabric tacky glue, spacing out every two rectangles to create the illusion of a spine (Figure 13-4a). The spaces between the foam rectangles allow the tail to swing and wiggle. However, the foam rectangles alone don't possess enough strength to support the tail when it swings back and forth, so glue rectangular Styrofoam pieces, narrower in width than the foam pieces, in the spaces between the foam and tape them with

Figure 13-4 (a) Glue the foam pieces to the canvas tail foundation. (b) Glue and tape Styrofoam pieces between the foam units. (c) Stitch the foam and Styrofoam pieces to the top edge of the tail canvas. (d) Completed the tail foundation.

black duct tape (Figure 13-4b). Styrofoam is lightweight and more rigid than foam, and will support the foam.

- Hand sew all the foam and taped Styrofoam pieces to the center top of the tail canvas to secure them (Figure 13-4c).
- Finally trim the foam rectangles with scissors, tapering them down to the tip of the tail. Cut and attach a longer tapered foam piece for the end of the tail (Figure 13-4d).
- Hand sew a diamond-shaped canvas piece between the belt and the start of the foam for reinforcement (Figure 13-4d).

Step Three: Sculpting the Crocodile with Clay

Sculpting the Head

The crocodile's head is built in two separate parts: the upper jaw and lower jaw. I recommend that you sculpt the crocodile's head on a sculpting table. (For this example, I did not have one in the shop, so I sculpted the head on a hat block that was set on the table. It worked with little difficulty.)

- Do research on crocodiles.
- Build up a wire frame around the mirror balls (eyes) and the hat block to support the modeling clay. (Aluminum wire was used for the frame in this example because it is lightweight and

easy to bend.) The wire frame has to be at least ½″ smaller than the clay surface all the way around, so plan ahead (Figure 13-5).

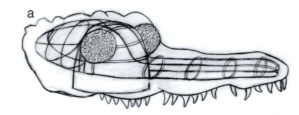

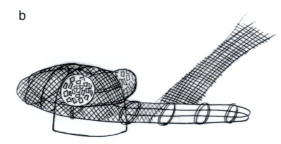

Figure 13-5 (a) Reference: Make the wire frame at least ½″ smaller all the away around than the clay surface will be. (b) Build up the wire frame over a hat block, attaching the mirror balls and wrapping the wire frame with wire screen strips.

- Cover the two mirror balls with thin plastic bags, and anchor the plastic bags on the hat block with T-pins or tie them to the wire frame (Figure 13-5a). The two mirror balls will be used as the crocodile eyes and will be inserted into the rubber crocodile head after it is made; the clay is molded around them to provide an accurate fit between the eyes and rubber skin. They are removed after the negative mold is made.

- Wrap wire screening (cut into strips) over the wire frame to seal the gaps between the wires (Figure 13-5a). This will reduce the weight of the upper head when the clay is added to the frame.
- Build clay up over the wire frame and sculpt the crocodile's upper jaw. The clay can be very heavy even though it is supported with wire. A couple of wooden cubes can be placed under the jaw for extra support (Figures 13-6 to

Figure 13-6 (a) Crocodile upper jaw molded with clay — ¾ view. (b) Crocodile upper jaw molded with clay — profile.

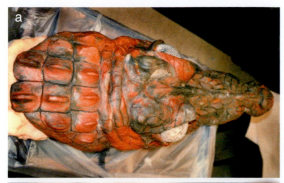

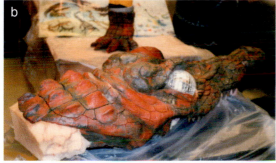

Figure 13-7 (a) Crocodile upper jaw molded with clay — top. (b) Crocodile upper jaw molded with clay — back.

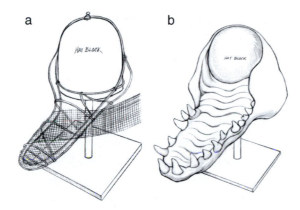

Figure 13-8 (a) Build the wire frame for the lower jaw over a hat block. (b) Build up the lower jaw with clay.

(Figure 13-2); the tail shape and size are based on the foam tail foundation that you built.

- Build up about $\frac{1}{2}''$ even thickness clay-sheet from the table surface first and then mold detailed crocodile scales on top of it. The crocodile's scales in this example were based on the natural beauty of a real crocodile's skin. The scales were balanced, carefully sculpted, and directly built up on the clay skin/sheet on the table (Figures 13-9 to 13-10; unfortunately, no photos are available of the finished tail, limb, or belly skins).

there was no sculpting table available when I made the lower jaw, I chose to make it separately. Repeat the same steps of modeling the upper jaw. There are no photos available of the lower jaw.)

Sculpting the Crocodile's Back, Tail, Limb, and Belly

- Model the skin for crocodile's back, tail, limb (only one sculpture is needed for the four limbs), and belly from clay individually and directly on a large table. The size and shape of the back, limb, and belly are based on the patterns for the foam foundation pieces

13-7). If the aluminum wire sticks out of the clay, knock it down with a hammer, but be careful not to distort the clay shape you just built on the wire frame.

- Create the lower jaw, building the clay up on a wire frame, just as you did for the upper jaw (Figure 13-8). (Technically, the upper and lower jaws should be built in one piece. Since

Figure 13-9 Completed clay crocodile back skin plus scales.

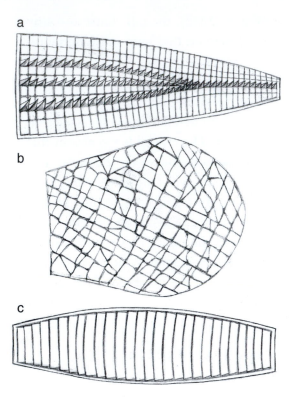

Figure 13-10 (a) Sketch of the clay crocodile tail skin and scales. (b) Sketch of the clay crocodile limb skin and scales. (c) Sketch of clay crocodile belly skin and scales.

Step Three: Making Negative Plaster Molds from the Clay Sculptures

All the crocodile parts sculpted from clay are needed to make a negative plaster mold so that you can make the rubber latex piece.

Pouring Molds for the Back, Tail, Belly, and Limb

- First, build a 2″-tall clay wall around each clay sculpture.
- Mix a ratio of 1 cup water with $2\frac{1}{2}$ caps plaster of paris powder. To do this, first, pour water into the mixing bowl, and then sprinkle plaster powder into the water, without stirring, until the powder reaches about $\frac{1}{4}$″ above the surface of the water. Then stir the mixture until it becomes a creamy paste.
- Pour the plaster over each clay sculpture, from the center out; pour it slowly to avoid creating air bubbles underneath. The negative plaster mold should be at least 1″ thick on all surfaces. If a second coat is needed, mix it thicker than the first coat.
- After the plaster becomes warm and starts cooling down, the mold can be removed from the clay sculpture. Use a screwdriver or sculpting tool to carefully loosen the edges around the negative mold, and turn the mold over. TWO people will be needed to turn it over because of its size (I tried to turn one of these over by myself and it cracked from the middle).
- After each mold is turned over and the clay sculpture removed, clean out the clay that's stuck in the deep scale

impressions of the mold with a sculpting tool. Clay can be easily removed from the scales when the mold is still warm.

Pouring the Mold for the Jaws

- No clay wall needed for pouring the upper and lower jaw negative molds, because of the dimensions of the clay molds. The plaster mixture for pouring the negative molds should be manageable, not too runny or too thick. Pour plaster over the upper and lower jaws in exactly the same way (but without dividers), following the directions for pouring the negative mold for the Dracula mask (Chapter 1; see Figure 1-26 for directions on mixing and applying plaster over the clay sculptured mold).

Step Four: Pouring Casting Latex into the Negative Molds

No mold release is needed when making rubber latex pieces.

Pouring Latex for the Back, Tail, Belly, and Limb

- Pour the liquid casting latex in a zigzag, swinging your arms back and forth across the surface of the negative mold of the back piece. You need enough latex to cover the entire mold. Two even coats of latex will be thick enough to form a durable rubber skin (Figure 13-11a).

Figure 13-11 (a) Negative mold of the crocodile back with casting latex poured in. (b) Negative mold of the crocodile limb with casting latex poured in. The clay limb mold sculpted by Patti Sweesy.

- The tail, belly, and limb pieces are done the same way as the back piece. Using the same limb mold (Figure 13-11b), pour the casting latex four times so that you have four limbs.

Pouring Latex for the Head

Rubber latex is floppy, it won't stay in shape by itself. The body latex pieces will be supported by the foam suit. For the crocodile head, you must insert foam strips and canvas strips so that it retains its shape. This is done in exactly the same way as when making rubber masks. (Chapter 5; see Figures 5-6 to 5-13 for how to insert foam strips into a negative mold.)

- Pour latex into the upper jaw negative mold, turn the mold around, and make sure the latex covers the entire surface of the mold, including the ends of the teeth. Set aside to dry.
- When the latex is half dry, pour the second coat of latex into the mold. Rotate the mold until the entire surface is covered with the second coat. Immediately place some precut foam strips around the inside edge of the upper jaw, on top of the upper jaw in the center, and in the nose tip. Insert canvas strips in the wet latex into the spaces between the foam pieces, except the eyes. After the latex dries, the jaw will be a flexible shell.
- Pour latex in the lower jaw negative mold in the same way as you did for the upper jaw.

Removing the Molds and Dyeing

- After the latex dries, brush baby powder along the edges of the latex before peeling each latex piece from its mold.

- Dye all the rubber pieces green. In the example, Rit dye was used. Precook the dye and pour it into a washing machine or large garbage can. Soak the rubber pieces in the dye until they are the desired color.

Step Five: Putting the Pieces Together

The Head

- Make a diagonal slash in the middle of each latex eye; turn about half of the slashed edges in and glue them down. Glue a mirror ball just behind this slashed opening. The sparkling mirror eyeballs will convey a lifelike illusion to the crocodile's eyes.
- Make a headdress foundation from buckram (Chapter 11; see Figures 11-10 to 11-13) or Fosshape (Chapter 12; see Figures 12-3 to 12-6).
- Hand stitch to attach the upper and lower rubber jaws the headdress foundation so they are one piece.
- Attach the lower jaw to the headdress foundation first. Step one: Cross-attach a double-layered canvas strip (1" wide and 10" long — needs to be fitted on actor's head) onto the sides of the back portion of the rubber lower jaw with casting latex and hand stitching, only attach down the ends (about 2") of the canvas strip. Step two: Hand sew the

middle portion of the canvas strip onto the top of the headdress foundation (about ear to ear cross up position).

- Properly position the upper jaw on the top of the lower jaw and secure it onto the headdress with casting latex (function as glue) and hand tacking stitches at the top and back portion of the upper jaw. The actor's head is completely covered by this crocodile headdress. The lower jaw is kept open so that the actor can breathe and see.

- Attach/glue a piece of red chiffon fabric to the throat with casting latex as a tongue; this will also conceal the actor's face. (In fact, crocodiles do not have a

tongue. I added a red tongue for a theatrical effect.)

The completed crocodile headdress is shown in Figure 13-12.

The Body

- Use leather glue-barge to glue the rubber skin to the crocodile's foam back, sides (limbs), belly, and tail. Sew two cotton fabric pockets (at neck and upper waistline areas) to the back of the outfit to holding ice packs to cool

the actor's body (the foam keeps the body very warm).

- Glue each latex limb on to its sleeve or leg foam support piece, and use an industrial sewing machine to stitch the side seam of each limb together.

- Sew the limbs to the torso. The thick layers of foam and latex are hard to handle when sewing, so use an industrial sewing machine.

The completed costume is shown in Figures 13-13 to 13-17.

Figure 13-12 Completed crocodile headdress.

Figure 13-13 Completed crocodile rubber costume; the rubber gloves and feet were also sculpted with clay and poured with casting latex as the same way of making the jaws. They were created by Patti Sweesy.

Figure 13-14 Publicity photo of Peter Pan and the Crocodile (before painted). *Becky Main played Peter Pan. Troy Gibson played Crocodile. Central Washington University Theatre Arts Department presentation.*

Figure 13-15 Actor Troy Gibson in crocodile outfit without headdress — profile.

Figure 13-17 Production photo of *Peter Pan. Troy Gibson played Crocodile. Becky Main played Peter Pan. David Shoup played Hook. Directed by Michael Smith. Scenic design by Mark C. Zetterberg. Lighting design by Dave Barnett. Costume design by James Hawkins. Animal costume design by Tan Huaixiang. Central Washington University Theatre Arts Department presentation.*

Figure 13-16 (a) Crocodile curtsying. (b) Crocodile in standing position — back.

Chapter 14   Fabric Outfits

MAKING A SWAN COSTUME

The inspiration for the swan costume used in *Elves and Shoemaker* (Figure 14-1) came from a ballet tutu with many layers of fabric closely attached to a dance trunk. The layered feathery fabrics were arranged in gradated colors that added flavor and an effective, interesting look to the whole outfit.

Figure 14-1 Costume design for *Elves and Shoemaker*.

PROCEDURE FOR MAKING THE SWAN COSTUME

Materials Required:

- Pattern paper
- Nylon organza (white)
- Nylon organza (from light to dark blue colors)
- White leotard
- White acrylic fur material
- Poly stuffing
- Small piece of felt
- Animal eyes
- Headband
- Sewing machine
- Needle and thread
- Scissors
- White dance trunk

Step One: Creating Patterns and Cutting Fabrics

- Create the patterns for the swan's head and the tutu. The pattern for the swan's head and neck is a long and narrow rectangle rounded at the head. The pattern for the tutu is developed from a square. Three corners of the square are cut and rounded off into a basic circular shape, with one square corner and an off-center waistline opening. The entire edge of the tutu is feather cut.

- Lay each pattern piece on the proper fabric and cut it out. Different shades of blue nylon organza fabric were used to make this tutu (Figure 14-2a); this fabric has a stiff and crisp texture so the feathered raw edges won't fray. The swan head/neck is made from acrylic fur fabric (Figure 14-2b).

Step Two: Assembling the Swan Head

Making the Neck

- Fold the neck piece with the fury sides facing each other, and stitch the side seam. Turn the stitched tube right side out.
- Stuff the neck tube with poly stuffing. For flexibility, don't stuff the neck too much.

Making the Swan's Bill

- Cut two pieces of felt following the swan bill pattern (Figure 14-2c), and top-stitch them together with a $\frac{1}{8}''$ seam allowance.
- Stuff the bill with poly stuffing; insert it into the head seam on the neck and stitch it down.
- Cut out the accent/trim of the swan bill pattern on leather (Figure 14-2d), and glue this over the stitching line on the bill (where the bill merges with the head) as an accent (Figure 14-2e).
- Sew eyes on the head. Attach a headband under the swan head/neck with hand-sewn stitches for securing it on the actor's head. Tie a ribbon around the head where the headband is attached as decoration.

Step Two: Making the Tutu

- Machine sew two rows of zigzag stitches over a heavy gathering thread around the inner edge of each tutu layer (Figure 14-3a). The inserted heavy thread is pulled to gather each tutu piece and fit it around the dance trunk.
- Attach each gathered layer of tutu to the dance trunk (Figure 14-3b). Start on the bottom row with the darkest blue pieces, position each layer about $\frac{3}{4}''$ apart, and continue up until the trunk is covered, ending with the white pieces.

Figure 14-2 (a) Pin the tutu pattern for the swan costume on layered organza fabric. (b) Pin the pattern for the swan head on the fur fabric. (c) Pin the swan bill pattern to felt. (d) Place the accent/trim of the bill pattern on black leather. (e) Swan bill and head/neck are cut, sewn, and jointed together.

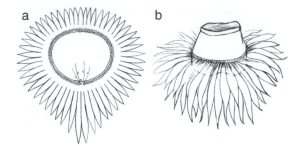

Figure 14-3 (a) Sew two rows of gathering stitches over a heavy thread to the inner edge of each tutu layer. (b) Attach the tutu layers to the dance trunk, starting at the bottom.

Figure 14-4 Completed swan tutu.

Figure 14-5 Production photo of the swan costume in *Elves and Shoemaker*. (a) *Swan played by Kyra McGough.* (b) *Colette Jones (left) played Mrs. Shoup. Kyra McGough (middle) played Swan. David Shoup (right) played Mr. Shoup. Directed by James Haskins. Scenic design by Dutch Fritz. Lighting design by Mark C. Zetterberg. Costume design by Tan Huaixiang. Directed by James Haskins. Scenic design by Dutch Fritz. Lighting design by Mark C. Zetterberg. Costume design by Tan Huaixiang. Central Washington University Theatre Arts Department presentation.*

The completed costume is shown in Figures 14-4 to 14-5.

MAKING A TREE COSTUME

In *Once on This Island*, Ti Moune falls in love with Daniel, but she later learns that Daniel's parents have already arranged for him to marry a girl from his own class. In despair and goaded on by the god of Death, Ti Moune tries to kill Daniel, but at the last moment her love for him triumphs. Ti Moune fulfills her promise to the gods, proving the power of love by giving her life in exchange for Daniel's and becomes a tree (Figure 14-6).

Banyan trees grow in the tropical islands where the story takes place. Their roots extend from their branches to the ground and weave and stretch out in unique patterns. It was logical to adopt the banyan tree as Ti Moune's tree costume, and the director approved it. Fleece was used to create this tree costume. Fleece has several advantages: (1) It is bulky and durable, providing enough body and volume for banyan tree roots; (2) it possesses the same color and texture on both sides of the fabric; (3) it does not ravel; and (4) it is stretchy, and if you pull the fleece on the cross-grain,

Figure 14-6 Costume design for *Once on This Island*.

both edges of the fabric strip will naturally curve and roll toward the center to create a 3-D banyan tree root (the best quality). Different shades and patterns of fleece pieces in the banyan-tree color range were used to create exquisite and artistic roots. Each 1-yard-long fleece was cut cross-grain into 7–10" wide × 60" long strips. Each strip was slashed, woven, twisted, stretched, and knotted in a unique way.

PROCEDURE FOR MAKING THE TREE COSTUME

Materials Required:

- Fleece fabric in different tones (highlights, middle tones, and shadows)
- Scissors
- Net or mesh tunic
- Decorative floral vine
- Needle and thread
- Safety pins
- Hat block
- ¾" diameter foam cord
- Copper wire
- Artificial leaves
- Fosshape headdress base
- Buckram
- Fabric clear tacky glue

Step One: Cutting Fabrics

- Based on the natural color of banyan tree roots, purchase 4–5 different shades of fleece fabric, 1 yard per shade.
- Cut the fleece cross-grain in 6 = 10"-wide strips (Figure 14-7).
- Natural roots split as they grow. To achieve that with fabric, make vertical cuts/slashes in each strip in different locations. Slash thick strips starting at one edge (designated as the top edge); more slashes (and thus thinner strips) should be made at the bottom edge of

Figure 14-7 Cut the fleece fabrics into strips.

the strip as natural roots split out (Figure 14-8). Evenly spaced slashes achieve a symmetrical balance, while unevenly-spaced slashes achieve an asymmetrical balance.

- Make small vertical holes near the end of each slash to create splitting branches. Make a small hole in the middle section of a strip or middle section of an entire root (these will be used to create a 3-dimensional texture (Figure 14-8).

Figure 14-8 Cut slashes and small vertical holes in the fleece strips.

Step Two: Creating Banyan Tree Roots

- Pull the slashed strips through the holes. Start from the top of the root (the end with the thicker strips) and work down. It doesn't matter whether the fabric is pulled from the front or the back. You can also pull some strips through the holes in other roots. Figures 14-9 to 14-11 illustrate this technique on the thick-strip ends/tops of the roots.

Figure 14-9 (a) Starting with the top of the root, insert the slashed strips into the holes. (b) Pull the strips straight through the holes.

Figure 14-10 (a) Insert a strip of the top edge through a hole in another strip. (b) Pull the strip through the hole.

- Apply the same technique to the thin-strip ends/bottoms of the roots. Then tie some knots at the very ends of the strips. Figures 14-12 to 14-14 illustrate the technique on the strips on the lower edge/portion of the roots.

Completed roots are shown in Figures 14-15 to 14-16.

Figure 14-11 (a) Insert all three top strips into a hole made at the middle of the entire root. (b) Pull the three strips through the hole. (c) Full view of the root.

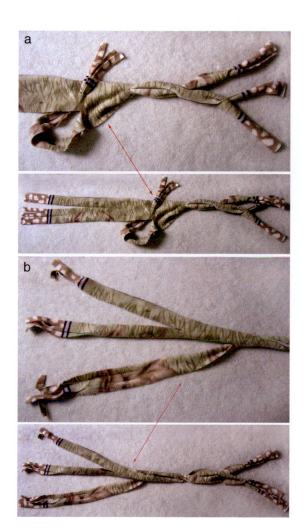

Figure 14-12 (a) On the lower portion of the root, insert a slashed strip into a nearby hole. (b) Pull the strip through the hole.

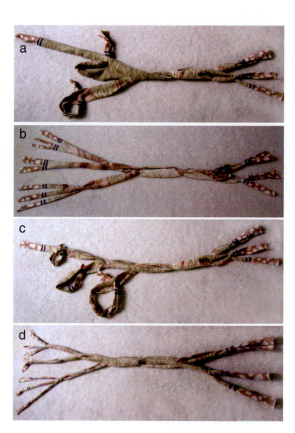

Figure 14-13 (a) Insert strips into nearby holes. (b) Pull the strips through to create more splitting roots. (c) Insert strips into holes made in the middle section of each strip. (d) Pull strips through to create 3-D splitting roots.

Figure 14-14 (a) On the very ends of each strip, tie knots to add character to the root. (b) Add more knots for more texture.

Figure 14-15 Example of a textured root in a different color and with different splits.

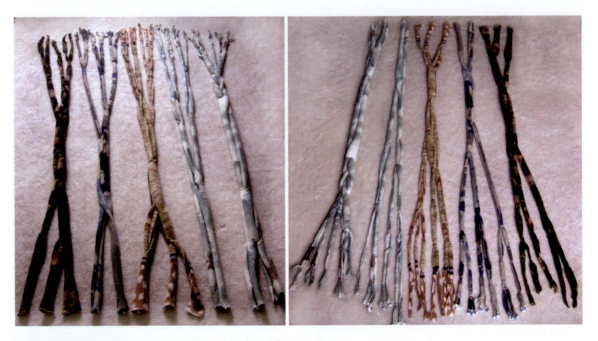

Figure 14-16 Completed roots in different shades of fleece strips.

Step Three: Attaching the Individual Roots to the Mesh Tunic

- Wrap and interweave a floral vine around some of the roots for decoration. Hand sew the vine to the root end that will be attached to the mesh tunic, and tie the loose hanging end of the vine and root together with the slashed fleece ends (Figure 14-17a).

- Safety pin each root to the mesh tunic, placing the roots at staggered intervals/ positions (Figure 14-17b). Pin the darkest roots to the tunic first as the bottom layer. Place the middle-tone strips on top of the darkest roots, and place the light-tone strips on top of the middle-tone roots as the top layer. This

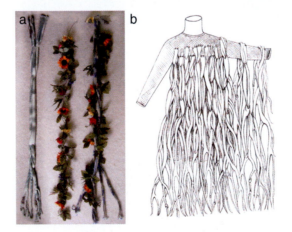

Figure 14-17 (a) Wrap floral vine around the root and secured it by tying the vines with fleece roots. (b) Attach the roots to the mesh tunic.

will highlight and accent the outfit to create depth and dimension.

Step Four: Making the Tree Headdress

The completed tree costume is accompanied with a tree headdress. This tree headdress needs a headdress foundation made from Fosshape and covered with fleece fabric, and branches made of foam cords and covered with fleece fabric strips. The process is similar to making the god of Water headdress waves (Chapter 12; see Figures 12-3 to 12-9), except no wooden base is added to the Fosshape base, but a buckram base instead.

- Make tree branches by inserting copper wire into various length of foam cords (Figure 14-18a).
- Attach a few small foam cords to the long ones to create split branches as desired. Wrap and tie leaves to the upper portions of the foam cords.
- Create a buckram base for attaching foam cord branches in the same way as the turban base (See Figures 11-9 and 11-10) but make it much shallower. Cut it with a 6″ diameter so it will perfectly fit on top of the headdress foundation and then wire the edge.
- Bend the bottom of each foam cord branch in a circle and bend it in a 45 to 90 degree angle (depends on how the branches spread out) relative to the base. Hand sew each circle to the buckram base with double Hy-mark threads.
- After all the branches are attached to the buckram base, then attach the buckram base to the Fosshape headdress base.

And then wrap each foam cord branch with fleece fabric strips (like the water waves in Chapter 12). Weave more fleece fabric strips around the buckram base and glue them down; hang a few fabric strips from the base as banyan tree roots to finish off the headdress. The completed headdress is shown in Figure 14-18b. The completed costume is shown in Figures 14-19 to 14-20.

Figure 14-18 (a) The banyan tree headdress creator, Bukki Sittler, a BA theater major student at University of Central Florida Conservatory Theatre, making tree branches. (b) Completed tree headdress.

Figure 14-19 Production photo of the tree costume in *Once on This Island. Ti Moune played by Kahliah Rivers.*

Figure 14-20 Production photo of the tree costume in *Once on This Island. Ti Moune played by Kahliah Rivers, music student. Directed by Earl Weavor. Music/Vocal Director by Jim Brown. Choreographed by Brian Vernon. Scenic design by Vandy Woods. Lighting design by David Upton. Costume design by Tan Huaixiang. University of Central Florida Conservatory Theatre presentation.*

MAKING A FRUIT COSTUME

This fruit dress and its headdress were used in the musical *Pippin* (Figure 14-21). For the dress, fruits and flowers are attached to a bra and dance trunk; the headdress is built on a bike helmet's inner support. They were created by Jonathan Waters (fruit costume) and Kisha Cobourne (headdress), both BFA design and technology students. They did a wonderful job.

PROCEDURE FOR MAKING THE FRUIT COSTUME

Materials Required:

- Bra and dance trunk
- 3 plastic shell-like dishes (two for the bra, one for the crotch)
- Spray paint
- Dremel tools
- Electric drill
- Needle and thread
- Artificial fruit and flowers
- Raffia
- 1"-wide elastic waistband
- Inner support from a bike helmet
- Hat block

Step One: Creating a Foundation and Attaching Fruit and Flowers to the Foundation

- Obtain a bra and dance trunk. Sew a 1"-wide elastic waistband to the dance trunk for added support.
- Attach the shell dishes to the two cups of the bra; center the third dish on the front crotch of the dance trunk. The shell dishes are for holding the fruit (small baskets can also be used in place of shell dishes). To do this, cut two of the shell dishes smaller with a Dremal tool to fit the bra cups. Drill holes on the edges of the shell dishes and hand sew the shell dishes through these holes to the bra and dance trunk (Figures 14-22a and c).
- Attach fruit, flowers, and raffia to the entire elastic waistband and to the shell dishes on the bra and dance truck as desired to complete the outfit (Figures 14-22b, d, and 14-23).

The completed dress is shown in Figure 14-24.

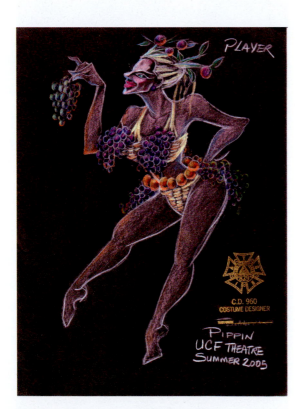

Figure 14-21 Costume design for *Pippin*.

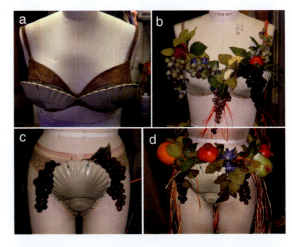

Figure 14-22 (a) Attach two shell dishes to the bra cup. (b) Attach fruit to the bra cups. (c) Attach the third shell dish to the dance-trunk crotch. (d) Attach fruit, flowers, and raffia to the dance trunk.

Figure 14-23 Jonathan Waters, a University of Central Florida BFA design/technology student, attaching fruit and raffia to the outfit.

Figure 14-24 Completed fruit dress.

Step Two: Creating the Fruit Headdress

A bike helmet's inner support (purchased from a thrift store) was used as the foundation of the fruit headdress. It is adjustable and lightweight.

- Remove the inner support from the bike helmet and put it on a hat block.
- Insert tufts of raffia into the holes existing on the helmet support band, tie into knots to secure, and basketweave the raffia tufts together over the helmet support to create a slightly dome-shaped headdress top (the helmet support itself is topless) (Figures 14-25c–d).

Figure 14-25 (a) Fruit headdress — front. (b) Fruit headdress — side. (c) Top of the headdress, showing the woven raffia. (d) Inside of the headdress showing the bike helmet inner support. It was made by Kisha Cobourne.

- Attach leaves and flowers with hand stitches around the circumference of the helmet support and raffia to complete the headdress.

The completed headdress is shown in Figure 14-25. The completed fruit costume is shown in Figure 14-26.

Figure 14-26 Production photo of the fruit costume in *Pippin. Pippin played by Justin Sargent, Fruit girl played by Christine Perez. Directed by John Bell. Set design by Joseph Rusnock. Lighting design by Eric Haugen. Sound design by Martin Wootton. Costume design by Tan Huaixiang. University of Central Florida Conservative Theatre presentation.*

Chapter 15 Wire-framed Headdresses

Wire-framed headdresses were used in the children's show *Just So*. The costumes for the show were plain and simple, mostly unitards and leotards with wraps; the focus of the costumes was the headdresses.

Full wire-framed headdresses were made for most of the characters in the show, including Eland, Rhino, Kolokolo Bird, Zebra, Bushbuck, Koodoo, Giraffe, Quagga, Alligator, Cooking Stove

(chimney), and Parsee (shaft hat). Half headdresses (ears only) were made for Dingo Dog, Jaguar, Leopard, and Kangaroo. Both the full and half headdresses were made of flexible

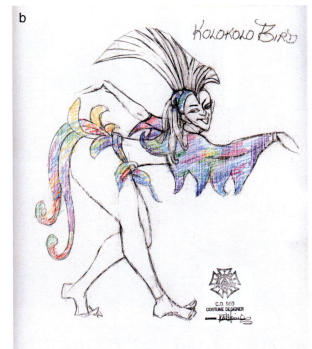

250 **Figure 15-1** Costume design for *Just So*, (a) Eland; (b) Kolokolo Bird and Rhino.

c

ZEBRA

KOODOO

Figure 15-1—Cont'd Costume design for *Just So*, (c) Zebra and Koodoo.

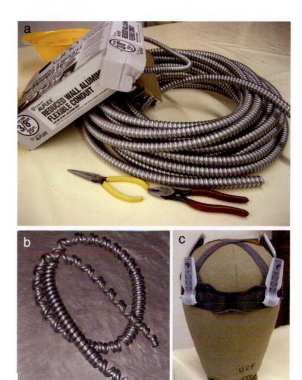

Figure 15-2 (a) Flexible aluminum conduit (curly) wire. (b) Partially uncoil one end of the flexible aluminum conduit wire; trim one of the sharp ends and bend into a rounded edge. (c) Place the inner support from a construction helmet on a hat block.

aluminum conduit wire (also used in housing construction) built on top of the inner supports of construction helmets. All the headdresses were made with very much the same methods and materials, but in different shapes. The Eland horn headdress is presented as an example here.

PROCEDURE FOR CONSTRUCTING A WIRED HEADDRESS

Materials Required:

- $^3/_8$" flexible aluminum conduit (curly) wire (Figure 15-2a)
- $^3/_4$" flexible aluminum conduit (curly) wire

- Inner support from construction helmets (quality is not very good, but I used it to save money) or from bike helmets (better quality but more expensive)
- Plastic package ties with gun
- Two pieces of 30"-long straight wire
- Wire cutters
- Working gloves and apron
- Hat block

Step One: Preparation

- Cut two pieces of coiled wire for each horn, one piece twice as long as the other. Cut one piece of straight wire for each horn (Figure 15-3a). Trim off the sharp corners and bend the ends inward into a little spiral to create a rounded edge (Figure 15-3b). Any cuts made on any pieces of wire should to be trimmed and bent in this same way for safety.

- Each spiral of the conduit wire has an upper rounded edge and a lower flat sharp edge and they are overlocked together. The spirals/coils can be pulled apart and stretched to loose spirals.

Figure 15-3 (a) Cut two curly wires and one straight wire; pull the ends of the curly wire loose. (b) Fold the longer curly wire in half, bending in the sharp ends and rounding them inward into a small spiral.

Stretching and loosening the spirals/coils (Figure 15-3b) will reduce its weight and also achieve a unique texture and look. Only one end of the flexible aluminum conduit wire can be easily pulled apart without destroying the coils. Pull and stretch from the rounded edge side of the spiral/coil. Keep partial wire fully coiled as desired (Figure 15-3a).

- Take out the inner support from a bike or construction helmet to use the foundation of the wired headdress. (The inner support from a bike helmet adjusts better and is more durable. If budget allows it, the bike helmet's inner supports should be the first choice.)

- Fit the helmet support on to a hat block 1″ bigger than the actor's head (Figure 15-2c).

Step Two: Creating Horns

Each horn is made from two pieces of coiled wire and one straight wire twisted together.

- Fold the longer coiled wire in half and bend the sharp corners on the ends inward to round them out into a small spiral (Figure 15-3b).

- Twist the unstretched portion of the folded coiled wire toward the direction of the spirals, and wrap the loosely

coiled portions of the wire together into one (Figure 15-4).

- Bend the straight wire, and insert the two ends of the straight wire into the openings in the folded coiled wire at the fold; push the straight wire into them (Figure 15-5a). The two ends of the straight wire will meet when they reach the portion where the coils are wrapped together.

- Join the short coiled wire to the long folded curly wire. To do this, connect the unstretched end of the short coiled wire to the folding point of the long wire by twisting and wrapping the short wire on top of the long wire (Figure 15-5b). This creates one Eland's horn (Figure 15-5c).

- Make the second horn in the same way.

Figure 15-4 (a) Wrap the loosely coiled portions of the folded wire together. (b) Completed wrapping.

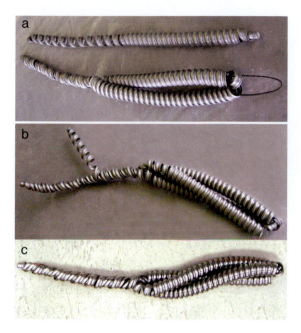

Figure 15-5 (a) Insert the folded straight wire into the hollow interior of the long coiled wire. (b) Twist the short coiled wire on top of the folded long coiled wire. (c) Completed horn.

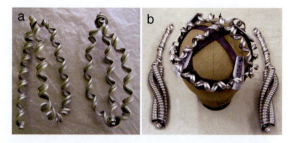

Figure 15-6 (a) Bend the wire into thirds; completed ear. (b) Tie the coiled wire to the foundation with plastic ties.

Figure 15-7 Ears and horns attached to the foundation with plastic ties — front view.

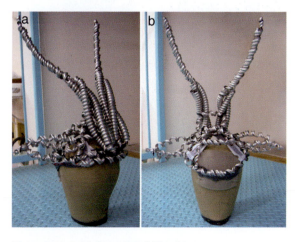

Figure 15-8 (a) Completed Eland horn headdress — side (b) Back of the Eland horn headdress showing the piece of curly wire attached behind the horns for support.

Creating Ears

- Cut a length of coiled wire. Loosen the coils and cut the wire to the desired length. Bend and round the two sharp ends. Bend the wire into thirds to form a flower-petal shape. This is one of the Eland ears (Figure 15-6a).
- Create the second ear in the same way.
- Cut a new piece of coiled wire to the proper size, pull it to loosen the spirals, and round the sharp cut ends. Overlap the ends 1–2″, and attach it to the headdress support with plastic tie (Figure 15-6b). How much it needs to be stretched, the number of pieces, and the arrangement depends on the size of the headdress. The curly wire can be stretched into tight or loose spirals. Keep in mind that the looser and more spread out the coils, the lighter in weight it will be; however, it may lose its curly texture. Tighter coils display a unique texture but add weight to the headdress. Experiment with it and make the proper adjustments.

Step Four: Attaching the Ears and Horns to the Headdress Foundation

- First attach the horns and then the ears with plastic ties. Add an extra piece of curly wire behind the horns for more support (Figure 15-8b).

The completed headdress is shown in Figures 15-7 to 15-8. The eland headdress and the other animal headdresses are shown in Figures 15-9 to 15-16.

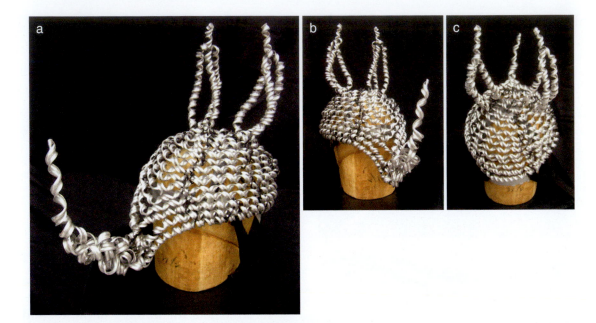

Figure.15-10 Rhino headdress: (a) ¾ view, (b) front, and (c) back.

Figure 15-9 Kolokolo bird headdress.

Figure 15-11 Koodoo headdress.

Figure 15-12 Bushbuck headdress.

Figure 15-13 Alligator headdress (made by Michael Steger).

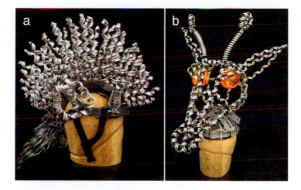

Figure 15-14 (a) Zebra headdress. (b) Giraffe headdress (made by Simon Warner).

Figure 15-15 (a) Production photo of Rhino and Parsee headdresses in *Just So*. (b) Production photo of Rhino and Cooking Stove headdresses in *Just So. Directed by Chris Jorie. Scenic design by Vandy Wood. Lighting design by David Upton. Costume design by Tan Huaixiang. Photograph from Orlando Repertory Theatre Collection. Orlando Repertory Theatre presentation.*

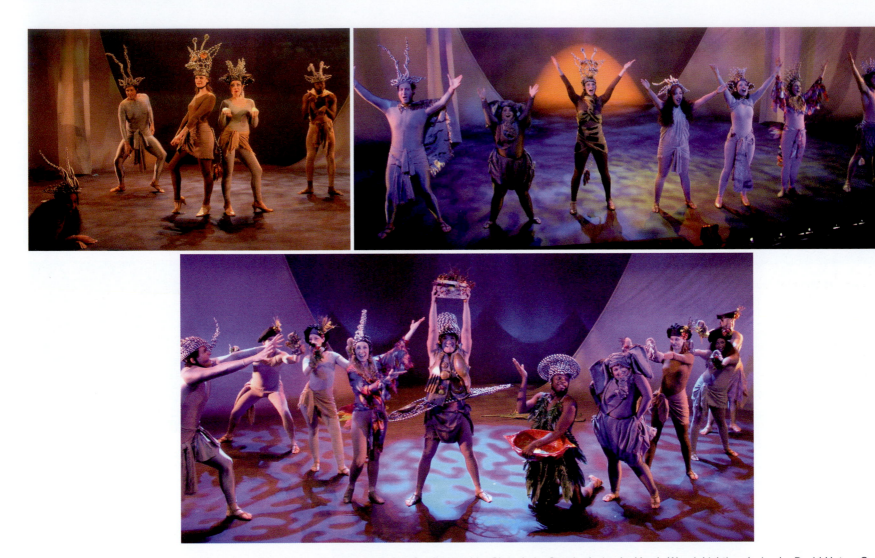

Figure 15-16 Production photos showing several wire headdresses from *Just So. Directed by Chris Jorie. Scenic design by Vandy Wood. Lighting design by David Upton. Costume design by Tan Huaixiang. Photographs from Orlando Repertory Theatre Collection. Orlando Repertory Theatre presentation.*

Figure 15-16—Cont'd

Chapter 16   Foam Headdresses and Costumes

Foam can be found at any fabric store. It is lightweight, fluffy and voluminous, easy and fast to work with, and effective on stage. I have experimented with foam when making several headdresses and costumes that I designed. Foam is one of my favorite materials for making theatrical costumes and crafts.

MAKING HORSE HEADDRESSES

In *Cinderella*, the Fairy Godmother magically creates a pumpkin carriage pulled by four horses to take Cinderella to the ball to meet the Prince (Figure 16-1). Four actors played the horses and also the guests who danced at the ball. When the clock struck midnight in the ball scene, the four actors had to quickly become horses and take Cinderella home. The solution was to have the dancers quickly put on the horse headdresses.

The headdresses were constructed with an aluminum wire frame and covered with ¼"-thick foam sheets. They seemed big,

Figure 16-1 Costume design for *Cinderella*.

but were lightweight and easy to handle by the actors on stage. The bells attached to the horses' necks made lot of noise at the first dress rehearsal, but a few drops of hot glue applied inside the bell silenced them. The foam was not painted but kept its natural creamy color, which worked well on stage.

258

PROCEDURE FOR MAKING A FOAM HORSE HEADDRESS

Materials Required:

- ¼"-diameter aluminum wire
- Millinery wire and tie wire
- Wire cutter
- ¼"-thick foam sheets
- Hot glue gun and glue sticks
- Scissors
- Headdress foundation
- Hat block
- Muslin fabric
- Elastic
- Velcro
- Rubber balls (for horse eyes)
- Gold trim (for halters)
- Bells (silenced)
- Plastic boa-like Christmas decorations (for horse manes)
- Needle and thread
- Pins
- Marker

Step One: Creating a Foundation Base for the Horse Headdress

- Make a headdress foundation from buckram (Chapter 11; see Figures 11-9 to 11-19 for how to create a buckram headdress foundation and line it with felt) or Fosshape (Chapter 12; see Figures 12-7 to 12-9).

- Place the foundation on a hat block.
- Draft a coif headpiece pattern, cut it from two layers of muslin fabric (one layer is the lining) (Figure 16-2a). For each layer, machine sew the center piece and two sides together (Figure 16-2b). With the right sides of the two finished coifs together, sew along the outer edges, keeping the center back seam allowance open so that you can turn the coif right side out (Figure 16-2c).
- Turn the coif right side out, and sew a piece of 3"-long elastic in the back and

pieces of Velcro under the chin of the coif (Figure 16-2d). Attach the coif over the headdress base.

Step Two: Creating the Wire Frame of the Horse Head

- Construct a silhouette of a horse head with aluminum wire on top of the headdress base (Figure 16-3). Tie each intersection of wire with thin tie wire. Add a few rows of millinery wire around the aluminum frame to reinforce the shape and fill in any large gaps between the aluminum wires.
- Cut one colorful rubber ball in half, and attach each half to the wire frame as the horse's eyes (Figure 16-3).

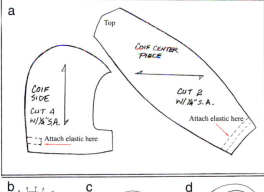

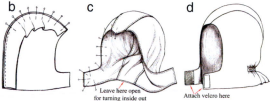

Figure 16-2 (a) Cut out two sets of coif pattern pieces from muslin. (b) Sew the center piece to the side pieces. (c) Sew the two coifs together. (d) After you turn the coif right side out, attach Velcro pieces to the front and an elastic piece to the back.

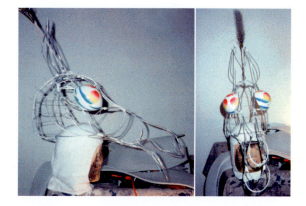

Figure 16-3 After you attach the coif to the headdress foundation on the hat block, build up an aluminum wire-frame horse headdress on top of the foundation base. Add eyes and a mane.

- Attach a plastic gold boa-like Christmas decoration between the two ears as the mane of the horse (Figure 16-3).
- Finally, hand sew the wire-frame horse head to the headdress base.

Step Three: Covering the Wire Frame with Foam

You now cover the wire frame in sections with ¼″-thick foam.

- Cover the ears first. Cut a triangular piece of foam for each ear. Wrap each foam piece around a wire frame ear from behind, and overlap and glue the seams at the mid-front.
- Cut a foam piece big enough to cover the entire horse head all the way down to the bottom of the coif. The headdress base (coif and buckram) becomes the horse's neck.
- Cut a heart shape at the top of this foam piece to go around the ear base (Figure 16-4a).
- Drape the big piece of foam over the wire frame and place the two ears inside the heart. Make sure the foam fits around the ear wire frame; pin the foam down the mane of the horse (Figure 16-4b).
- As you drape the foam over the wire frame, make marks with a light colored marker on the foam in the following

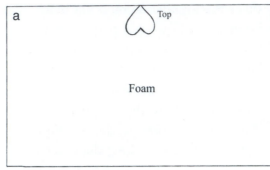

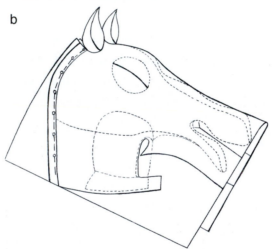

Figure 16-4 (a) Cut a heart shape out at the top of the large foam piece. (b) Drape the foam over the wire frame, fit and pin it, and mark cut lines on the foam (the figure shows one side, mark the other side in the same way).

places: across the middle of the eyes; along the silhouette of the neck and chin, including an underchin flap to overlap; on the mouth opening; and along the pins (at the center back, down the mane) (Figure 16-4b).

- Remove the foam from the wire frame, and cut it following your marks. Include a ½″ seam allowance only at the pinned part (the mane).
- Apply hot glue down the center front of the wires from the ears to the lips (between the eyes). Drape the foam over the wire frame as before, and press it on to the glue.
- Lift one side of the foam up, and apply hot glue to the exposed wire, one section at a time (because hot glue dries fast, do not attempt to apply hot glue to all the wires) (Figure 16-5a). Don't apply glue to the rubber eyes. Press the foam on to the glue and wire. Then hot glue the foam to the wire underneath the lip and chin. Trim off the excess edges of foam around the wire forming the lower lip.
- Glue the opposite side of the horse's head in the same way.
- Glue the back portion of foam to the wire one side at a time.
- Cut the mark you made previously across each eye with scissors. Trim the upper edge of the eye to the desired shape, following the rubber ball eye. Then fold the bottom edge under (Figure 16-5b).
- At the nose tip, extra foam material will be hanging down in two corners. Roll each corner back, and glue

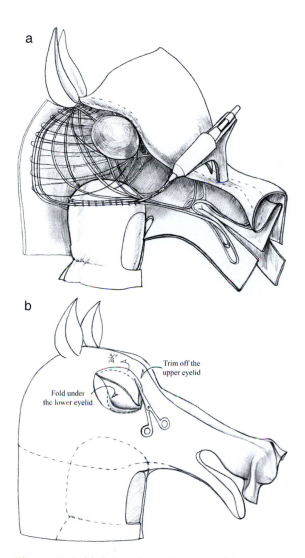

them to create the nostrils (see Figure 16-6a).

- Cut an almond-shaped piece of foam 3″ longer than the eye. Insert ⅓ of the almond beneath the upper eyelid, and fold the rest over the outside of the upper eyelid; glue down the edge to create a 3-D upper eyelid (Figures 16-6a–b).

- Cover the inside of the mouth with foam. To do this, cut a rectangular piece of foam a little bigger than the

Figure 16-5 (a) Cut the foam; lift up one side of the foam, and apply hot glue to the wire frame. (b) Trim the upper eyelid, and fold the lower eyelid under, gluing it in place.

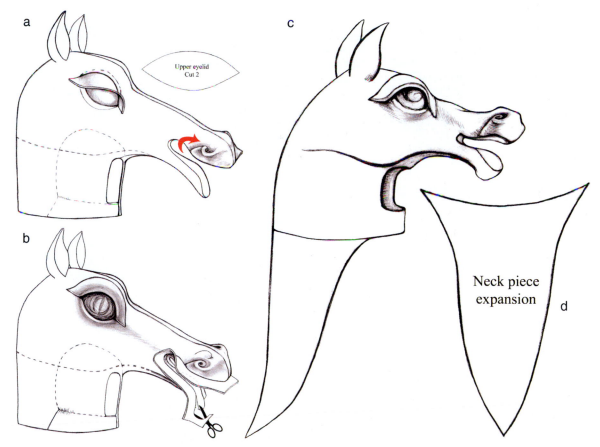

Figure 16-6 (a) Roll back the foam corner at the nose tip to create a nostril; insert an almond-shaped piece of foam beneath the upper eyelid. (b) Fold up the almond-shaped foam on the upper eyelid, and glue it to create a 3-D eyelid; glue a piece of foam to the inside of the mouth opening and trim off the excess edge. (c) Add the expansion piece to the back neck. (d) Neck expansion piece pattern.

inside of the mouth, and hot glue it to the roof and bottom of the mouth. Then trim off the excess edges (Figure 16-6b).

- Add a tapered triangle piece to expand the horse's neck (Figures 16-6c–d).

Step Four: Decorating the Horse Head

- Sew bells on the gold-trim halters, and glue the halters to the foam horse headdress.
- Attach an additional mane (Christmas decoration gold and silver boa) to the

headdress. The foam is kept its natural cream color.

The completed horse heads are shown in Figures 16-7 to 16-8.

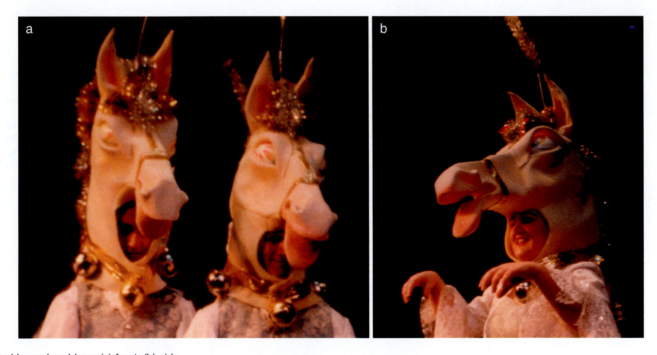

Figure 16-7 Completed horse headdress (a) front; (b) side.

Figure 16-8 Production photos of the horse headdresses in *Cinderella*. Horses played by Greg Miller, Ericka Davis, Keith Edie, and Jasmine Grevstad. Cinderella played by Leslie Webb. Godmother played by Athena Karageorges. Buttons played by David Shoup. Adaptation by Wesley Van Tassel. Directed by James Hawkins. Scenic/lighting design by Mark C. Zetterberg. Hair and wig design by Poulette Bond. Costume design by Tan Huaixiang. Central Washington University Theatre Arts Department presentation.

MAKING MOLE AND SQUIRREL HEADDRESSES

There are many animal characters in the children's play *Frog and Toad*, including three moles, two squirrels, three birds, a turtle, a lizard, a frog, a toad, and a snail. Headdresses were created for all of these characters. The moles, squirrels, turtle, and snail headdresses were made of 1"-thick foam sheets. The mole and squirrel headdresses are the examples presented here (Figure 16-9).

MOLE HEADDRESS

PROCEDURE FOR MAKING THE MOLE HEADDRESS

Materials Required:

- 1"-thick foam (²⁄₃ yd per mole)
- Pattern paper
- Animal eyes
- Scissors
- Marker
- String (to tie foam)
- Needle and thread
- Spray paint
- Fabric tacky clear glue

Figure 16-9 Costume design for *Frog and Toad*.

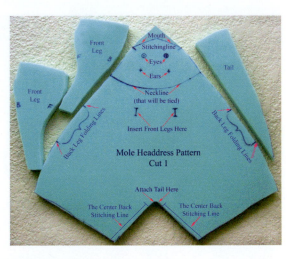

Figure 16-10 Mole patterns.

Step One: Creating the Pattern

- Create a pattern by playing with a piece of foam to get the desired size and shape. Make marks on a piece of experimental/mock-up foam, and transfer the shape to a paper pattern or use the experimental foam as a pattern.

- Transfer the marks from the pattern to an actual foam piece that you plan to use using straight pins. Push the pins through the marks made on the pattern to the actual foam piece; carefully lift up the pattern and mark where the pin locations are on the foam. Cut out the shapes (Figure 16-10).

Step Two: Creating the Ears

- A mole has tiny ears and eyes. The eyes will be glued on later. Cut two $^3/_8$"-thick and 5"-long foam strips for the ears.

- Use a scissors to poke holes in the foam body that you made in step one, to show where the ears are located (Figures 16-11a and c). Fold each foam strip in half and insert it into one of the holes (Figures 16-11b and d). The looped side is the ear. Pull the ear strips through the ear holes to the wrong side of the foam and glue down the two ends (Figures 16-11e–f).

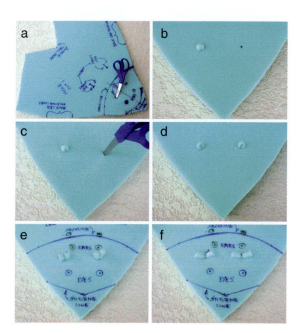

Figure 16-11 (a) Poke an ear hole in the body piece. (b) Insert one ear. (c). Poke the other ear hole. (d) Insert the second ear. (e) Turn the body piece over; note the ends of the ear strips. (f) Glue down the ends of the ear strips.

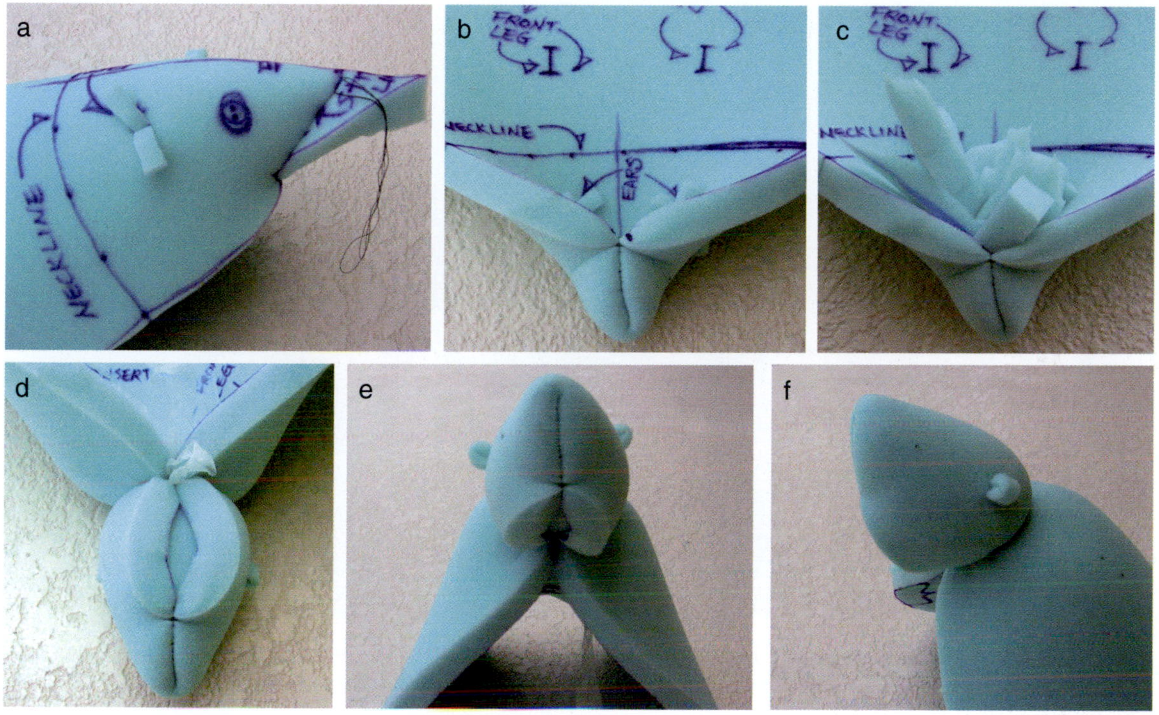

Figure 16-12 (a) Stitch the nose. (b) Turn the nose right side out. (c). Stuff the nose and head with foam pieces. (d) Tie off the head at the neck with string. (e–f) Mole head.

Step Three: Creating the Head

- Take the body piece. With the right sides of the foam together, follow the stitching marks and hand sew the nose tip with $\frac{1}{4}''$ back stitches using double thread (smaller stitches will rip the foam) (Figure 16-12a). The uneven seam allowance around the stitching line is for stuffing the nose tip.

- Turn the body piece right side out, and stuff the head and nose with small foam pieces (Figures 16-11b–c). Tie the foam tightly along the neckline marks to form a mole head using any nonstretchy string (Figure 16-12d). This completes the mole head (Figures 16-12e–f)

Step Four: Attaching the Tail

- With the right sides of the foam together, hand-stitch the center back seam together to form the butt; leave about $\frac{3}{4}''$ at the end of the seam unsewn to insert the tail (Figure 16-13a).

- Fold the foam tail and hand sew the edges together with large slanted hem stitches to create a cylinder-shaped tail (Figure 16-13b).

- Turn the body right side out (Figure 16-13c). Insert the tail through the hole

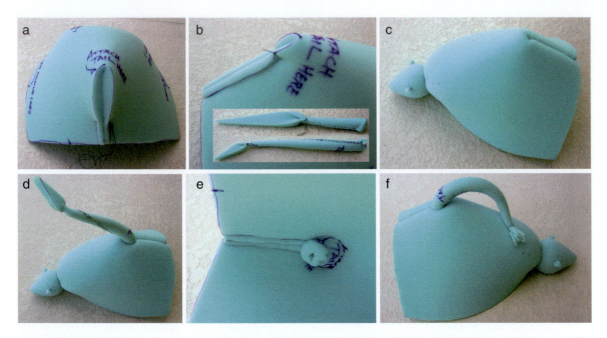

Figure 16-13 (a) Hand sew the center back seam. (b) Sew the tail together. (c) Turn the body foam right side out. (d) Insert the tail into the hole left in the seam. (e) Glue the tail end down inside the body. (f) Sew the other tail end to the foam body.

Step Six: Creating the Front Legs

- Find the front leg marks on the foam body, and slash them open with scissors (Figure 16-15a). The slashes you make should be four times smaller than the width of the leg to be inserted. The foam can be stretched.
- Fold the ends of one leg piece twice so it's round (Figure 16-15b), and insert it into one of the slashes, pushing and pulling it to the wrong side of the foam (Figures 16-15c–d); secure it with glue to the inside of the foam body. Insert the second front leg in the same way (Figure 16-15e).
- Tie the ends of the front leg together with a string (Figure 16-15f). Hand-stitch with tacking stitches the lower portion of the front leg to the body (Figure 16-15g).
- Cut the paws with scissors (Figures 16-15h–i).

that you left in the back seam (Figure 16-13d), and glue the inserted end to the inside of the foam (Figure 16-13e). Sew the other end of the tail to the foam body (Figure 16-13f).

Step Five: Creating the Back Legs

- Make two back legs from two big pleats made in the foam body. To do this, fold the "back leg folding lines" toward the head, pin them down, and hand-stitch them together with three large tacking

stitches in the middle of the leg (Figures 16-14a–e).
- After you sew both legs, trim the paws with scissors (Figure 16-14f).
- To create a thigh, make a 1"-long stitch at the upper portion of each leg (Figure 16-14g). Then, from the inside of the foam body, pull the two threads until an indentation appears on the outside of the foam (the thigh); then tie the threads together into a knot and secure the knot with glue (Figure 16-14h). This completes the thigh (Figure 16-14i).

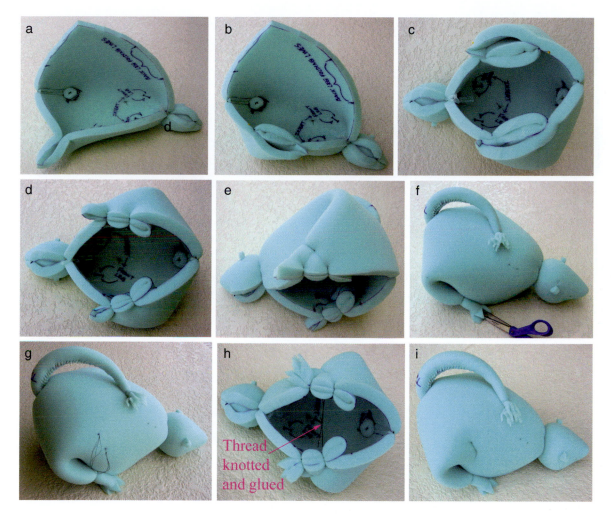

Figure 16-14 (a) Fold on the "back leg folding line." (b) Fold the pleat toward the head. (c) Pin the two pleats down for sewing. (d). Make two large tacking stitches on each leg. (e) Sew a third tacking stitch on the folding edge. (f) Cut the paws with scissors. (g) Make a large stitch at the top part of the leg. (h) Pull both stitches tight from the inside and knot them. (i) The thigh defined with a large stitch.

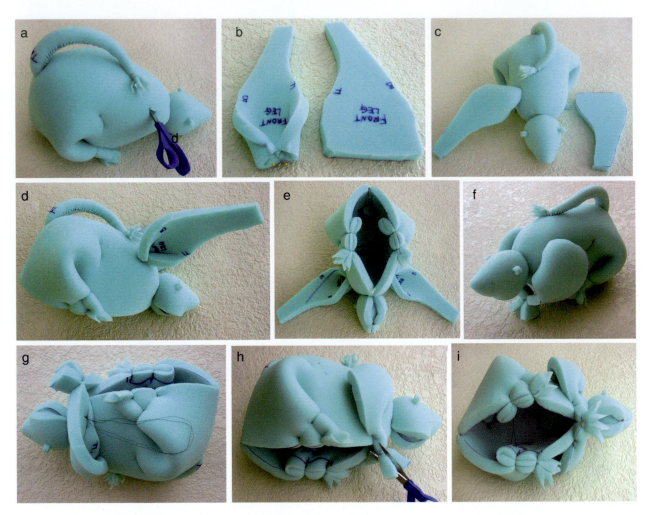

Figure 16-15 (a) Slash the front leg openings on the foam body. (b) Fold the end of the front leg. (c) Insert the leg piece — top. (d) Insert the leg piece — bottom. (e) Insert the second leg. (f) Tie the ends of the front leg together. (g) Sew the front leg to the body foam from the underside of the leg. (h) Create the front paws. (i) The completed paws.

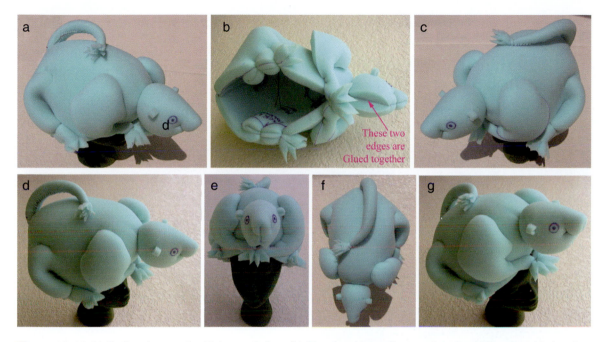

These two edges are Glued together

Figure 16-16 (a) Outline the mouth with large stitches. (b) Glue the chin portion together. (c–g) The assembled mole.

Figure 16-18 Completed moles used in production of *Frog and Toad*. *Orlando Repertory Theatre presentation.*

Step Seven: Finishing Up

- Make large stitches across the front of the face to outline the mouth (Figure 16-16a). Close the opening of the chin together with fabric tacky glue (Figure 16-16b).
- The stomach is left open; it is the opening for the actor's head (Figures 16-16c–g).
- Use spray paint to make the foam the color of a mole. Brush on highlights and shadows using acrylic paints.
- Glue the eyes on.

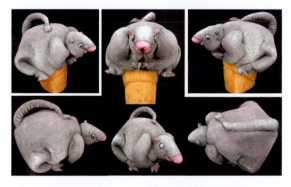

Figure 16-17 Completed moles, painted by Virginia McKinney.

The completed moles are shown in Figures 16-17 to 16-18. (No production photos are available.)

SQUIRREL HEADDRESS

PROCEDURE FOR MAKING THE SQUIRREL HEADDRESS

Materials Required:

- 1″-thick foam (22″ square per squirrel for body)
- ¼″-thick foam (thinned from 1″-thick foam)
- Animal eyes
- Scissors
- Marker
- String (to tie foam)
- Needle and thread

- Spray paint
- Fabric tacky clear glue
- Scarf

Step One: Creating the Pattern

- The squirrel headdress pattern is a 22" square of 1"-thick foam (Figure 16-19). No cuts or no seams are made in the foam piece. As you did with the foam for the mole headdress, play with a piece of foam to get the desired shape and size, and develop a pattern from that. You are making only the head; the body of the squirrel will be covered with a scarf.
- Cut the ears from ¼" thick foam (thinned from 1" thick foam) (Figure 16-19).

Step Two: Creating the Eyes and Ears

- Poke holes with scissors through the eye marks (Figure 16-20a). Insert the eyes in their positions (Figures 16-20b–c).

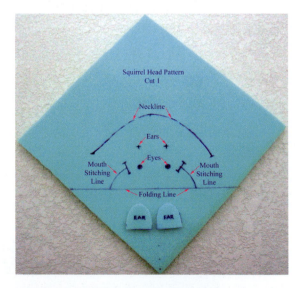

Figure 16-19 Squirrel headdress pattern.

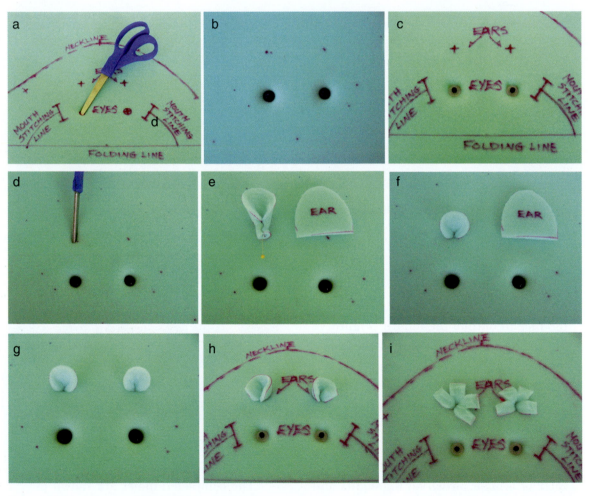

Figure 16-20 (a) Poke out the eye holes. (b) Insert the eyes. (c) Secure the eyes with their back pieces. (d) Poke out the ear holes. (e) Roll the end of one ear. (f) Insert the ear. (g) Insert the second ear. (h) Turn the body over. (i) Clip ear ends and glue them flat.

- Poke holes through the ear marks (Figure 16-20d). Fold and round out the ends of the ear pieces and insert them into the holes (in the same way as for the mole) (Figures 16-20e–g).
- Turn the foam over; make a few clips on the back ends of the ears, and glue them to the body (Figures 16-20h–i).

Step Three: Creating a Squirrel Head

- Fold a corner of the square to the foam's folding line; fold again on the folding line toward the center (Figures 16-21a–b).
- Fold the two sides of the foam toward the center (Figures 16-21c–d). Bring the folded edges together toward the center, and tie the foam along the neckline to create the neck (Figures 16-21e–f).
- Outline the mouth by making large cross-stitches on the cheeks. Make a large stitch using four strands of thread on each side of the cheek to create the corners of the mouth (Figure 16-21g). Pull the stitching threads tight, and tie them in a knot (Figure 16-21h).
- Insert a needle with four strands of thread under the mouth corner stitch, and bring the thread across the mouth opening (Figures 16-21i–j). Pull them tight and tie a knot at the middle that will be hidden inside a foam fold

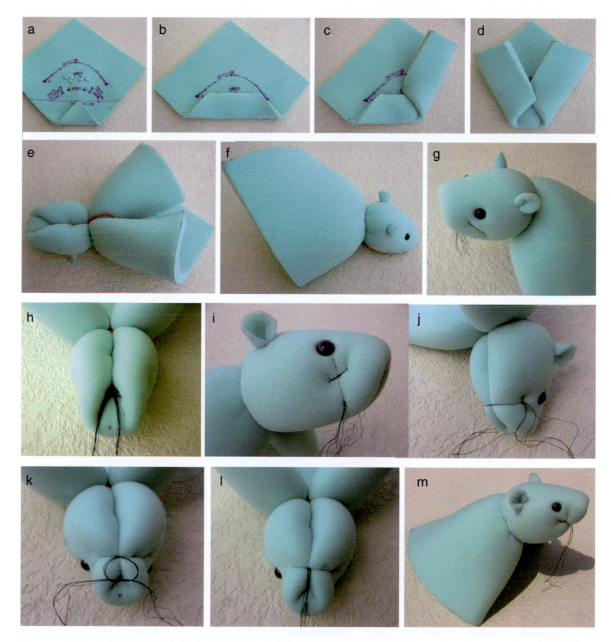

Figure 16-21 (a) Fold the corner to the folding line. (b) Fold it again on the folding line. (c) Fold one side of the foam to the center. (d) Fold the second side to the center. (e) Tie the neck — underside. (f) Tie the neck — top. (g) Stitch the mouth corner stitch on each cheek. (h) Tie the mouth corner threads in a knot. (i) Insert a needle under the mouth corner stitch. (j) Bring the inserted threads across the mouth opening. (k–l) Tie the threads in a knot. (m) The completed mouth opening.

(Figures 16-21 k–l). This completes the mouth opening (Figure 16-21m).

Step Four: Finishing Up

- Trim the edges of the folded foam to a tapered edge to reduce bulk and create a smoother surface on the inside (Figures 16-22a–b). Glue down the folded foam to form the shoulders (Figure 16-22c). This is the opening for the actor's head (Figures 16-22d–f).

- Use spray paint to make the headdress the colors of a squirrel, and brush in highlights and shadows.
- Add a scarf over the squirrel's shoulders to tie under the actor's chin.

The completed headdress is shown in Figure 16-23. (No production photo is available.) The headdresses for Turtle and Snail were made in the same way (Figures 16-24 to 16-25).

Figure 16-23 Completed squirrel headdresses, painted by Virginia McKinney and used in *Frog and Toad. Orlando Repertory Theatre* presentation.

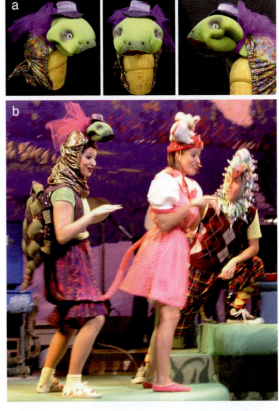

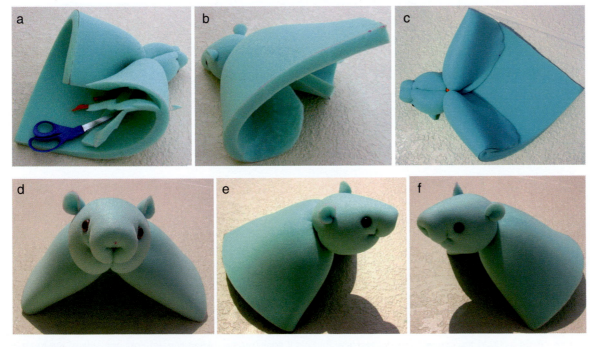

Figure 16-22 (a) Trim the foam to a tapered edge with scissors. (b) One side of the foam edge is tapered. (c) Glue the folded foam edges down to create the shoulders. (d–f) Assembled squirrel foam headdress.

Figure 16-24 (a) Turtle headdress, painted by Virginia McKinney. (b) Production photo of the turtle headdress in *Frog and Toad. Dera Lee played Turtle. Elizabeth Block played Mice. Kane Prestenback played Lizard. Directed by Chris Jorie. Musical Director, Jim Brown. Sound design by James E. Cleveland. Scenic design by Guy Petty. Lighting design by David M. Upton. Costume design by Tan Huaixiang. Orlando Repertory Theatre* presentation. *Photos from the Orlando Repertory Theatre collection.*

Figure 16-25 (a) Costume design for Snail in *Frog and Toad*. (b) Production photo of the snail headdress in *Frog and Toad*. *Kane Prestenback played Snail. Robert Pigott played Frog. Directed by Chris Jorie. Musical Director, Jim Brown. Sound design by James E. Cleveland. Scenic design by Guy Petty. Lighting design by David M. Upton. Costume design by Tan Huaixiang. Orlando Repertory Theatre presentation. Photo from the Orlando Repertory Theatre collection.*

MAKING HALLOWEEN COSTUMES

ALIEN COSTUME

PROCEDURE FOR MAKING ALIEN COSTUME

Materials Required:

- ½″-thick foam (25 × 50″)
- Foam cord (2½″ diameter and 18″ long)
- Sheer fabric
- Styrofoam cones
- Animal eyes
- Fabric clear tacky glue
- Scissors
- Spray paint
- Acrylic paints and brush

Step One: Taking Body Measurements

- Measure the wearer from the head to the knees and across the shoulders. These measurements are the base for the length and width of the costume.
- Measure the armhole locations.

Step Two: Creating the Pattern and Cutting the Foam

- Develop the Alien costume pattern from a rectangular silhouette. Use the wearer's body measurements as a reference, and add extra inches to the width for body movements. The Alien costume in this example was made for a 12-year-old girl; the measurements for the foam were 24″ wide (the manufactured width of the foam) and 42″ long (Figure 16-26).
- Locate where the arm holes will be and draw them on the foam.
- Measure 4″ in from each edge toward the center, and draw a line, tapering down to the shoulder, to create the Alien head. (The amount of tapering depends on the desired head shape. Add an overlapping seam allowance.)
- Measure the head-opening circumference. Based on the shape of the head opening on the body foam, cut an oval foam lid with a ½″ seam allowance.
- Cut another oval lid ¾″ smaller. Glue this under the larger lid for reinforcement.
- Cut a smiling mouth over the eye area (to function as a peephole). Glue a piece of sheer fabric across the peephole from inside.

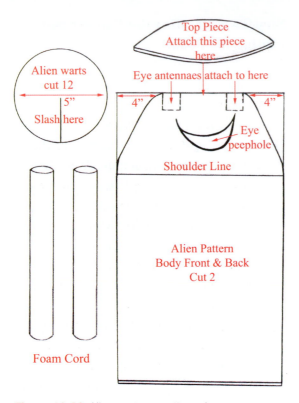

Figure 16-26 Alien costume pattern pieces.

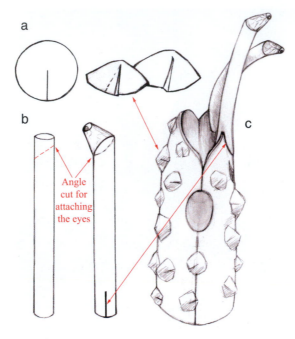

Figure 16-27 (a) Create the warts by forming the circles into cones by overlapping the cut edges. (b) Cut the end of the two pieces of foam cord at an angle and attach eyes; make a slash at the bottom of each eye antennae. (c) Form the body into a cylinder; attach the warts and eye antennas to the body.

• Cut twelve 5″-diameter circles; these are the Alien warts.

Step Three: Putting It Together

• Complete the Alien warts by cutting a slit from the edge of each circle to the center. Overlap the cutting edges, and shape the circles into cones (Figure 16-27a). Space them as desired on the body, and glue them on (these warts

can also be glued on later, after all pieces are put together) (Figure 16-27c).

• Glue the body foam seam together to make a cylinder by meeting the edges together; do not overlap them (Figure 16-27c).

• Cut an angle in the top ends of the foam cord antennas in the direction you want the eyes. Glue the Styrofoam cones to the ends as the eyes, and glue

a pair of animal eyes to the very ends of the cones (Figure 16-27b).

• Make a 3″ vertical slash in the antennas' bottom ends (Figure 16-27b).

• Insert the front of the top body edge into the slit made on the bottom of each antennae. Glue the antennas to the body. Use scissors to trim and round off the angular corners to merge the antennas with the body (Figure 16-27c).

• Glue the oval foam lid across the top of the cylinder, matching the edges together (Figure 16-28a).

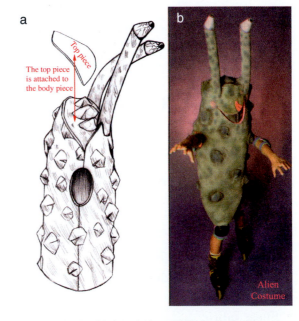

Figure 16-28 (a) Attach the oval lid to the body. (b) Completed Alien costume.

- Spray paint the entire foam body green; emphasize some darker spots for texture and to achieve an alien look. Add shadows and highlights to contour the warts.
- Draw blood vessels on the eyes (Styrofoam cones) with a fine brush and acrylic paints.

The completed costume is shown in Figure 16-28b.

BUTT COSTUME

My daughter and her friend wanted a creative Halloween costume one year and jokingly thought about being a butt. I overheard their idea and decided I would go ahead and make the costume for them. After I made it, they were both surprised and happy that they would have one of the most unique Halloween costumes that year.

PROCEDURE FOR MAKING THE BUTT COSTUME

Materials Required:

- $\frac{1}{2}$"-thick foam
- Thin knit fabric in any color (for lining)
- Fabric tacky glue
- Four pairs of large denim jeans
- Safety pins
- Scissors
- Suspenders

Step One: Creating a Hip Silhouette

- All foam sheets are 24" wide. The hip circumference of the costume is determined by personal preference; for my butt costume I used a foam piece 24" long and 96" wide (the widest part of butt cheeks).
- Line the entire foam rectangle with knit fabric using spray adhesive. Cut the knit fabric 2" wider than the foam all the way around. Wrap the extra fabric over the edges of the foam and glue it to the other side.
- Meet the edges of the foam together (no overlapping), and glue them together with fabric tacky glue.
- Make a few darts marks in the foam as desired around the top (waistline) and bottom of the butt. Slash the darts, overlap them, and glue them together to create a hip-shaped silhouette.
- Spray paint the foam cheeks a flesh color.

Step Two: Covering the Foam with Jeans

- Cut one pair of jeans at the entire center back crotch and the entire inseam seams open. Safety-pin this pair of jeans onto the front of the butt costume with waistband $\frac{1}{2}$" above the edge of the foam.
- Cut a second pair of jeans at the entire center front crotch and the entire inseam seams open. Cut out two large holes in the back of jeans (keep the back pockets) to expose both cheeks. Safety-pin this pair of jeans onto the back of the butt costume with waistband $\frac{1}{2}$" above the edge of the foam.
- Cut the third and fourth pairs of jeans at the entire crotch and entire inseam seams open. Safety-pin each pair of jeans to the each side of the butt costume with the waistband $\frac{1}{2}$" above the edge of the foam (for extra large size) or with the hem side up (for large size).
- Make a cross-cut and shorten all the jean-pieces including 2" hem (based on the length of the foam butt costume).
- Overlap, connect, and fit all the seams (from waistband down to the hem, trim off some of the seams as necessary) of the four pairs of jeans over the butt foam structure. And then fold the seam allowance of the top layer of each jean piece under for a nice finish. Safety-pin the pieces together. Vertically and closely positioning the safety pins on the seams here become part of the

Figure 16-29 Completed butt costume, modeled by Yingtao Zhang.

Figure 16-31 Completed butt costume, modeled by Nina Blankenship (right) and Yingtao Zhang (left).

Figure 16-30 Completed butt costume, modeled by Nina Blankenship (front) and Yingtao Zhang.

decorations. The butt costume is held up over wearer's body with two pairs of clipped suspenders.

The completed costume is shown in Figures 16-29 to 16-31.

MAKING A SNAKE HEADDRESS/COSTUME

A huge snake is required in the musical production *Godspell*. In the costume I designed the snake was played by five actors performing together. One actor played the head of the snake, and the others played the snake's body. Each actor had a black cape trimmed with snakeskin scales in the center back. The trim width was tapered from the head to the end of the tail. The snake head was big, with movable eyes and a wide-open mouth. The eyes were operated by the first actor's arms, the movable mouth was operated by the second actor pulling the fish strings attached to the inside of the snake mouth, and actors formed the snake's body by each one putting his head under the cape of the actor in front of him to form a long body. The snake-scale trims on the cape backs formed a whole and accompanied the actors' movements. The trim became fluorescent, glimmering and shimmering and gave an illusion of a huge snake body on stage.

PROCEDURE FOR MAKING THE SNAKE HEADDRESS/COSTUME

Materials Required:

- Egg carton foam
- $\frac{1}{4}''$ foam sheet (smooth textured)
- Scissors
- Green shiny fabric
- Red shiny fabric
- Dryer hose

- Green felt (light and dark)
- Wonder under
- Iron
- Sewing machine
- Mirror balls
- Fishing line
- Metal rings
- Spray paint
- Acrylic paint
- Fabric clear tacky glue

Step One: Cutting the Foam

- Measure actor's head circumference.
- Lay a piece of egg carton foam flat on the table.
- Measure and draw an oval head opening 2″ bigger than the actual head circumference in the center of the foam. Cut it out.
- The snake head was developed from a 25 × 50″ foam piece (Figure 16-32a). The upper and lower jaws are one piece. Make the upper jaw slightly bigger than the lower jaw. Cut another piece of smooth textured ¼″ or ½″ thick foam in a half oval-shape to symbolize the hood of the copra snake, it will be glued onto the cape just blow the lower

Snake Costume Sketch
Godspell

Figure 16-32 (a) Costume design for Snake. (b) Egg carton foam used for making the snake head.

jaw and connected/joined at the front neckline opening.

- Make the eye openings big enough for a big hand to pass through because the actor puts his hands through these openings, freely moving the eyes while on stage.

Step Two: Decorating the Head

- Spray paint the inside of the jaws red. Brush-paint the fangs and lower teeth white with acrylic paint.
- Cover the outer side of the jaws and the snake hood part with the shiny green fabric.
- To make the eyes, sew red fabric into a tube and pull it over a piece of dryer hose. Repeat this for the second eyestalk. The snake eyes move when the actor reaches his arms and hands through the fabric tubes/dryer hose.
- Attach a mirror eyeball to each fabric/dryer hose tube with fabric clear tacky glue. Hand sew two small rubber snakes (shape them to two circles) onto the snake hood piece to symbolize the characteristic of the copra.

The completed snake costume is shown in Figure 16-33.

Figure 16-33 (a, b) Production photos of the snake in *Godspell*. (c) Showing the snake mouth open. *Snake head operated by David Plant. Craig Zagurski (Top right) played Jesus. Directed by Blair Bybee. Scenic design by Mark C. Zetterberg. Lighting design by Dutch Fritz. Costume design by Tan Huaixiang. Central Washington University Theatre Arts Department, presentation.*

SECTION FIVE *Armor*

Ten sets of armor were needed for the musical production *Pippin* presented at the University of Central Florida Conservatory Theatre. One of them was borrowed from the Orlando Shakespeare Festival (many thanks to them) and the other nine sets of armor had to be built. We needed a fast and easy way to construct the vast amount of armor needed for the production. In addition, the armor had to be beautiful as well as flexible so as to not restrict the actors when they danced. The final products were fantastic and effective on stage.

The concepts for the costume design were simplicity, symbolism, and style. Mesh was the theme for the costume design in the show. The main character, Pippin, searches for extraordinary meaning in his life. But after experiencing many things, Pippin did not feel complete or extraordinary but felt trapped. A mesh design symbolized a net that trapped Pippin and was repeatedly emphasized on several of Pippin's costumes including his tunic, helmet, armor, and T-shirt. Other characters' costumes had mesh on the armor breast plates and masks.

The inspiration for the armor design came from 15th century iron corsets. The patterns on the iron corsets caught my attention. There were open designs on them that resembled today's laundry baskets, so I brought this idea of actually using laundry baskets for the armor to the director, John Bell, and he approved it.

Plastic laundry baskets are lightweight, durable, and flexible enough for dance movements and are also the cheapest material for making armor (the ones I used were $0.94 each). One small laundry basket was cut to fit each the player. The helmets were made from kitchen materials and polished aluminum clamp-light covers, which are lightweight, durable, and metallic.

I am not the first one to use nontraditional or unusual materials to create costume pieces for the stage. Many professionals have created extraordinary craft pieces from unusual materials for their productions too. The key to making crafts is selecting the proper materials for your projects. Research is always necessary for instigating and carrying out your design. Before I made my sketch, I went window-shopping at local inexpensive stores (Wal-Mart, Big Lots, Michaels Craft, Dollar Store, and several secondhand stores), searching for items that might work for making armor and helmets. I made several trips to the stores and also researched websites and books for mask-making materials in order to successfully accomplish my design concept.

The major craftworks needed for *Pippin* included ten masks, nine armor breast plates, one fruit outfit, a beard, and a wig. So much needed to be built in so little time! Producing these craftworks was challenging, and I had do this in a time-efficient manner while still constructing fantastic products.

Chapter 17   War Helmets from Household Items

The helmets for *Pippin* (Figure 17-1) were made from kitchen materials and polished aluminum clamp-light covers, which are lightweight and durable and show a metallic surface. There were four helmet designs (Pippin, Lewis, the male chorus, and the female chorus), but all were made similarly.

MAKING THE HELMET BASE

The base is used for all four styles of helmet.

PROCEDURE FOR CREATING THE HELMET BASE

Materials Required:

- Fosshape (#600 requires one layer to support the helmet, #300 requires two layers)
- Hat block
- $\frac{1}{2}$-inch-wide elastic straps

- Steamer
- Scissors
- Craft spray paint or shoe color
- Small buckles

Step One: Forming the Helmet Base

- Cut a piece of Fosshape large enough to cover the hat block. Use elastic to tie the Fosshape to the hat block (Figure 17-2a). (Fosshape #600 was used for this example.)
- Use both hands to pull the Fosshape down. Manipulate the material as best you can to get rid of the wrinkles along the elastic-tied area of the hat block (Figure 17-2b). Fosshape is like felt and can be easily stretched.
- Use a steamer to harden and set the shape (Figure 17-2c).
- After the base has hardened, separate it from the head block (Figure 17-2d).

- Fit the helmet base to the actor's head (all the metal pieces will be attached to this base). Trim the fitted base (Figure 17-2e).

Step Two: Painting the Base

- Use colored craft spray paint or shoe color to coat both the inside and outside of the helmet base black.
- Sew the elastic straps with the attached buckle on to the base to fit under the actor's chin (Figure 17-3a).

MAKING THE FOUR HELMET STYLES

The helmet bases are decorated with various metallic and other objects (Figure 17-3b), put together with pop rivets. (Many thanks to Bill Brewer, who was a guest costume designer for our summer season production *Wizard of Oz*. He is an extraordinary designer and craft expert,

Figure 17-1 Costume designs for Pippin.

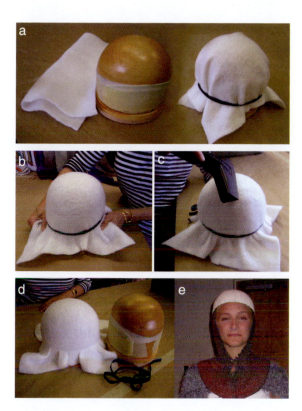

Figure 17-2 (a) Tie a piece of Fosshape on a hat block with an elastic strap. (b) Smooth the wrinkles by pulling and manipulating the material. (c) Steam the Fosshape from the top to bottom. (d) Separate the Fosshape base from the hat block. (e) Fit the helmet base on the actor's head; trim the edge as necessary.

and he recommended the use of pop rivets for attaching the pieces together; it worked very well!)

Materials required:

- Polished aluminum clamp light covers
- Burner covers

Figure 17-3 (a) Completed helmet bases with attached elastic straps and buckle. (b) Parts used for the helmets (aluminum clamp-light covers and plastic funnels).

- Plastic funnels
- Metal dishes
- Metal steamer baskets
- Feathers and feather boas
- Pop rivets and pop rivet gun
- Electric drill and drill bits for metal
- Hot glue gun and glue sticks
- Black acrylic paint and paint brushes

- Silver and gold metallic paint
- Eggbeater (whisk part)

PROCEDURE FOR CREATING THE MALE AND FEMALE CHORUS HELMETS

Step One: Attaching the Helmet Pieces to the Helmet Base

- Glue feathers (a boa was used for these helmets) into a funnel, and put all

helmet pieces together in the order you want, starting from the very top piece and working your way down. Line the helmet parts up and drill holes in them (Figure 17-4a)
- Line up the holes in the helmet parts, and attach all pieces together with pop rivets.
- Then attach the assembled helmet parts to the Fosshape base with pop rivets (Figure 17-4b). It is easier to do this if you first put a small amount of hot glue

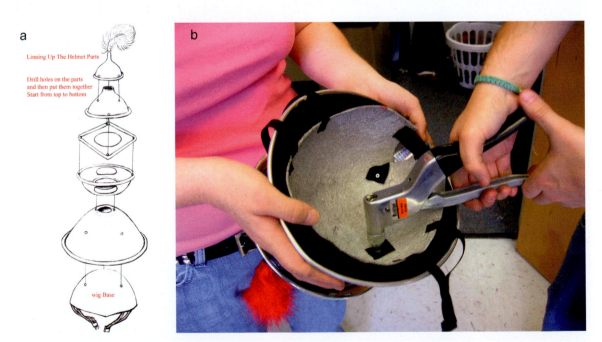

Figure 17-4 (a) Line up the helmet parts for drilling the holes. (b) Attach the helmet parts to the helmet base.

between the helmet metal parts and the Fosshape base to temporarily hold them together before putting pop rivets in the holes.

Step Two: Painting the Helmet

- Since the aluminum clamp-light covers have a shiny metallic look, paint on dark shadows to add depth and weight and to achieve the illusion of iron metal.
- The plastic funnels I used were black, so I highlighted them with silver metallic paint for a metallic look.

The completed helmets are shown in Figures 17-5 to 17-6.

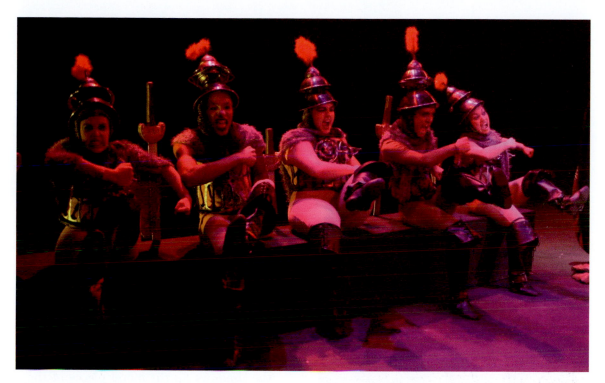

Figure 17-6 Production photo of the chorus helmets in *Pippin*. *Players (from left to right) played by: Andrea Dunn, Steven Gatewood, Denver Clark, Jason Whitehead, Tiara Young. Directed by John Bell. Set design by Joseph Rusnock. Lighting design by Eric Haugen. Sound design by Martin Wootton. Costume design by Tan Huaixiang. University of Central Florida Conservative Theatre presentation.*

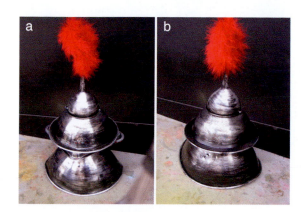

Figure 17-5 (a) Completed male chorus helmet. (b) Completed female chorus helmet.

PROCEDURE FOR CONSTRUCTING PIPPIN'S HELMET

Step One: Attaching the Helmet Pieces to the Helmet Base

- Glue feathers into a funnel.
- Pippin's helmet was constructed of kitchen stuff and light covers (Figure 17-7). The funnel is the top. Line up the helmet pieces in the desired order.

Figure 17-7 Helmet parts for constructing Pippin's helmet.

Cut the metal pieces so they fit with other parts of the helmet (Figure 17-8).

- Drill holes in the lined-up helmet pieces.
- Use pop rivets to connect all the parts together. Start from the bottom layer (the base) and work up to the top because of the shapes of the metal pieces (Figures 17-9 to 17-10).

Figure 17-8 Jonathan Waters (left) and Danny Davilla (right), both BFA design technology students, cutting a metal piece to make it fit with the other parts.

Figure 17-9 Pippin's helmet in progress.

Figure 17-10 Pippin's assembled but unpainted helmet.

Step Two: Painting the Helmet

- Use black acrylic paint and use a dry-brush feather-stroke techniques to add the shadows on the metal pieces of the helmet.
- Apply gold metallic paint to the middle piece of the helmet for a rich look.

The completed helmet is shown in Figures 17-11 to 17-12.

Figure 17-11 Pippin's completed helmet.

Figure 17-12 Production photo of the helmet in *Pippin*. Justin Sargent played Pippin. Directed by John Bell. Set design by Joseph Rusnock. Lighting design by Eric Haugen. Sound design by Martin Wootton. Costume design by Tan Huaixiang. University of Central Florida Conservatory Theatre presentation.

PROCEDURE FOR CONSTRUCTING LEWIS'S HELMET

Step One: Attaching the Helmet Pieces to the Helmet Base

- Glue feathers into the whisk part of an eggbeater.
- All the metal pieces used for Lewis's helmet were kitchen supplies and light covers. A gold-toned metal piece was chosen for Lewis's helmet. Line up the pieces in the desired order. (The order in this example is eggbeater with feathers, plastic funnel, small light cover placed upside down, golden fruit bowl, and a large light cover with metal steamer-basket pieces.)
- Drill holes in the lined-up pieces (except the steamer-basket pieces) and assemble them with pop rivets, using the same method as before.
- Attach the metal pieces to the base.
- Use a hot glue gun to glue on the metal pieces from the steamer baskets along the outer edge of the bottom part of the helmet; this creates a more elaborate design (Figure 17-13a).

Step Two: Painting the Helmet

- Add black shadows to the helmet with black acrylic paint.

The completed helmet is shown in Figures 17-13b–c and 17-14.

Figure 17-13 (a) Lewis's helmet, assembled and unpainted. (b–c) Lewis's completed helmet.

Figure 17-14 Production photo of Lewis's helmet in *Pippin*. *Players (from left to right): Michael Navarro, Christine Perez, Steven Gatewood, Denver Clark, Christopher Pearson Niess, Tiara Young, Jason Whitehead, Andrea Dunn, Robert Stack (as Lewis), Mark Brotherton (as King). Directed by John Bell. Set design by Joseph Rusnock. Lighting design by Eric Haugen. Sound design by Martin Wootton. Costume design by Tan Huaixiang. University of Central Florida Conservatory Theatre presentation.*

Chapter 18   Body Armor

MAKING ARMOR FROM HOUSEHOLD ITEMS

Two types of armor were made for the Pippin production: breastplates for the Chorus and a set of full armor for Pippin. They were made from small plastic laundry baskets.

THE CHORUS'S BREASTPLATES

PROCEDURES FOR MAKING THE CHORUS'S BREASTPLATES

Materials Required:

- Round-shaped laundry baskets
- Marker
- Steamer baskets (for the female breastsplates)
- Gold tie wire
- Needle
- Fishing line
- Pliers
- Tin snips
- Eggbeater (whisk part)

- Magna-Tac clear glue, 809 permanent adhesive
- Dremel tools (Figure 18-1a)
- Heat gun or stove
- Black plastic spray paints
- 1"-wide black elastic strips
- Small buckles
- ½"-wide black elastic strips
- Silver metallic paints
- Paint brushes

Step One: Cutting the Laundry Baskets

- Outline the shape of the breastplate on a laundry basket with a marker (Figure 18-1b). The size of the breastplate is based on the actor's chest and waist measurements. Use the natural pattern on the laundry baskets to determine the sizes of the plates. Keep an extra warp (see Figure 18-2) on each side at the bottom of the basket for the larger breastplates. Cut the laundry basket following the markings with tin snips or a dremal cutter (Figure 18-1b).

Figure 18-1 (a) Dremel tools for cutting and sanding rough edges. (b) Outline the breastplate on the laundry basket, and cut it out.

287

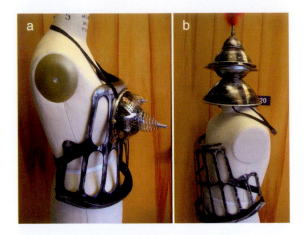

Figure 18-2 (a) One extra warp is kept at each side for small breastplates. (b) Two extra warps are kept for large breastplates.

- Use a Dremel sander to sand down sharp edges and corners. Heat the plastic edge of the laundry basket using a stove or heat gun (Figure 18-3a); it will become soft and easy to bend. Bend in the two end edges of the plate to achieve a better fit to the curves of the body (Figures 18-3b and 18-4).
- Spray both sides of the breastplate with black plastic spray.

Step Two: Creating Breasts for the Female Breastplates

- Steamer baskets are used to make breasts that will be attached to the breastplate (inspired by the 15th-century iron corsets) (Figure 18-5).

Figure 18-3 (a) Heat the edges and corners of the breastplate using a stove. (b) Danny Davilla, a BFA design technology student, bending the corner of the cut edge of the plate.

- Thin the petals of the steamer by pulling off every second and third petal from the steamer basket (Figure 18-5b). This reduces the weight of the breasts and also helps define the design patterns on the breasts.

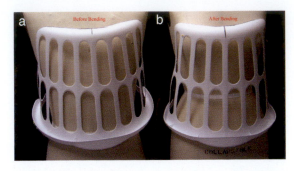

Figure 18-4 (a) Before the breastplate is bent. (b) After the breastplate is bent.

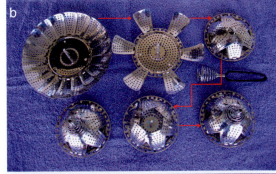

Figure 18-5 (a) Pictures of 15th-century iron corsets. (b) Remove petals from the steamer basket. (c) Sew the remaining petals together to the center pole with fishing line.

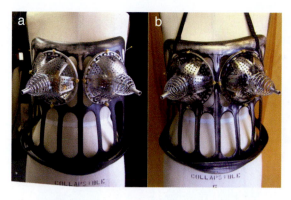

Figure 18-6 (a) Fit the breasts on the breastplate. (b) Danny Davilla, BFA design technology student, attaching the steamer-basket breasts to the breastplate with tie wire.

Figure 18-7 (a) Attach the steamer-basket breasts to the breastplate. (b) Completed female breastplate.

Figure 18-8 Completed female breastplate with elastic strips attached in places.

- Close the rest of the petals toward the center of the steamer basket, and then sew them together to the center pole with a needle and fishing line (Figure 18-5b). Sew the whisk part of an eggbeater on the top of the breast.
- Use Fabric-Tac clear glue to secure the fishing-line knots.
- Attach the finished breasts to the breastplate with tie wire (Figures 18-6 and 18-7a).

Step Three: Completing the Breastplate

- Loop 1″-wide elastic strips on each side of a buckle and attach the elastic strips to either side of the breastplate (Figures 18-8b–c). Also, attach a ½″-wide elastic strip around the neck as a halter to help hold up the breastplate (Figures 18-7b and 18-8a).
- Highlight and paint the black plastic breastplate with silver metallic paint

using a feather-stroke painting technique to achieve a metallic look. The completed breastplates are shown in Figures 18-7b and 18-8 to 18-9. The male breastplates were made in the same way but without breasts (Figure 18-10). The players wore a gray, textured cape that covered their backless breastplates.

Figure 18-10 Completed male breastplate.

Figure 18-9 (a, b) Production photos of the female breastplate in *Pippin*. (c) *Players (from left to right): Andrea Dunn, Tiara Young, Paul Gebb. University of Central Florida Conservatory presented.*

PIPPIN'S ARMOR

PROCEDURE FOR MAKING PIPPIN'S ARMOR

Materials Required:

- Tall oval laundry basket
- Leftover pieces from the Chorus's round laundry baskets
- Heavy-duty scissors
- Safety pins
- Gold screw posts
- 1"-inch thick black elastic strips
- Silver buckles
- Black craft spray
- Spray adhesive #77
- Gold and silver metallic paints
- Gold-leaf adhesive
- Paint brushes
- Dremel tools

Step One: Cutting the Laundry Basket

- Outline the shapes of the armor both front and back plates with a marker on an oval plastic laundry basket (one side for front and the other side for back piece) (Figure 18-11a); cut the shapes out.
- On pieces left over from the laundry baskets used to make the Chorus's breastplates, outline the shoulder straps; cut them out (Figures 18-11b–c).

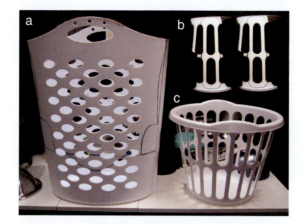

Figure 18-11 (a) Outline Pippin's armor pieces on a large oval laundry basket. (b) Cut the shoulder straps from the leftover pieces of the Chorus's laundry baskets. (c) Round laundry basket was used for the Chorus's breastplates.

- Cut/slash the top center edge of the front piece about 5″ deep, and overlap the slashes to better fit the curvature of the actor's chest.
- Create a decorative center piece by cutting a long strip from the laundry basket and making a few notches on both sides, so it can curve along with the curves of the front breastplate (Figure 18-12a).
- Use a Dremel cutting tool to cut halfway through the thickness of the plastic center piece, down the middle of the strip, creating a groove line down

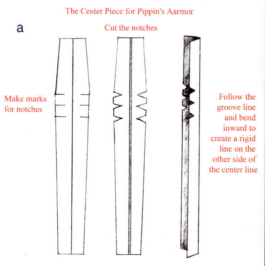

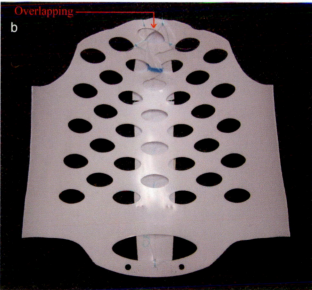

Figure 18-12 (a) Diagram of the steps for creating the center strip. (b) Attach the center strip to the breastplate.

the wrong side of the strip (for trouble-free bending and to create a rigid edge on the right side of the strip) (Figure 18-12a).

- Temporarily pin the center piece, the shoulder straps, and both front and breastplates onto a proper sized dress-form for necessary adjustments (Figures 18-12b and 18-13a–c).

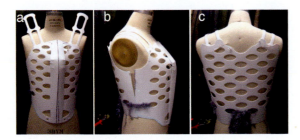

Figure 18-13 (a) Attach the decorative center piece and the shoulder straps temporarily to the breastplate. (b–c) The assembled armor.

Step Two: Painting the Armor

The plastic laundry basket used for Pippin was different from the laundry baskets used for the Chorus members. Pippin's basket was softer, smoother, and taller. I had difficulty keeping the plastic spray paint on the surface of Pippin's laundry basket (it kept peeling off), even though it had worked well for the round-shaped laundry baskets. To solve the problem, spray adhesive #77 was used to hold the paint on the armor.

- Evenly coat the armor pieces with spray adhesive #77, and wait for it to dry.
- Then spray the armor pieces with black craft spray over the dried spray adhesive #77 (Figure 18-14a), and let it dry (shoe color spray also works but costs more).

Figure 18-14 (a) Danny Davilla and Hannah Kugelmann spraying the plastic armor pieces. (b) The assembled armor.

Step Three: Connecting the Armor Pieces

- Drill holes on the center piece and breastplate, both shoulder straps, and the top edge of the breastplate and back piece of the armor. Then use gold screw posts to attach them together (Figures 18-14b and 18-15).
- Drill holes on the sides of the breastplate and back piece, and insert the posts through the holes to attach the buckles to the armor pieces (Figures 18-14b and 18-15b).

Figure 18-15 (a–c) Insert gold screw posts to hold all the pieces together. (b) Attach the buckles to the sides of the armor.

Step Four: Highlighting the Armor

- Coat the black paint with gold-leaf adhesive to reinforce the paint before highlighting the armor.
- Highlight the armor with metallic paint (Figure 18-15).

  The completed armor is shown in Figures 18-15 to 18-16.

Figure 18-16 Production photos of the armor in *Pippin*. Justin Sargent played Pippin. Directed by John Bell. Set design by Joseph Rusnock. Lighting design by Eric Haugen. Sound design by Martin Wootton. Costume design by Tan Huaixiang. University of Central Florida Conservatory Theatre presentation.

ALTERING AND DECORATING EXISTING PLASTIC ARMOR

The set of armor discussed here was created for *The Frog Prince* (Figure 18-17), staged at the Cornell University Department of Theatre Arts. Alterations were made to a set of plastic

Figure 18-17 Costume design for *The Frog Prince*.

white armor by adding a shoulder cap, neckbands, and waistbands to make it look handsome.

PROCEDURE FOR ALTERING EXISTING ARMOR

Materials required:

- Set of plastic armor that includes helmet, gauntlets, greaves, and front and back plates
- Black spray paint
- Gold metallic paint
- Black felt
- Grommet tool and grommets
- Dress form
- Hot glue gun and glue sticks
- Black vinyl or leather
- Black nylon fabric
- Gold trim

Step One: Painting and Lining the Armor

- Spray the outside of the white plastic breastplates black as a foundation.
- After the paint dries, add highlights with gold metallic paint (if it's a set of silver armor, use silver paint); the black foundation will provide depth to the painting.
- Cut a piece of black felt larger than the plates. Spray adhesive on the side of the felt, and stick it to the wrong side of the plates for added comfort and to reinforce the thin plastic plates. Then trim off the excess felt with scissors.
- Add grommets on the sides of the plates using grommet tools as fasteners for lacing up the armor.

Step Two: Creating Patterns for the Parts to Be Added to the Armor

- Put the breastplate over a dress form; drape the basic organic-shaped shoulder cap pattern (Figure 18-18a) around the shoulder.

- Cut out a couple of slashes in a diamond shape to better fit the shoulder. It is both functional and decorative for the shoulder cap. Make a diamond-shaped slash in the first third of the cap, starting from the bottom up (Figure 18-18a).
- Make two ½" darts at the bottom of the cap toward each corner of the slashed diamond (Figure 18-18a).
- Slash the bottom center of the cap and overlap the two exposed edges in a tapered manner, overlapping the cut ends ¼" at the very bottom to add a round curve to the pattern (Figure 18-18a). This overlapping can also be achieved with a dart, but overlapping the cut edges achieves a flatter seam.

- Fold rows of 1"-deep knife pleats for the middle part of the sleeve (Figure 18-18c). The pleats provide a decorative look and increase the flexibility during arm movements. Attach a cuff to finish off the sleeves.
- Create two decorative scallop-shaped sleeve cuffs to finish off the sleeves (Figure 18-18b).
- Follow the curves along the armor's neckline and waistline, and drape neckband and waistband patterns (Figure 18-18d) to complete the armor.

Step Three: Constructing Shoulder-Cap Pieces for the Armor

- Cut the shoulder caps out in vinyl or leather. Fold two darts under the two

corners of the slashed diamond. Then trim the diamond-shaped slashed areas with thin trim and trim the outer edge of the cap with thicker trim (Figure 18-19a).

- Cut out the pleated sleeves pattern on stiff black nylon fabric and pleat it (Figure 18-18c). Decorate each folded edge with gold braid-trim to define the lines and shapes of the sleeve (Figure 18-19b).

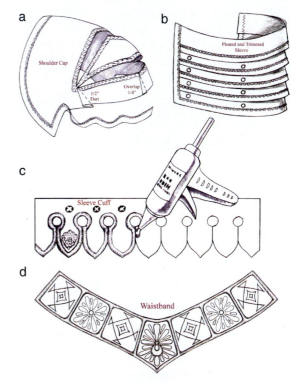

Figure 18-19 (a) Decorate the shoulder cap. (b) Put trim on the pleated sleeve. (c–d) Using a hot glue gun, create designs on cuff and neckband.

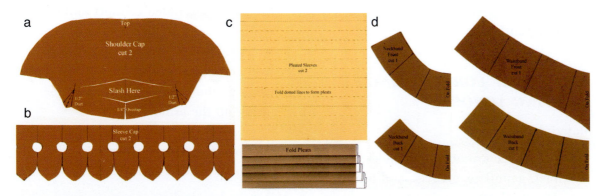

Figure 18-18 (a) Shoulder cap pattern. (b) Scalloped cuff pattern. (c) Flat pleats pattern and folded pleats. (d) Neckband and waistband patterns.

- Fold under the seam allowances on both sides of the pleated piece and finish the edge with trim.
- Insert two rows of metal studs on the pleated sleeves to achieve a metal-textured appearance.
- Use hot glue to add 3-D designs at the neck, waistband, and sleeve; after this has cooled, paint the designs with gold metallic paint (Figures 18-19c–d).
- Attach the sleeve cuff to the pleated sleeve first, and then attach this to the shoulder cap (Figure 18-20a).
- Do not sew the underarm seams together; keep them open instead. Attach an elastic strip to each sleeve's underarm opening to hold the sleeves in place (Figure 18-20b).

- Attach the sleeves, neckband, and waistband to the armor's front and back pieces with metal studs.

The completed armor is shown in Figures 18-21 to 18-22.

Figure 18-22 Production photo of the armor in *The Frog Prince. Palace Guard played by David Fishbach and Jeff miller. Directed by Ken Westerman. Scenic design by Julie Gallager. Lighting design by Patrick Gill. Costume design by Tan Huaixiang. Cornell University Theatre Arts Department presentation.*

Figure 18-21 Completed armor.

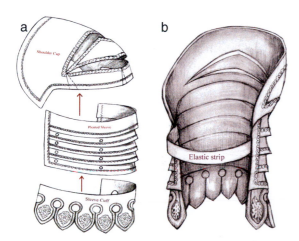

Figure 18-20 (a) Attach the three pieces together. (b) Add an elastic strip to the underarm of each sleeve.

SECTION SIX *Leather Products*

These chapters cover inexpensive ways
to make shoes/boots, a jacket, and a
shoemaker's apron. (See also Chapter 21,
which has instructions for making leather
mittens.)

Chapter 19   Suede Leather Shoes and Boots

I made many pairs of inexpensive soft suede leather shoes and boots for *Robin Hood*, inspired by my mother when she made embroidered shoes that I loved very much for me during my childhood.

Robin Hood is set during the medieval period. There was no period boots or shoes that could be pulled from stock. Many of the boots and shoes were made from deerskin (available at tanneries), which is a natural yellowish brown color. Some of the dark shoes and boots in the production were made from cut suede leather coat material purchased from secondhand stores.

Three types of footwear were made for *Robin Hood*: tall boots, ankle boots, and shoes (Figure 19-1). They were all put together with an industrial sewing machine and leather needle.

MAKING BOOTS

PROCEDURE FOR MAKING SUEDE BOOTS

Materials required:

- Deerskin (purchased from a local tannery)
- Brown suede leather jacket
- Industrial sewing machine
- Leather needle
- Sole rubber material

Step One: Creating a Boot Pattern

- To develop a pointed-sole pattern, trace the wearer's feet and lengthen the front of the toes (Figure 19-2c).
- Cut two upper pieces for each individual boot. The shoe/boot will have center and back seams.

- The boot cuffs were included in the measurement for the height of the boots (Figure 19-2d). For example, if the desired height of the boot is 15″ tall, add a 3″ cuff to the pattern for a total height of 18″. The cuff can be also attached separately.
- For a boot that laces up, mark where the lace will start and end on the pattern (Figure 19-2d); then cut the side opening where the boot will lace up. Add facing directly behind the opening to strengthen it. Then put eyelets or grommets along both sides of the opening. The example presented here does not lace up.

Figure 19-1 Costume design for *Robin Hood*.

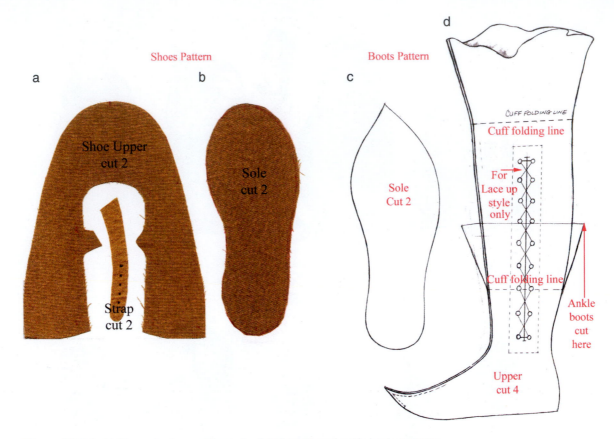

Shoes Pattern

Boots Pattern

a

b

c

d

Shoe Upper
cut 2

Sole
cut 2

Strap
cut 2

Sole
Cut 2

CUFF FOLDING LINE

Cuff folding line

For
Lace up
style
only

Cuff folding line

Ankle
boots
cut
here

Upper
cut 4

Figure 19-2 (a–b) Women's shoes patterns. (c–d) Tall boots and ankle boots patterns.

Step Two: Putting It Together

- Constructing women's shoes (Figures 19-2a–b) is little different from constructing boots. There is only one back seam on the upper piece. Attach the strap, and sew the back seam together. Sew the sole to the upper in the same way as the boots (Figure 19-4a). (These shoes cannot be seen well in the production photos.)
- Constructing angle boots with cuffs will be done the same way as making tall boots (Figures 19-3a–c).
- Constructing tall boots: With the right sides together, machine sew the center front and back upper seams together. If the boots have cuffs, stop the stitches at the cuff-folding line (Figure 19-3a). The edge shapes of the boot cuffs were the natural edges of the hide.
- If the boots have cuffs, make small clips at the edges of the folding line ⅛″ away

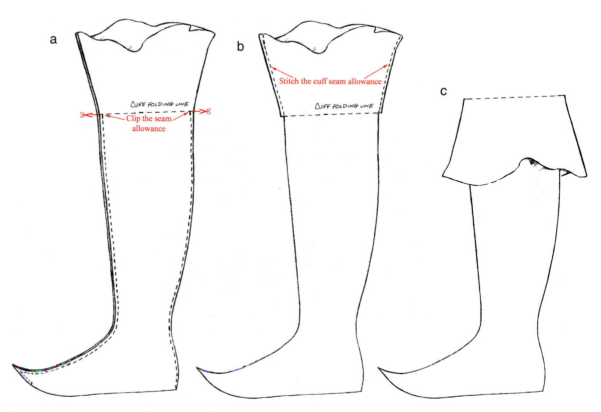

Figure 19-3 (a) Stitch the upper together; stop the stitches at the cuff folding line, and clip the cuff folding line of the seam allowance of the boots. (b) Turn the boot upper right side out, and stitch the cuff seam allowance together. (c) Turn the stitched cuff down.

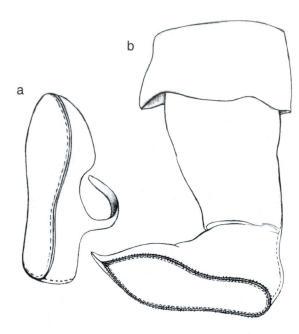

Figure 19-4 (a) For women's shoes, sew the back seam together and attach the sole to the upper. (b) For boots, stitch the boot sole to the boot upper, and zigzag stitch the seam allowance together.

from the ends of the stitching line (Figure 19-3a.).

- Turn the boot right side out. Pull the clipped seam allowance out, and stitch the cuff seams together (Figure 19-3b). After rolling the cuffs down, the seam allowance will be hidden (Figure 19-3c). (Boot cuffs can be also attached as a separate piece)

- Pin the sole and boot together with the right sides facing each other, and machine stitch them together. Use a 4 or 4½″ stitch length to sew leather. Don't use small stitches.

- After finishing the straight stitches, zigzag stitch all the seam allowances together for reinforcement (Figure 19-4b) and then turn the boot right side out.

The completed boots are shown in Figure 19-5. Constructing ankle boots (Figure 19-2d) employs the same method as making tall boots.

Figure 19-5 (a) Production photo showing the soft leather boots in *Robin Hood. From very back left to right: Robb Padgett played Little John, Torina Smith played Mother Meg, Paul Wickline played Monk, Vanessa Hespe played Old Lady, Jared Vallejo played Scarlet, David Plant played Robin Hood, David Shoup played Sheriff of Nottingham, Tom McNelly played Casper, performance students.*

Figure 19-5—Cont'd (b) Production photo showing the soft leather ankle boots in *Robin Hood*. *Vanessa Hespe played Wife of the Sheriff. David Shoup played Sheriff of Nottingham.* (c) Production photo showing the soft leather boots in *Robin Hood. From left to right: Torina Smith played Mother Meg. Robb Padgett played Little John. David Shoup played Sheriff of Nottingham. Abra Stanley played Lady Merle.* (d) Production photo showing the soft leather boots on stage in *Robin Hood.* Note two of the boots are in laced-up style. *Keith Edie (middle) played Dale, Jared Vallejo (left) played Scarlet, and Little John played by Robb Padgett, performance students.*

Figure 19-5—Cont'd (e) Production photo showing the soft leather boots on stage in *Robin Hood*. *Directed by James Hawkins. Set design by Tim Stapleton, Lighting design by Mark C. Zetterberg. Costume design by Tan Huaixiang. Central Washington University Theatre Arts Department presentation.*

Chapter 20   Leather Apron and Jacket

MAKING A LEATHER APRON

A leather apron was needed for *Elves and Shoemaker* (Figure 20-1). Here is an economical way to make one.

PROCEDURE FOR CREATING AN ECONOMICAL LEATHER APRON

Material Required:

- Old leather jacket
- Apron pattern
- Sewing machine
- Leather needle
- Scissors

Step One: Cutting Out the Apron

- Pull from stock or purchase an old jacket large enough to cut a full apron from. If there is not enough material, piece it together.
- Lay an apron pattern on top of the leather and cut it out. Also cut out a halter strap and two tie straps.

Figure 20-1 Costume design for *Elves and Shoemaker*.

Step Two: Assembling the Apron

- Machine sew the pieces together. The completed apron is shown in Figure 20-2.

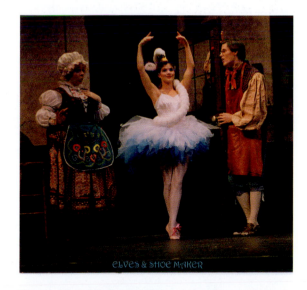

Figure 20-2 Production photo of the apron on stage in *Elves and Shoemaker. Colette Jones (left) played Mrs. Shoup. Kyra McGough (middle) played Swan. David Shoup (right) played Mr. Shoup. Directed by James Haskins. Scenic design by Dutch Fritz. Lighting design by Mark C. Zetterberg. Costume design by Tan Huaixiang. Central Washington University Theatre Arts Department presentation.*

305

MAKING A COLORFUL LEATHER JACKET

A leather jacket was needed for Terry in the production *Extremities* (Figure 20-3). This one was created from many small colorful leather pieces sewn together with machine zigzag stitches.

Materials needed:

- Small leather pieces in different colors
- Leather trim strip
- Fabric tack glue
- Scissors
- Sewing machine
- Jacket pattern
- Lining fabric

Step One: Assembling the Leather Pieces into Pattern Pieces

- Place the leather pieces (without changing their shapes) on top of the jacket pattern with their edges overlapping.
- Stabilize the sewing edge of the leather pieces with small amount of fabric tacky glue and then stitch them together (sew on one piece a time) with machine zigzag stitches in a contrasting thread to form the jacket pieces.

Step Two: Assembling the Jacket

- Sew together the jacket pieces.
- Trim all outer edges of the jacket with a folded leather strip.
- Make a full lining for the jacket, and sew it on.

The completed jacket is shown in Figures 20-4 and 20-5.

Figure 20-3 Costume design for *Extremities*.

Figure 20-4 Completed leather jacket.

Figure 20-5 Production photos showing the leather jacket in *Extremities*. Terry played by Leslie Seidel. Directed by Jim Howard. Scenic design by Tom Begley. Lighting design by Jim Hart. Costume design by Tan Huaixiang. University of Central Florida Conservatory Theatre presentation.

Chapter 21   Jewelry and Mittens

MAKING CHEAP JEWELRY

The accessories used for *Once on This Island* can be very expensive and hard to find in a store, so I made them using cheap, yet effective materials. The costumes and accessories for the production displayed Caribbean-influenced tropical patterns, colors, textures, and styles that harmonized with the Caribbean rhythms and culture. The costumes and accessories were kept simple to portray that the characters could make them themselves.

The accessories — headbands, turbans, kerchief scarves, earrings, necklaces, armlets, and anklets — all exhibited this primitive flavor. They were created from colorful wooden beads and cotton batik fabrics that were left over from the costumes.

PROCEDURE FOR MAKING FABRIC NECKLACES, BRACELETS, AND ANKLETS

Materials Required:

- Fabric
- Scissors
- Large beads
- Needle and thread

Step One: Cutting the Fabrics

- Cut a bias strip 4 ft long by 5″ wide (this is the main portion of necklace), and then cut some other shorter bias strips of various lengths and widths (e.g., 1 ft long by 2″ wide; 8″ long by 1″ wide) in a variety of colors to insert on to the main portion of the necklace. Cutting on bias provides the necklace with flexibility.
- Make a slit at each end of the strip (to add beads to the necklace).

Step Two: Adding Beads

- Fold the strip in half and tie several symmetrical knots (tie as many as desired) on either side of the strip.
- Make small slashes between each knot, and insert the shorter strips. Tie each one in a knot to secure it, and string a bead on to each strip. Tie another knot after adding the bead to secure the bead in place. Repeat this process until you get the desired look.
- Bring the two split ends of the necklace together, insert them through a large bead, and tie knots to form a closed loop and finish the necklace.

Completed necklaces are shown in Figures 21-2 to 21-7. Simple string necklaces, bracelets, and anklets were made in the same way, but no splits were made in the strip. Instead, knots were tied and beads were added between the knots.

307

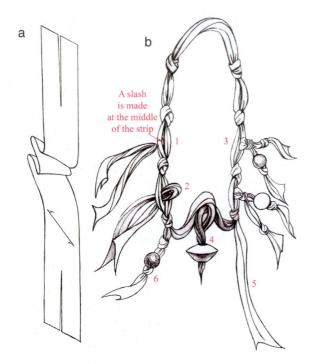

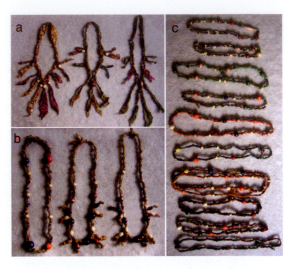

Figure 21-1 (a) Cut a long bias strip, and cut slashes in the ends. (b) Add shorter fabric strips and beads.

Figure 21-2 Completed female characters' necklaces.

Figure 21-3 (a) Completed female characters' necklaces. (b) Completed male characters' necklaces. (c) Bracelets and anklets.

Figure 21-5 Production photo of the necklaces and bracelets in *Once on This Island*. *Ti Moune (middle) played by Kahliah Rivers. Storytellers: Patrice Lois Bell (left), Tiara Yong (right).*

Figure 21-6 Production photo of the necklaces and bracelets in *Once on This Island*. *Storytellers from left to right: Wes Miller, James Edward Coleman II, Patrice Lois Bell, Down Pryor.*

Figure 21-4 Production photo showing necklaces, bracelets, and anklets in *Once on This Island*. *Marjorie Thomas played Mama. Reginald Woods played Tonton. Taylor Pryor played Young Ti Moune. Directed by Earl Weavor. Scenic design by Vandy Woods. Lighting design by David Upton. Costume design by Tan Huaixiang. University of Central Florida Conservatory Theatre presentation.*

Figure 21-7 Production photo of the necklaces and bracelets in *Once on This Island*. *Storytellers from left to right: Back Row: Taylor Pryor (Young Ti Moune), Wes Miller, Rubert DuPont, Middle Row: Kris Sprouls, James Edward, Regina Fernandez, Patrice Lois Bell, Annie Forgione. Front Row: Rita Coleman, Desmond Newson, Jamie Phipps.*

A necklace can also be made by stringing premade objects together. God of Death's necklace was made from bone pieces and a skull strung together (Figure 21-8).

Figure 21-8 Production photo of the god of Death in *Once on This Island*, showing a necklace put together from premade objects. *Westley Todd Holiday played Papa Ge/Death God.*

MAKING LEATHER MITTENS

During religious ceremonies in Alaska, dancers wore ornamental fillets of caribou, wolf, ermine, bird skin and feathers, wristlets or arm bands, caribou teeth or crab-joint belts and bracelets, and special

Figure 21-9 Costume design for *Walker in the Snow*.

pants. They never danced with bare hands. They wore long gauntlet mittens made of seal skin with puffin beaks or metal attached by short cords, which also provided rhythm for the dancer's motions. When the character Shaman/Pikok in *Walker in the Snow* (Figure 21-9) wore the mittens, he could manipulate the spirits and had power over them. These mittens were very important props in the production.

The mittens in this production were made of reddish-brown suede leather. The ornaments on them were fish and shells shapes cut from steel food cans and attached to the mittens with strong thread. The mittens were trimmed with black fur and colorful patters were painted on the cuffs with acrylic fabric paints. Shaman wore the mittens when he danced, and the metal ornaments tinkled and created a soft magic sound that accentuated the atmosphere.

PROCEDURE FOR MAKING LEATHER MITTENS

Materials Required:

- Suede brown leather (can be cut from a used leather jacket)
- Metal cans
- Metal cutters
- File
- Drill
- Leather needle
- Thread
- Fur
- Acrylic paints and brush
- Fleece babric lining

Step One:

- Create mittens pattern and cut out from reddish-brown suede leather for outer

layer of the mittens, fleece fabric for its lining.

- With right side of the fabric together, pin and machine stitch the seam allowances together, and then turn inside out. Repeat the same steps to stitch the lining.
- Brush-paint a 2½″ wide boarder with colorful patters around the cuffs with acrylic fabric paints for decoration. After the paint dries, trim the cuff edge of the mittens with black fur.
- Cut ornaments (fish and shells shapes) from steel food cans. Drill a small hole on each fish or shell. File all the sharp edges of the holes to smooth and hand sew the pieces onto the back of the mittens with strong thread (Figure 21-10). Shaman wore the mittens when

he danced, and the metal ornaments tinkled and created a soft magic sound that accentuated the atmosphere.

The completed mittens are shown in Figures 21-10 to 21-11.

Figure 21-11 Production photo showing the mittens in *Walker in the Snow. Pikok played by Robert Herderson. Fantasia played by Annette Johnson. Directed by Lynda Linford. Scenic design by Sid Perkes. Lighting design by Steve Twede. Costume design by Tan Huaixiang. Utah State University Theatre Arts Department presentation.*

Figure 21-10 Completed mittens.

Changing Cheap Clothing into
Elegant Garments

There are many ways to alter a modern garment into a period one. Changes made to the original garment depend on its style and condition. The methods of altering modern garments discussed here are those I used on these garments for them to work effectively on stage. (See also Chapter 8 for instructions on altering a modern hat to a period hat.)

Chapter 22   Altering Women's Dresses

ALTERING AN OLD-FASHIONED DRESS TO A 1920s–30s WEDDING DRESS

This dress, first modified for *Crazy for You* (Figure 22-1), was used again and again for different productions. It was purchased from a second-hand store; then the sleeves were removed and extra fabric was added to lengthen the dress.

PROCEDURES FOR ALTERING A MODERN DRESS TO A PERIOD WEDDING DRESS

Materials Required:

- Second-hand dress (can be pulled from stock)
- Fabric (to add length to the garment)
- Scarves
- Sewing machine
- Seam ripper
- Scissors

Figure 22-1 Costume design for *Crazy for You.*

Step One: Removing the Sleeves

- Pull from stock or purchase a dress (Figure 22-2), and analyze the style. (The dress used in this example was a beaded dress.)

- Detach the sleeves from the dress (Figure 22-3a) and undo the sleeve seams from the armpit down to the beginning of the beads cuff (Figure 22-3b).
- Remove some beads around the armholes and recut the armholes to narrow the width of the shoulders.
- Hem the armholes with uneven slipstitches or slanted hem stitches.

Step Two: Reconstructing the Dress

- Attach the two beaded sleeves that you removed to the dress's front and back hipline to expand and continue the beautiful beaded pattern. To do this, join one beaded sleeve to the front beaded pattern at the dress's front hipline and join the other sleeve to the back beaded pattern at the dress's

Figure 22-2 Dress before alteration.

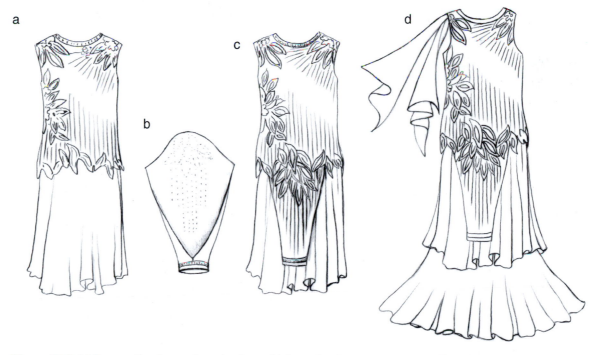

Figure 22-3 (a) Remove the sleeves from the dress. (b) Open the sleeve seam to the cuff. (c) Add one sleeve to the front left and one sleeve to the back right of the dress. (d) Add extra fabric to the bottom of the lining of the dress; attach scarves to the shoulder.

hipline for an asymmetrical balance; attach only the top sleeve-cap seam line to the dress and let the rest of the sleeve body dangle loose (Figure 22-3c).

- To achieve a 1920s flapper look, attach a few fabric kerchiefs on to the skirt lining of the dress to lengthen the dress (Figure 22-3d). To achieve the 1930s flair-out look, add two circles of the fabric to the skirt lining to lengthen the dress (Figure 22-3d).

- Finally, attach two hanging scarves to one side of the shoulder (Figure 22-3d) to add elegance and complete the dress.

The completed dress is shown in Figure 22-4.

Figure 22-4 Production photo showing the dress in *Crazy for You*. Polly played by Julie Ruth; Bobby played by Daniel Lee Robbins. Directed by Mark Brotherton. Scenic design by Joseph Rusnock. Lighting design by Richard Harmon. Costume design by Tan Huaixiang. University of Central Florida Conservatory Theatre presentation.

Figure 22-5 Costume design for *Blithe Spirit*.

ALTERING A USED DRESS TO A 1920s–30s EVENING DRESS

This dress was altered for the character Mrs. Bradman in *Blithe Spirit* (Figure 22-5). It was also purchased from a second-hand store. The silhouette of this dress was excellent for the 1920s and early 1930s look that was needed. The major change was to make the long sleeves into short sleeves to add elegance to the evening dress.

PROCEDURE FOR ALTERING A MODERN DRESS TO A PERIOD EVENING DRESS

Materials Required:

- Second-hand dress (can be pulled from stock)
- Fabric (for sash)
- Sewing machine
- Marker
- Seam ripper
- Scissors

Step One: Shortening the Sleeves

- Pull from stock or purchase a dress.
- Detach the sleeves from the dress (Figure 22-6a), and undo the sleeve seams. Lay the sleeves on the cutting table, pin the two sleeves together on top of each other, and draw a new sleeve style on the two original ones (Figure 22-6b). The new sleeve style in this example had rounded corners.
- Cut the sleeves following the new sleeve outline. Finish the freshly cut edges.

Step Two: Reconstructing the Dress

- Attach the new sleeves to the dress. Instead of sewing each sleeve into a tube, sew only a portion of the sleeve to the upper part of the dress armhole (Figure 22-7). The new sleeves now possess volume and flow, draping down to achieve the women's dress fashion of the 1920s and 1930s.

The completed dress is shown in Figures 22-7 to 22-8c.

Figure 22-8 (a) Production photo showing the dress in *Blithe Spirit*. From left to right: Charles played by Donte Bonner, Dr. Bradman played by Michael Swickard, Mrs. Bradman played by Ayla Harrison. (b) Production photo showing the dress in *Blithe Spirit*. From left to right: Charles played by Donte Bonner, Dr. Bradman played by Michael Swickard, Mrs. Bradman played by Ayla Harrison, Ruth played by Patrice Bell, Edith played by Ashiey Barnette, Madame Arcati played by Charita Coleman.

Figure 22-6 (a) Sketch of the original dress with one sleeve detached. (b) Draw the new sleeve design on the original sleeve pieces.

Figure 22-7 Attach the new sleeve style only to the upper part of the dress armhole.

Figure 22-8—Cont'd (c) Production photo showing the dress in *Blithe Spirit*. *From left to right: Mrs. Bradman played by Ayla Harrison, Dr. Bradman played by Michael Swickard, Madame Arcati played by Charita Coleman, Ruth played by Patrice Bell, Charles played by Donte Bonner. Directed by Jim Helsinger. Scenic design by Bert Scott. Lighting design by Jim Hart. Costume design by Tan Huaixiang. University of Central Florida Conservatory Theatre presentation.*

Figure 22-9 Costume design for *Romeo and Juliet.*

Figure 22-10 (a) Sketch of the original dress before alteration. (b) Square trim the stomach; slash the sleeves for inserting the decorative fabric; lengthen the skirt with a train made from the decorative fabric.

ALTERING AND DYEING A MODERN DRESS TO A RENAISSANCE GOWN

This dress was created for Juliet in Shakespeare's *Romeo and Juliet* (Figure 22-9). In the production, Juliet's family wore warm-toned costumes; Juliet's dress was a maroon–brick red color.

The original dress pulled from stock was a high-waisted, floor-length dress with no train and light yellow-green brocades (Figure 22-10a). It was dyed to suit her family's colors. Extra fabric with contrasting color and texture was added to the dress to achieve Renaissances period fashion.

PROCEDURE FOR ALTERING A MODERN DRESS TO A RENAISSANCE GOWN

Materials Required:

- Floor-length dress pulled from stock (or purchased)
- Decorative contrasting fabric to add to dress
- Rit dye and dye pot/vat
- Sewing machine
- Scissors

Step One: Dyeing the Dress and Fabric

Rit dye was used to separately dye both the dress and the added fabric. Because there was no dye vat available in the shop, the dress was dyed in the washing machine.

- Pull a dress from stock or purchase one.
- Preheat and mix the proper amount of dye and water and pour it into the washer.
- Wet the dress and prewash it if needed before putting it in the dye water. (Dry fabric creates uneven dyeing.)
- Dye the fabric in the same way. (The dress had a shiny, smooth texture. For better contrast, a piece of fabric with velvet floral patterns was chosen for altering the dress. The fabric had a bright yellow background made of synthetic fibers with velvet orange floral patterns made of natural fibers. The two different fibers were an advantage. After they were dyed, the fabric turned out perfectly: the velvet floral pattern turned a deep wine color and contrasted with the bright yellow background, which did change much in the dye. The sharp contrast to the velvet floral pattern worked very well for decorating Juliet's dress.)

Step Two: Modifying the Sleeves

- Slash the dress sleeves open to make a place for the decorative fabric (Figure 22-10b).

Step Three: Reconstructing the Dress

- Use the dyed decorative fabric to square trim the stomach and use it to decorate the front and bottom, expand the length, and create a back train of the dress (Figure 22-10b).
- Insert decorative fabric into each sleeve seam and sew it in. Attach pairs of ties along the seam lines; space them out about 3″ to 5″ apart from shoulder cap down to the cuff; and tie each pair of the tie to a bow-knot to create Italian-style slashes on the sleeve (Figure 22-11).
- Add lining to the layer added to the bottom of the skirt.

The completed dress is shown in Figures 22-11 to 22-12c.

Figure 22-11 Completed dress.

Figure 22-12 Production photos showing the dress in *Romeo and Juliet. Juliet played by Sara Hill; Romeo played by Keith Edie. Directed by Brenda Hubbard. Scenic design by Tim Stapleton. Lighting design by Mark C. Zetterberg. Costume design by Tan Huaixiang. Central Washington University Department of Theatre Arts presentation.*

Chapter 23   Altering Men's Jackets

There are many changes that can be made to men's jackets or coats. These can be as simple as changing the lapels, collars, pocket flaps, or sleeve cuffs; edging the entire jacket; or making double pleats at back of the jacket.

ALTERING A MODERN JACKET TO A SMOKING JACKET

This jacket was altered for a production of *13 Rue de L'Amour* (Figure 23-1). Changes were made to the jacket's lapels, collar, pocket flaps, and sleeve cuffs.

PROCEDURE FOR ALTERING A MODERN JACKET TO A SMOKING JACKET

Materials Required:

- Maroon blazer jacket (from stock)
- Plastic clear sheet
- Marker

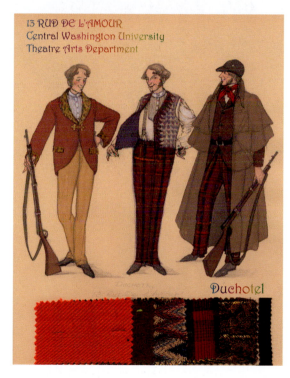

Figure 23-1 Costume design for *13 Rue de L'Amour*.

- Pins
- Dress form
- Quilted gold fabric
- Maroon-colored lining fabric
- Sewing machine

- Needle and thread
- Scissors

Step One: Marking the Changes

- Lay a piece of clear plastic on top of the jacket wherever it needs to be altered or changed (in this example, on the jacket's lapels, collar, pocket flaps, and sleeve cuffs).
- Pin the plastic sheet in place. You may have to clip the plastic around the curved areas.
- Use a marker to trace the folding edge (faces the neck) on the collar and lapels; then outline a new style for the collar or lapel on the plastic at the collar's outer edge (Figure 23-2a). In this example, a shawl collar was created.
- Remove the outlined plastic collar pattern from the jacket and add seam allowances to all cutting edges: add a 2″ seam allowance to the collar's inner edge, which will be folded under and attached to the

321

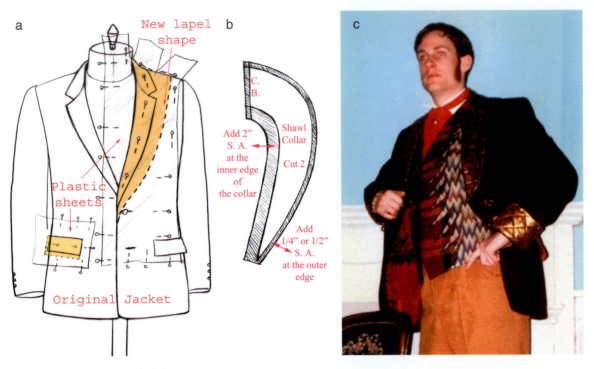

Figure 23-2 (a) Create a shawl collar pattern on a clear plastic sheet. (b) Add seam allowance to the plastic pattern. (c) Completed alteration of smoking jacket.

Figure 23-3 Production photo showing the smoking jacket in *13 Rue de L'Amour*. From left to right: Duchotel played by Craig Zagurski; Moricet played by David Foubert; Leontine played by Tricia Thiel. Directed by James Hawkins. Scenic design by R. Dutch Fritz. Lighting design by Mark Zetterberg. Costume design by Tan Huaixiang. Central Washington University Theatre Arts Department presentation.

inside of the jacket and add a ¼″ seam allowance on the collar's outer edge (Figure 23-3b).

- Cut out the shawl collar from quilted fabric, and cut the lining from fabric lining.
- With the right sides, stitch the outer edge of the quilt and lining together, turn the new collar right side out, and press. Serge or zigzag the raw edge.

Step Two: Reconstructing the Jacket

- Place the jacket on a dress form, place the new shawl collar over the lapel, and pin it to the outer jacket.
- With both the lapel and collar folded, lay the shawl collar over the jacket collar and fold the inner shawl edge over the jacket's folding line. Doing this

while the collar and lapel remain folded keeps the shawl collar naturally flat on the jacket collar.

- Hand sew the inner edge of the shawl collar to the inside of the jacket to attach them.
- Machine or hand sew the quilt fabric to the pocket flap and the sleeve cuffs.

The completed jacket is shown in Figures 23-2 to 23-3.

ALTERING A MODERN JACKET TO A LATE-NINETEENTH TO EARLY-TWENTIETH CENTURY JACKET

This jacket was modified for a production of *Tintypes*. In this example, the collar shape on the jacket was not changed; only the collar fabric was changed.

PROCEDURE FOR ALTERING A MODERN JACKET TO PERIOD JACKET

Materials Required:

- Men's modern medium length jacket (here purchased from a second-hand store)
- Brown velveteen fabric (to trim the collar)
- Scissors
- Sewing machine
- Clear piece of plastic
- Marker
- Needle board
- Iron

Step One: Marking the Changes

The only change made on the jacket was trimming the back collar of the jacket with contrasting colored fabric.

- Place a piece of clear plastic on top of the back collar and trace the exact shape of the collar with a marker (Figure 23-4a).
- Remove the plastic piece from the jacket and add a ½″ seam allowance around the pattern.
- Cut out the pattern from a piece of brown velveteen fabric.
- Machine sew a straight stitch line all around the edges of the collar piece. Fold the edge at the stitch line toward the wrong side of the fabric, and press it over a needle board, making sure the folded edge is neat.

Step Two: Reconstructing the Jacket

- Hand sew the new velveteen collar to the jacket's collar with slip stitches (invisible stitches).

The completed jacket is shown in Figures 23-4b and 23-5.

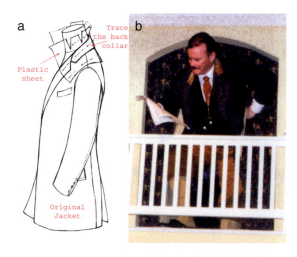

Figure 23-4 (a) Trace the collar pattern on top of the clear plastic. (b) Completed coat with velveteen collar.

Figure 23-5 Production photo of *Tintypes*. *Teddy Roosevelt played by Mark Brotherton, Emma Goldman played by Michelle Knight. Directed by Bruce Allen Earnest. Scenic and lighting design by Richard Dunham. Costume design by Tan Huaixiang. University of Central Florida Conservatory Theatre presentation.*

The men's jackets were altered in a similar way for a production of *The Importance of Being Earnest* (Figure 23-6). John Worthing's white jacket was edged with satin cords to add a period flavor to it. Algernon Moncrieff's the collar and lapels are trimmed with plain green satin fabric to create a contrasting texture and a period appearance. High, stiff turn-of-the-century-style shirt collars were also attached to their modern white dress shirts to complete the look.

Figure 23-6 Production photo of *The Importance of Being Earnest*. *John Worthing played by Chris Taylor, Algernon Moncrieff played by Jason Flora. Directed by Jim Helsinger. Scenic design by Paul Lartonoix. Lighting design by Eric Haugen. Costume design by Tan Huaixiang. University of Central Florida Conservatory Theatre presentation.*

Chapter 24   Aging and Distressing Costumes

WAYS TO AGE AND DISTRESS COSTUMES

There are many ways to age costumes for theatrical purposes. The methods can also be combined, depending on the needs of the character and the play.

Materials Most Commonly Used:

- Scissors
- File
- Cheese grater
- Wire brush
- Sandpaper
- Dyes
- Shoe spray paints
- Craft spray paints
- Fabric acrylic paints
- Paint brushes
- Sawdust
- Gesso
- Spray adhesive
- Acrylic mix

AGING COSTUMES BY SCRUBBING

- Use a cheese grater, wire brush, or file to create an aged impression by scrubbing the garment surface where it would naturally appear worn out, such as around the collar, lapels, pockets, buttonholes, edges, elbows, cuffs, hem, knees, and buttock area. Scrubbing creates a ragged appearance on the costume.
- To create bigger holes in the garment, cut small holes and scrub them with a file or cheese grater for a natural torn look.
- Cut the bottom hems off, and scrub them to achieve aged raw edges on the garment.

AGING COSTUMES BY DYEING AND PAINTING

- Dye a garment to change a bright color to a dull color and mute down the contrasting patterns on the garment.

- Use spray paint to add highlights and shadows to imitate color fading and a washed-out appearance.
- Use paints to create stains on the garment according to the character's occupation.

AGING COSTUMES BY BLEACHING AND WASHING

- Bleach the garment to remove some color from the garment for a faded look. Test the garment before putting it in the bleach-water solution. (A color remover can also be used for garment aging, but it is costly.)
- Wash the garment (if washable) several times without pressing it.

AGING COSTUMES BY BUILDING 3-D TEXTURE

- Simulate dirt and food stains. Obtain some sawdust from a scene shop, and pour liquid dye or paint into the sawdust to simulate soil or dirt.

325

- Spray adhesive on garment areas that easily attract dirt; sprinkle and smear dyed sawdust over the glue and let it dry.
- Sew colorful and textured patches using contrasting thread to achieve more signs of aging on the garment.
- Sew ragged fabric pieces to display torn ragged edges.

AGING COSTUMES BY CREATING WRINKLES

- Press crisp lines flat on the garment.
- Put the garment in a small net washing bag, and put it in the dryer to heat it and help set the wrinkles.

EXAMPLES OF AGED/ DISTRESSED COSTUMES

You may combine all the methods mentioned in this chapter as desired for the ideal aged look. The production photos here show costumes that have been aged.

The first set of examples is from the production *The Visit* (Figures 24-1 to 24-2). The costumes at the beginning of the play reflect that the village and townspeople suffered under the curse of some inexplicable blight, depriving them of everything but basic necessities. The

Figure 24-1 Costume design for the townspeople in *The Visit.*

costumes should contrast from the beginning to the end as the characters' clothing change from poor to more prosperous.

Mixed aging methods were used to transform the costumes from dull colors to vivid colors, from rough to smooth texture, and from old to new. Spray paint

Figure 24-2 Production photos of aged costumes in *The Visit. Directed by Mark Brotherton. Scenic/lighting design by Vandy Wood. Costume design by Tan Huaixiang. University of Central Florida Conservatory Theatre presentation.*

was used on dry clean-only garments, while washable garments were dyed to tint and change the original color and texture to suit each character. Scrubbing and 3-D texture were applied on both garment types. Adhesive, gesso, and sawdust were added to shoes to simulate dirt. The leather surface of the shoes was filed for a worn-out look. The aged/distressed costumes are shown in Figure 24-2.

The next group of consists of the production photo for *The Grapes of Wrath* (Figure 24-3) and the costume design and production photo for *Big River* (Figures 24-4 to 24-5); the costumes in this group were, dyed, patched, and spray painted.

BIG RIVER
UCF THEATRE
Spring 1999

Figure 24-4 Costume design for *Big River*.

Figure 24-3 Production photo of aged costumes in *The Grapes of Wrath*. *Ma played by Dude Hatten; Rose played by Leslie J. Webb, performance student; Grandma played by Milo Smith. Directed by Wesley Van Tassel. Scenic and lighting design by Dutch Frit. Costume design by Tan Huaixiang. Central Washington University Theatre Arts Department presentation.*

Figure 24-5 Production photos of aged costumes in *Big River*. Huckleberry Finn played by Daniel Robbins, Pap Finn played by Shane T. Serena. Directed by Donald Seay. Scenic design by Joseph Rusnock. Lighting design by Richard Dunham. Costume design by Tan Huaixiang. University of Central Florida Conservatory Theatre presentation.

Chapter 25   Supply Sources and Safety Tips

SUPPLY SOURCES

3-D MAKEUP MATERIALS

Common prosthetic pieces are usually made form foam latex/hot foam, cold foam, gel-foam, or liquid latex.

- Foam latex/hot foam (a four-part system) is a very flexible, lightweight material that moves wonderfully with the actor's movements. Foam latex is more complex than other materials and should be considered an advanced technique. It needs certain equipment to complete the process such as positive and negative molds, an electric mixer, a gram scale (a postal scale will work), and an oven. Because foam latex is baked, it is often called hot foam. The positive and negative molds used with hot foam should be made of Ultracal 30, fiberglass, or silicone rather than plaster of paris because they're stronger for baking. Ultracal 30 is a cement material that is the most economical. (Dracula's full mask in Chapter 1 is made of foam latex/hot foam and the molds are made of Ultracal 30).

- Cold foam/soft foam is a two-part system, mixed together to produce facial and body appliances. The average prosthetic takes about 25 minutes to cure, and the mold is ready to be used again immediately. No oven curing is required. It is called cold foam because it does not need to be baked. Necessary equipment includes a gram scale, electric mixer (only for making large prosthetic pieces; small pieces can be done by hand), and containers. Cold foam is quick and easy to make and use, but it is not as flexible as hot foam. It can be used with positive and negative molds made of plaster of paris because no baking is required. (Cyrano's nose in Chapter 1 is made of cold foam.)

- Gel-foam is gelatin foam that comes in cubes and in different colors. It is economic, translucent, flexible, extremely soft, easy to work with, and excellent when used in small quantities.

Gel-foam requires both positive and negative molds, just like hot and cold foam, but it involves a much simpler process. Heat the gel-foam cubes in a microwave about 1 minute (depending on the size of the prosthetic piece being made) to a gelatin-like consistency; pour the hot gelatin into a negative mold, and then close it with a positive mold. It is ready to be demolded in about 30 minutes. The gel-foam is extremely soft and flexible, but heavier than foam latex. It is best for making small pieces or overlapping small pieces to create a large piece. It can be made with any type of positive and negative molds. Gel-foam can be reused several times (any extra edges trimmed off from the prosthetic piece can be melted and reused). (The Witch nose in Chapter 1 is made of gel-foam.)

- Liquid latex has been used for theatrical makeup for quite some time. Makeup artists use liquid latex to create instant wrinkles, scars, cuts, wounds,

329

masks, or prosthetic pieces. Liquid latex can be directly applied over the skin or be poured into molds. It air-cures at room temperature and dries faster at higher temperatures (with a hair dryer). It can be combined with cold foam or gel foam to make the prosthetic piece more durable and increase the flexibility of the cured latex. Liquid latex also can be combined with some objects to create textured 3-D forms. It can be dyed or painted. (The Witch's nose, Cyrano's nose, and some masks in this book are made of liquid latex.)

Foam latex, cold foam, gel-foam, liquid latex, and life casting and mold-making materials can be purchased from the following sources.

- Alcone Company Inc. (Paramount theatrical supplies):
  1. Alcone LIC (mail-order warehouse), 5–49 49th Avenue, Long Island, NY 11101; Tel: (718)-361-8373; Fax: (718) 729-8296, 1-800-466-7446; www.alconeco.com.
  2. Alcone NYC (retail store), 235 West 19th Street, New York, NY 10011, Tel/Fax: (212) 633-0551.
- FX Warehouse, Inc. (supplies for FX artists and scenic studios), www.fxqarehouseinc.com.
- Gel-Foam Make-up Designory; 129 S. San Fernando Blvd, Burbank,

CA 91502; Tel: (818) 729-9420; www.mudshop.com.
- GM Foam, Inc., 14956 Delano St., Van Nuys, CA 91411; Tel: (818) 908-1087 or 1-888-648-8810; Fax: (818) 908-1262 or (801) 936-9763; www.fxsupply.com, www.gmfoam.com, www.getspfx.com.
- KRYOLAN Corporation, 132 Ninth Street, San Francisco, CA 94103; Tel: (415) 863-9684; Fax (415) 863-9059.
- Joe Blasco Cosmetics, www.joeblasco.com.

DENTAL SUPPLIES

Materials for making false teeth such as dental trays, alginate, dental stone, and liquid and powder acrylic can be purchased from the following sources.
- Local dental supply stores
- FX Warehouse, Inc. (supplies for FX artists and scenic studios), www.fxqarehouseinc.com.

MILLINERY SUPPLIES

Materials such as buckram, Fosshape, and Wonderflex can be used for making hats, crowns, and headdress and wig bases. These materials can also be used to make props, masks, and armor.
- Buckram is a loosely woven material, with glue sizing in it. When dry, it is

stiff and coarse; when wet, it is pliable and moldable on a hat block or mask mold. It can be cut and molded in shapes. It is excellent as a support structure in costumes, wigs, hats, headdresses, masks, and armor. It works very well in dry-climate areas, but it will not hold its shape well in the humid climates without being treated with a waterproof spray.
- Fosshape is a unique, nonwoven, heat-activated fabric. It is soft and looks like white felt, but is pliable and can be formed, shaped, and molded into the desired shapes with steaming, heating, or ironing; it then remains in this shape. The procedure for using it is extremely easy and fast. The lightweight material serves well as a structure support for hats, wigs, headdresses, armor, masks, and other crafts; it can be sewn, layered, painted, and dyed. The degree of stiffness is achieved by adjusting temperature, duration of heat, and pressure applied. After it is heated and molded, it is waterproof and won't stretch. It is not necessary to wire the edge. It will hold the shape well in either dry or humid climates.
- Wonderflex is a type of thermoplastic material that is also molded with heat. It can be softened with a heat gun, hair dryer, or hot water, and then molded

over a mold. Wonderflex and Fosshape are both strong, flexible, lightweight, and easy to work with. They can be painted or decorated with a variety of artisan coatings and paints. Wonderflex is an ideal material for making armor, props, and masks. Wonderflex headdress foundations breathe less and are uncomfortable on the head; therefore Fosshape works better for this purpose.

Buckram, Fosshape, and Wonderflex can be purchased from the following sources.

- Foss Manufacturing Company Inc. (Fosshape — engineered fabrics #300 and #600), 380 Lafayette Road, P.O. Box 5000, Hampton, NH 03843-5000; Tel: (201) 549-1000, (877) 232-9426 (East Coast) or (877) 432-9426 (West Coast); www.dazian.com.
- California Millinery, 721 South Spring Street, Los Angeles, CA 90014; Tel: (213) 622-8746; Fax: (213) 622-0438; E-mail: calmil@bursline.com.
- Manny's Millinery Supply Co., 26 West 38th Street, New York, NY 10018; Tel (212) 840-2235; Fax (212) 944-0178; www.mannys_millinery.com.
- Colorado Allyns Millinery Supplies, Inc., 2306 E. Sixth Avenue, Denver, CO 80206; Tel: (303) 377-4969; www.allynsfabric.com.

MASK-MAKING SUPPLIES

Mask-making supplies include Varaform, Wonderflex, Casting latex, and Elmer's glue and paper.

- Varaform and Wonderflex are rigid, self-adhering, nontoxic, rapid and easy to use, lightweight, remoldable, biodegradable, and not wasteful (all cut-off pieces can be reused).
- Casting latex is much thicker than liquid latex. It is used for making masks, body parts, and rubber suits. It is durable, dryable, printable, and stitchable. It has excellent detail reproduction and a fast demolding from the mold.
- Elmer's glue and paper (paper towels or brown-pattern paper) make an excellent economical mask-making material that can be purchased in any local store.

Varaform can be purchased from the following sources. (Sources for Wonderflex are listed under Millinery Supplies.)

- Douglas and Sturgess, Inc. (sculpting tools, materials, and supplies),
  1. (warehouse and store), 1023 Fastory St., Richmond, CA 94801.
  2. (store), 730 Bryant St., San Francisco, CA 94107; Tel: (510) 235-8411; Fax: (510) 235-4211; www.artstuf.com.

Sculpt or Coat — an easy working, non-toxic plastic cream for all your construction needs. Dries clear if applied thinly or translucent if applied thickly. Commonly used for coating sculptures or masks or for aging costumes for the stage. Available in quarts or gallons.

- Norcostco, (800) 743-0379, www.norcostco.com.

Casting latex can be purchased from FX Warehouse, Inc. (supplies for FX artists and scenic studios), www.fxqarehouseinc.com.

CRAFT PAINT AND ADHESIVES

These can be purchased from the following sources.

- Display & Costume Supply, 11201 Roosevelt Way NE, Seattle, WA 98125-6225; (206) 362-4810.
- Joann's Fabric
- Home Depot
- Wal-Mart
- Michaels Crafts
- Any Art Supply Stores

OTHER MATERIALS

- Foam comes in varying thicknesses from $\frac{1}{4}$" to 2" thick. It can be purchased from Joann's Fabrics.

- Foam cord comes in varying thickness from ½″ to 2″ in diameter. It can be purchased from
  1. Waterproofing Supply, Inc., www.fwsi.us.
  2. Display & Costume Supply, 11201 Roosevelt Way NE, Seattle, WA 98125-6225; (206) 362-4810.

SAFETY TIPS

The most hazardous materials used for costumes and makeup are dyes, spray paints, spray adhesive, and glue. These materials contain toxic chemicals that diffuse harmful fumes into the environment. Be cautious and careful when using them.

TOXIC MATERIALS SAFETY RULES

- Always read the material safety data sheet (label on the container) before using products.
- Work with the proper safety equipment and in ventilated areas (outdoors is best).
- Always wear masks, gloves, aprons, and goggles in the working area to protect yourself, others, and the environment.
- If you are pregnant, avoid working with toxic chemicals.
- If any chemicals get on your skin or in your eyes, rinse the area immediately and thoroughly with COLD WATER. Warm water increases the chemical reaction and causes more damage.
- Keep a first aid kit in the shop for emergencies.
- Keep lids/covers on their containers (dye jars, glue bottles, or tubes).
- Cover the working area with paper or plastic sheets before starting a messy project and clean the working area when the work is done.
- Keep all flammable materials in safety cabinets.